FLASH TECHNIQUES FOR

# MACRO AND CLOSE-UP PHOTOGRAPHY

Published by:
Amherst Media, Inc.
P.O. Box 586
Buffalo, N.Y. 14226
Fax: 716-874-4508
www.AmherstMedia.com

Publisher: Craig Alesse
Senior Editor/Production Manager: Michelle Perkins
Assistant Editor: Barbara A. Lynch-Johnt
Editorial assistance provided by Chris Gallant, Sally Jarzab, and John S. Loder

ISBN-13: 978-1-60895-290-8
Library of Congress Control Number: 2010940510
Printed in Korea.
10 9 8 7 6 5 4 3 2 1

# CONTENTS



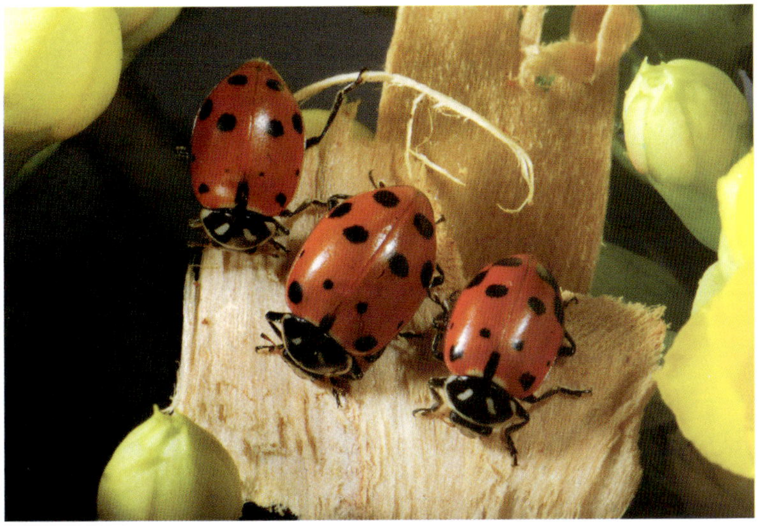

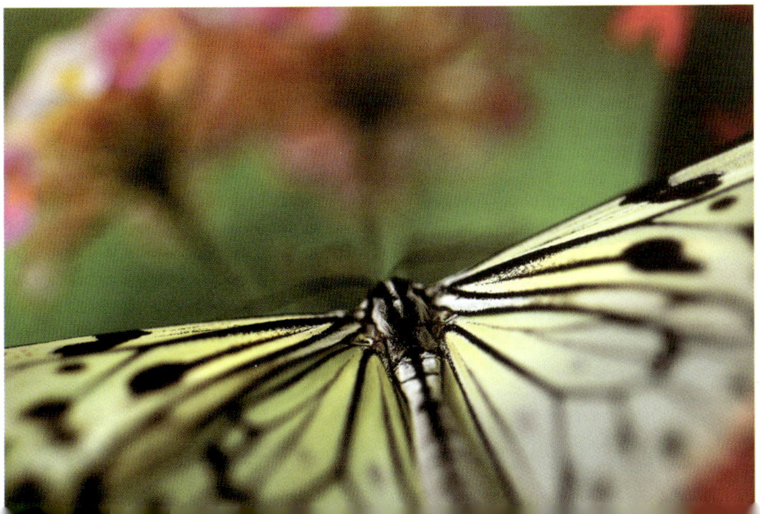

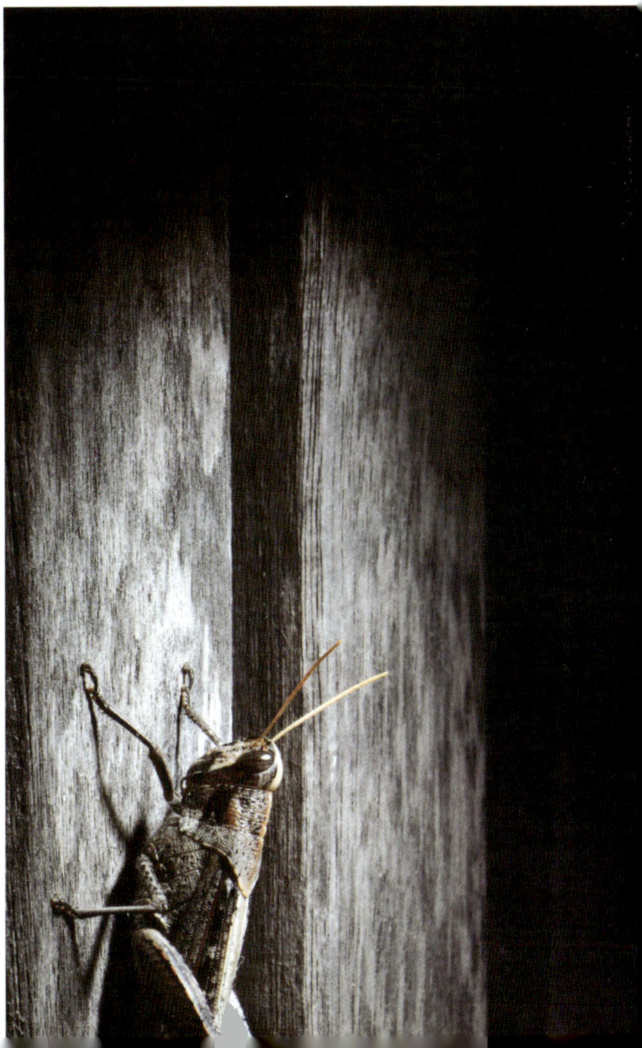

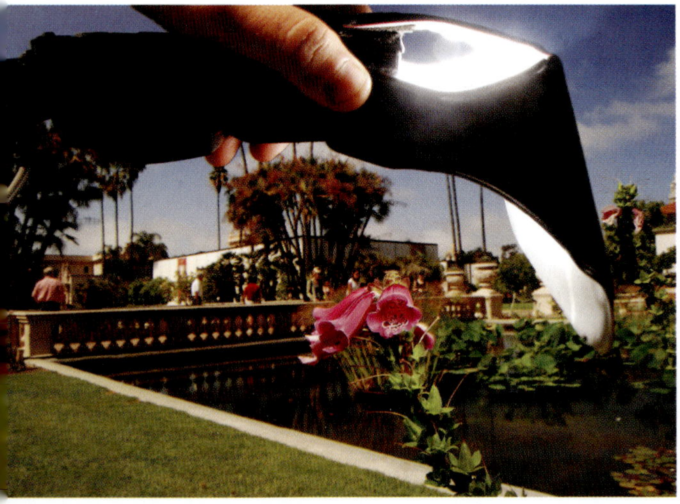

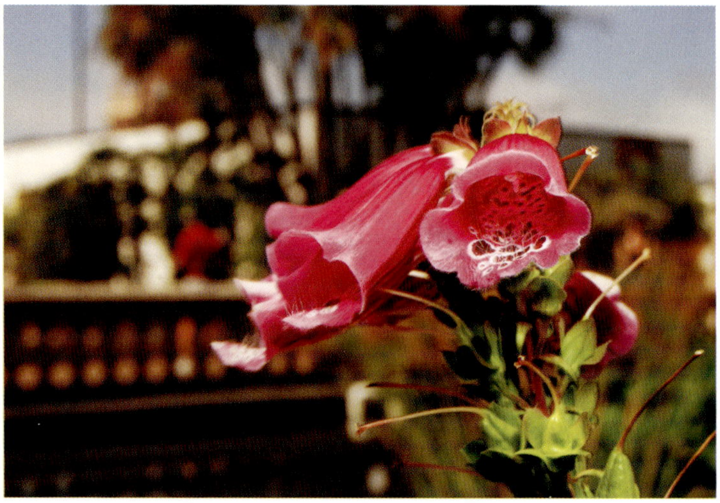

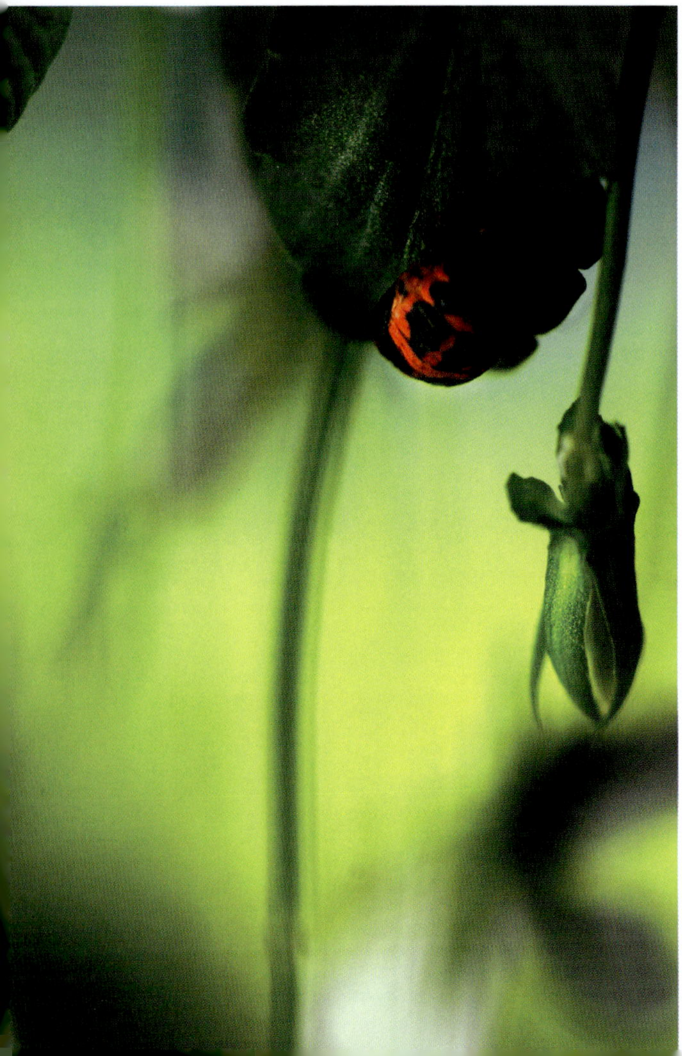

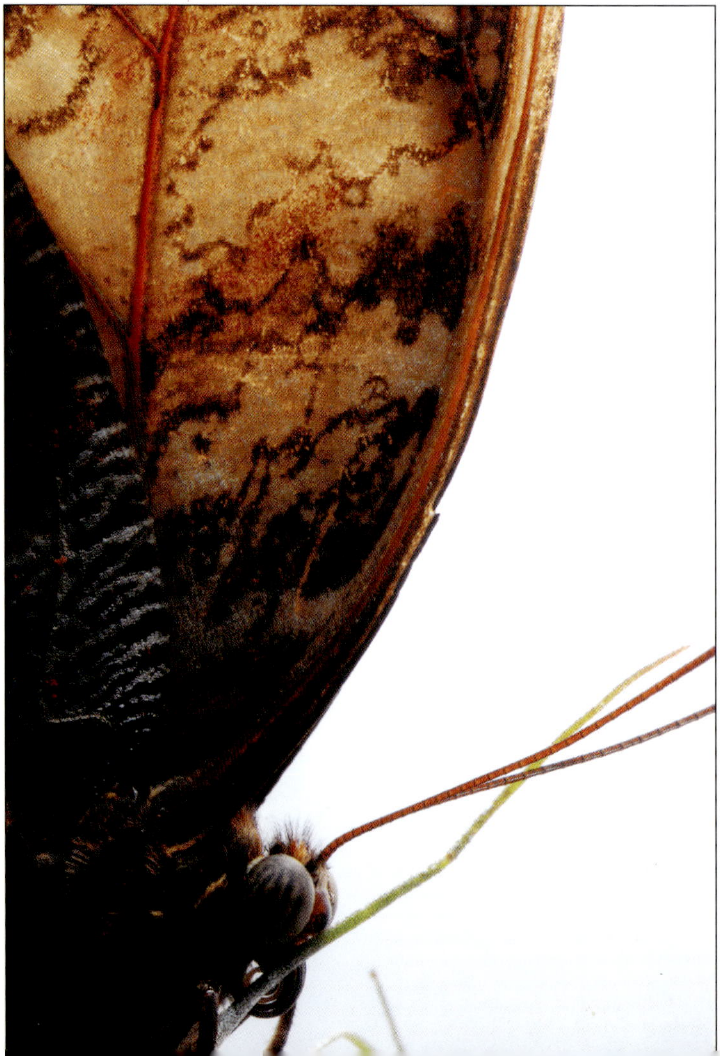

***Foreword***

We have always held firm that it's the journey that's most important—that from these experiences we grow as artists, as photographers, and as people. Through our lifelong exploration of the smaller side of light (and life), we've learned to appreciate the minuscule and see options hidden to most. It's passion, courage, and insight that makes it all happen—that and a few beautiful and amazing tiny creatures and plants. Sadly, not all photographers share our outlook or reverence. They view these small living creatures as objects that can be photographed and tossed away. They talk (and write) of kill jars, stunning insects into submission, and even worse options. This is not just bad advice, it's simply wrong. We would like to offer another way of photographing them. We've discovered that with enough care, patience, and understanding anything is possible—without causing any damage or undo stress. If you take your time, if you offer the respect due, these tiny subjects will welcome you. It will happen, and your images will prove it.

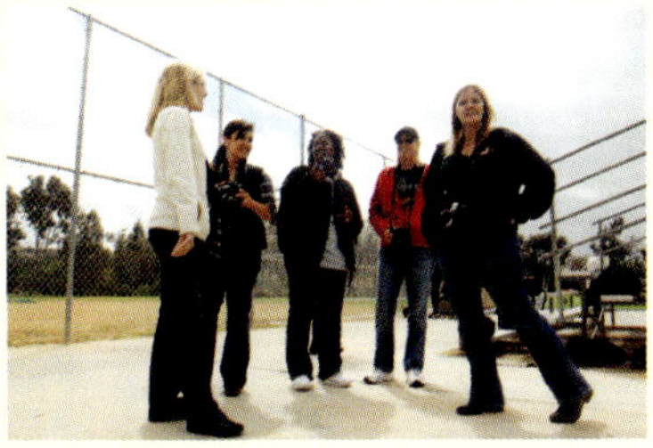
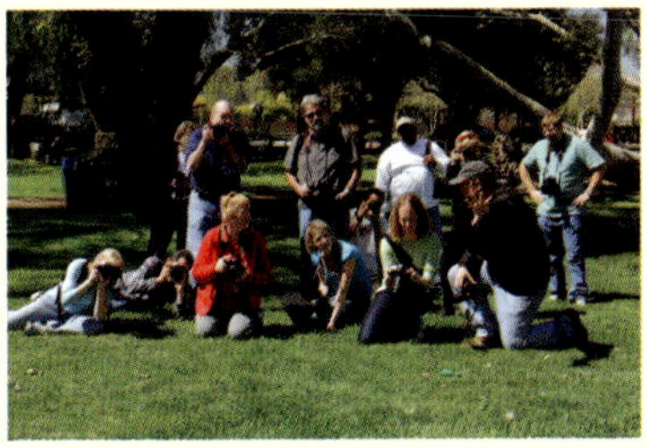
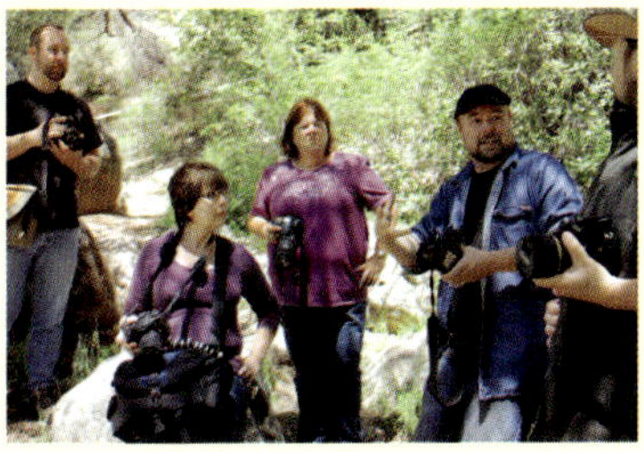

*In our courses, we instill a sense of respect and admiration for the world around us, showing that expressionism and nature can go hand-in-hand.*

## ABOUT THE AUTHORS

Award-winning fine art photographers, veteran newspaper editors, and acclaimed photography instructors Rod and Robin Deutschmann have been teaching people to be artists with their cameras for years. Taking a practical approach to modern photography, the duo strips the nonsense from the facts and the hype from the truth. They believe that creativity lies in the artist's soul and not his camera bag. Touting the advantages of manual control, they offer a fresh view of photography that rebels against the norm. Their innovative approach and down-to-earth style have garnered them a loyal following of fans. Visit their Web site at www.IFLCSanDiego.com.

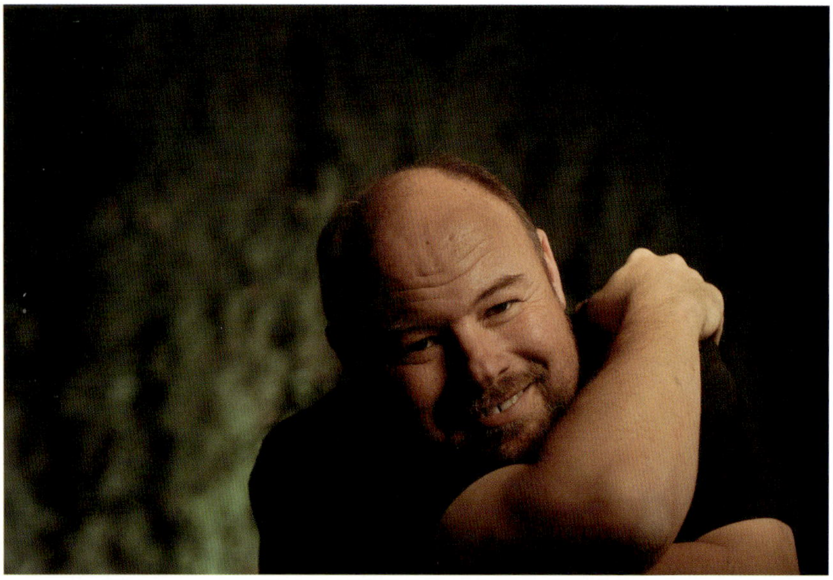

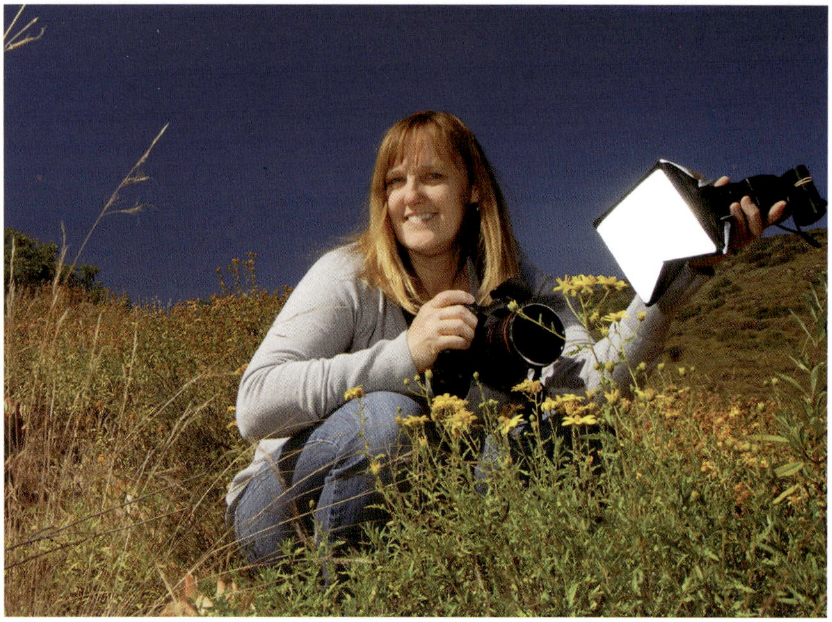

# 1. THE MAGIC OF MACRO

This is not just about taking pretty pictures of insects, flowers, and water drops—it's about garnering the experience and knowledge to become the artist-with-a-camera that you know you can be.

There is something magical about really good macro and close-up images. They provide a glimpse of a world few ever see and fewer still understand. When done well, these images put us in touch with the essence of being, like nothing else. They let us know we are not alone and that every living thing—no matter how small—is important. But let's not kid ourselves. There is a reason these images only come from master photographers, real artists with cameras. This type of work requires a high level of mechanical competency and unrestrained vision. Relatively few photographers today are willing to sacrifice the time and energy needed to master their own equipment and focus their vision on such a specific and ethereal goal.

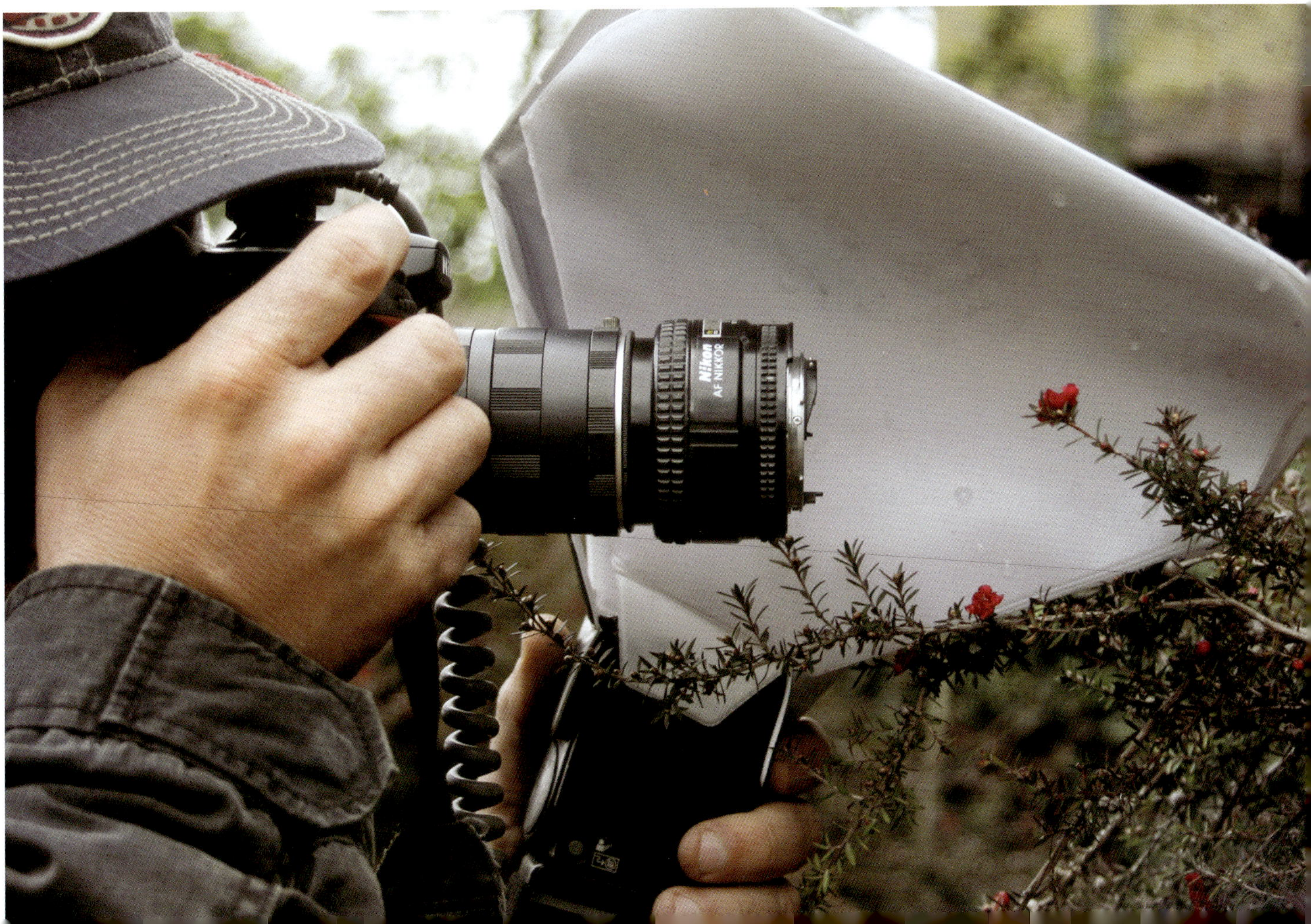


Here, a photographer uses a modified off-camera flash, three extension tubes, and a flipped 50mm lens. This gear choice wasn't random. It was the only collection of tools that allowed his vision to shine. Granted, it may not be the most glamorous (or traditional) of photographic setups, but it gets the job done as nothing else can. For the macro and close-up artist, it's not just about looking the part, it's about accomplishing a goal and speaking your mind.

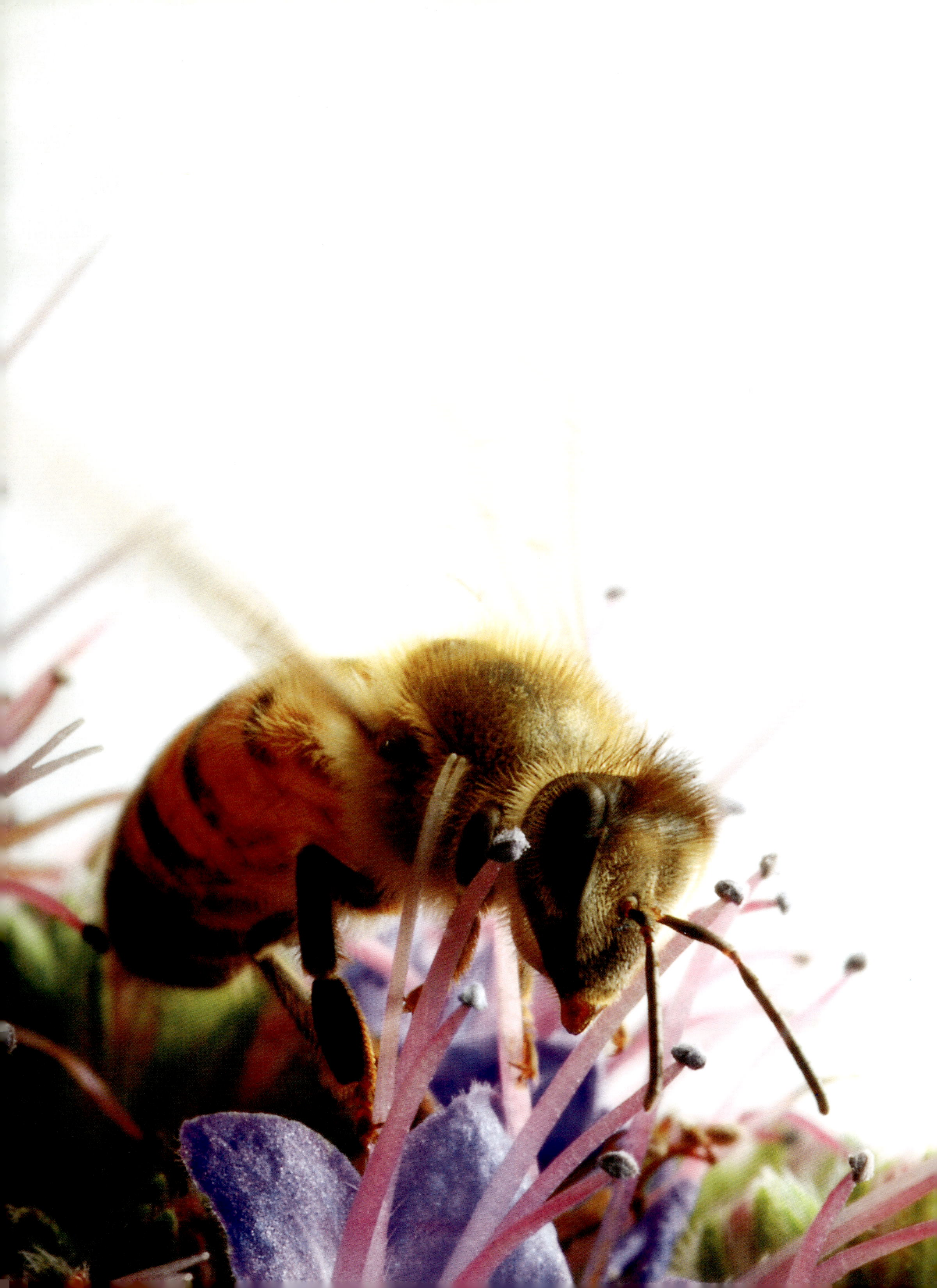

**Facing page**—Getting up close and personal with life and nature—no matter how small it might be—is something that every macro/close-up artist adores. While the techniques and mechanics required to capture dramatic macro images like this one may prove challenging at first, with patience, dedication, and love anything is possible. Great macro and close-up photographs aren't taken by technicians, they are created by caring, loving, and knowledgeable artists. **Right**—You are in full control when using an off-camera flash; you can manipulate the scene, adding or taking away light to your heart's content. If you want to add light to the background instead of the subject (as in this photo), then do it. That's the beauty of having a flash off-camera: your creativity is not restrained. Every tier of graphic information can be lit a different way. This is power, this is magic, this is what you want to do—it's who you want to be!

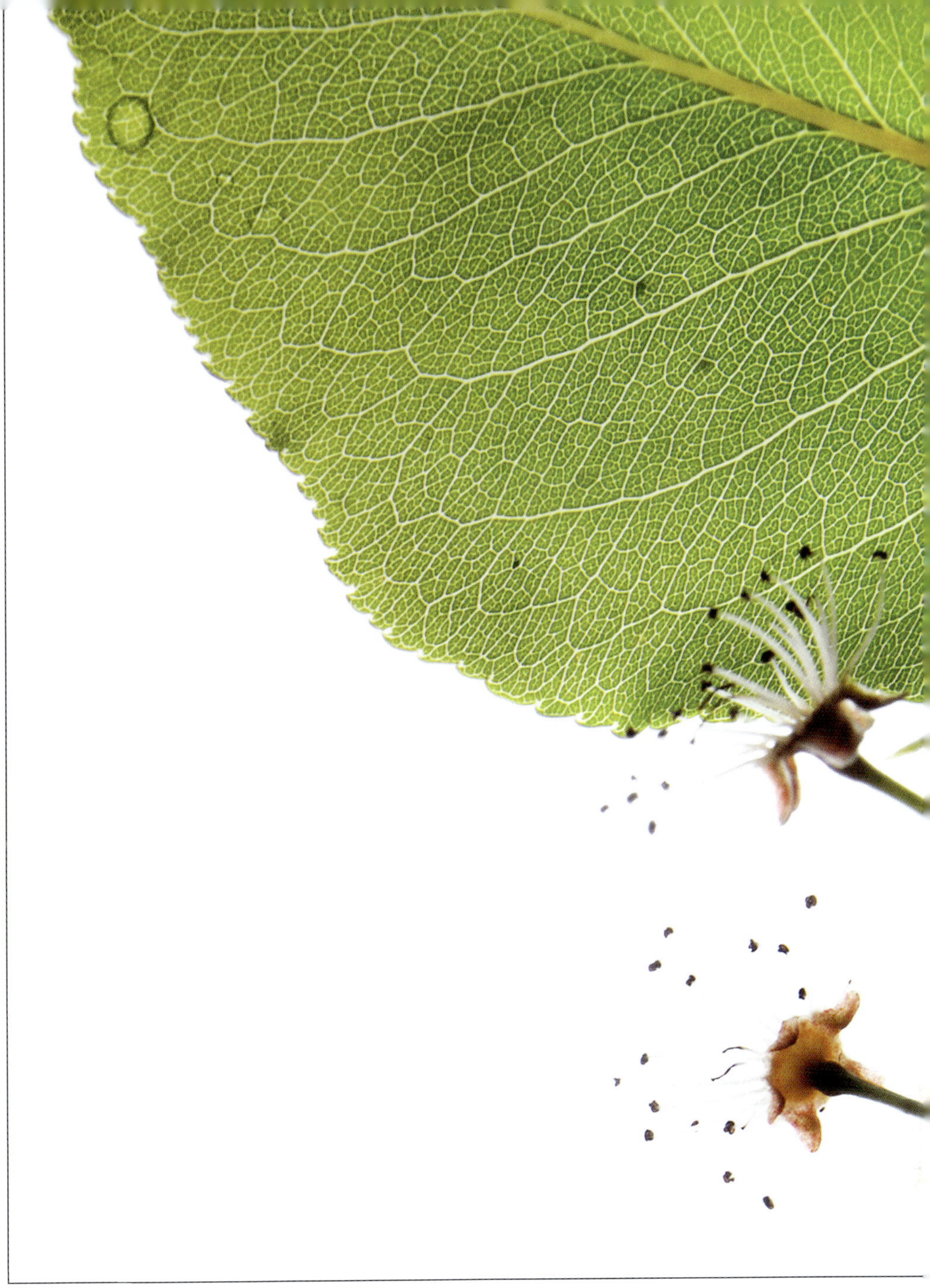

Yet, here you are, searching for answers, looking for tips, hunting down tricks. Bravo on your decision, your courage, and your interest in flash techniques for close-up and macro photography! We applaud your tenacity and foresight. By simply buying this book you've shown that you have the drive required to create amazing images. The only question remaining is this: Do you have the perseverance to make it happen?

## THE TRUTH

Macro and close-up photography have their own very stringent set of rules that must be followed—break them ever so slightly and your image falls apart. Follow them and your images rock. You're also probably aware

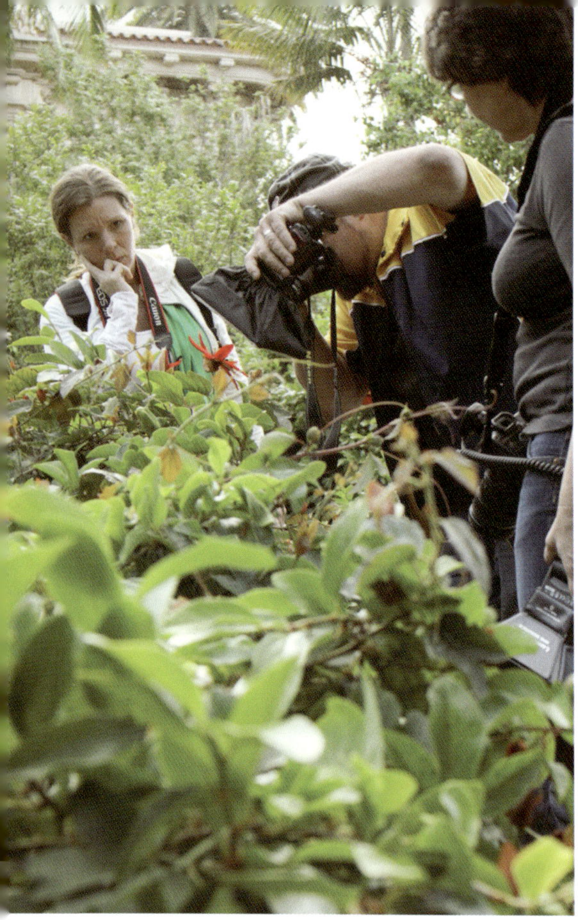

Yes, manual photography is hard—and macro and close-up photography with an off-camera flash is even harder. Rest assured though, that you can do it. Don't give in. Just as our students (pictured here) are doing, push yourself. Learn everything there is to learn about close-up photography, then learn some more. And then, when that can't get you want you want, start creating your own techniques to solve your own problems.

of the power that adding off-camera flash affords, allowing for the addition of light from every possible angle. Combined, they offer a chance to strike out against the norm and truly express yourself.

The flash is the key, of course. Once flash is employed, the usual close-up/macro problems disappear. No more will you need to worry about limited depth of field or camera shake. Wind blowing? No problem. Shaky hands? No such thing. Subject moving too quickly? So what? Believe it or not, you can even leave your tripod at home. (We don't use them to hold the camera and would never think of it.)

You can even turn your camera off of auto and set your lens and flash to full manual with complete confidence. (After all, an artist does not rely on a machine to make vital choices for him; he chooses the amount of light, depth of field, contrast, saturation, and white balance.) With enough practice, you can break free of the need to "manipulate" images later in the computer. You can create close-up beauty quickly, routinely, and get what you want when you want it. As a matter of fact, what you learn here can seriously change the way you think about "regular" photography, too.

Off-camera flash for macro and close-up photography will change your life—and, trust us, your pictures are going to prove it.

## INSIGHT

So, how does all this magic happen then? What does it take? What settings do you need?

First, you'll have to be in full manual control of your camera and flash. Sorry! We know that hurts, but there really isn't any other choice. A camera or flash set to "auto" anything is designed to do one thing: to give you average or normal images. We don't think that is what you want or why you bought this book. If you were okay with "normal" or "average" pictures, you probably wouldn't be looking for guidance on something as technical and artistic as macro and close-up photography.

No, our guess is that you want something more from your images. To do that, you must take full responsibility—and that means shooting in pure manual. As photography instructors, we've asked thousands of new photographers to give up the pursuit of "simple" photography and push themselves and their equipment even farther. We ask them to think about a goal and chase a dream instead of just reacting to stimuli. Granted, this is more like walking up a steep hill than anything else, but we believe in the human spirit and in true artistic expression. A photograph can and should say something about the person who shot it. It should speak of them and how they felt about what was in front of them, not just show us what something looked like.

The best part of all of this is that if you're not already completely confident with your manual skills, you will be after you master close-up and macro photography with an off-camera flash. There won't be a choice; you will have to learn how to do it all in-camera or your images will fail.

To help, we've got a great walk-through just a few chapters away—something that you can do in the privacy of your own home. No stress, no worries. It'll get you up and running with the whole manual camera approach and even teach you the basics of adding light with a manual flash. You'll love it.

***Making Mistakes (and Learning from Them)***

To be an artist, you have to learn from your mistakes. Automatic modes are designed to eliminate mistakes—to take from you the very things you need the most: experience, vision, and foresight. If you want to be the best you can be, then you have to make the worst mistakes possible and learn from each of them. Give your auto settings a rest—each and every one of them. A camera cannot make creative decisions—and you can't either if the machine you're using is trying to give you average pictures!

Great close-up or macro images begin with determination and confidence. You need to build a strong foundation in the basics before attempting something this complicated. If you are new to the idea of shooting in pure manual or using an off-camera flash, concentrate on learning the basics. Then you can truly start pushing the envelope of creativity and tackle the complexities of macro and close-up photography with an off-camera flash.

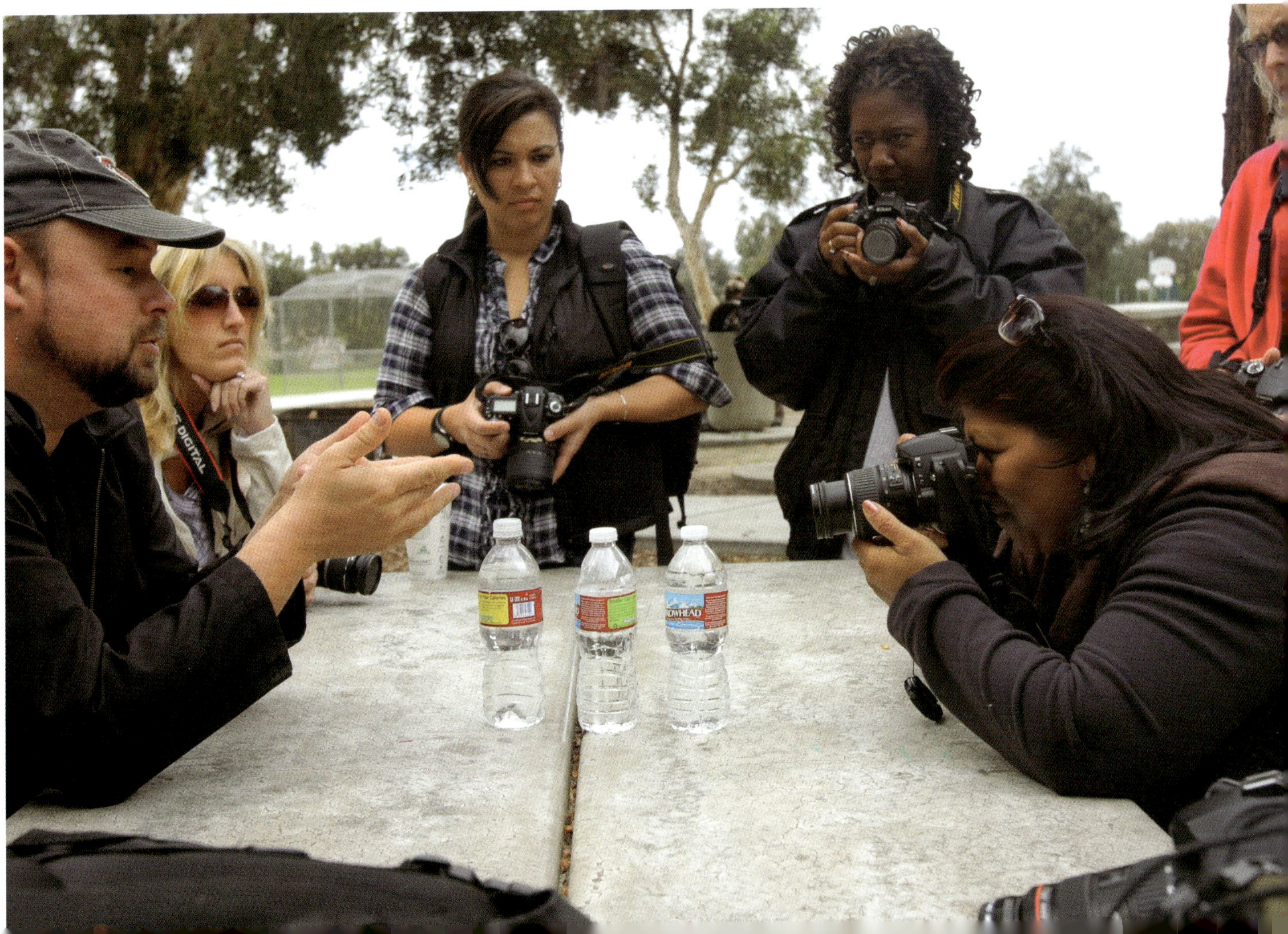

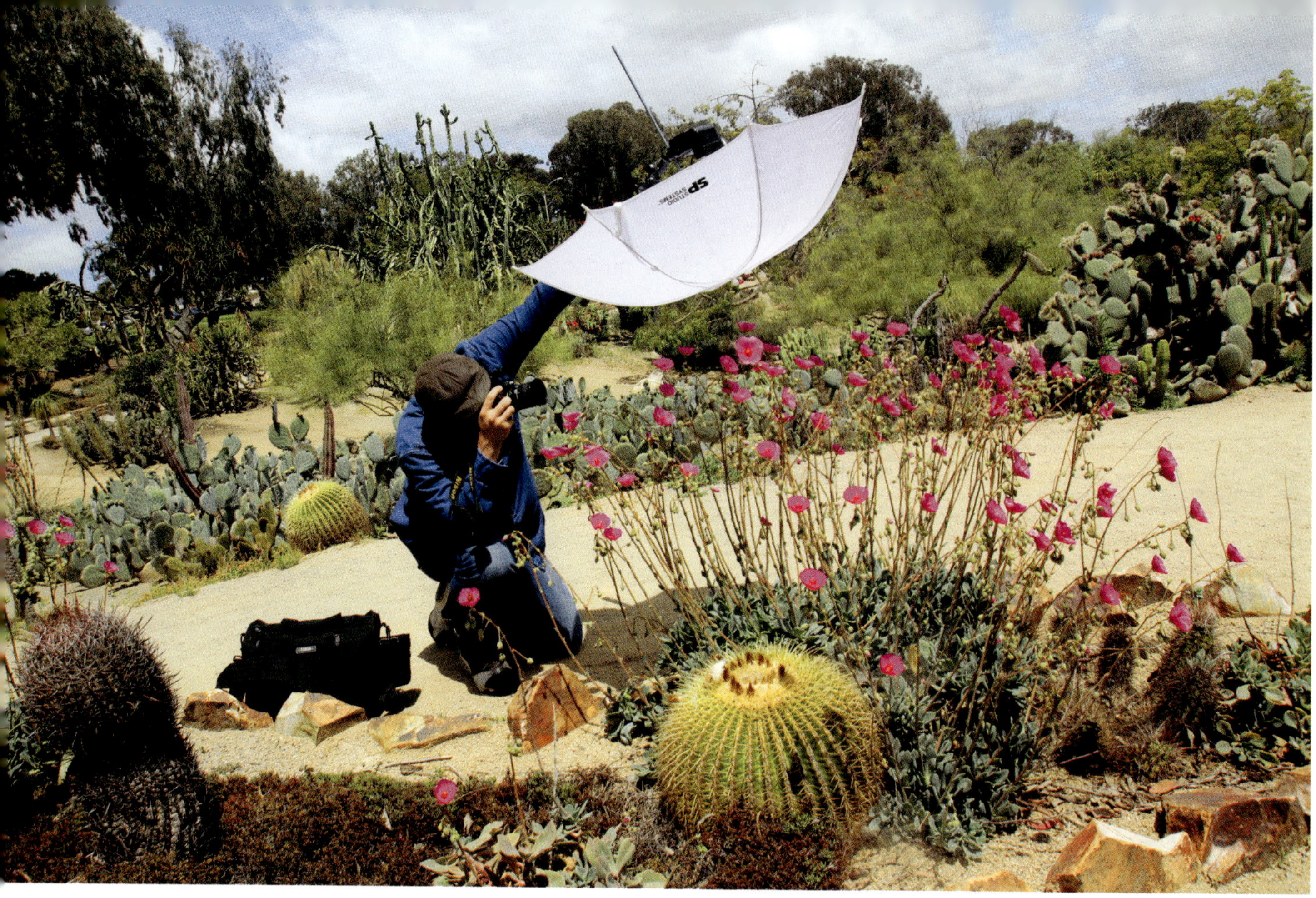

You don't need the latest or greatest gear to create amazing close-up or macro images. Grab some old gear and just start using it. A manual shooter is never without options or ideas. In this photo, an old studio umbrella was employed to enlarge the flash. Remember, this is not about "looking the part," it's about getting the images you want. Use what you have—and use it well.

## ABOUT THE GEAR (THIS IS THE BRILLIANT PART!)

As a manual shooter, all you need is a camera, a lens, and a flash. You don't need anything fancy and certainly nothing expensive. Any lens will get you close (each lens has a minimum focal distance). Every flash will add light (that is its job), and every SLR (digital or not) will allow you to adjust the aperture and shutter speed (as long as the camera is in manual mode).

It's nice, of course, to have some extra equipment, as well. Softboxes, umbrellas, light sticks, specialty lenses, and macro tubes can all make the chase for close-up perfection that much more fun—but they are not the important part. It's your artistry and drive that counts. Without an initial vision and understanding of your equipment, nothing works. There has to be a *reason* to use that equipment, to employ that flash, to attach that modifier. You need to know *why* you need the stuff before you buy or use it.

Creativity doesn't come from a camera bag, an automatic setting, or a computer. It comes from the heart of an artist and takes time, dedication, and perseverance to develop. There are no shortcuts. For this reason, we emphasize the value of visualization. For example, depth of field and lighting are paramount when shooting macro and close-up images. If you make a mistake here—if you don't choose the right aperture, shooting angle, or power setting on your flash—there is no fixing it later in the computer (trust us!). You either get this stuff right in-camera or you go home with nothing. This is why it is critical to think through the message-building process completely. Once you identify your objectives, you can easily work through what gear is required and make wise decisions when purchasing it. When trying to create amazing close-up or macro images, it's not so much about the amount or the expense of the gear you have;

***Exploring the Unknown***

Traversing the unknown is an amazing thing. A world unlike anything you've ever seen is waiting—usually just a few feet from your front door. Don't take anything for granted or think that something is so beneath you that it doesn't warrant some close-up attention—you may be shocked at what this small world offers. Through the delicate play of light, color, and shapes, a tapestry of magic can unfold in the most unlikely of places. Exploring, challenging, inventing, and expressing are what it means to be a close-up/macro photographer—and a true artist.

Whether you decide to play in an ethereal world of abstract shapes, colors, and textures (such as in the close-up image of the dead flower) or go for a more traditional macro interpretation of a living plant and water drops, you need to know the basics and to have the options an off-camera flash provides. In both of these images, an off-camera flash proved vital. In the dead-flower image, it was used to illuminate the background behind the plant. In the water-droplets image, it was used to light the flower after a very small aperture in the camera was chosen. The smaller aperture was needed to achieve the crisp depth of field.

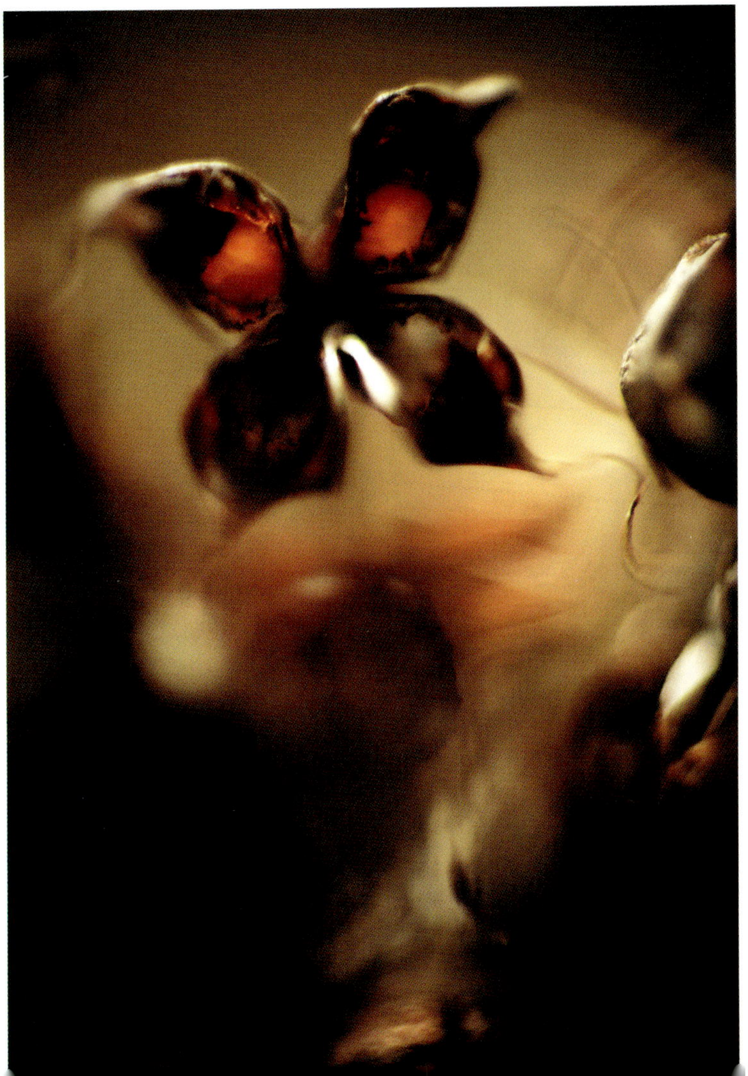

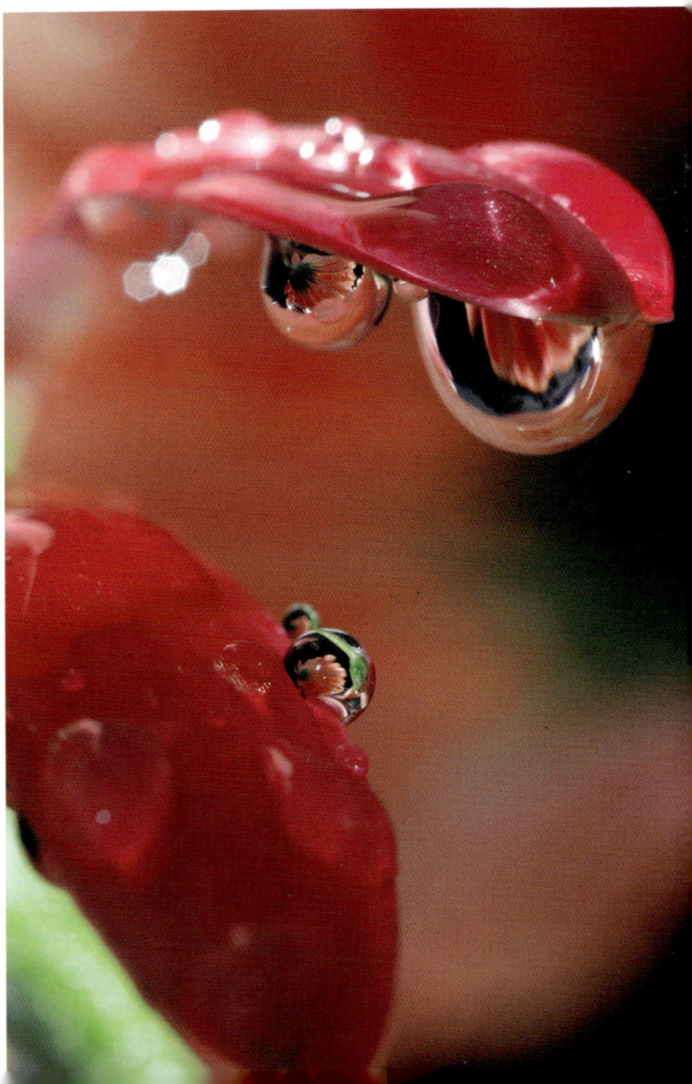

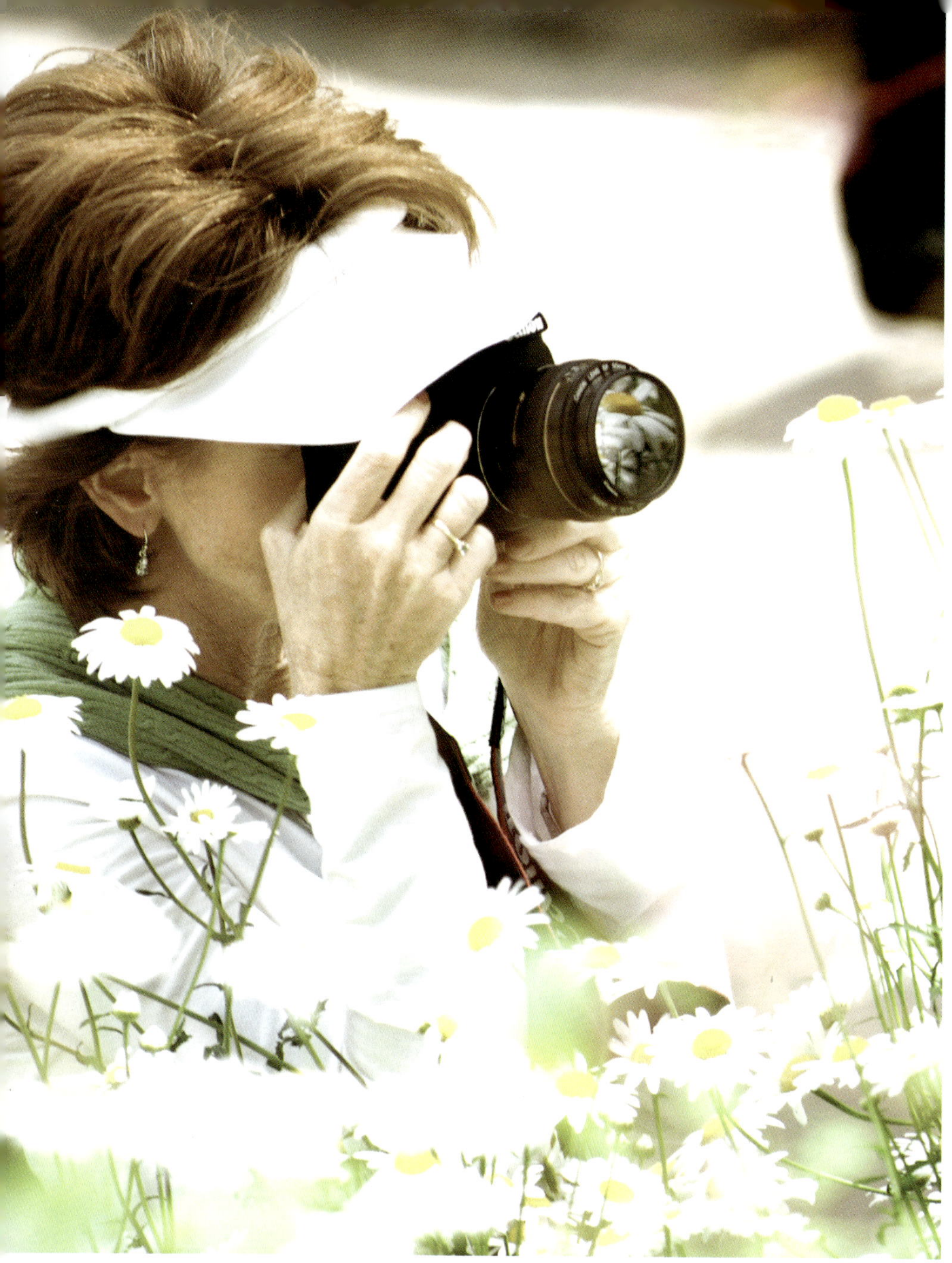

Start simple. Get close to something and shoot as this image demonstrates. Don't worry about adding light with an off-camera flash until you know the exact limitations of your gear without it. Having a reason before you begin shooting with an off-camera flash will make the whole journey that much more enjoyable and rewarding.

your success will be a direct result of the courage you show when using those tools.

## ABOUT SHOOTING IN RAW

We suggest that you shoot only in JPEG while learning your craft. We find that shooting in the RAW format often provides students with an excuse not to concentrate on some very vital parts of the message-building process. Shooting RAW files allows you to correct your images after the fact, weakening your resolve and giving you an excuse for not creating a perfect image while in the field. That's not something you want to happen. Instead, we encourage you to make mistakes and learn from them while in the field—to fix things immediately and do everything manually.

This, as you can imagine, also eliminates most of the time spent at the computer—an added bonus!

Think of it like this: What if there weren't any mistakes in your image? What if you taught yourself to dial-in your white balance, contrast, saturation, hue, and sharpness settings *before* you took the picture (based on how you felt about what was in front of you and not what you imagined others would like)?

What if you picked the perfect aperture that nailed the required depth of field? What if you chose the perfect amount of light by adjusting your shutter speed or ISO or employing a flash? What if you could dial-in

Subtle shifts of perspective, light, contrast, and saturation need to be visualized before you take the photos. It's not just about getting close to something, it's about making that something ring true to your own unique vision. It's all about interpretation, not recollection.

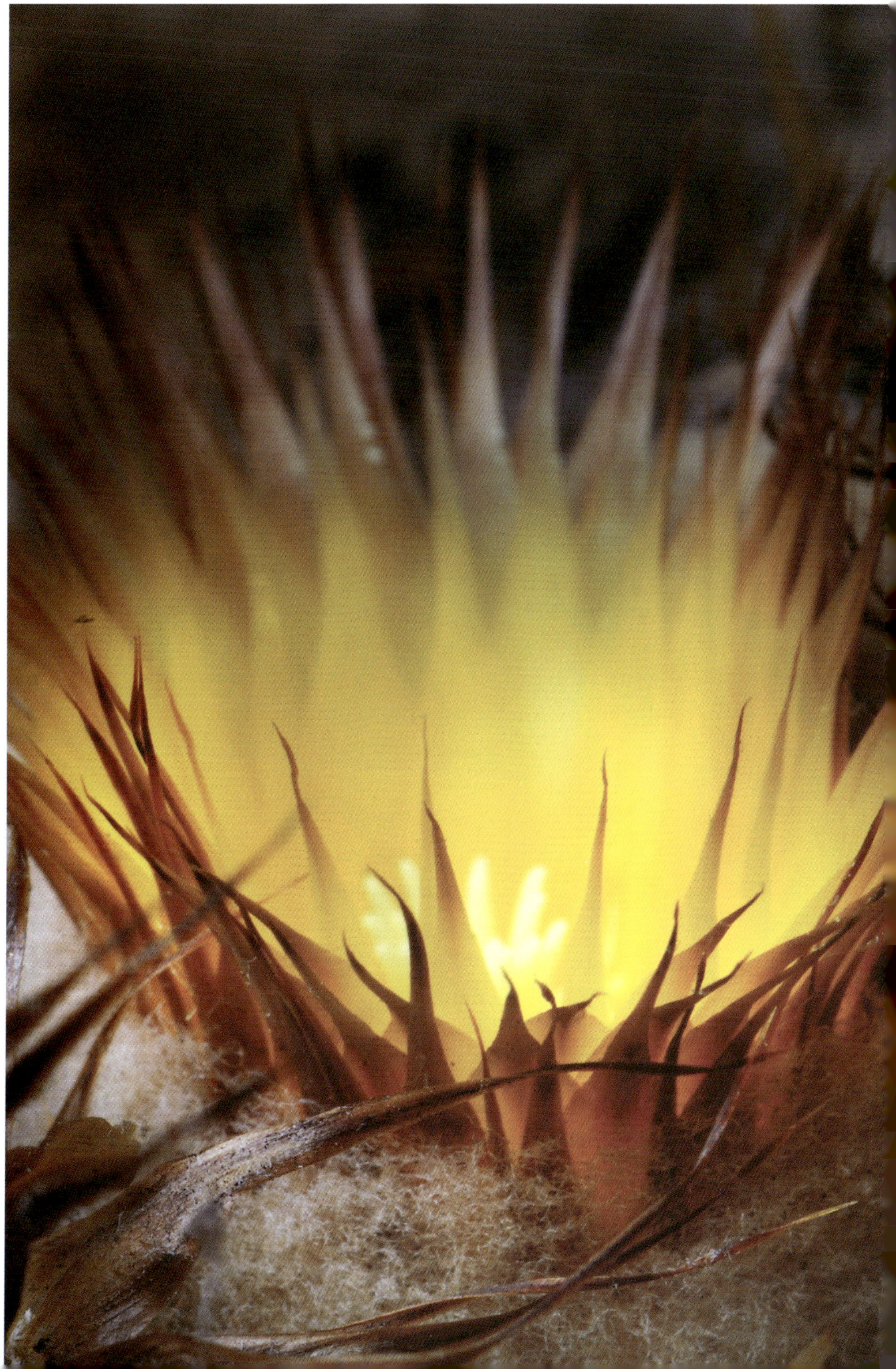

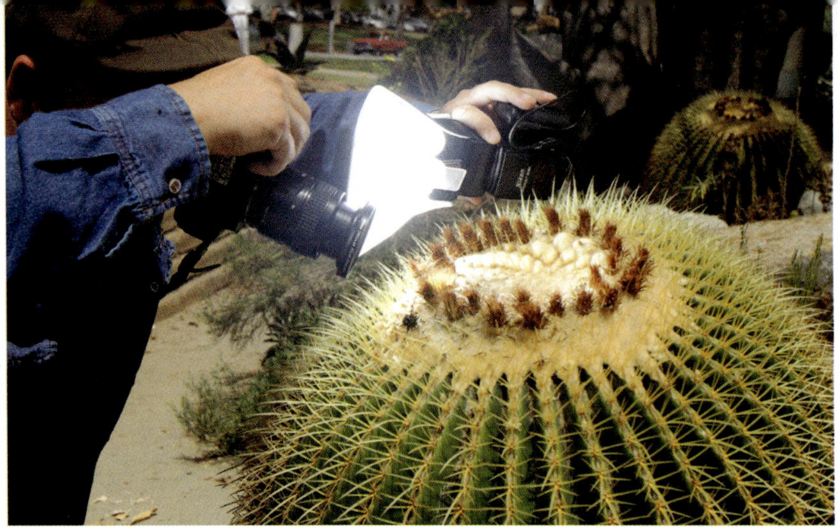

The mechanics of capturing great images aren't that hard. What's tricky is visualizing the end result first.

mood? What if you did everything right and your photo looked great coming out of the camera? If you did all that, what would you need to correct?

Now, imagine making that your goal. Imagine becoming a true artist with your camera—having the skill, foresight, and visualization techniques to make every image you shoot perfect right out of the camera. That kind of changes things, doesn't it? It actually sounds like a real goal.

## ABOUT THIS BOOK

There are no shortcuts to perfection, no button that can make you more creative, and no auto approach that will ever work. You have to know what you want, recognize the obstacles in the way, and solve each and every problem—before it even happens.

Is it possible? Can you do it? Yes you can! So stop pushing for normal and start striving for perfection. Learn your craft, use your tools, and start creating something memorable instead of just taking pretty pictures. Be the artist you can be and don't ever settle for less.

To get to that point, you've got a lot of work to do—and that's where this book comes in. We'll guide you through the complicated and confusing waters of off-camera flash when shooting macro and close-up images. We'll offer our advice, guidance, and even some tips.

And don't worry if your skill level with manual control isn't up to par. Macro and close-up photography with an off-camera flash is actually a wonderful place to start your journey—with macro, you really have no other choice but going manual. You will have to learn how (and why) to adjust your shutter speed, your aperture size. You will have to deal with focus and depth-of-field issues, you will need to change your contrast and saturation before you shoot, and you will most definitely have to start building messages with an off-camera flash.

As you work through this process, keep in mind that there are already thousands of photographers out there, taking thousands of close-up photographs every day. However, there is only one of *you*. Your vision is unique and your images can be, too—this we promise!

**Facing page**—*Top left:* Natural light illuminated the flower, but it took two off-camera flashes to light the background. We could have made the lighting brighter, we could have put more on the petals in the front—but we chose not to. Great macro/close-up photography takes insight and vision. Start creating images that sing of you—instead of just another picture that records the "stuff" around you. *Top right:* The beauty of macro and close-up photography can be found in its apparent simplicity—colors, lines, shapes, and texture for the pure joy of it all. But looks can be deceiving. In this image, for example, an off-camera flash had to be used to highlight the extreme blur and beautiful colors of the background. The flower petals in the foreground were lit with natural light but the background was in deep shadow. Many would have ignored this scene as it was, but an artist is always evaluating the possibilities—even when they are hidden in darkness. *Bottom:* A world once reserved for professionals is just beyond your door. An indescribable universe of lines, shapes, patterns, and colors will emerge—unlike anything you have ever seen. But keep in mind that none of this is possible if you choose to approach it with an automated mentality. You have to want to "create," not just "take."

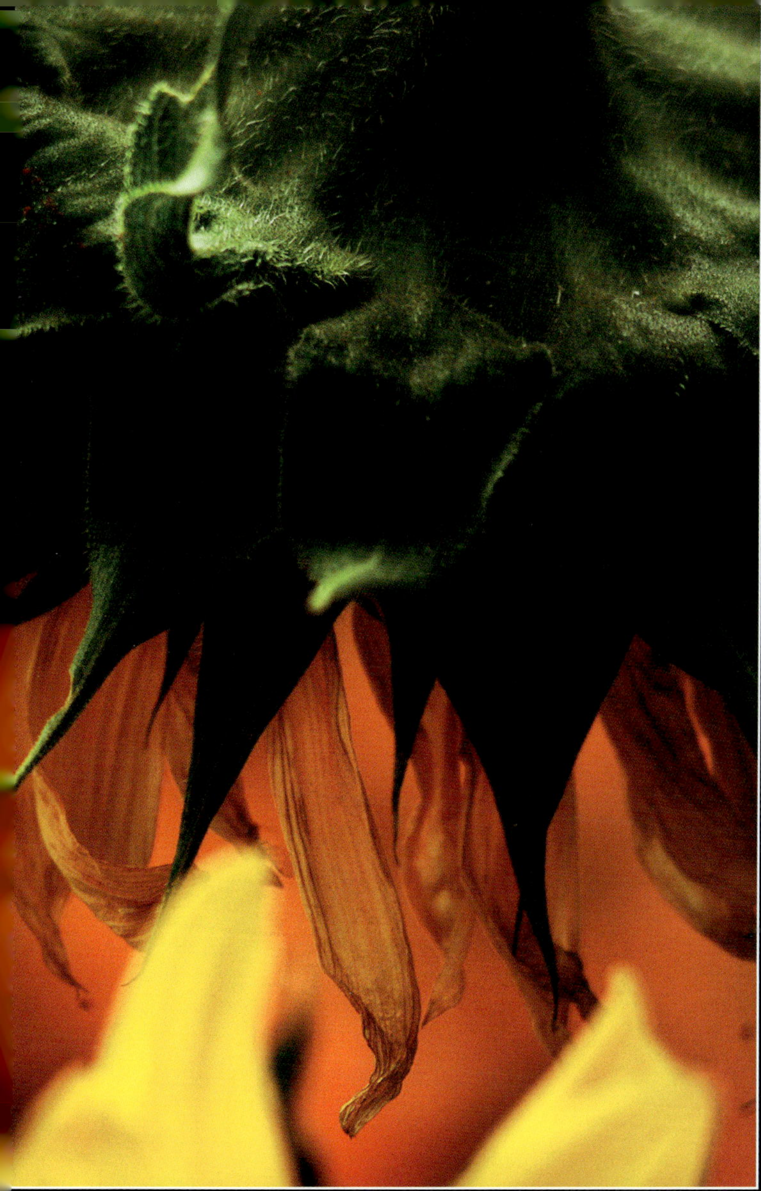
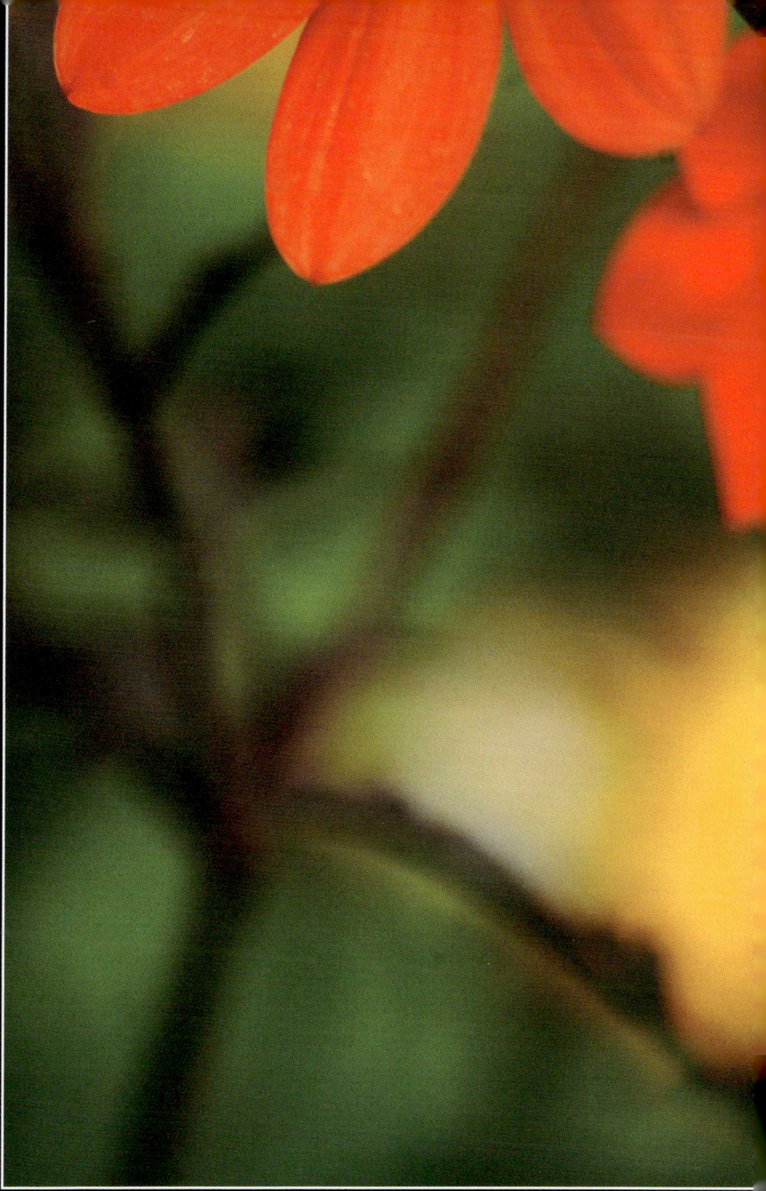
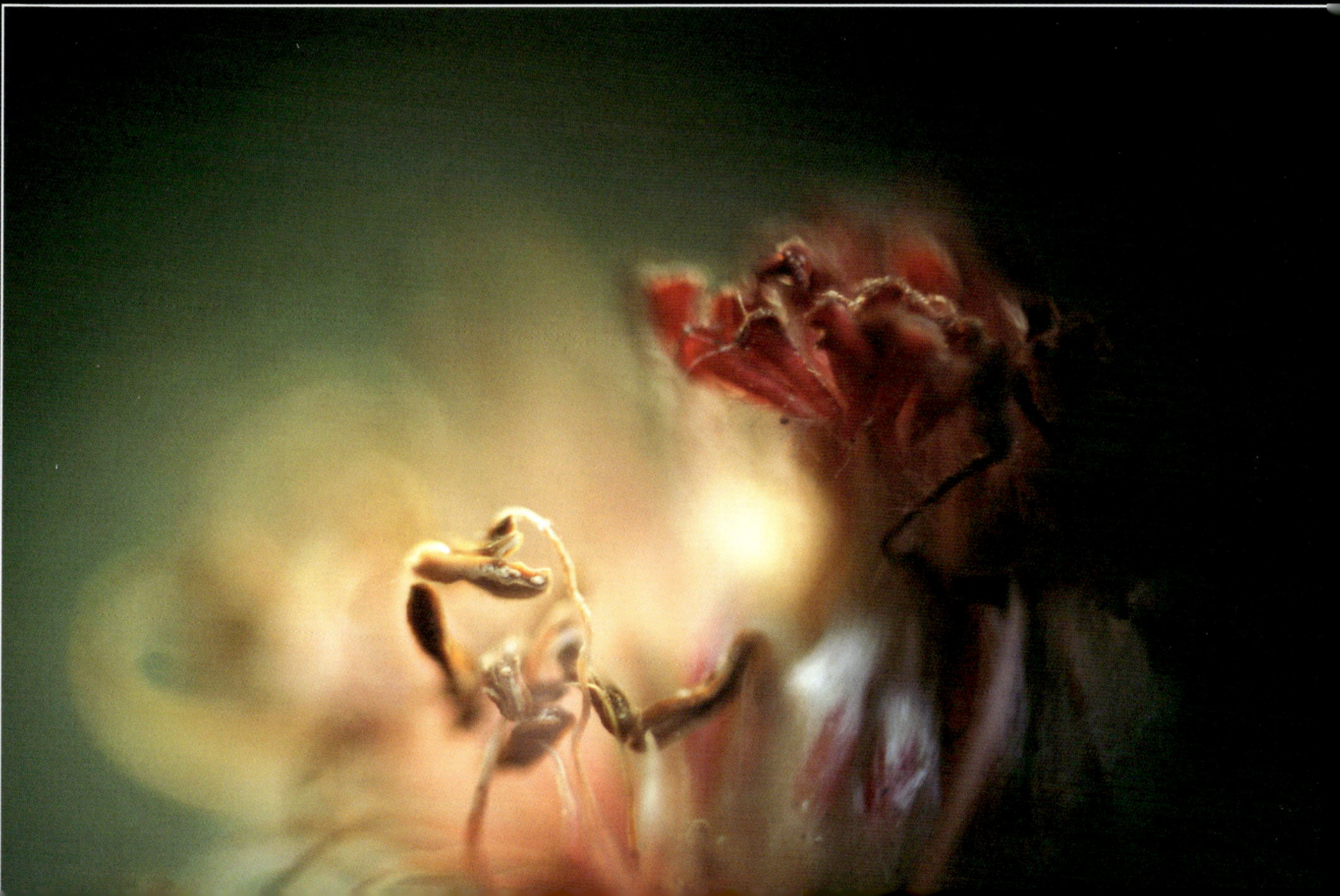

# 2. KEY TECHNIQUES

Before we get into adding light, let's discuss what macro and close-up photography really are—and zero-in on some key techniques.

### CLOSE-UP *VS.* MACRO

While related, macro and close-up photography are considered vastly different by most traditional and classically-trained photographers. For an image to be "macro" a certain size relationship between the actual subject and its appearance on the film/sensor is required; a near life-size (1:1 or greater) representation is the benchmark. For instance, if you were shooting a fly and the size of the fly recorded on your sensor/film was the same (or nearly the same) size as the fly in real life, it would be classified as a macro photograph. If the image didn't live up to this standard, then it would simply be termed a "close-up" picture.

Knowing the difference between a close-up image (such as this one) and a macro photograph (such as the image of the bee in the previous chapter) is pretty important.

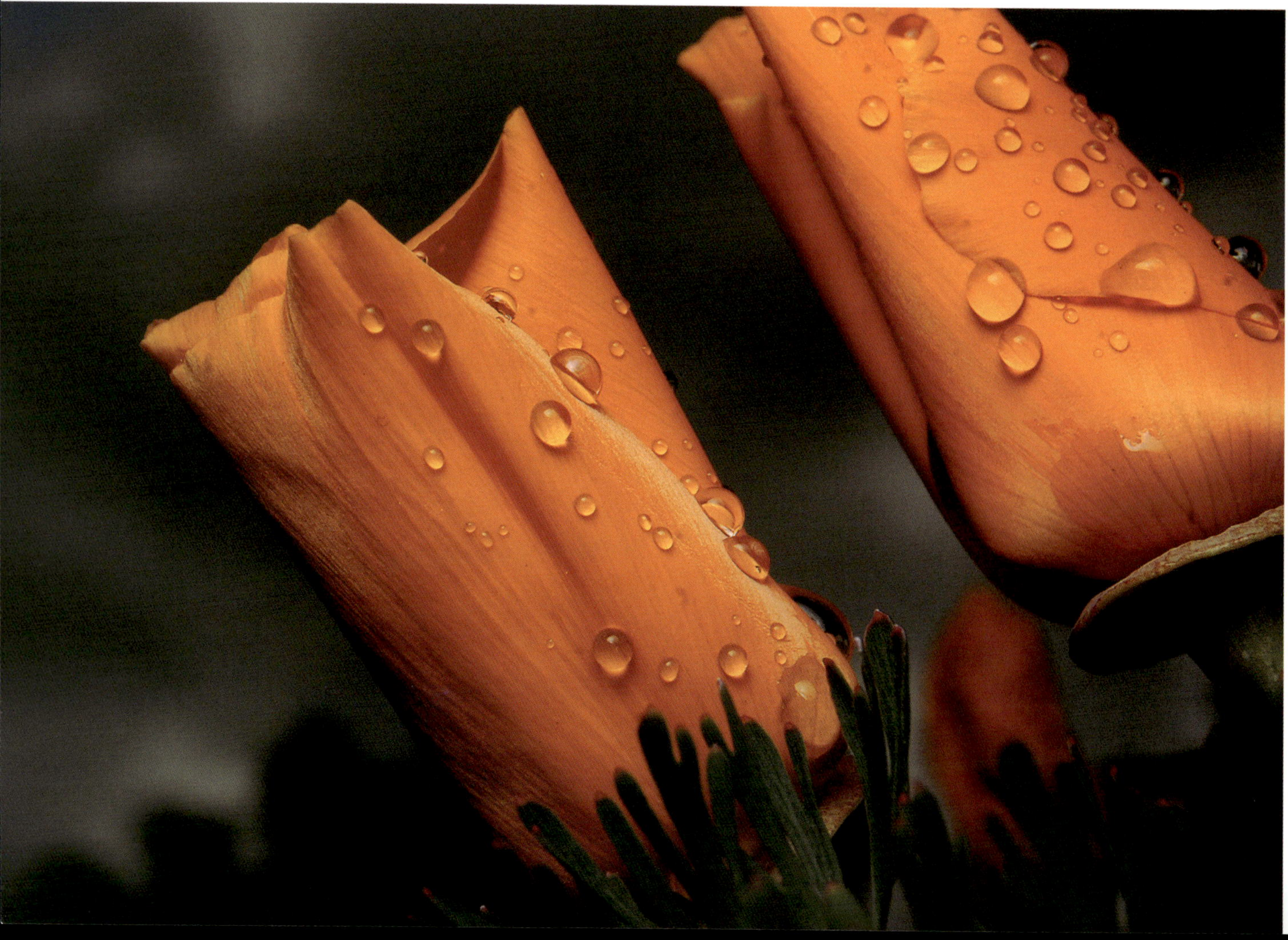

Top—To add just the right amount of light to this close-up image, the photographer asked a friend to hold her off-camera flash. With a rather large modification tool in place (a LumiQuest Big Bounce) the assistant held the flash over the flowers while the photographer triggered it with an inexpensive radio transmitter. Right—In this series of images, you see a graphic representation of the various distances (from camera to subject) required by different lenses when all have been set to their minimum focal distance. It's important that you understand what each of your lenses offers. If you've never tested this, or are unfamiliar with your gear, spend some time taking close-up test shots. It can only help.

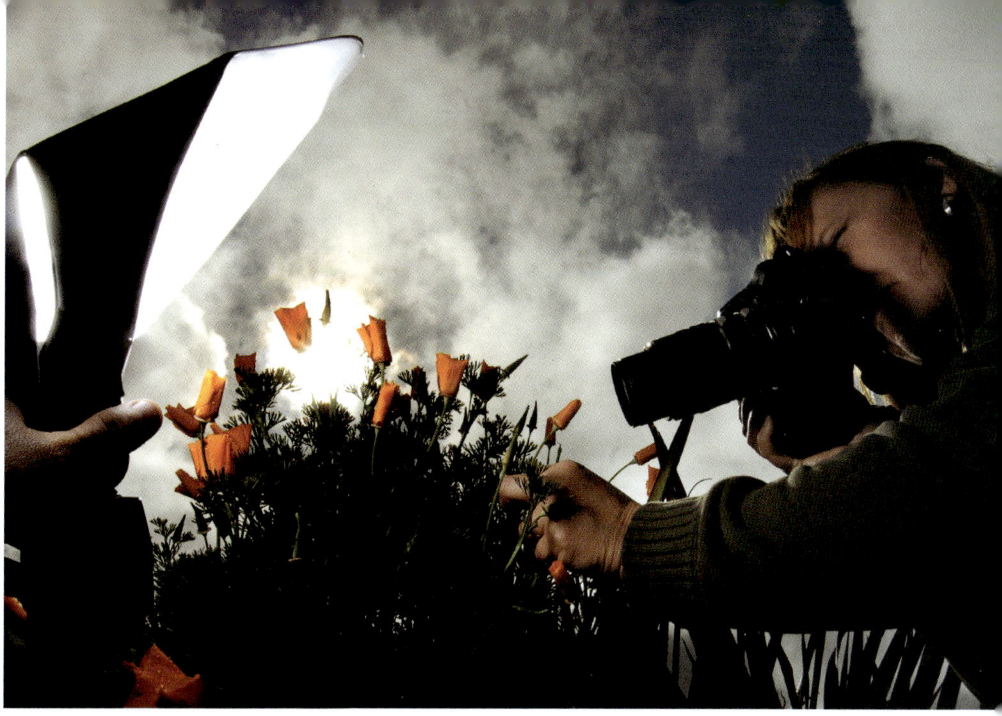

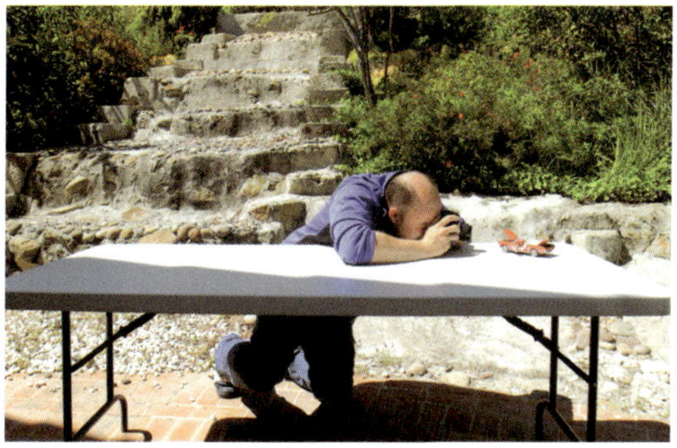

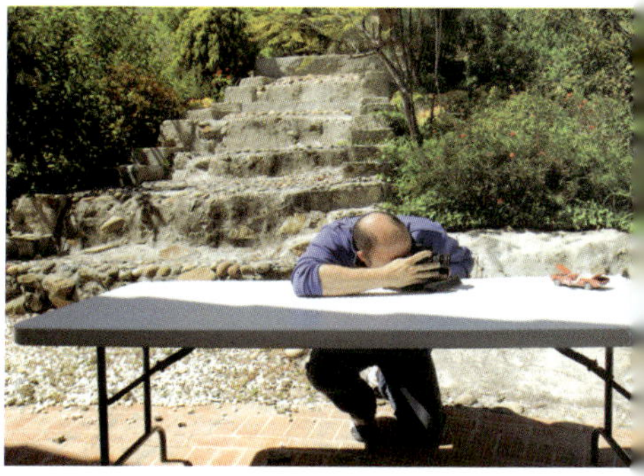

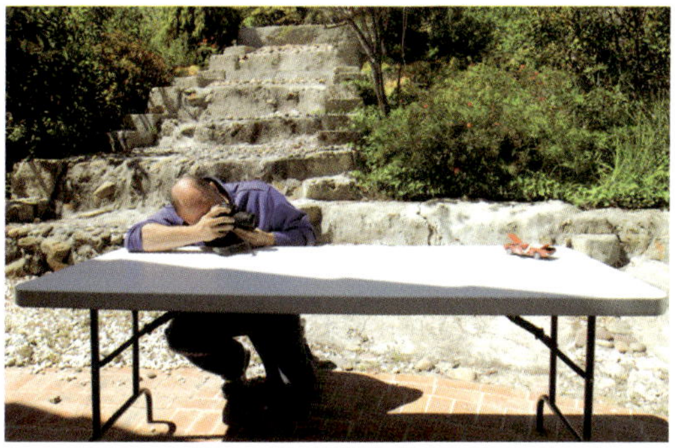

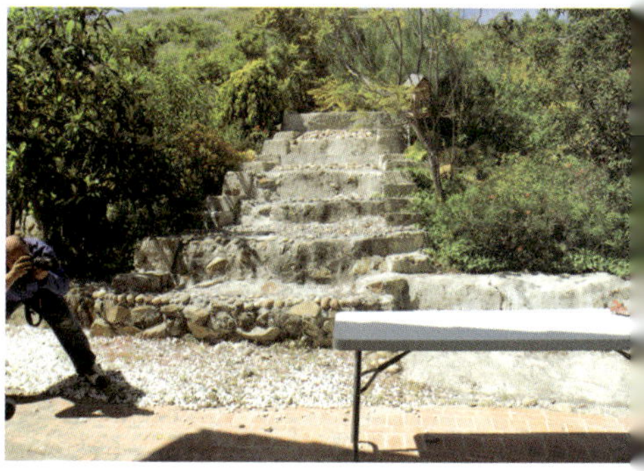

Over the course of time, these standards have weakened. Today's macro and close-up artists tend to mix these definitions a bit liberally, sometimes lowering the traditional standard of 1:1 representation to fit their own unique situation (or personal marketing strategy) by calling their work "macro" art when it's just good close-up photography. Camera and lens manufacturers have also clouded the issue by adapting the word "macro" (denoted by the iconic flower symbol) to describe equipment that barely achieves a 1:4 size relationship.

While this wordplay may prove great marketing, it does make things a bit confusing. We've found that these ever-changing definitions prove

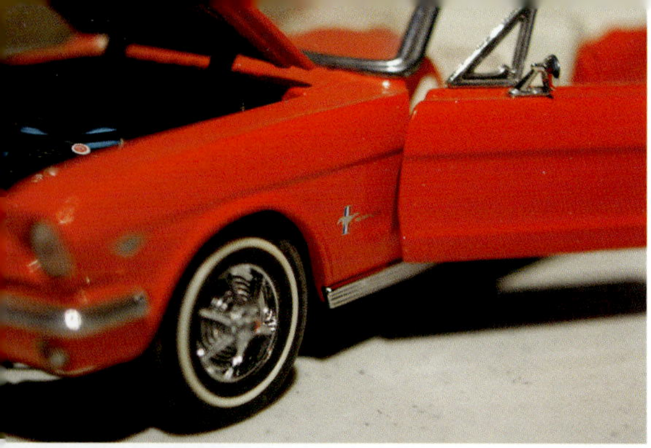

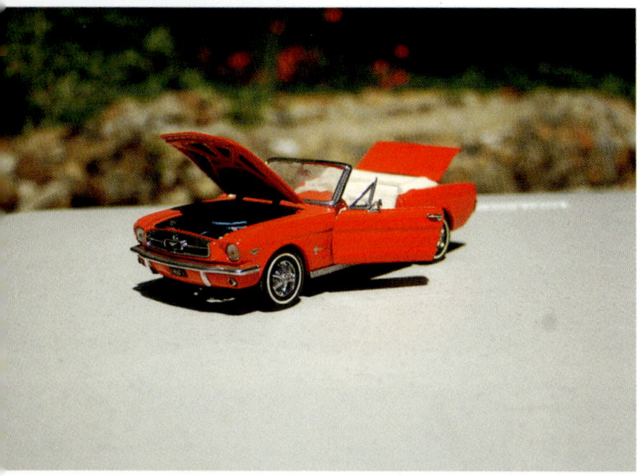

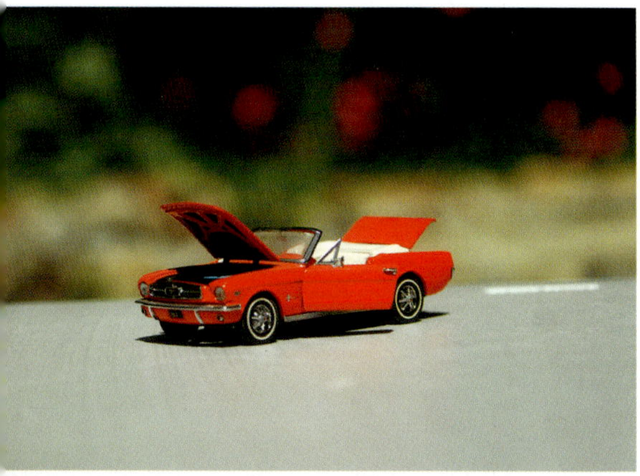

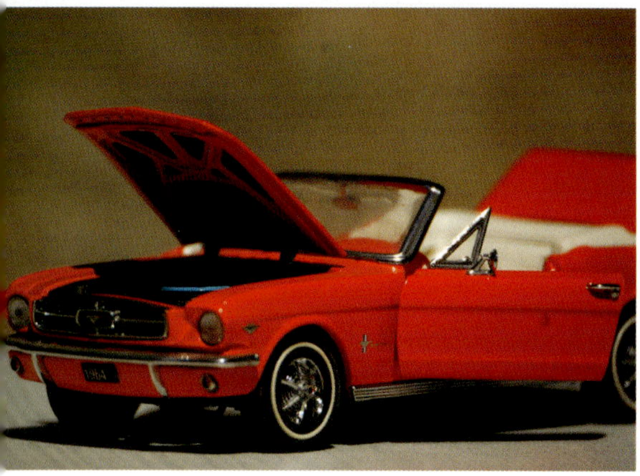

a stumbling block and actually slow the learning process. After all, how can you learn something if the words used to describe it keep changing? For the sake of clarity, we'll be using traditional standards and definitions in this book. Close-up photography simply means you're close to your subject; macro photography means you're achieving a near life-size (1:1 or greater) relationship on your sensor.

Fortunately, no matter what you plan on calling these images, the tools, methods, physics, and mechanics used to create them are identical.

Each lens you own will probably have a different minimum focal distance and, in turn, offer you a different type of close-up image. In the images to the left you see examples of several different lenses. Notice how the blurred area increases and decreases. It's important that a close-up/macro photographer know these details about all of their lenses.

## CAMERA AND LENS SETTINGS

Anyone with any camera can shoot extreme close-up images—you don't need anything special for that. Simply get close to something, manually adjust the focus ring to its minimum focal distance, then shift your body (and camera) back and forth until the focal point hits your subject . . . and shoot. Voilà—a close-up image! While taking a close-up image is pretty easy, controlling your results and creating something special is a completely different story.

**How It Works.** The first thing you'll notice when shooting a close-up image is the disturbing lack of focus. Controlling this focus area (making it wider or narrower) is one of the many challenges you'll face as a close-up/macro artist—and it's the most important one to conquer. To do so, you will have to be in full manual control of your camera, lens, and flash (you knew we'd say that, right?). You will also have to be familiar with some basic physics, camera mechanics, and flash truths to pull it off. So let's get started!

As illustrated here, when shooting close-up images you may notice a disturbing lack of depth of field. This is something to be expected and can easily be controlled. Adjusting this depth is critical to any photographer and is one of the main reasons why we employ an off-camera flash.

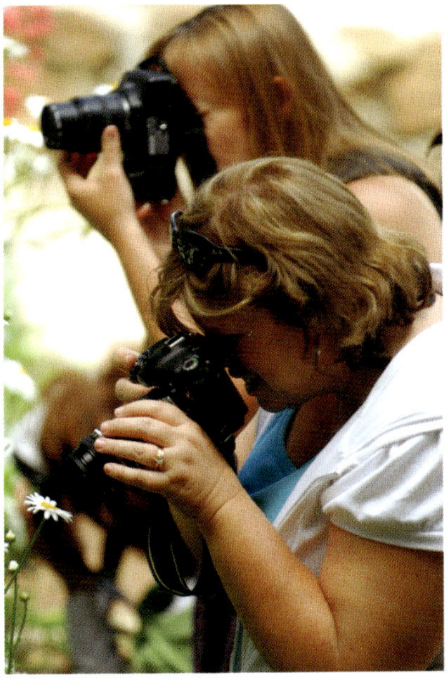

**Focal Distance.** There is only one spot in your image that is ever razor sharp—that's where you focused. Radiating from this spot (in front of and behind your focal point) is an area of apparent focus called the depth of field, which stretches from your focus point to well beyond, gradually fading into a blur at both ends. Exactly when it stops being in focus and starts being a blur is a personal decision and is based on the aperture you select.

To experiment with this, find a small object for your subject (in the examples to the left we used a toy car). Working in full daylight, set this up on a clean table—our mini-studio for this exercise—outside your house. Grab all of your lenses and start taking test pictures. Dial in your camera's largest aperture (smallest f-number) and choose a shutter speed that gives you the best possible exposure. Do not use any autoexposure mode and do not use autofocus. Turn your focus ring to its closest setting and then simply move your body back and forth, adjusting the small plane of focus until it hits your target. Take note of how close you can get and how shallow the depth of field is. You may be quite shocked at just how close you can get with each of your lenses.

**Depth of Field.** The depth of field can be changed by setting the appropriate aperture in the camera. You can lengthen it to cover an entire flower (by using a much smaller aperture) or pull it back to include just the edges of a petal (by using a larger aperture). It's an artistic choice.

Depth of field is governed by three factors: focal distance (how close you are to your subject when focusing on that subject); focal length (the

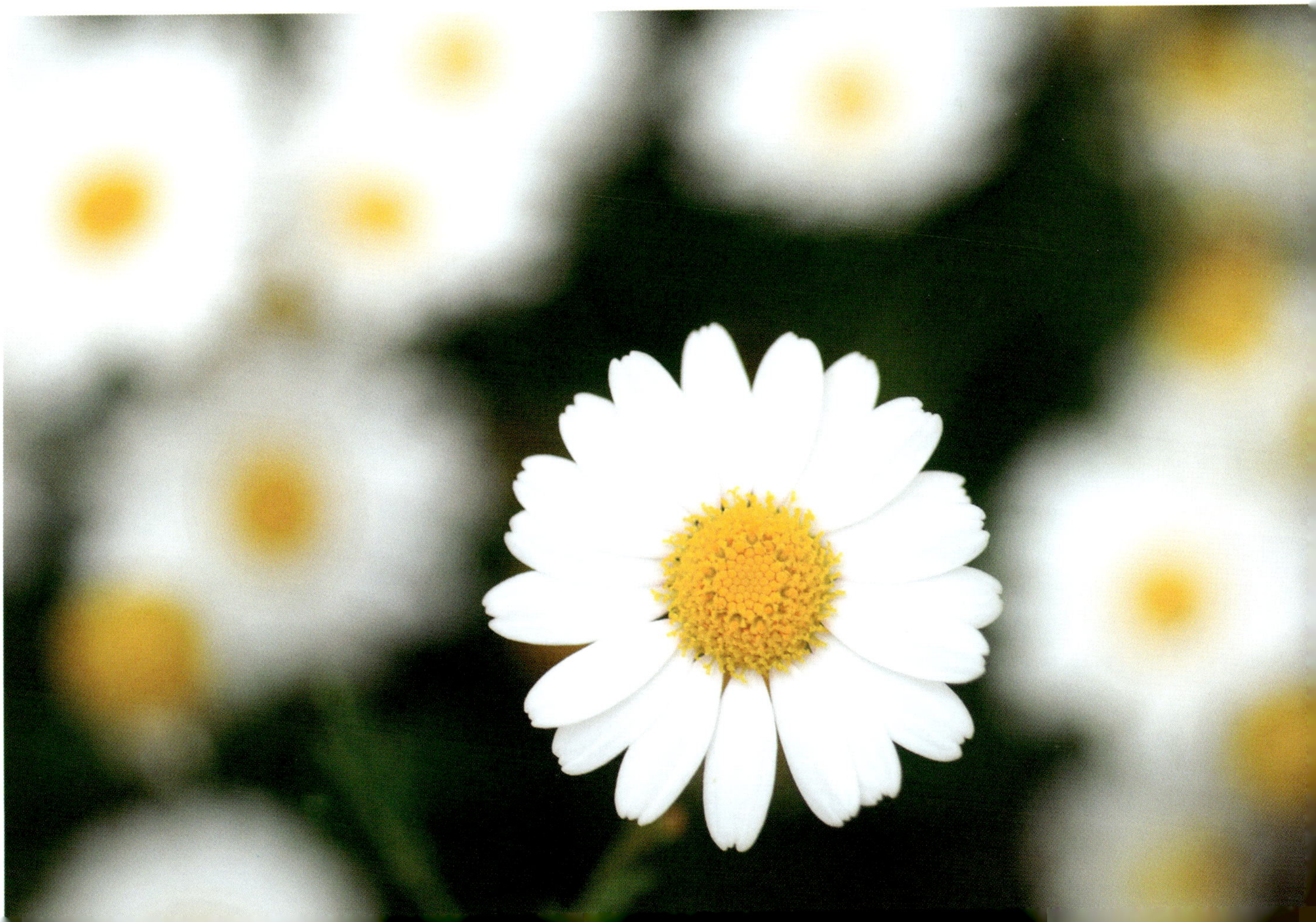

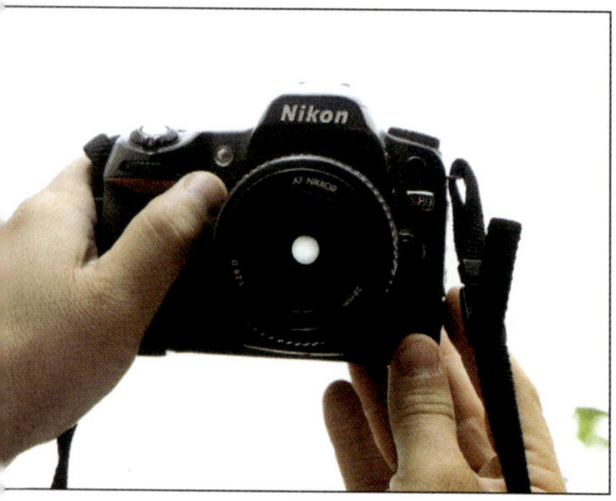


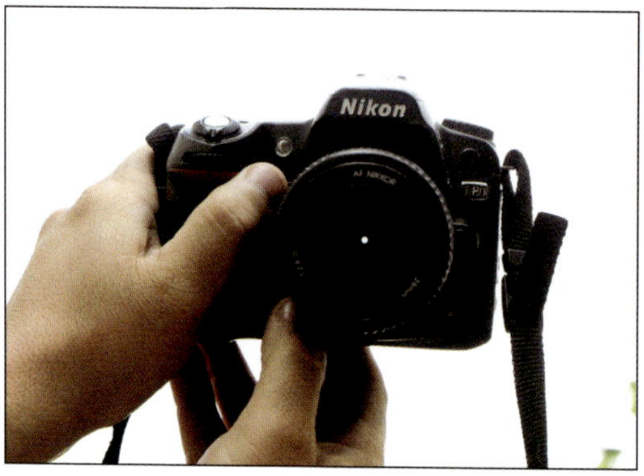


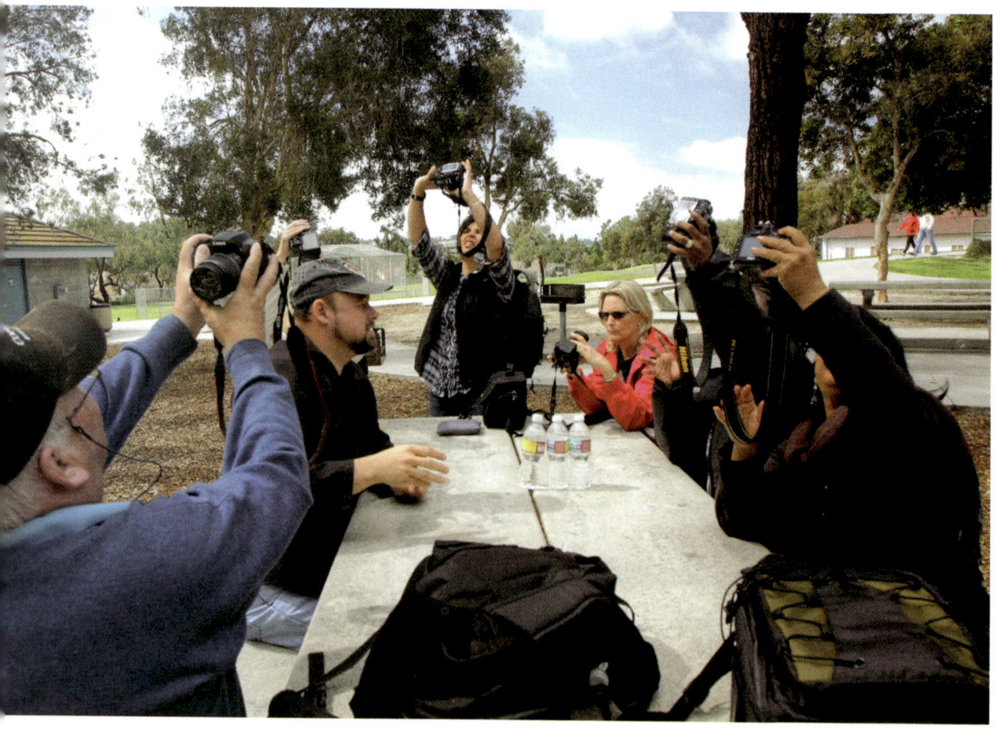

**Top left**—Aperture size remains constant in your lens until the shutter button is released—no matter which aperture you've chosen. **Top right**—When the depth-of-field preview button (found on the bottom right side of this model) is depressed, the size of the aperture shrinks to its dialed-in size. **Bottom**—Photography students inspect the results of activating their depth-of-field preview button during an outdoor training session. When the camera is held backwards (such as this) you can see the aperture shrink when the depth-of-field preview button is employed.

lens you are using); and the aperture size you have chosen. Adjust any of these (even slightly) and your depth of field changes. Through the camera's viewfinder you can quite easily see the effects that focal distance and focal length have on your depth of field. However, the third factor (aperture size) cannot be seen through your viewfinder unless you employ your camera's depth-of-field preview button.

**The Depth-of-Field Preview Button.** Nearly every SLR today uses an automated aperture system. This system keeps the aperture large until the shutter button is depressed. Then and only then does it shrink the size of the aperture to what you have chosen. While this keeps the viewfinder bright when trying to focus, it does not give you an accurate view of what will be in focus in your recorded image—unless you happen to be shooting at the lens's largest aperture setting. Since the scene through the viewfinder reflects only the depth of field associated with the largest aperture (no matter what you have dialed in) you cannot trust what you see. (*Note:* The depth-of field preview button is not relegated to just macro and close-up photography. An artist-with-a-camera uses it all of the time—whether he is shooting a mountain range, a model, or a butterfly. Yes, it's that important.)

To see the real focus depth you have to employ the depth-of-field preview button. When activated, it disengages the automatic aperture system, allowing the aperture to shrink to its current setting. Once this button is engaged (and held in) you will be able to see the actual depth of field. Yes, the scene will appear darker though the viewfinder as well (smaller apertures take away light), but that needs to be ignored; it means nothing to the final image. Remember, this button simply gives you a preview of your depth of field (hence its name), not of your final exposure.

***Live View***

On many digital cameras today, the live-view feature may also give you an accurate preview of the given depth of field. However, using live-view promotes bad camera handling habits, so we suggest simply getting used to the depth-of-field preview button—and using it religiously.

Depth of field is paramount when shooting close-up images. To pull off the depth you see in these photos, an aperture of f/22 was used. A shutter speed of $^1/_{200}$ second was then chosen to darken the sky. A modified flash (set to $^1/_{16}$ power) was used to brighten the flowers.

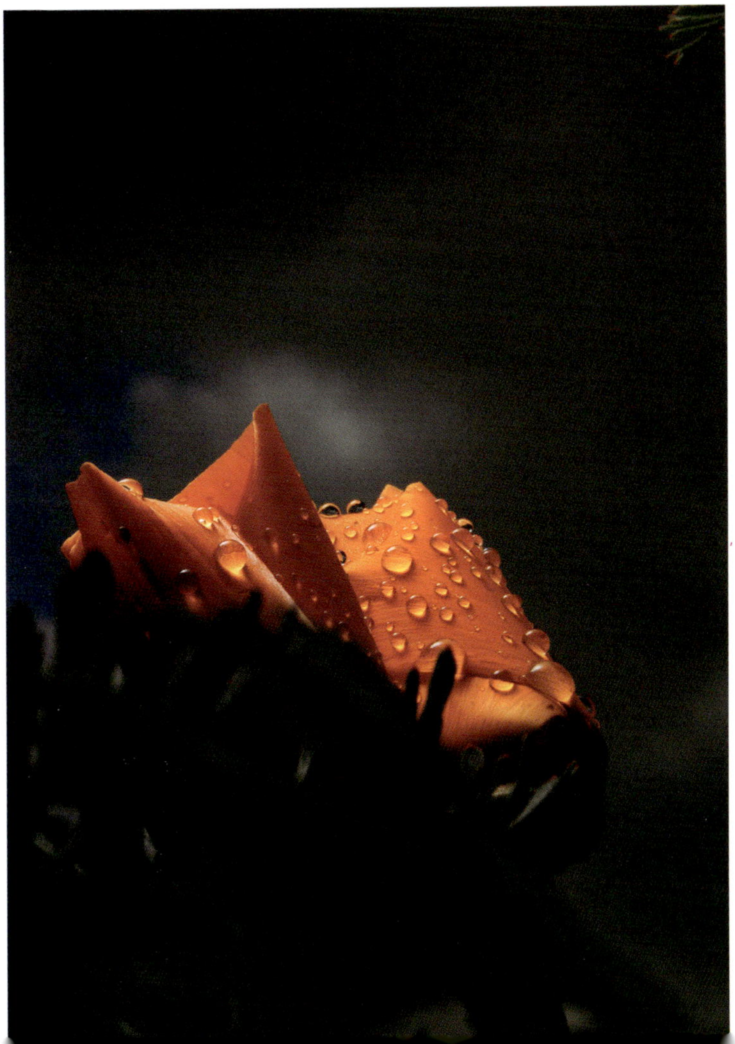

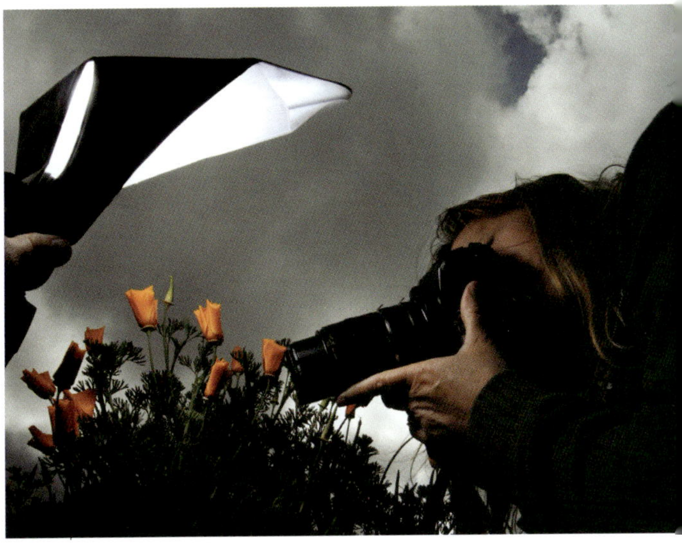

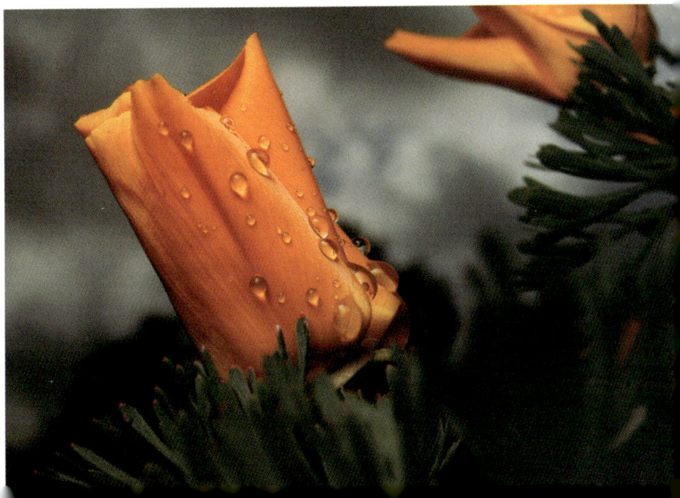

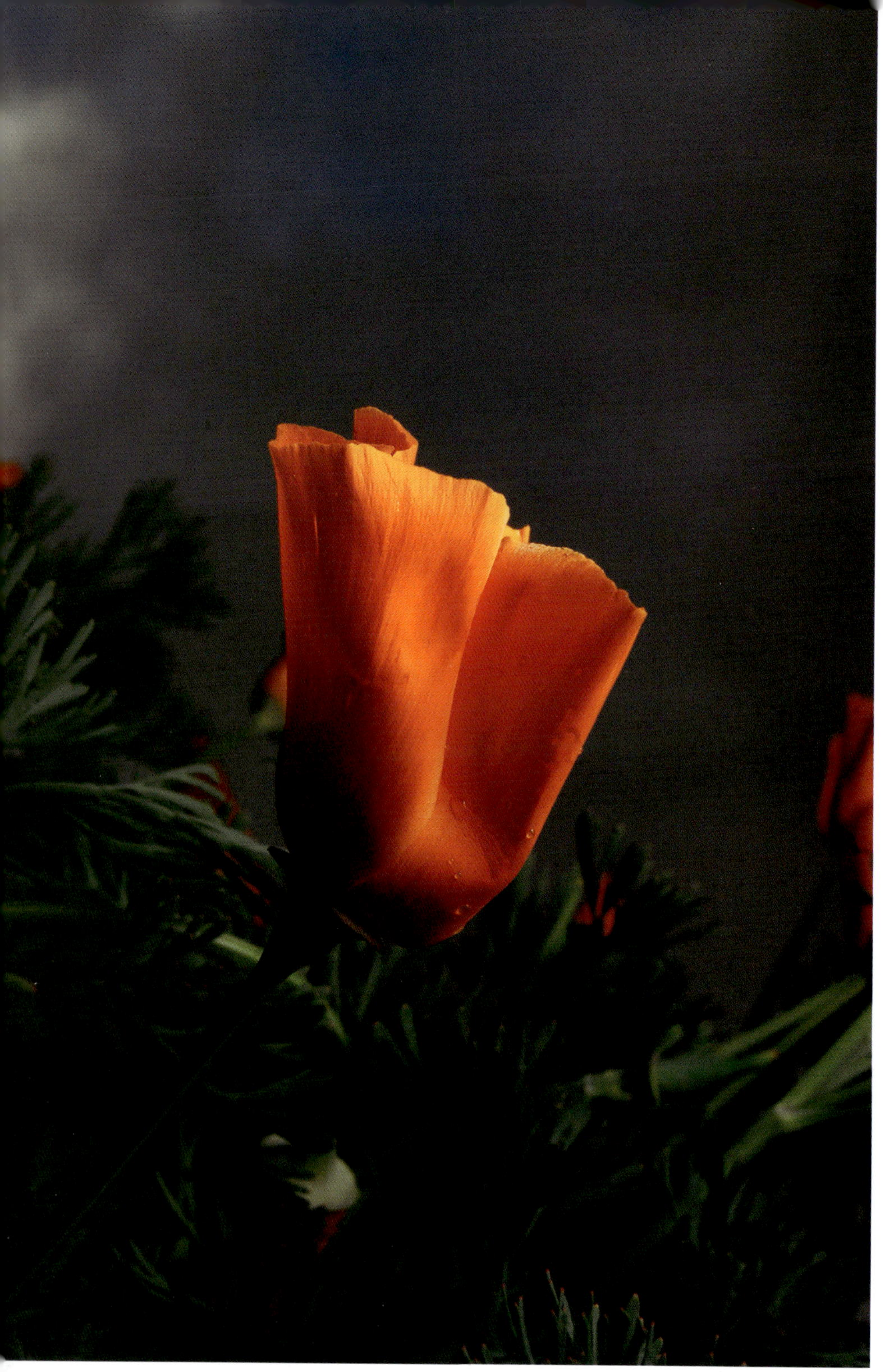

The amazing colors, contrast, focus, and depth of field in this photo were all achieved in-camera. No post-processing was required. Learning how to shoot macro and close-up images well with an off-camera flash is an amazing goal . . . one that needs to be taken seriously by each photographer in search of true meaning in their images. Give it the time it deserves. It will change your life and open your eyes to a world few ever see, let alone capture with their camera.

Check your camera manual for the location of the depth-of-field preview button; it moves around quite a bit between camera manufacturers and models. On Nikons, look for it on the lower (or middle) right side of the camera. Canon owners should look for it on the bottom left side of their cameras. Sadly (as many of you will soon discover) the physical location of this button is a pretty important feature. When working with off-camera flash, you may be hand-holding your flash in your left hand . . . in which case, having the depth-of-field preview button on that side of the camera may prove a problem—unless, of course, you're really good at juggling (or have purchased a third arm). Using a light stand to support your flash may help, but it's still not perfect.

To be quite honest, it is quite annoying to have to move your hand back to the depth-of-field preview button and then forward again to your lens/camera before you shoot each picture. Canon is one of the few camera manufacturers that continue to put the depth-of-field preview on the left (wrong) side of their cameras. Oddly enough, though, not all of their cameras are like this; on their most expensive (professional) versions, the depth-of-field preview button is actually on the right side of the camera—right where it belongs.

While this left-side placement may irritate many Canon owners, it's nothing when compared to what Nikon has done. On their newer entry-level cameras, they have actually taken this button off the machine or hidden it, stripping a vital tool from the very people who need it the most. How can you grow if your camera doesn't even offer the most basic of options? Couple this with the fact that most lens manufacturers have stripped the depth-of-field scale from their lenses and it's a wonder that anyone understands depth of field anymore.

So, our advice is this: when choosing a digital camera, make sure it has a depth-of-field preview button. Please, don't buy one that won't allow you to grow. If you already own a camera and find that it lacks a depth-of-field preview button, get a new camera (seriously). You can't live without it.

Now that we've tracked it down, let's check out the function of this handy button. To do this, set your camera to manual and adjust your aperture to f/22. Then, flip your camera around and point your viewfinder to a bright light. Look into your lens and take note of the physical size of the aperture. Now, activate your camera and push in (and hold) the depth-of-field preview button. The aperture will shrink to f/22 (a much, much smaller hole).

Lighting this image was actually the easy part. Choosing the correct aperture, focal length, and shooting distance to keep the toy car in focus—while still blurring the background—proved more challenging. Without the aid of the depth-of-field preview button, this image would have been much more difficult to achieve.

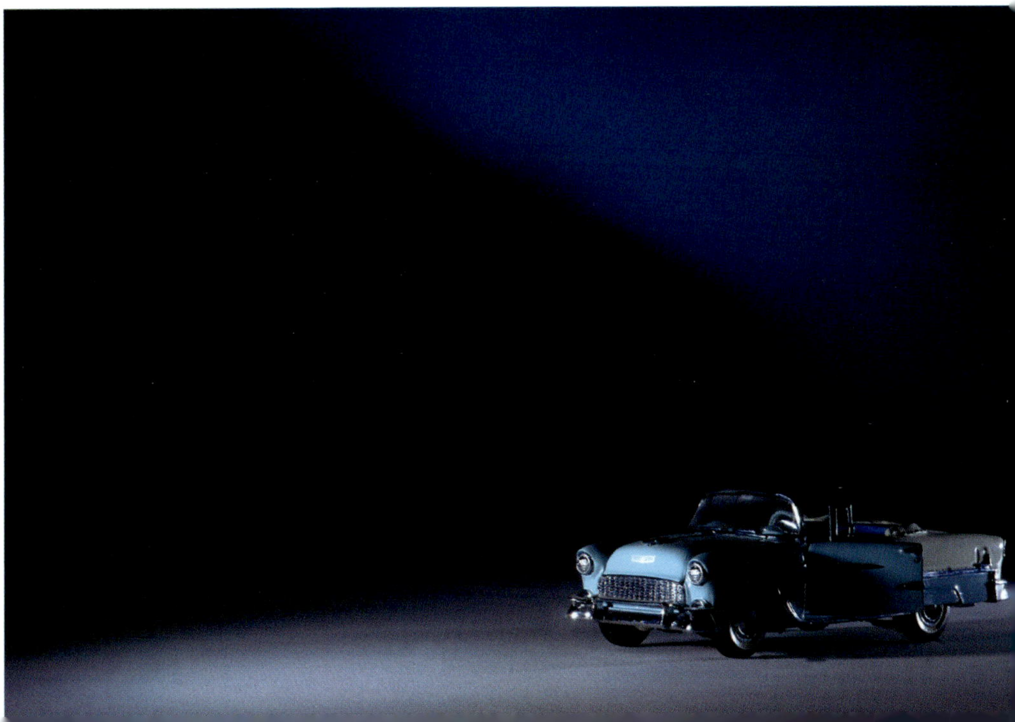

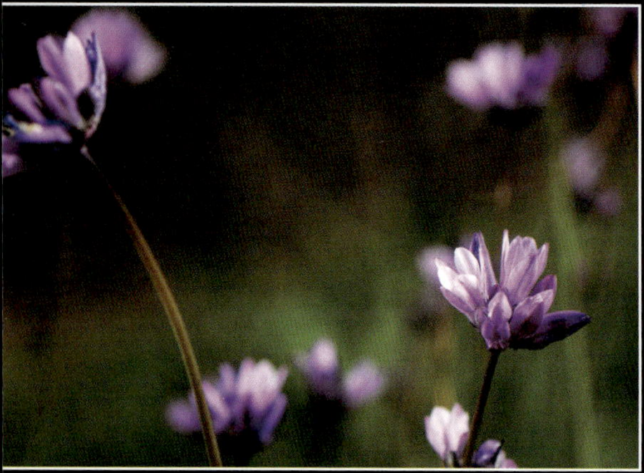

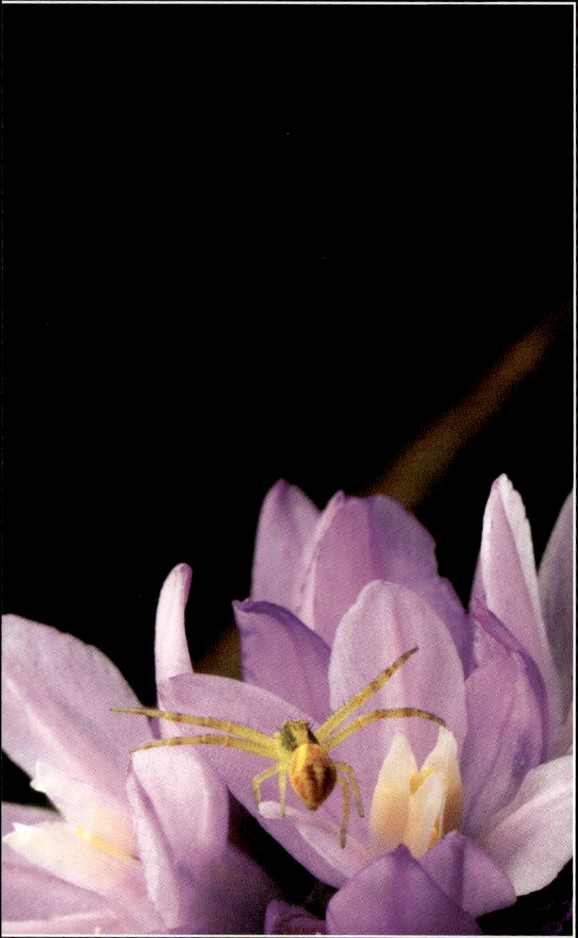

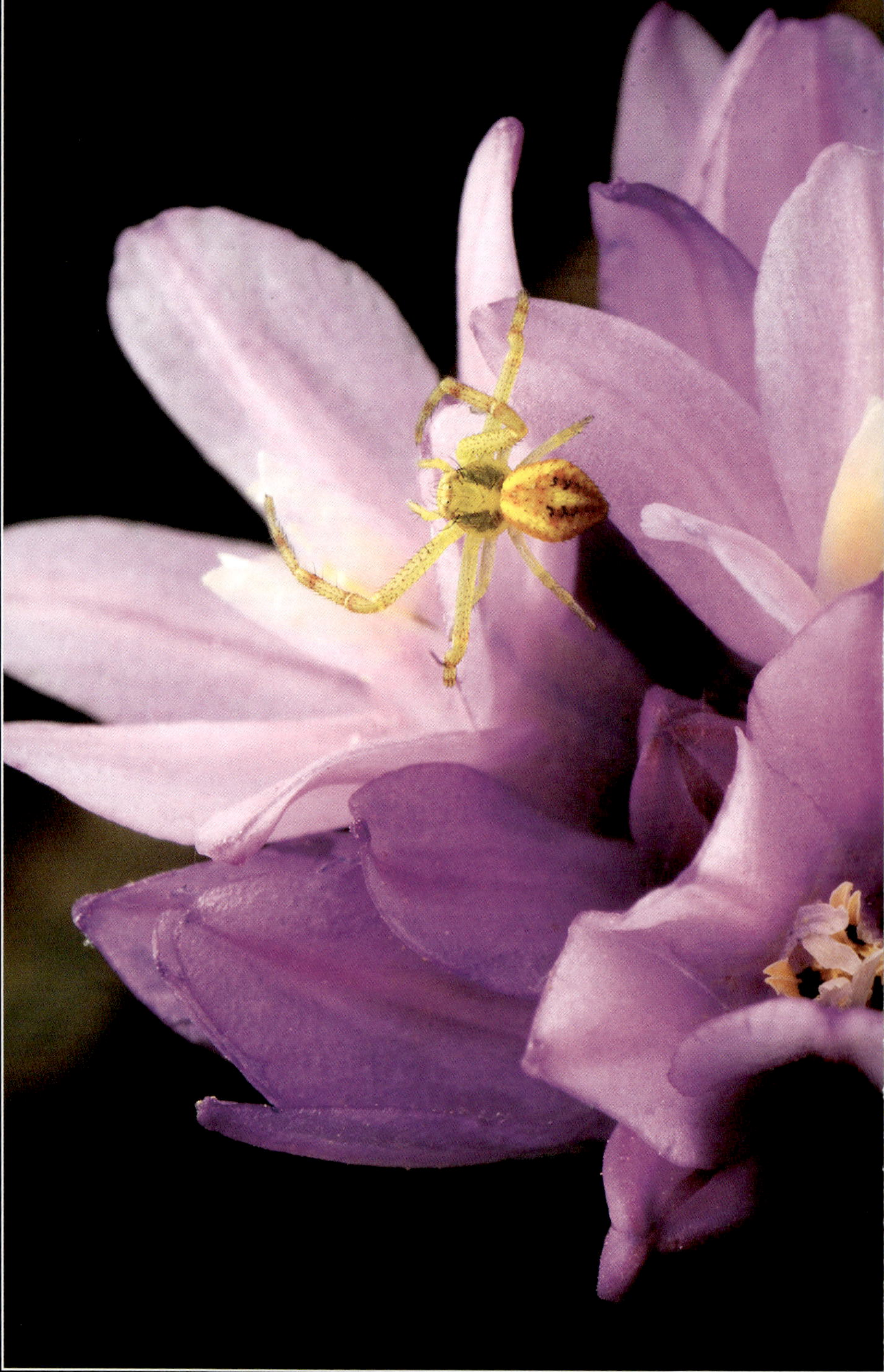

**Top left**—An aperture of f/5.6 was required to keep the front flower in crisp focus. A shutter speed of $^{1}/_{800}$ second was then applied to create the background. Adding a flash ensured crisp focus on the foreground tier. **Bottom left**—An aperture of f/36 was needed to stretch the depth of field far enough to reach from the front of the flower to the back. With the depth-of-field preview button depressed, we simply moved the camera forward and back until the entire spider sprang into focus. The shutter speed and ISO settings were dictated by the desired background brightness and a flash was employed to brighten up (and isolate) the entire depth of field. **Right**—Larger flash modifiers offer you the chance to light several graphic tiers with one flash. Achieving the rich detail on this spider and illuminating the entire background required simply one hand-held flash modified with a very large LumiQuest softbox.

Being able to preview the image at the aperture you've chosen lets you make a well-informed decision. If the focus range isn't deep enough, you can adjust the aperture and check it again with your depth-of-field preview button. If it still doesn't reach far enough, you can again make your aperture smaller and recheck. Repeat the process until you see through the viewfinder exactly the depth of field you want.

Basically, it works like this: the closer you are, the more you zoom, and the larger the aperture you use, the less sharpness and more blur you will see (the depth of field will be narrower). Conversely, if you want more things in focus, you've got to go the other way around with one or more of the key depth-of-field factors—moving away from the subject, zooming out, or selecting a smaller aperture to produce greater depth of field.

Choosing a shutter speed is critical; it's what dictates how bright or dark the background will be. (If fast enough, it also helps to eliminate motion blur.) In these images, we see the effect of changing shutter speeds; the aperture and power settings of the flash remained constant. As the shutter speed increased, notice that the amount of ambient light decreased—yet the light coming from the flash remains unaltered. Shutter speed has no effect on the output from flashes (unless you surpass the camera's flash sync speed). Eventually, as the last image in this series shows, a black background can spring forth from a day bathed in bright sunlight. This black background can then be used to isolate your subject(s). If you've got enough flashes (three were used in these images), you can make anything happen.

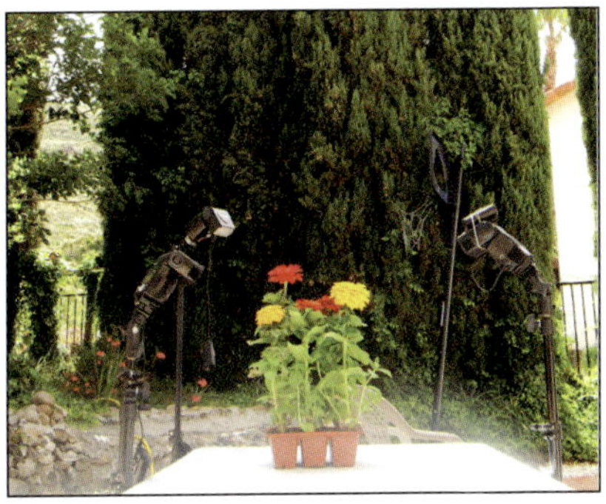
f/22, 1/5 second with the flashes off

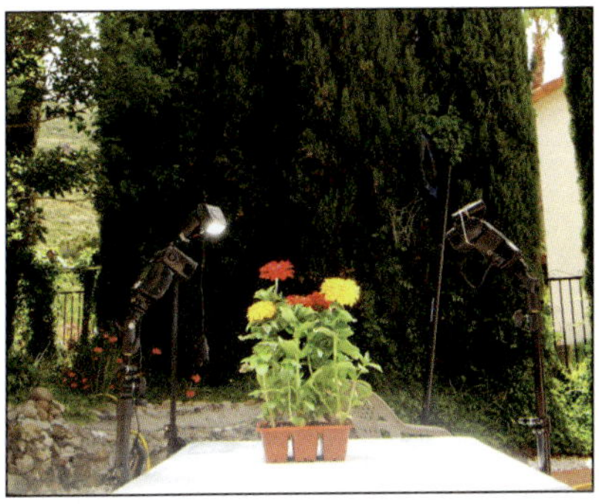
f/22, 1/5 second with the flashes on

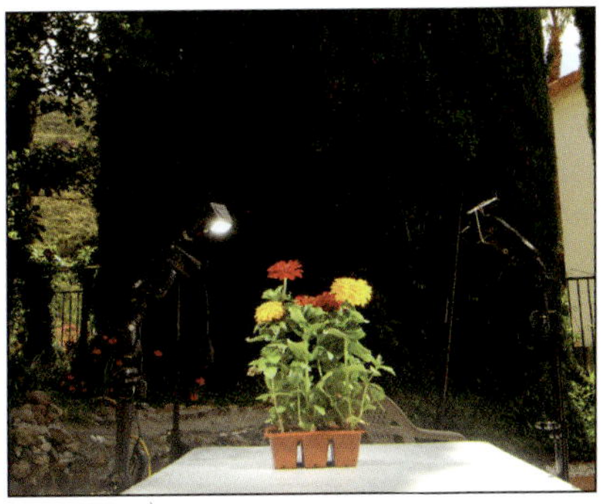
f/22, 1/13 second

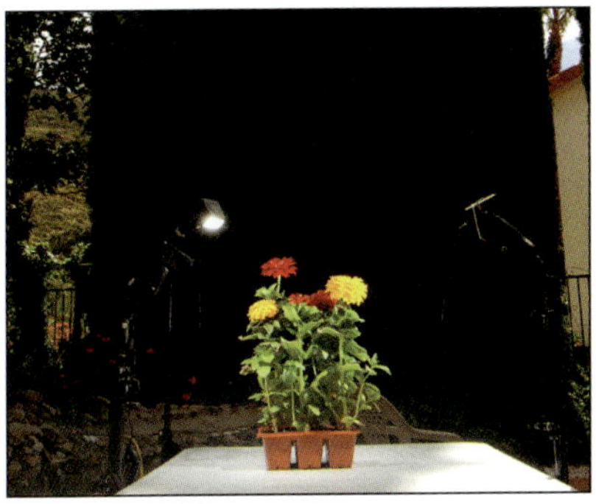
f/22, 1/30 second

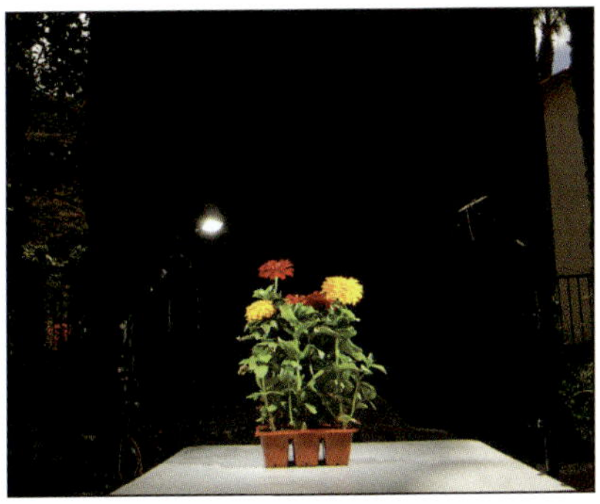
f/22, 1/80 second

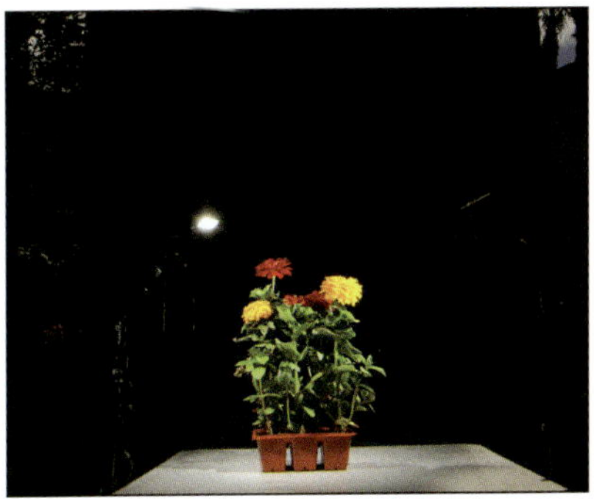
f/22, 1/200 second

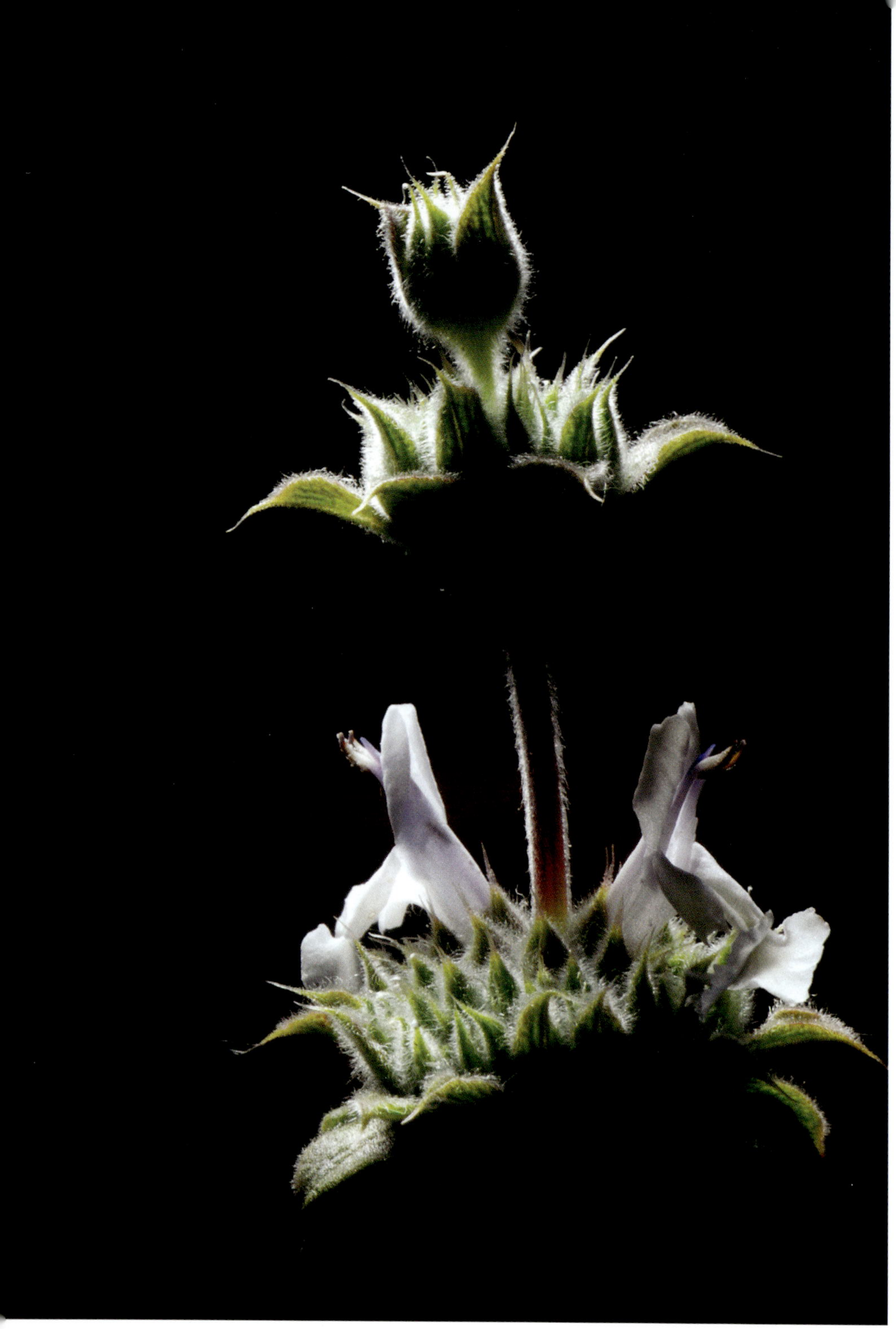

It's a two-stage process when adding light with an off-camera flash. An unmodified flash was held directly above the plant in this image, but it was employed because we made our background dark first. This image, surprisingly, was shot in the middle of the day under direct sunlight. We didn't like the way it looked, so we changed it. We chose an aperture and shutter combination that would produce a dark background and keep the flower in focus. Then we simply added light to brighten our flower. Remember, you are not always trying to capture something the way it looks—with an off-camera flash, you can create something completely different.

## FLASH PHOTOGRAPHY

Flash photography is a two-step process, whether or not it's for close-up/macro photography. You have to light both your foreground and background, balancing (if you so choose) ambient and man-made light. Sometimes you can light both with your flash/flashes (especially when shooting close-up and macro images) and sometimes you can't.

**Camera Settings.** When you have to use natural light in your image (to illuminate a background, for instance) we suggest dialing that in with your shutter speed or ISO setting right after you choose an aperture size. Some photographers change their aperture to adjust their lighting; we don't do this. Instead, we choose the aperture setting based on the desired depth of field. We want a specific amount of focal distance to appear in our image and we work very hard to make sure it's perfect. Giving up that control makes no sense whatsoever.

Keep in mind, though, that as you begin choosing smaller and smaller apertures for greater depth of field, the apparent power output from your flash will dwindle. Smaller apertures strip light from ambient sources and cut the amount of usable light coming from your flash. When shooting with smaller apertures, be prepared to use more powerful flash settings.

You'll also have to come to grips with certain modification issues. We'll cover the modification choices you have later, but for now it's important to remember that as your light source increases in size (such as when using a softbox), the apparent power output of your flash diminishes. This can be solved quite easily by moving the flash closer to your subject, decreasing the size of the modification tool, increasing the actual power output of the flash, or choosing a larger aperture (again, not recommended).

**Flash Sync Speed.** When using an off-camera flash, whether for close-up work or not, you have to work within or around your camera's flash sync speed. Surpassing this will prove detrimental to your image. The flash

Each camera has a flash sync speed—a speed at which full flash coverage is attained. If you choose a shutter speed faster than this, a portion of your scene will not be lit by the flash, as illustrated in this series of images. The more you exceed the sync speed, the larger this blacked-out area will become.

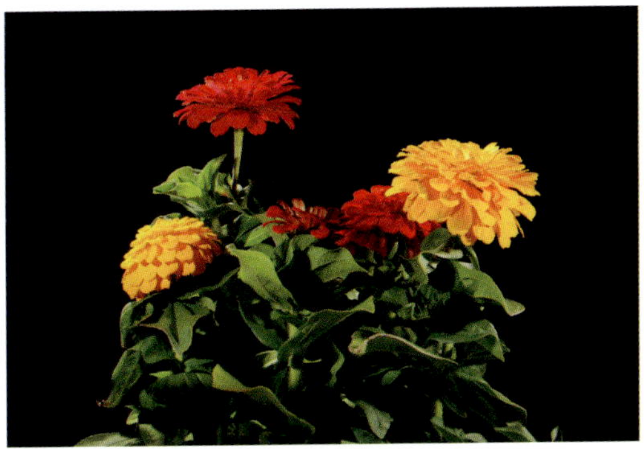
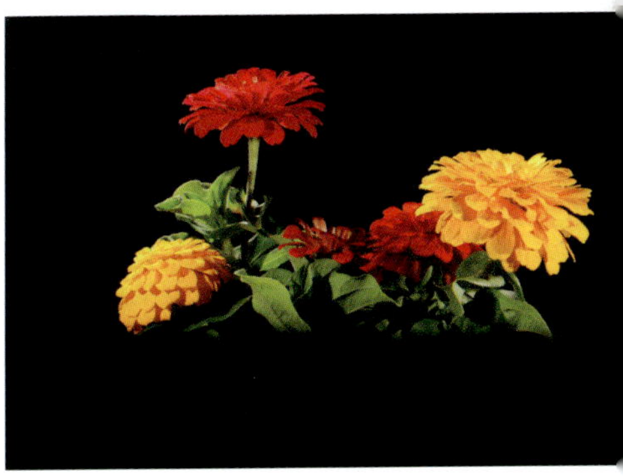

**Left**—This image was shot at the camera's flash sync speed of 1/200 second. **Right**—Shutter speed of 1/300 second.

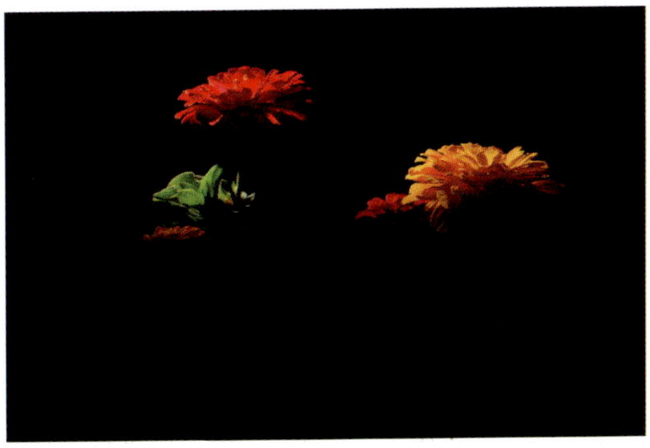
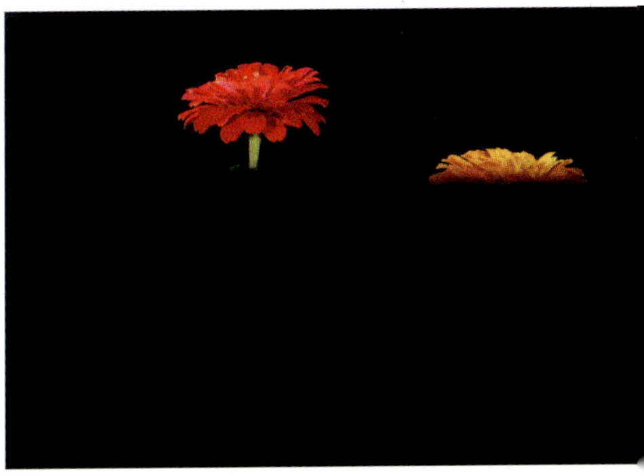

**Left**—Shutter speed of 1/400 second. **Right**—Shutter speed of 1/500 second.

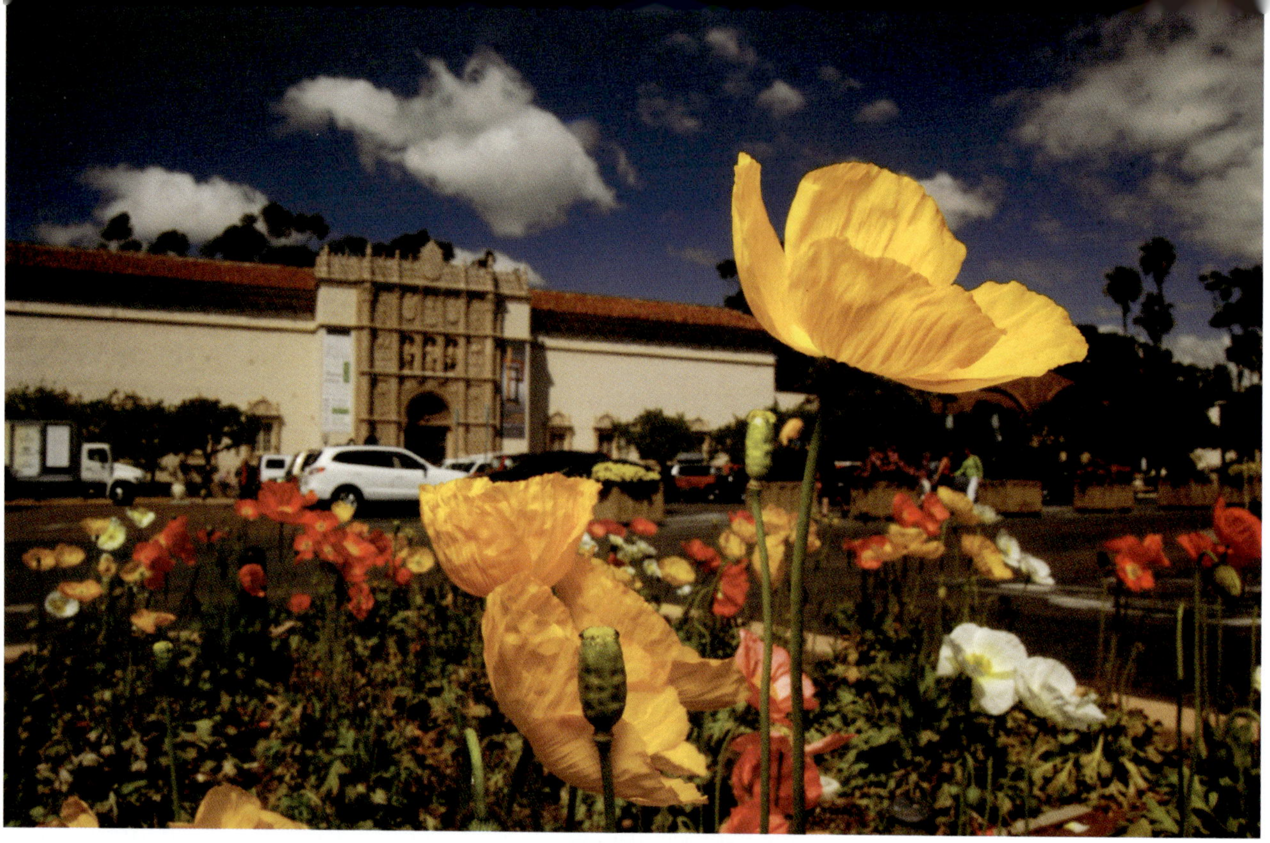

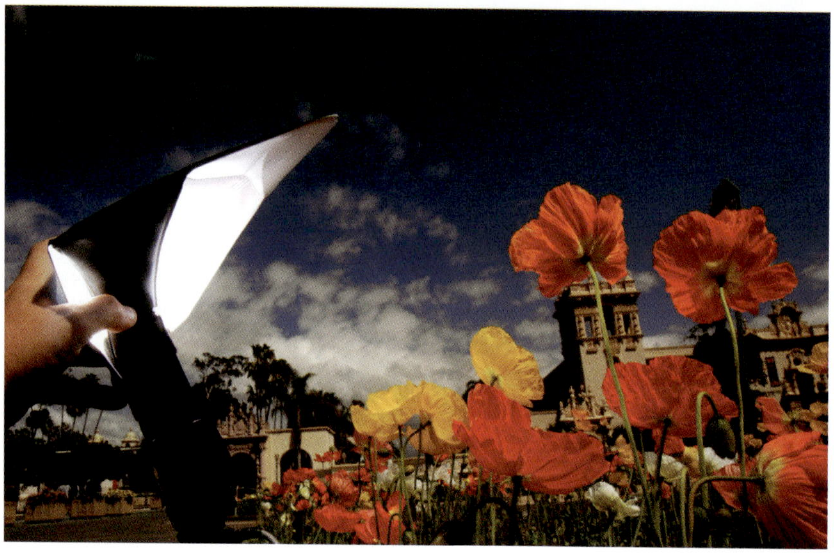

Even though it was the middle of the day, the bold colors, rich mood, and crisp focus in this image would not have been possible if it weren't for the addition of flash. Remember that a scene does not have to be lit the way it appears. By simply visualizing an alternative and adding a flash (employed off-camera as shown in the bottom image), you can make the magic happen with any camera, at any time, in any location.

sync speed is the fastest possible shutter speed your camera can shoot at and still acquire all the light emitted from your flash. (Check your camera's manual if you are unsure of what this shutter speed is.) If you shoot with a shutter speed faster than this, then a portion of light emitted by the flash will be hidden by the camera's internal shutter blades—provided, of course, that you are using a standard digital camera; there are several camera models today that employ an electronic shutter where this will not be an issue.

**High-Speed Flash Sync.** To circumvent the flash sync speed, you can purchase a special flash that allows for full flash coverage well beyond your camera's flash sync speed. This high speed sync option will require very specific camera and flash combinations and is usually quite expensive—plus it's a power hog. Using this system means that your flash is actually firing many times, very quickly, during one exposure. This does fill in any gaps created by the traveling shutter blades, but it cuts the available flash power substantially. This can be a huge problem if you're already using a large light modifier or smaller apertures.

**Camera Filters to Cut the Light.** Thankfully, there are other ways of cutting light that don't cut the apparent power from the flash—ways that won't break the bank, as the high-speed sync option might.

One option is to use neutral-density filters instead to cut the excess amount of light. Another option is simply to cross two linear polarizers. This is an ages-old technique that is growing in popularity again as more and more photographers experiment with off-camera flash. Simply stack two linear polarizers in front of your lens, rotate the bottom one to eliminate glare and turn the top one to eliminate ambient light. It works like a charm—creating what is, essentially, a variable neutral-density filter. (*Note:* From our experience, the polarizers do have to be *linear* for this to work—and not all brands play the same. Stacking two circular polarizers produces nothing but shifting colors throughout your image.)

As you can see from these images, a simple adjustment to the in-camera contrast setting created two very different images of the same subject. In the left-hand photo (where the setting was set low), a softer impression is made. In the right-hand photo, we see the strength and aggressive "flavor" that a higher contrast setting offers. If you begin incorporating how you feel into the development stage of your message-building process, your pictures can only get better.

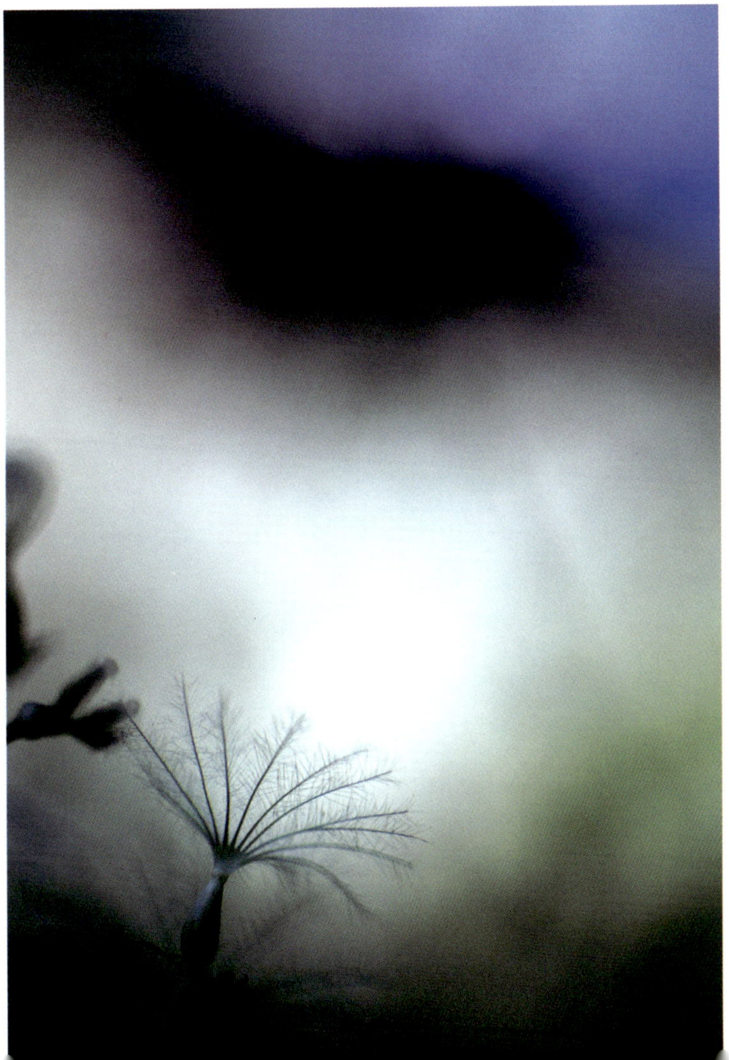

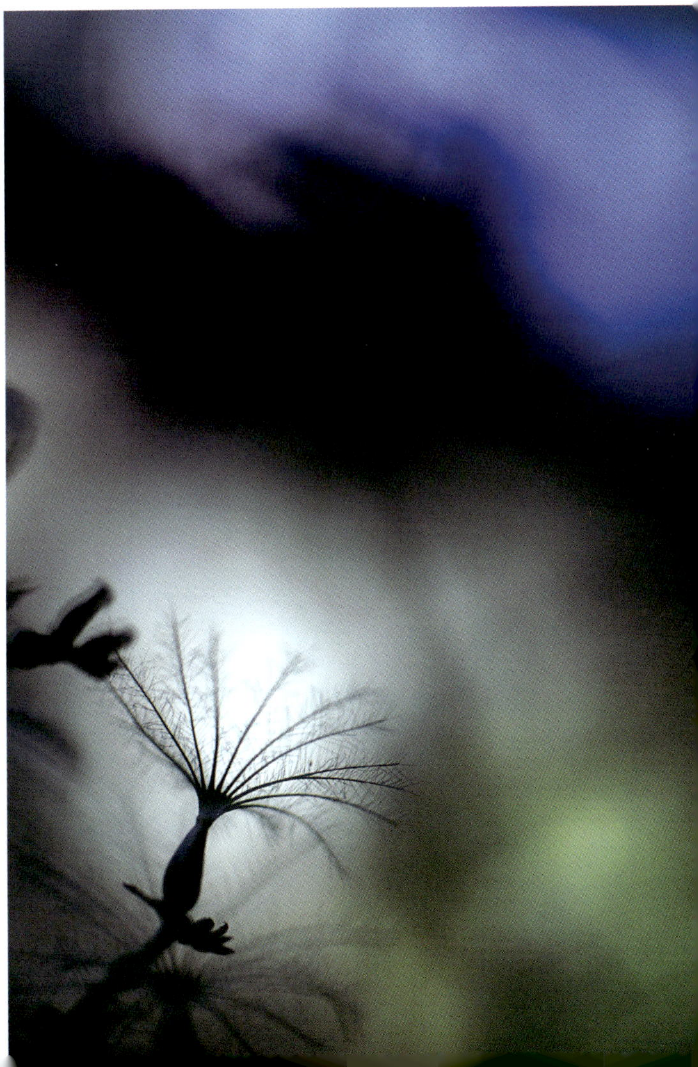

## THE MESSAGE-BUILDING PROCESS

If you care about the image you are creating—if you want something special—then you'll want to invest a bit of time and thought into the project. Think beyond what you see, then do whatever it takes to make that vision happen. It all comes down to choices.

**Start with an Idea.** Know deep in your heart what it is you're trying to say and what you're trying to convey. Don't just take a simple picture of flower. Think about what that flower means to you. Do you like the colors? Or is it the lines, the shapes, or perhaps the rhythm that draws you to it? Is it important that the whole thing is in focus? Or could just a

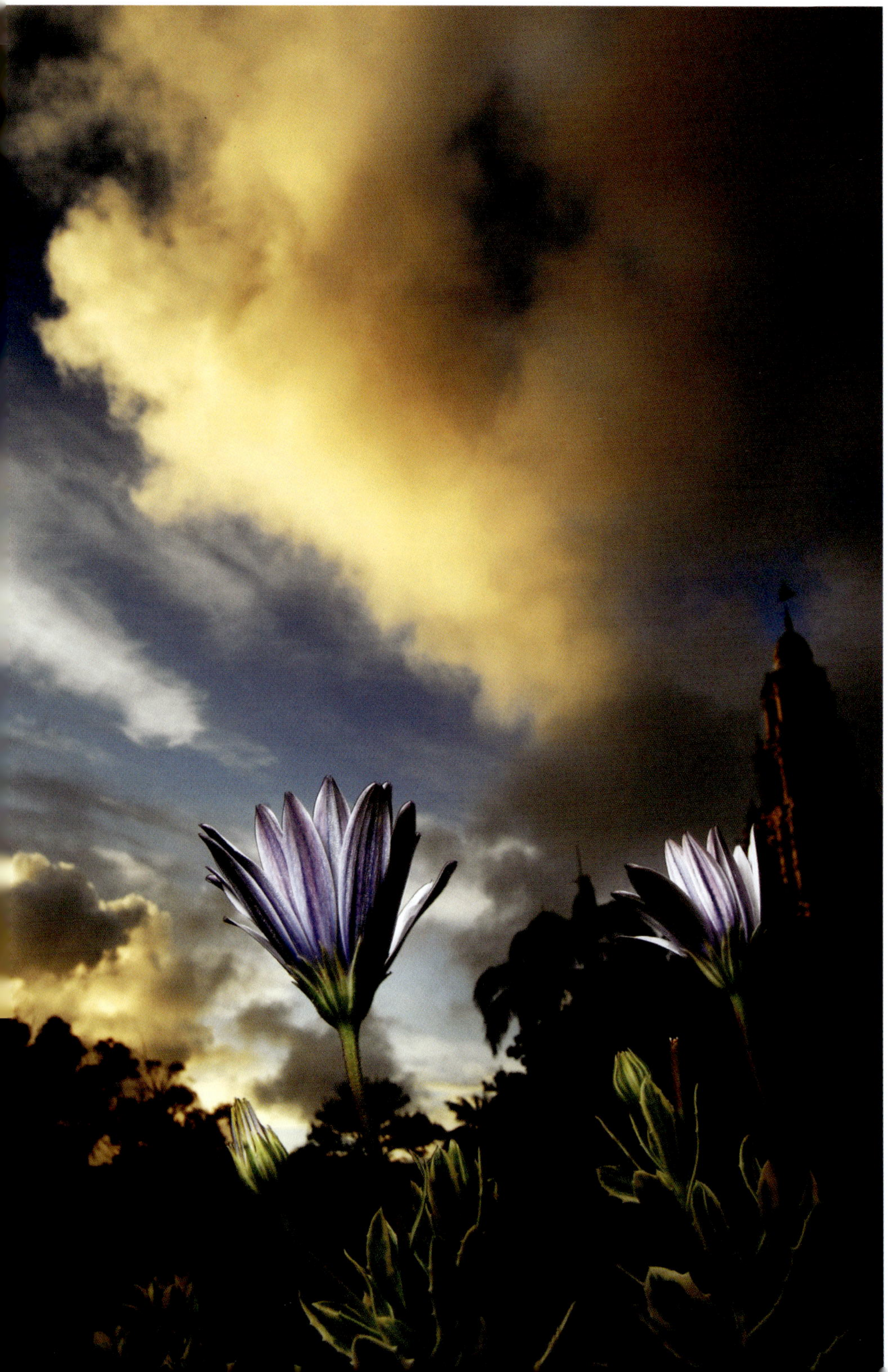

There is only one secret when it comes to creating amazing close-up images: start building your message from the back, then work your way forward. In this image, we began by choosing an aperture that gave us the right amount of focus depth for our flowers (checking it for accuracy with our depth-of-field preview button), then selected a shutter speed that allowed for the amazing background you see. Sadly, though, this shutter speed was beyond our camera's flash sync speed—which meant our flash would be useless and our flowers would remain hidden in shadow. To solve the problem, we employed a neutral density filter. These dark filters sit atop your lens and strip light from your image. This solved the lighting problem; we could now easily add light to our flowers, keeping our shutter speed at the camera's sync speed.

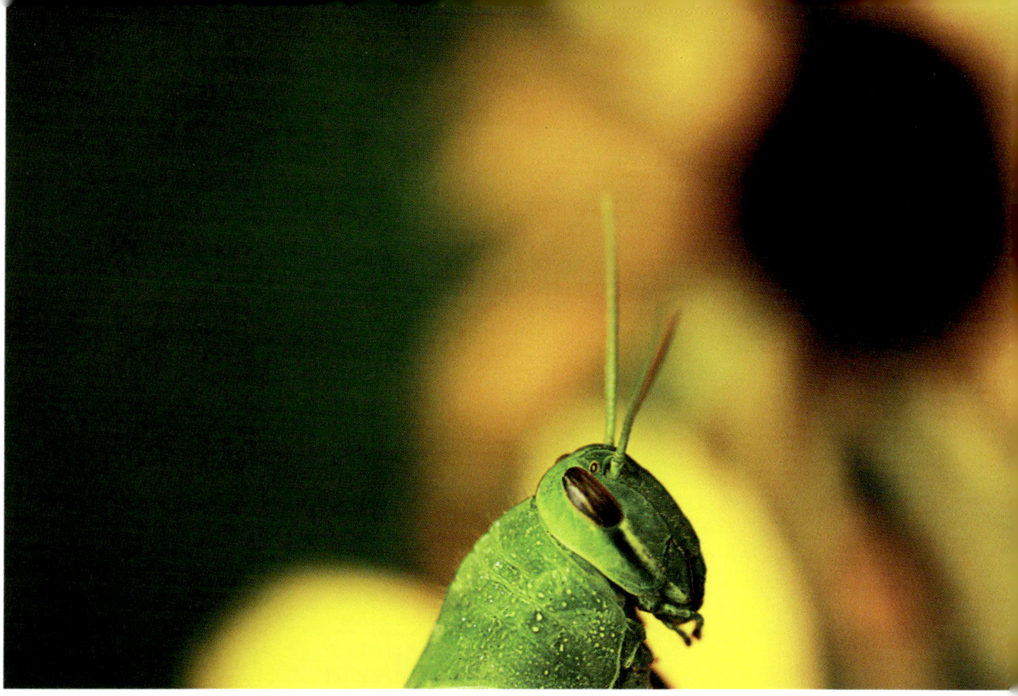

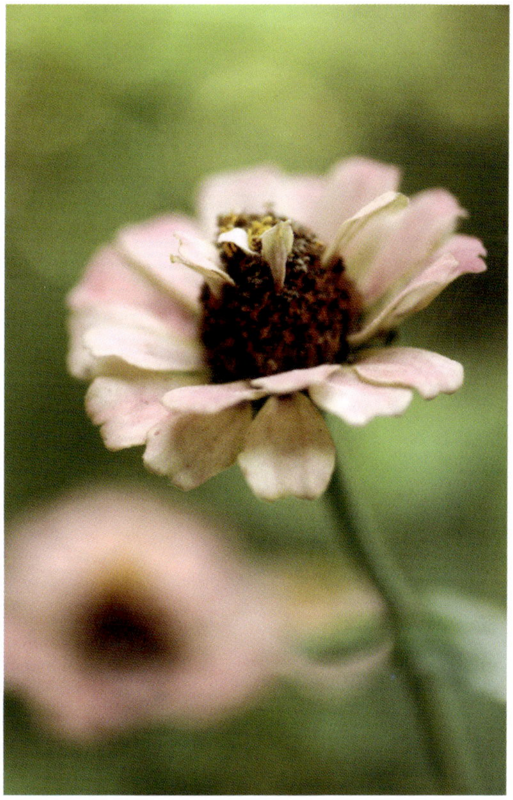

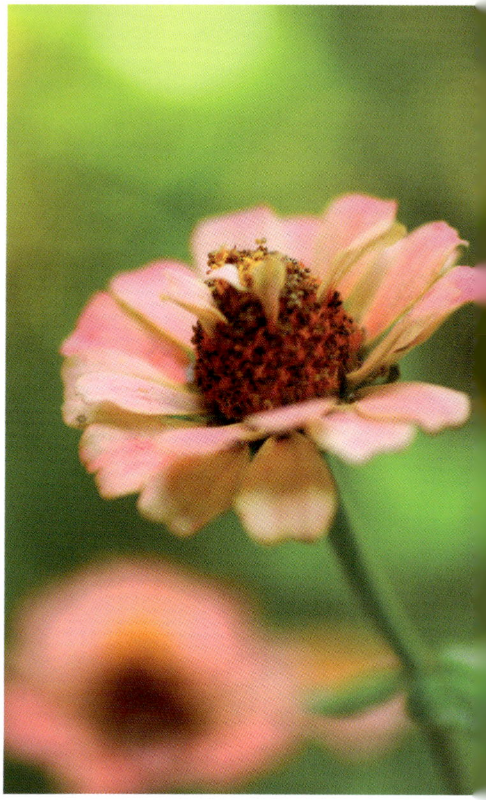

**Top**—When focusing, use your depth-of-field preview button as much as possible. Once employed, simply move the depth of field "range" into position, covering your intended subject. This can be tough if you are holding a flash in your left hand, shooting with a Canon camera (where the depth-of-field preview button is also on the left side), and trying to photograph a creature that moves very quickly—as the grasshopper in this image did. With enough practice, though, you will begin to visualize the depth of field without actually using the depth-of-field preview button. It takes hard work and a lot of practice on things that don't move, but you can do it! Experience is an amazing thing, so garner as much of it as you can. **Bottom**—These images illustrate the options you have when the saturation is adjusted in-camera. The left-hand photo shows a low setting, while the right-hand photo shows a high setting. Yes, we realize you can make these adjustments after the fact in a computer—but when do you think you are more in touch with how these flowers make you feel? When they are right there in front of you or two days later when you're sitting at home behind a computer? Why put off what you can do now?

portion of the bloom be sharply focused? Knowing what it is you want to capture before you actually try to capture it will make your trip through meaningful photography that much easier.

**Choose the Camera Settings.** Next, dial in how it makes you feel. Most digital cameras today allow you to adjust the contrast, saturation, hue, white balance, and sharpness in-camera. We suggest adjusting these *before* you begin shooting, basing your choices on how you feel about the image you are creating.

If you have never played with these settings, take the time to discover their magic. Work your way through the settings, testing each one. What you'll discover is a new avenue of approach, a chance to literally dial-in how something makes you feel before you shoot—virtually eliminating the need for post-processing corrections. It's a liberating experience.

**Determine the Perspective.** How the graphic tiers of information contained within your image align is important. It's the groundwork of all composition. This is controlled by your shooting location; each inch closer to or further away from your subject will change your story dramatically. Choose your shooting spot for a reason—don't just stand and shoot. Move your body, find the perfect location, line up those graphic tiers, change their apparent size relationships, and work hard to create the best possible image you can.

**Select the Focal Length.** Next comes focal length choice (or which lens you'll be using). Pick your lens for a specific purpose. Does it allow you to get close, crop more than the others, or offer better aperture choices? At first, this will prove a difficult decision, but as you practice more and get to know what each of your lenses offers it will come more naturally.

**Set the Depth of Field.** Now, chose an aperture that gives you the required depth of field. At this point, you will have to employ your depth-of-field preview button; without it you cannot know what will be in focus and what won't. Remember that your camera is lying to you unless you activate this button.

**Choose the Shutter Speed and ISO.** After this, things get simple (and fun). Critical thinking is a must. You will choose a shutter speed that makes your background (and sometimes your subject, if you're not using a flash) sing. Keep in mind that if you choose too slow a shutter speed, you may run into a problem with camera shake or subject movement. This is easily fixed with a change of ISO—bearing in mind that as the ISO number increases, the actual quality of your image (in terms of contrast, saturation, and color) wanes. At high settings, you'll also end up with a lot of digital noise.

**Consider Adding Flash.** If you're unhappy about your choice of ISO, you could employ a flash to add light, allowing for a lower ISO setting to give you the clarity and quality you want. If you are unhappy with the lighting on any tier of graphic information, that would be another reason to add flash—and maybe more than one flash, adjusting and changing each power setting and modification option to suit your vision.

***A Few Words on Flash***

There are few things you must know about flash photography before you begin your close-up journey. First off, know the flash is just a simple tool—no matter how many buttons or modes the manufacturer put on it. Don't give it any more credit than that. Sure, it may have cost a bundle, but it simply adds light—nothing more. It can never choose the perfect amount of light for your individual message. It can't create art. It must be controlled, modified, and supported.

**Facing page**—*Top:* Sometimes, natural light just won't do. Even though this flower (which was actually much brighter than the left-hand image illustrates) is bathed in light, it wasn't enough. A slightly modified flash, at a very low power setting, was employed to add just a touch of light to the flower without overwhelming the background. *Bottom:* For crisp focus, nothing beats a flash—just dial in the appropriate aperture. You'll know what's "appropriate" by employing your depth-of-field preview button. Choose a shutter speed/ISO that gives you the perfect background, then add light to whatever needs it. In this case, it was our in-focus foreground plant.

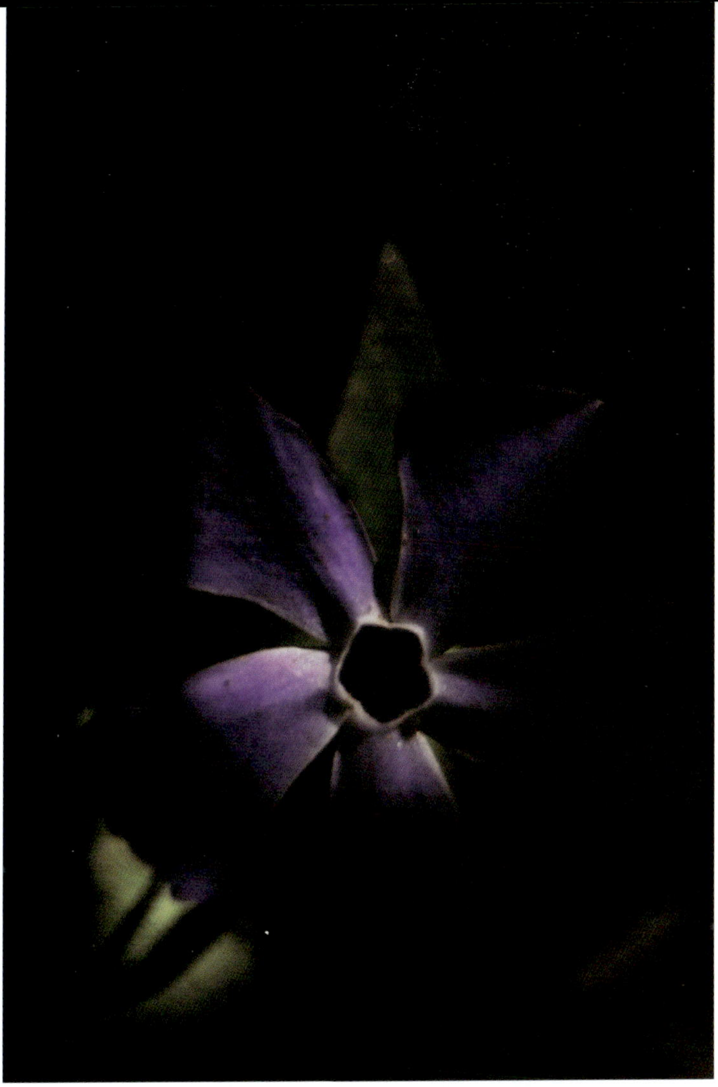
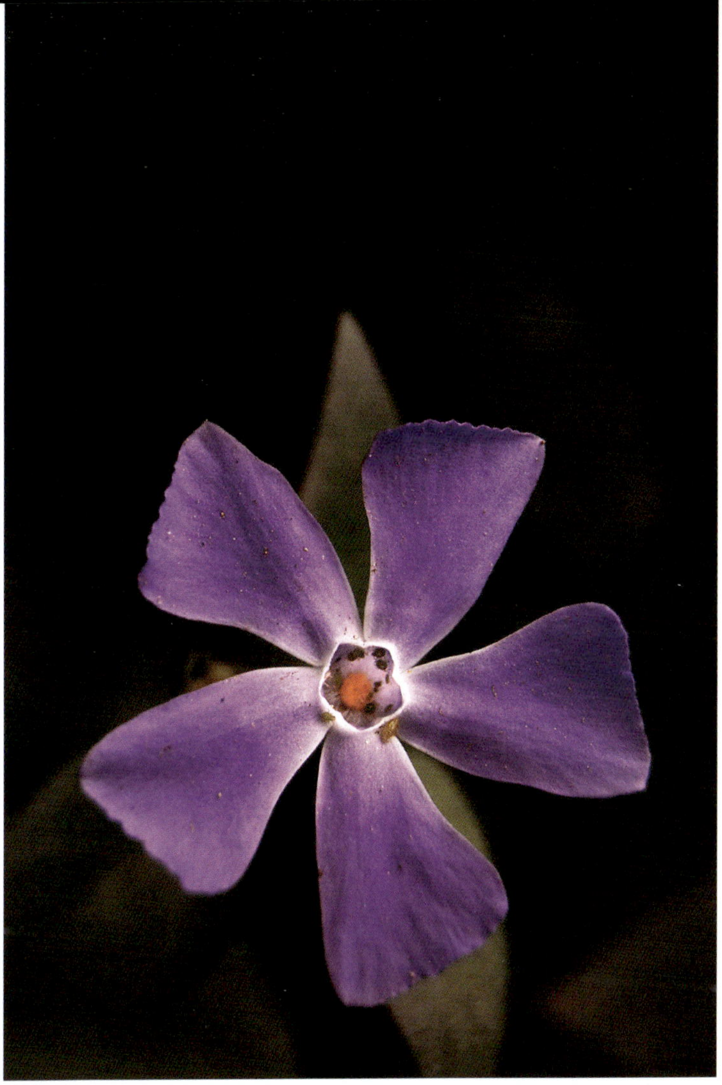
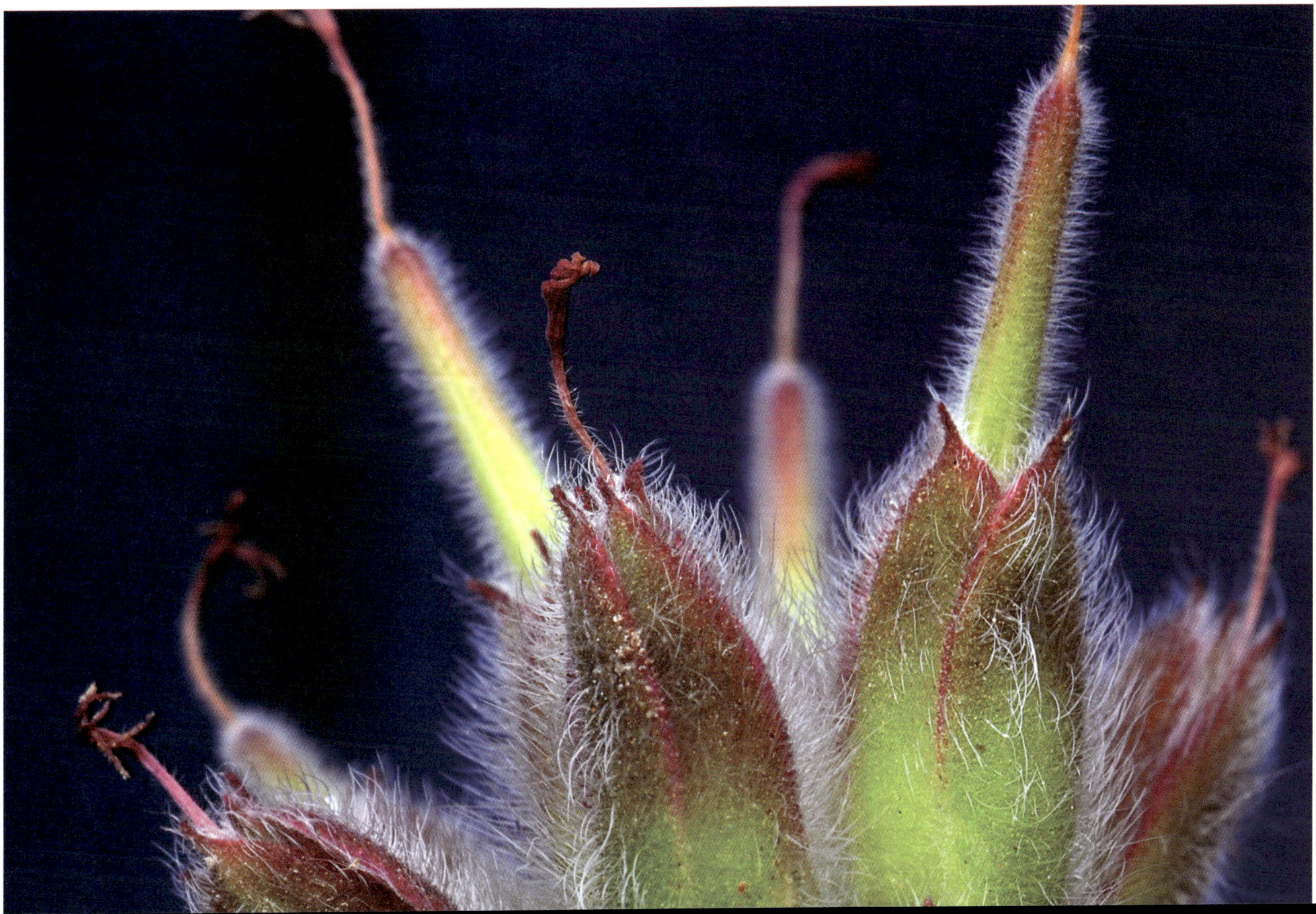

**Shoot.** If you've done everything well, you have the perfect image—one that does not need to be corrected after the fact. You have an image that is in the perfect light, with pure focus and an obvious intent. This image will most assuredly be more about you than what you were focusing on. It should reflect you as an artist and not just your gear or the subject you chose to shoot. That's why close-up and macro photography is so much fun—because it's so individual.

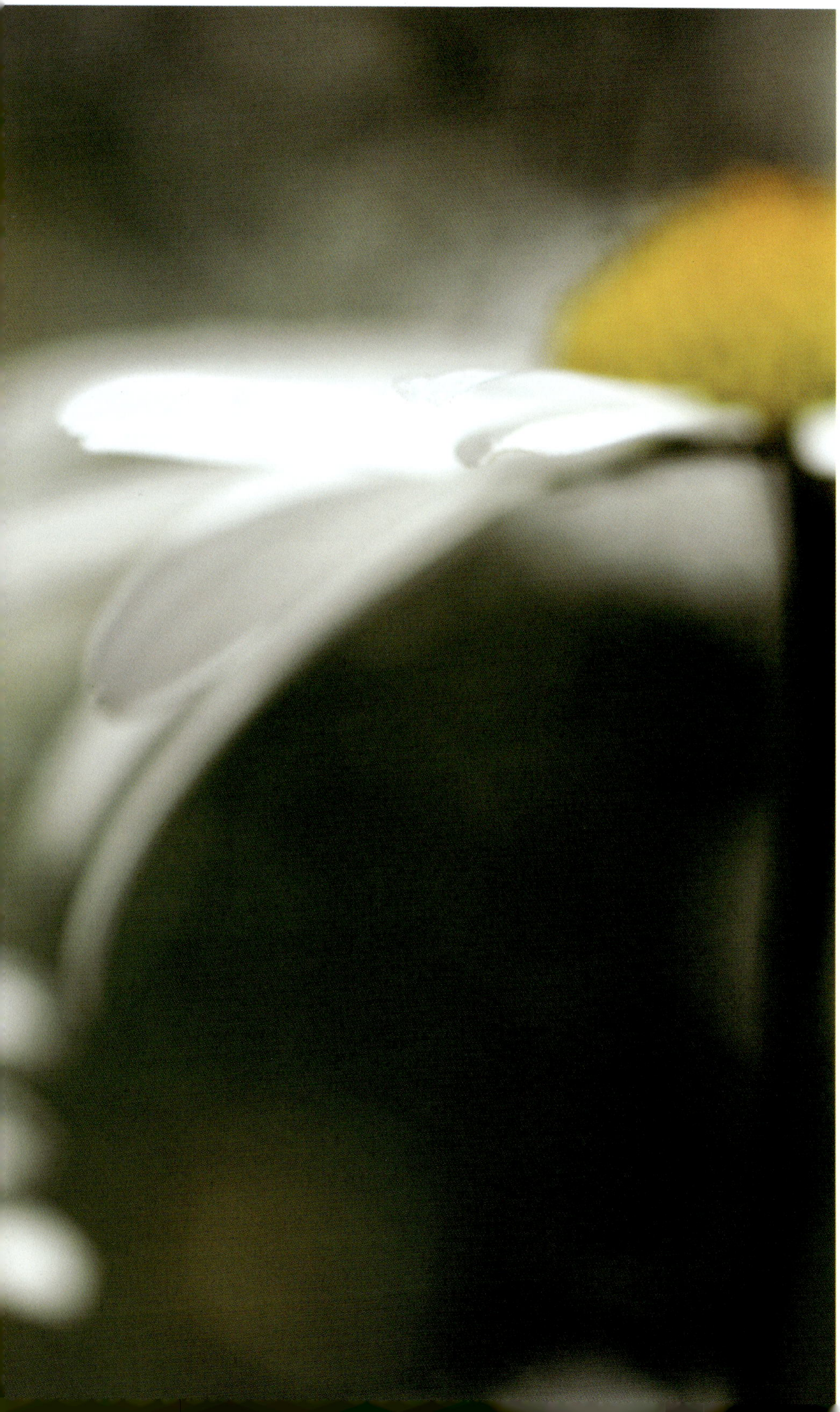

As a macro/close-up artist you are responsible for making the tough choices. Do you try to keep everything in focus in your image? Or do you use the option of extreme blur to your advantage? In this image, the photographer chose to explore her feelings about the flower instead of just shooting the flower. An off-camera flash was needed to properly illuminate her message.

# 3. THE GEAR

You will need some specialized gear to get super close.
The good thing is, it doesn't have to be expensive.

It's all about a vision, a picture in your head that just won't go away. Sometimes, creating that is easy; sometimes it's not. Luckily, the rules that govern macro and close-up photography are the same as in any other type of photography. If you know the basics, you shouldn't have a problem. However, you will need some specialized gear if you hope to achieve the 1:1 (or greater) size relationship that true macro photography demands.

When purchasing macro gear, you have a choice: you can either buy a macro lens (specifically designed to get that 1:1 representation) or you can choose from a variety of close-up/macro attachments for the lenses you already own. Neither choice is correct and neither is wrong. Each of them will allow you to create some fantastic images.

Achieving the amount of magnification needed to separate a good macro image (such as the one here) from a simple close-up image may mean the purchase of some specialized gear. Luckily, this gear need not be expensive. For less than $30, a manual photographer can pick from a variety of gear—extension tubes, reversing rings, couplers, and more.

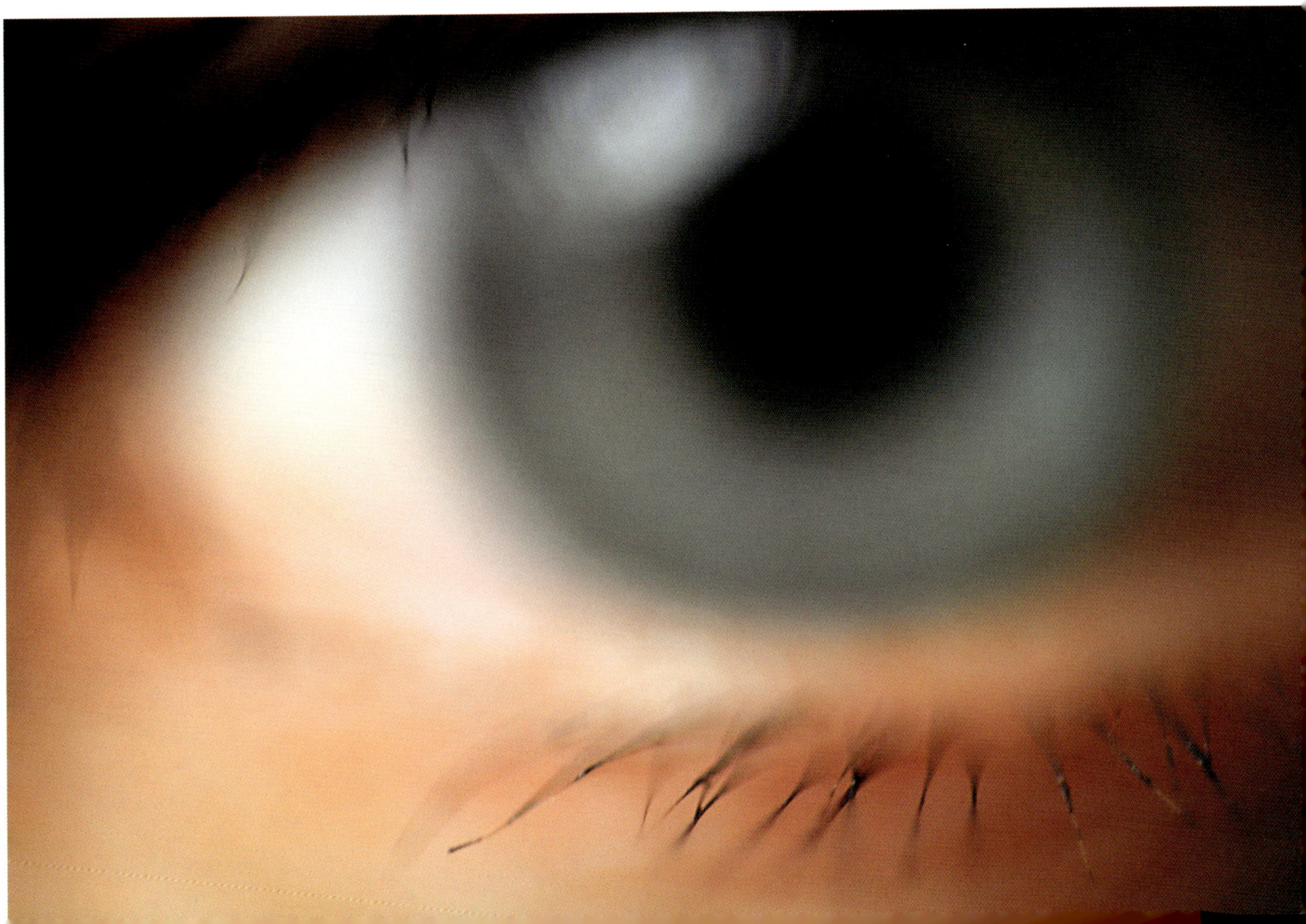

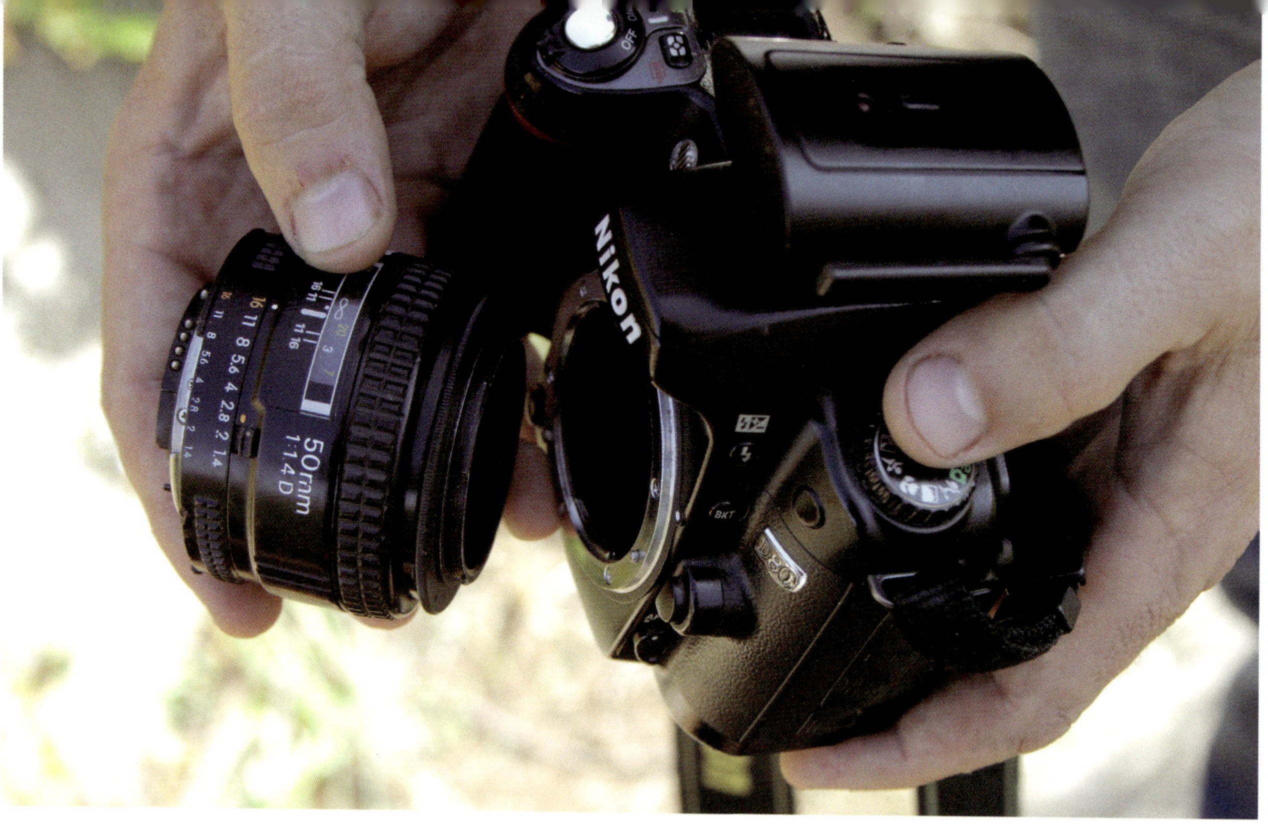


Never discount the power of simply getting close to a subject. When you want to get *really* close, though, you will have to either modify your current equipment (such as "flipping" a normal lens) or shoot with a true macro lens.

## START WITH WHAT YOU HAVE, BUILD AS YOU GROW

As the parents of five children, we have always kept things on the inexpensive side, using more traditional tools and cheaper accessories. Therefore, we suggest you hold off on purchasing anything at first. Instead, start with what you already have. Look at all your options and figure out just how close they can get you on their own. If your goal is to simply create art and explore the world around you, it doesn't have to cost an arm and a leg.

This does not mean that you shouldn't purchase the more expensive gear if you really want to—it will certainly work just as well. However, we find that the majority of our close-up students have never truly explored the limitations of their own gear. Often, they'll come to class after purchasing some very expensive piece of close-up/macro equipment and want us to show them how to use it. When asked why they bought it (given that they obviously don't know how or why to use it), they always reply, "Because I thought I needed it."

When it's time to add gear to your macro kit, deciding on the right tools can prove quite a challenge. There are literally dozens of options out there—and when multiplied with the variety of flashes, modifiers and support choices you have . . . well, it can get a little overwhelming (and quite expensive) if you let it.

In the beginning, there are so many choices and decisions that it's best to stick with what's simple. Concentrate on your true goal. Think before you buy. If you just want to get close to something, you might not need anything. If you want a true macro picture, explore the inexpensive options first. When you reach a point where your current gear can't give you what you need, move on to something different.

Weeding through the rhetoric often proves the most frustrating aspect of this process. With so many camera and lens manufacturers promising the world—and even more professional photographers offering their own advice (which often contradicts the manufacturers' suggestions)—it's a wonder anyone even attempts this type of photography, let alone masters it. The sad truth is that once you find the best way of getting close, once

Achieving life-size (1:1) stature is surely an impressive thing, but when you get this close to your subjects, depth-of-field issues will be smack in your face. You are going to have to deal with limited focal depth in ways that are unfamiliar. You can try to eliminate it by choosing smaller and smaller apertures (and then using your flash to add light) but you should also explore the extreme blurs it offers. The images below show the effects of depth-of-field control. You can either make precise focusing decisions, as in the top-left image where only one strand of the vine is crisp, and the right-hand image where the entire water drop is in focus (yet nothing else is). Or you can really go for the blur and examine the true meaning of your subject, as in the bottom-left image.

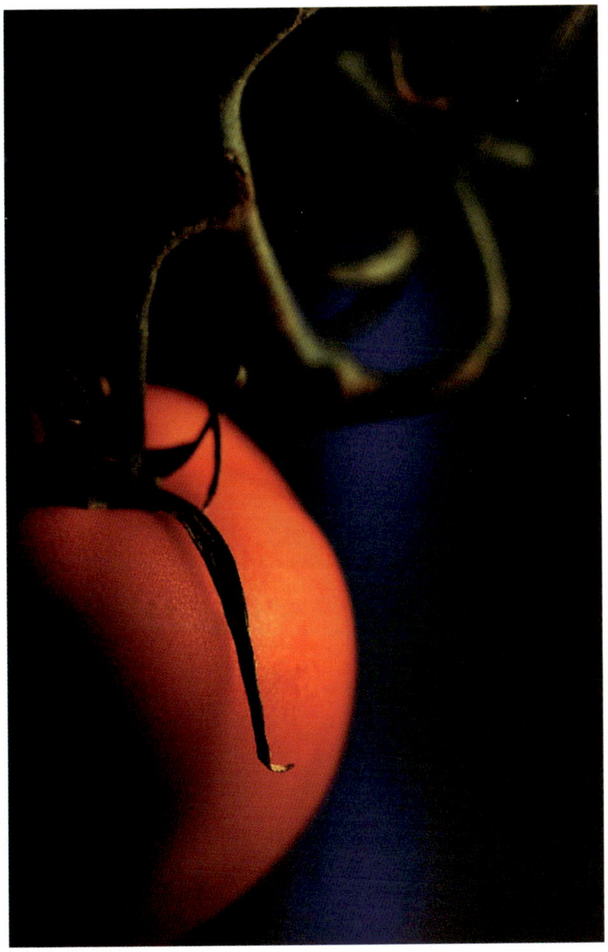

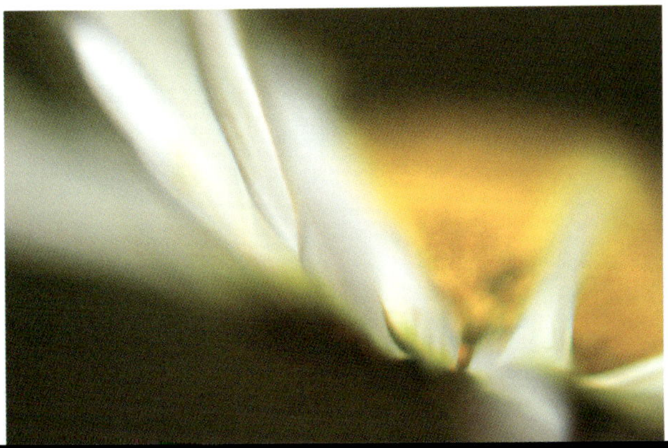

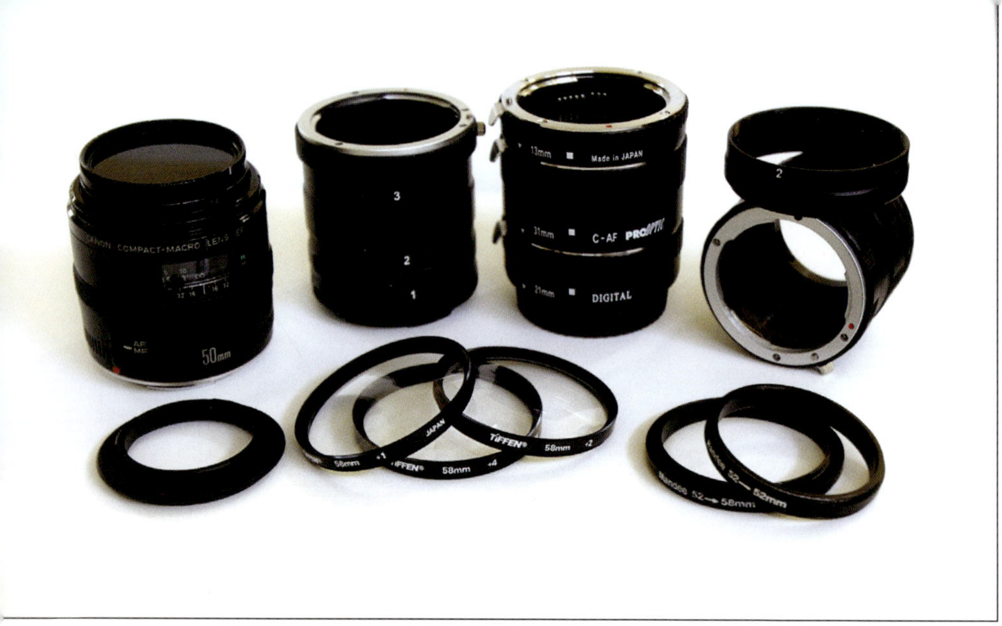


**Top**—This is a collection of various inexpensive macro and close-up gear we use. *Top row:* A 50mm macro lens, a set of non-electrical extension tubes, the electrical (automatic) alternative, and another set of extension tubes. *Bottom row:* Reversing ring, close-up filters, and coupling rings. **Bottom**—We already know every lens lets us get close—and we mean every lens. Even very long telephoto lenses, such as the 70–200mm lens, can produce some rather dramatic close-up images. Sure it's a little awkward to hold (especially if you intend to use an off-camera flash, as well), but it can be done.

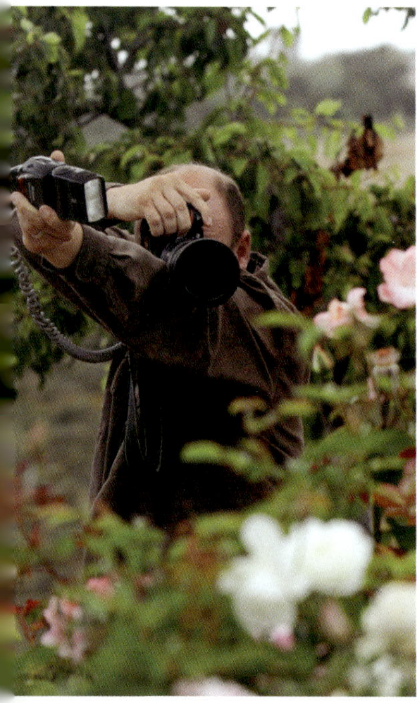

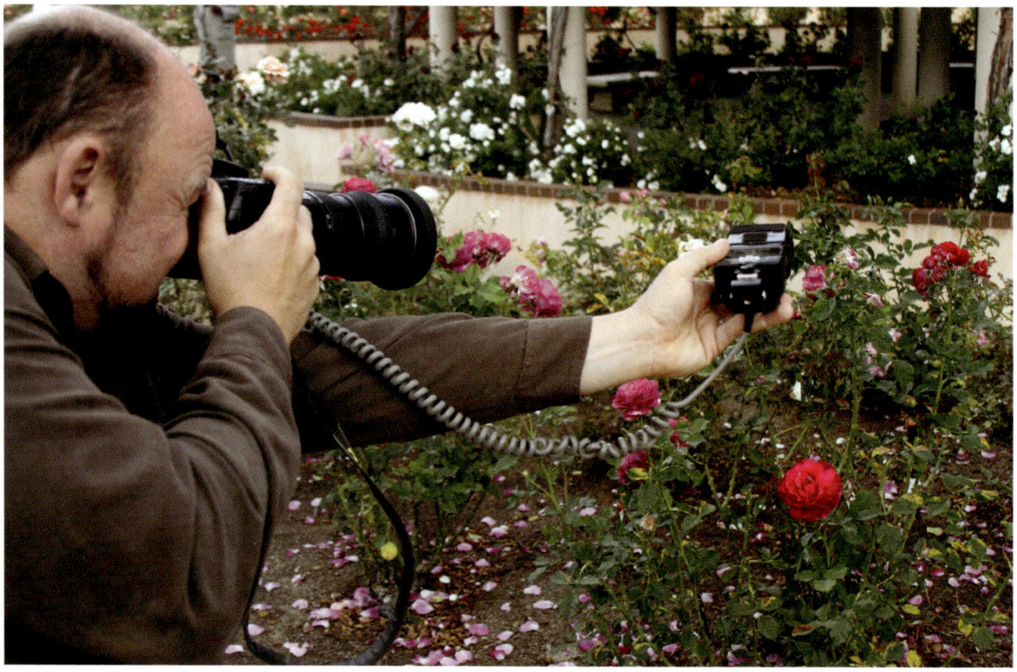

you think you've got macro and close-up photography understood, someone will undoubtedly find an even better way of doing it.

Our advice is to stop chasing the bull. There will always be the "next best piece of gear." Just use what you have for now. Get out there and start shooting. Learn what your own equipment can do. Push your vision, not your bank account.

## TELEPHOTO LENSES

For your first forays into close-up photography, try using your longest (telephoto) lenses. Telephoto lenses already offer the chance to crop quite tightly on something, so why not put that power to use? Just because most people use their long lenses to shoot things far away, doesn't mean we all should. That lens (and every other lens) has a minimum focal distance—and sometimes it can be quite close. The point is, you won't know until you try. Of course, longer lenses offer their own challenges when shooting with an off-camera flash; the mere physical weight of the lens and the fact that you may be holding your flash with one hand could prove too much of a challenge. Give it a shot, though (sorry for the pun!). You might just surprise yourself.

## TELECONVERTERS

If none of your lenses afford the crop factor you're looking for or you don't want to practice off-camera flash with a telephoto lens, you may want to purchase a simple teleconverter (sometimes called a doubler) for your shorter lenses. This simple device sits between the lens and the camera and, in essence, doubles your focal length. (*Note:* There are various types of teleconverters; some provide less magnification.)

A teleconverter does not get you physically closer to your subject—only your legs or a different lens can do that. Your lens's minimum focal dis-

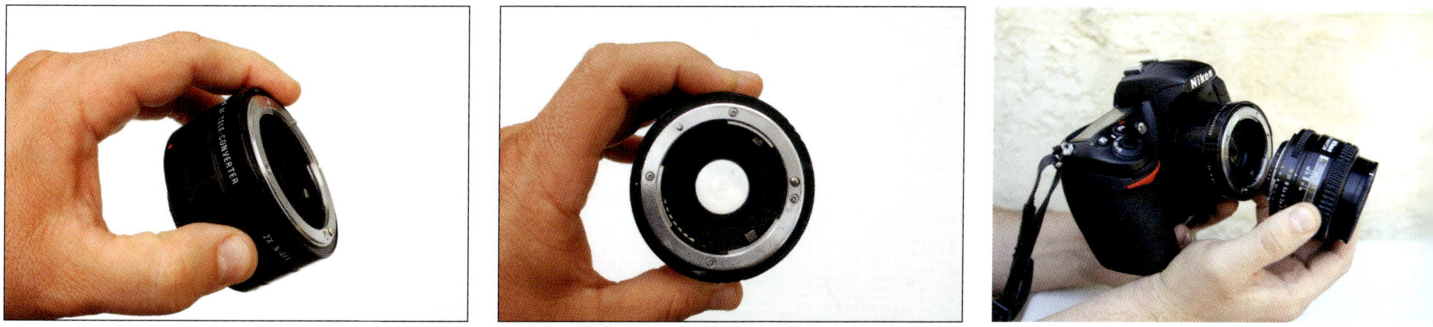

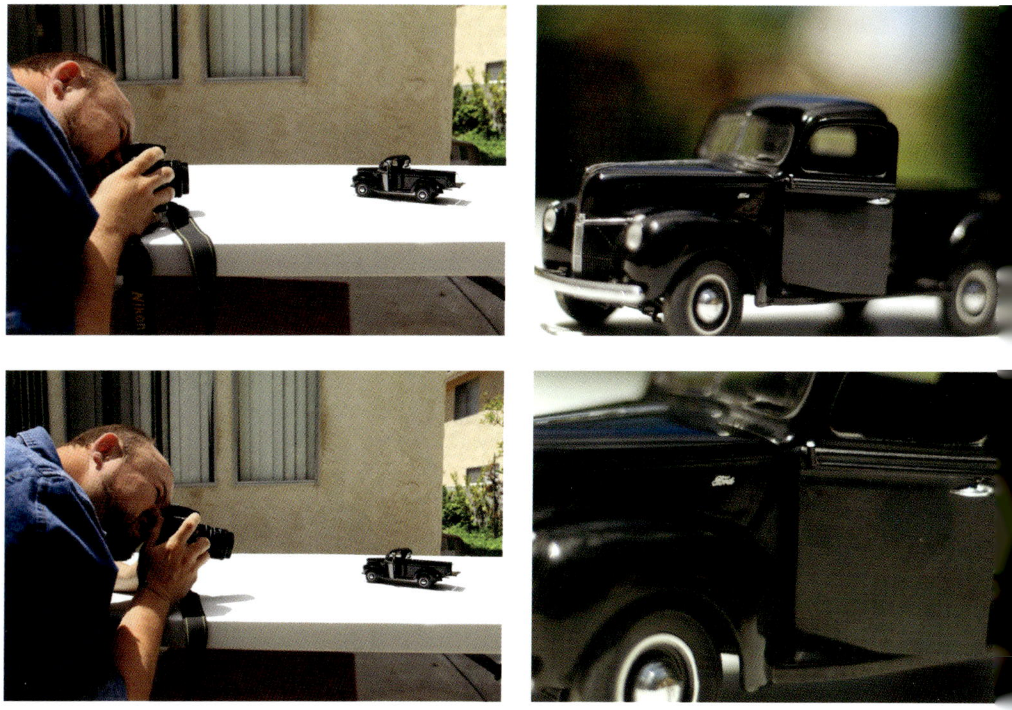

**Top row**—The teleconverter (or doubler) is a simple device that sits between your camera and lens. **Center row**—In the left-hand image you see the minimum focal distance rendered by a 50mm lens. The right-hand image shows the end result. Notice how you can see the entire vehicle from this vantage point. **Bottom row**—In the left-hand image you see that the addition of a teleconverter does not change the lens's minimum focal distance. However, the much tighter angle of view produces a more close-up view of the subject, as shown in the right-hand image.

tance is still your minimum focal distance, with a teleconverter attached or not. The only thing that changes with the addition of the teleconverter is the offered crop factor. For instance, if you're shooting with a 50mm lens, adding a teleconverter means you now have a 100mm lens. This will give you pretty dramatic close-up images, converting every lens you own into a close-up treasure.

Many professionals downplay the doubler and recommend against it, complaining of the loss of clarity and of ambient light. However, as off-camera flash shooters who are already adding light and using smaller apertures to increase the depth of field, we've found these concerns to be a bit unfounded. While the warnings are real (you really do lose light and the image may soften), the flash evens out the odds. Many of the images in this book were shot with a teleconverter—and we wouldn't have done it any other way.

### FLIPPING (OR REVERSING) A LENS

While the teleconverter will give you a tighter crop factor, it doesn't do much else. If you want to actually reduce the minimum focal distance, getting you closer to your subject, you have to do something about the lens you're using. You must either change lenses or change the physics behind the lens. For instance, instead of putting your lens on the camera the "right" way . . . you could try putting it on *backwards.*

This technique, called flipping a lens, is a traditional approach that works amazingly well in the digital age. After all, the physics still hold

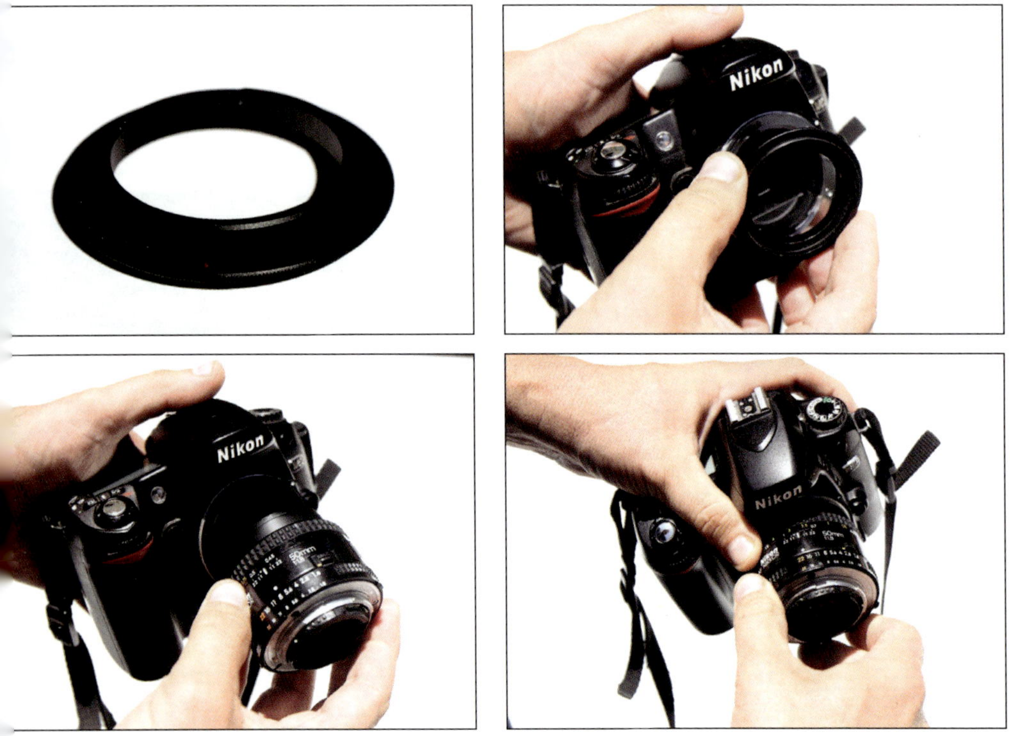


**Top**—A reversing ring is a very simple tool. It's a metal ring (as shown in the left photo) that attaches directly to the camera's lens mount (right photo). **Bottom left and right**—Once the ring is attached firmly, the lens is screwed into place.

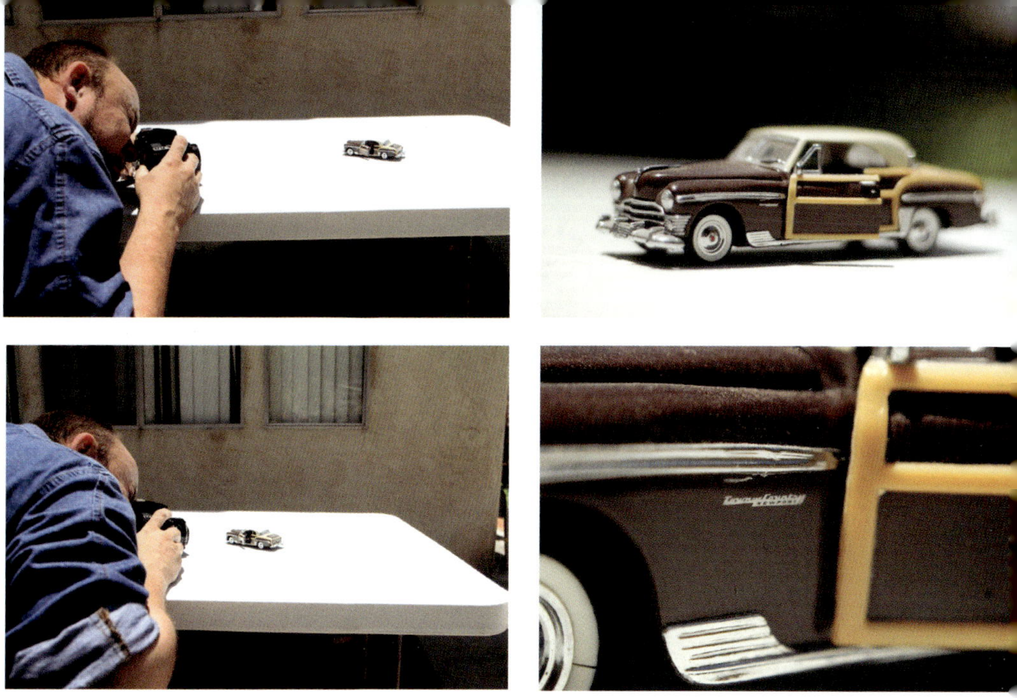

In the top left image, we see the minimum focal distance of a 50mm f/1.8 lens (roughly two feet). In the top right image, we see the resulting image. In the bottom left image, we see the adjusted minimum focal distance (now, roughly six inches) with the lens reversed. This obviously affords a much tighter angle of view and surprisingly larger-than-life image (roughly 2:1). Hello true macro photography!

true. This reversal can be done with the aid of a reversing ring, or without one. Metal reversing rings can be found at better camera stores or online and cost roughly $10. The ring is attached to your camera's lens mount, then the lens attaches to the ring backwards. Simply flip your lens, screw it onto the reversing ring using your lens's filter threads, and—poof!—your lens is on backwards. This changes the physics of the lens, moving its available focus point and allowing you to focus much more closely than before.

While it looks odd, reversing your lens does give you some amazing (and very real) macro options. It achieves a much greater size relationship (sometimes up to 2:1 or even 4:1) and, physically, gets you much closer to your subject. (*Note:* Whether this technique will work for you will depend on the focal length of the lens you are trying to flip. Too long or too short of a lens will put the focal point *inside* the lens—making the whole process pointless. We find that a flipped 50mm lens works best, though you should at least try this with every lens you have.)

To reverse a lens you will have to be in full manual—this isn't just a suggestion, it's a must. Once the lens is removed from the camera, all electrical connections are lost, meaning the machine has no idea what shutter speed to employ, it can't control your aperture, and it has lost all focusing power. Chances are the camera may not even fire if the camera is in any automatic setting.

However, if you're a manual shooter, there's nothing to worry about—especially if you employ an older lens that has an adjustable aperture ring. If this is present, you can still manually adjust your aperture, changing the focal depth just as you would with the lens attached to the camera. Admittedly, this technique is a bit old school—but when something works, it works.

## EXTENSION TUBES

An even more traditional way of achieving larger-than-life images (or simply getting much closer) is with the use of extension tubes. Tubes are an easy and economical way of getting up-close-and-personal with any subject, adjusting the focal point just as before. Extension tubes are hollow pieces of metal with a bayonet fitting. Usually they come in sets, allowing you to increase or decrease the length of the extension by adjusting the number of tube pieces you employ. The longer you make the tube, the closer you can focus.

Manual shooters will be able to use the most inexpensive of tubes (sometimes less than $20 for an entire set). Automatic shooters will need to purchase more expensive tubes that share electronic information between the camera and the lens.

You can put extension tubes on almost any lens, giving you a plethora of close-up options while in the field—no matter what gear you have. You can also double-up on techniques. For instance, you can flip a lens in front of a tube, use your macro lens with a tube, and more. A set of extension tubes is a pretty standard piece of gear in our camera bags.

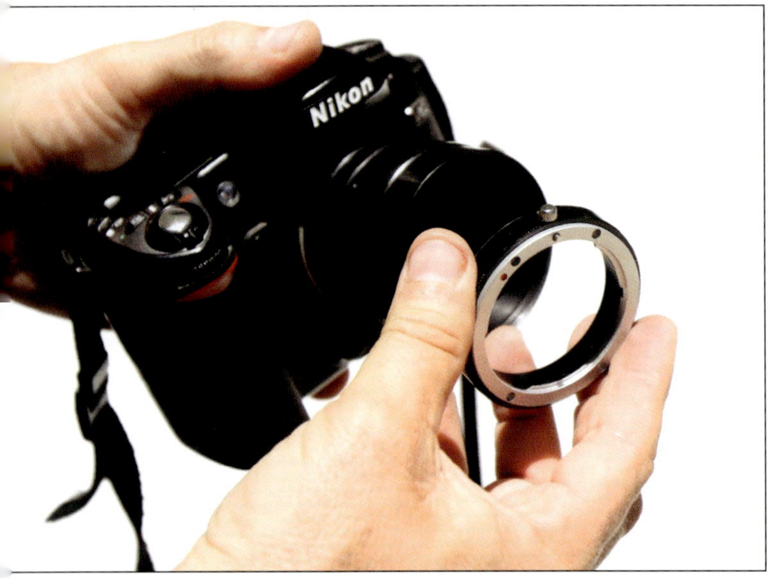

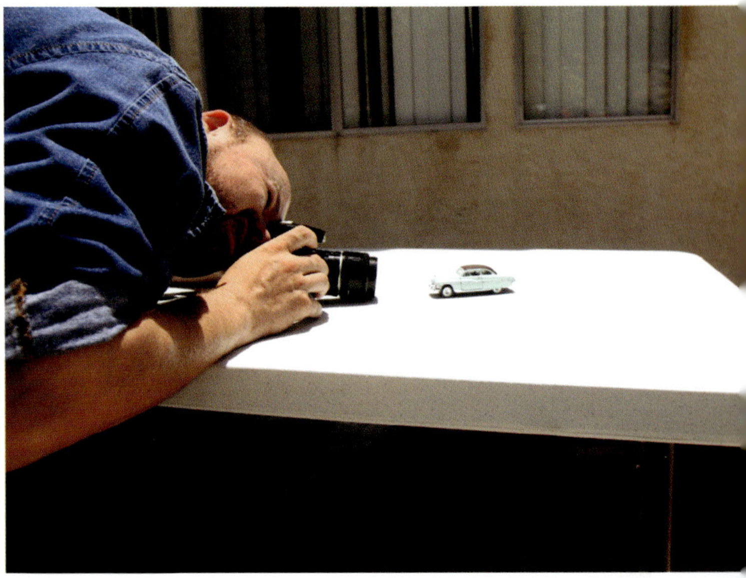
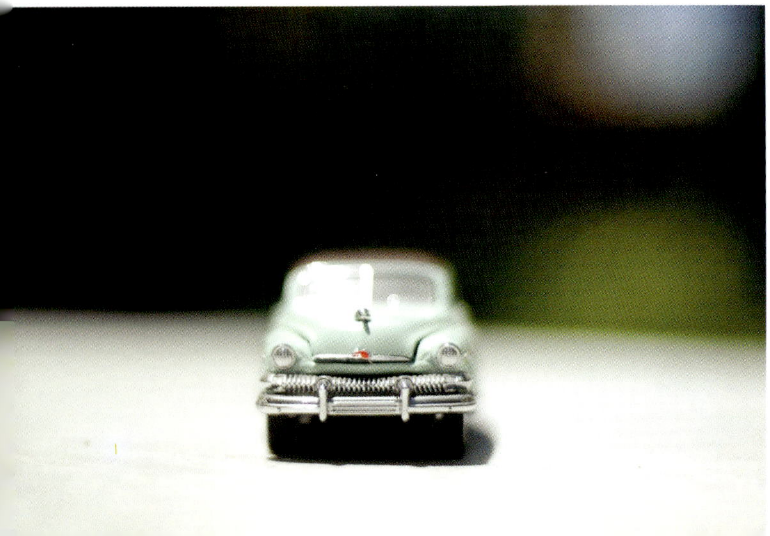
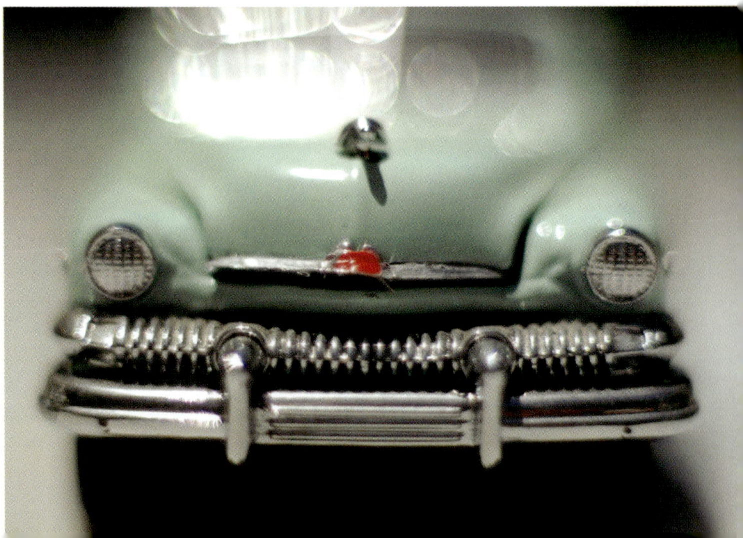

Extension tubes give the photographer the power of macro shooting without the need for a macro lens. By simply attaching one, two, or even three hollow tubes, you can get closer and closer and closer to your subject. For the price, they are by far one of the best ways of getting a macro image with just about any lens.

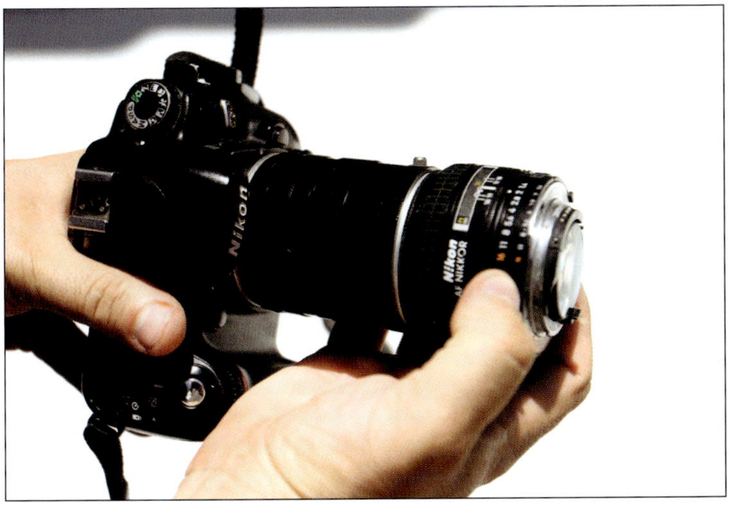

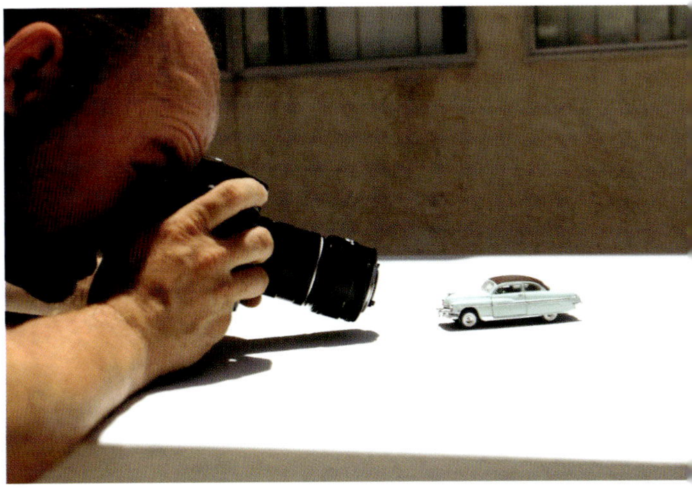

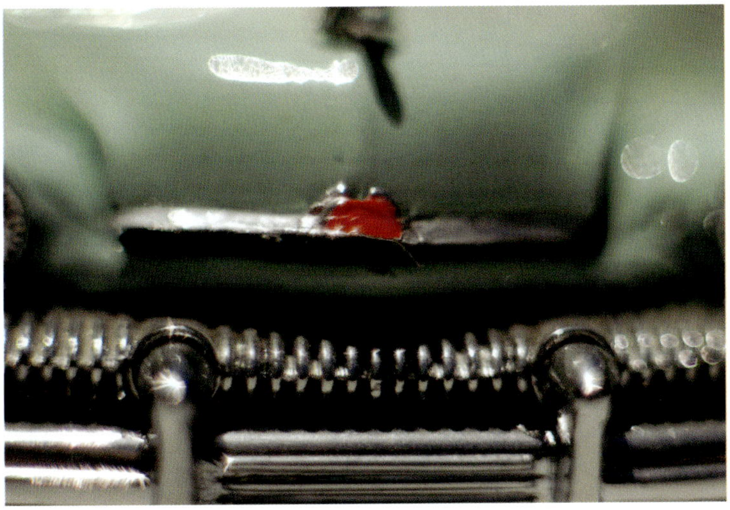

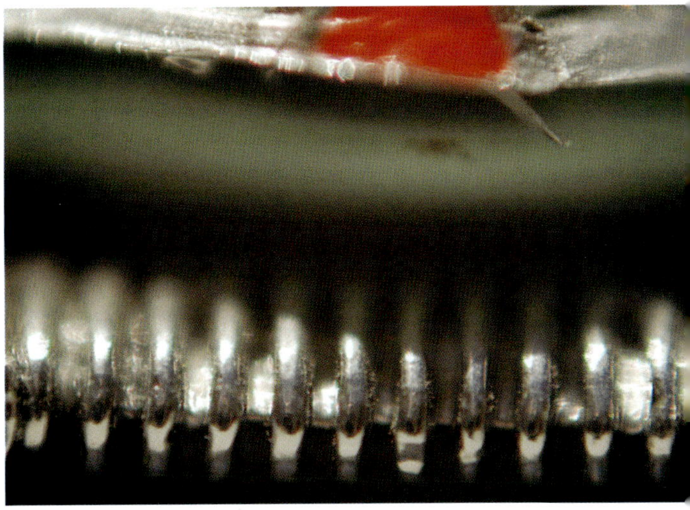

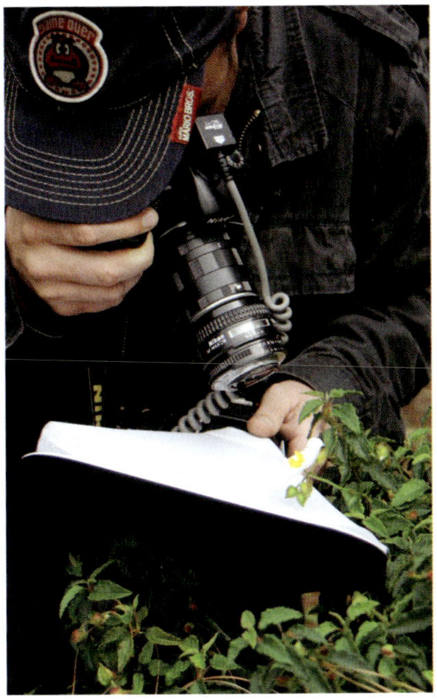

**Above**—You can try some outlandish techniques with an extension tube. Here, you see the implementation of a reversed 50mm lens on a set of tubes and the resulting macro images. **Left**—Here, you see the use of three extension tubes and a flipped 50mm lens as well as a corded, highly modified, hand-held flash.

## BELLOWS

An even older-school (yet still highly effective) approach is using a bellows system. This tool is, in effect, an adjustable extension tube. The bellows—made of paper, rubber, or sometimes even cloth—opens and closes like an accordion. It sits atop a built-in track system, allowing the photographer to adjust the length of the bellows based on the desired focal distance and magnification.

Many non-flash photographers use the bellows system, as it sits atop a tripod quite nicely. This makes precise focusing possible while in the field (as long as there is no wind blowing). However, the whole mechanism is a bit awkward for the off-camera flash shooter who usually has his hands full with a flash and flash-modification equipment.

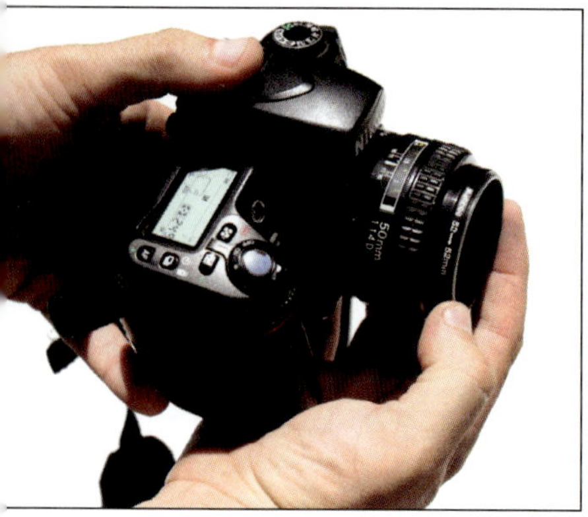
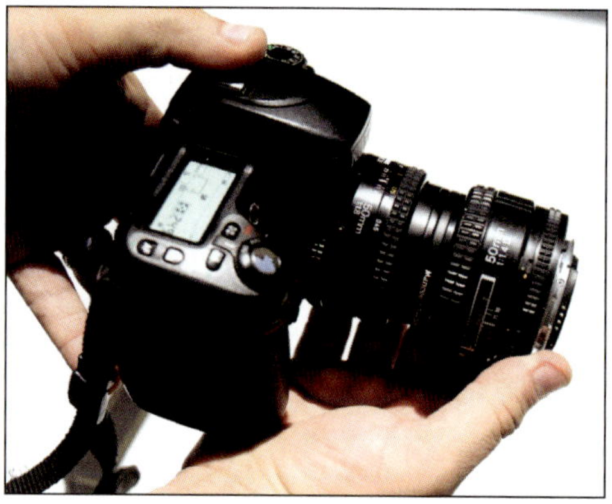
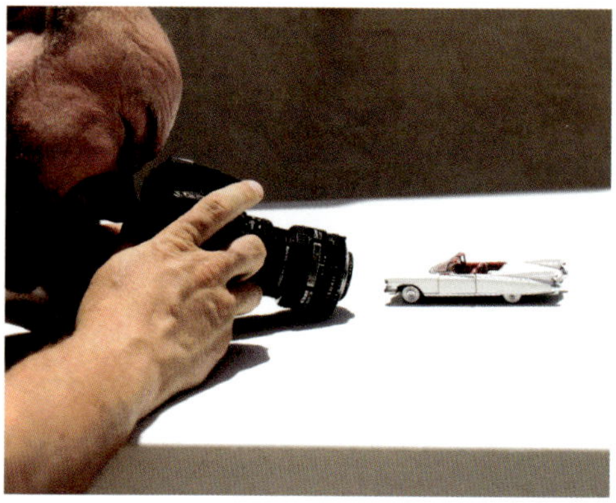

You can go face-to-face with certain lenses; we find that two 50mm lenses offer the best and most powerful combination. In essence, you are turning one of the lenses into an extension tube and then flipping the other. It's quite an effective means of getting close, offering some unbelievable magnification options.

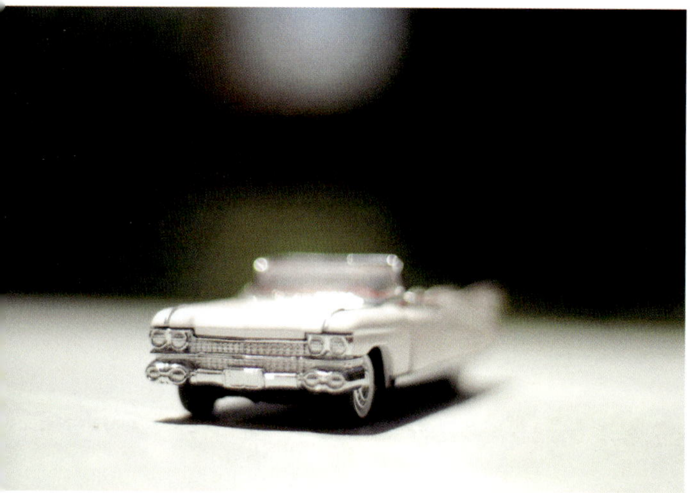
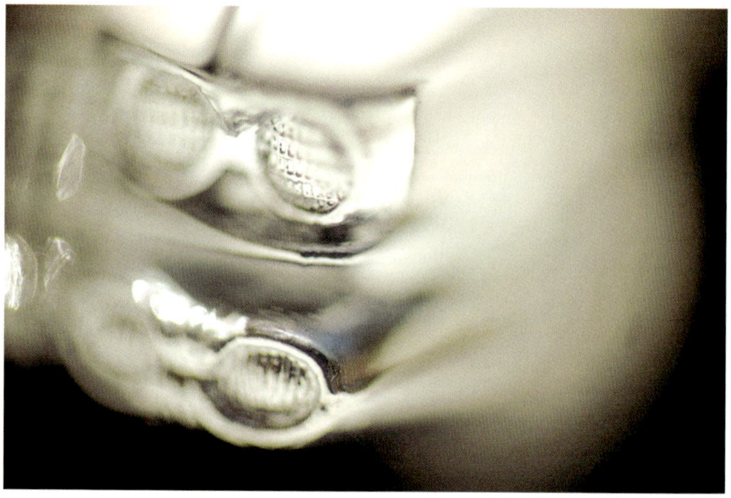

**Left**—This image shows the effects of a straight 50mm f/1.4 lens. **Right**—Here we see the unbelievable magnification that is achieved when two lenses are used at once.

## FACE-TO-FACE LENSES

You can also play on the extension tube idea by simply stacking two lenses face to face. To do this, you'll need to purchase a coupling ring. The metal ring sits on the filter holder of the first lens and then is screwed onto the filter holder of the flipped second lens. If you're looking to save money or really want close and extremely large magnification levels (8:1, 10:1, or more), this is the technique for you.

Depending on the lenses involved and the apertures you've chosen, you may see quite a bit of vignetting around the edges when using this technique. If this happens, try using a larger aperture—or simply take the shot and crop the vignetted portion out of the final image with your computer.

## THE MACRO LENS

Of all the options, the most versatile—and, our opinion, best—option is a macro lens. Designed specifically for macro work, macro lenses allow you to retain all the automatic functions (if needed). As a manual shooter, these lenses free you to shoot from any location, at any angle, to manually focus, to use the camera's meter if you feel the need, to employ the depth-of-field preview button, and much, much more. Of course, macro lenses are a bit more expensive than the previously discussed choices, but they are certainly worth the investment.

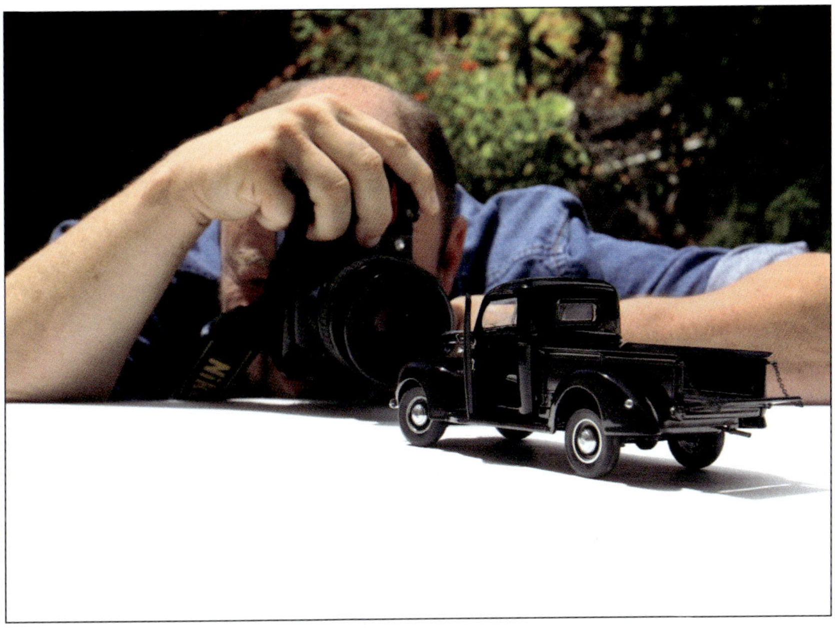

A true macro lens offers you the flexibility of in-camera aperture adjustments, perspective changes, autofocus, and autoexposure (if you need it). The images below illustrate the extreme closeness and variations of angles you can achieve when using a macro lens.

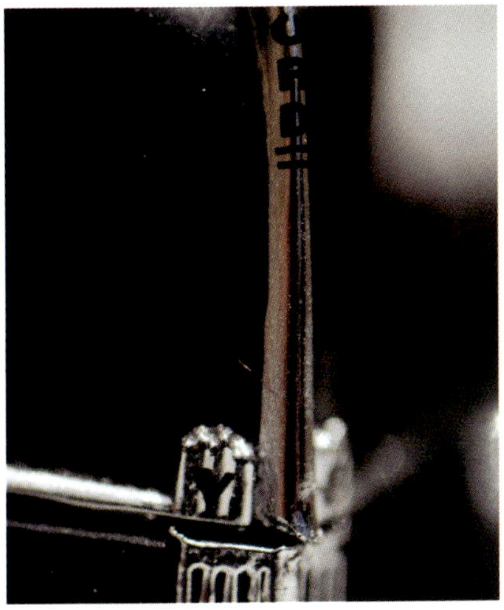

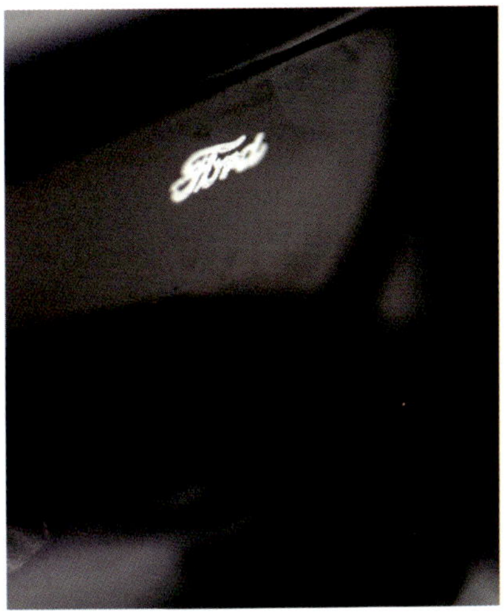


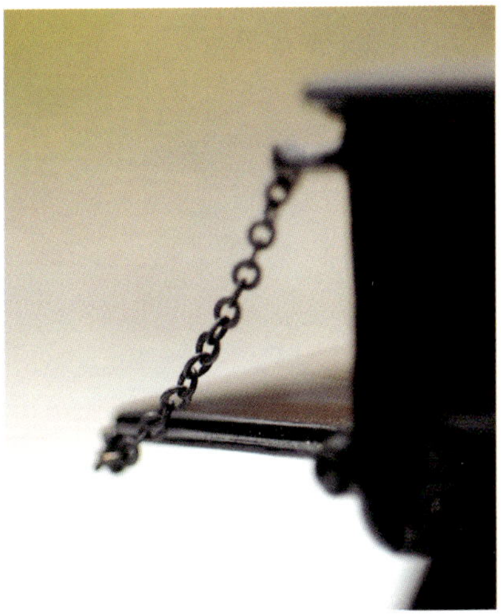

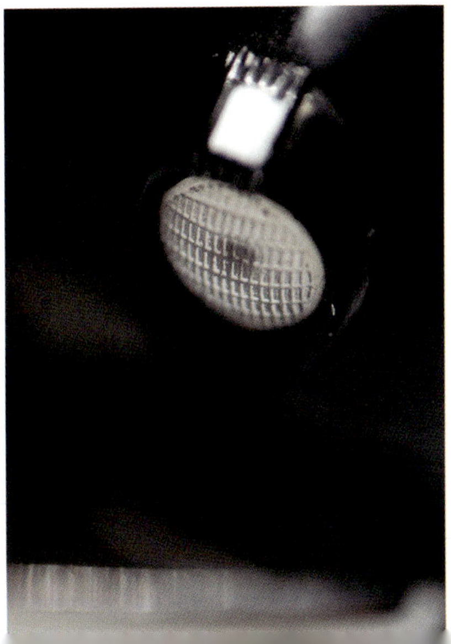

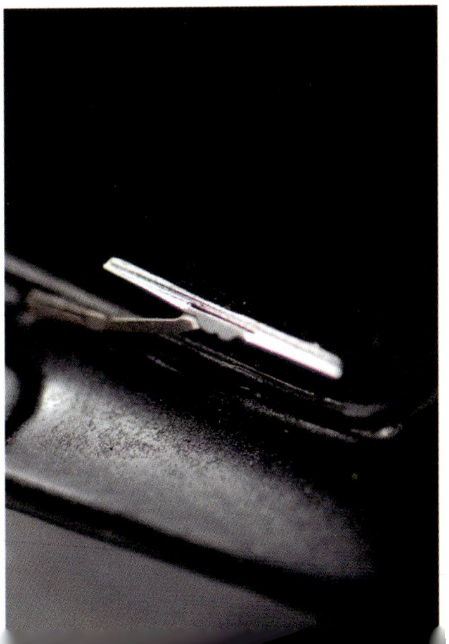

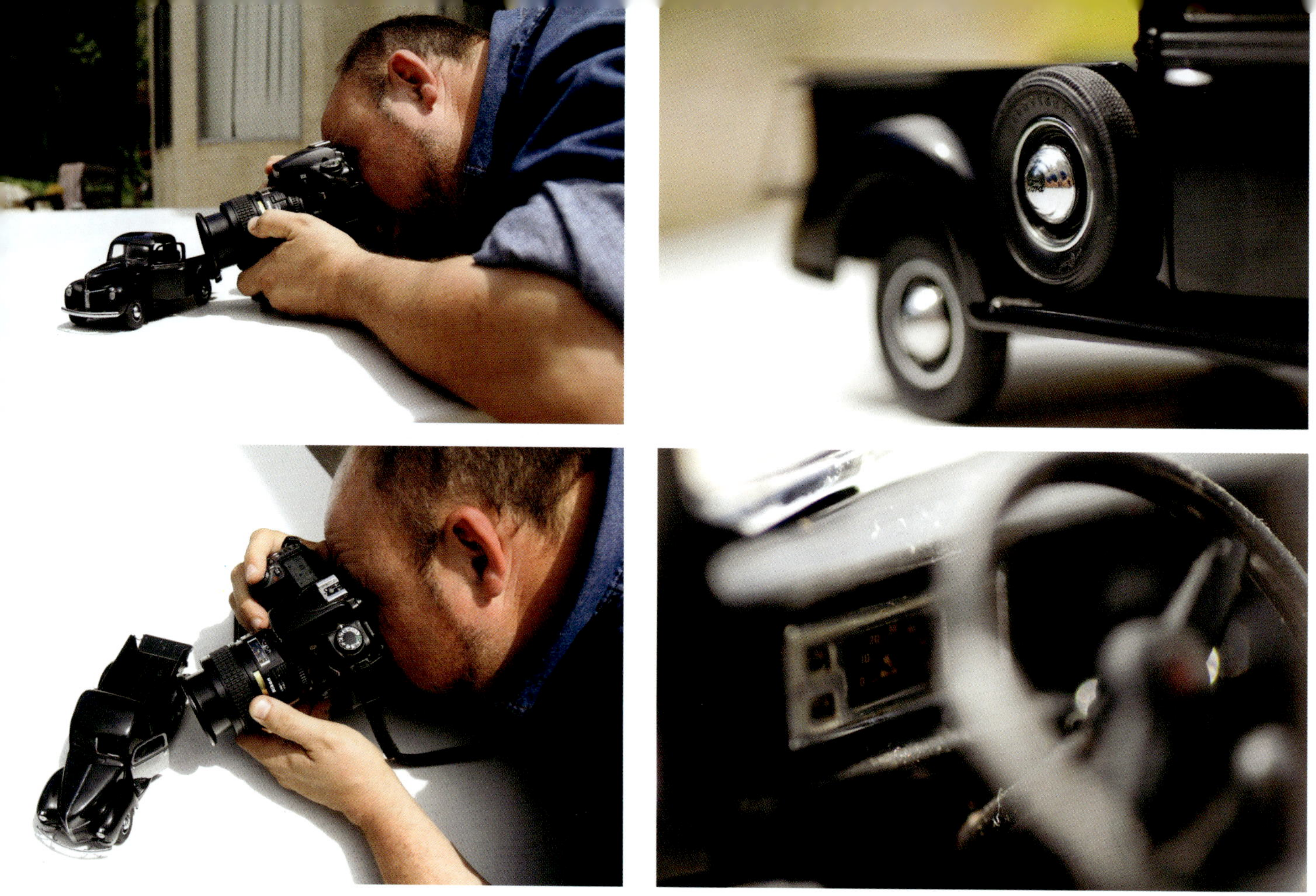

When you are close to your subject, the amount of blur in your image will increase dramatically. You can fight this depth-of-field reduction by using a smaller aperture.

Macro lenses come in a variety of focal lengths, and all will get you close to a subject (some, admittedly, closer than others). Usually, macro lenses range in focal lengths from 50mm to 200mm. Many people like the longer (more expensive) focal length macro lenses, believing them a necessity for shooting insects. Personally, we've never found that to be the case. With the right attitude and calm demeanor, you can get extremely close to insects in the wild. We do it all the time. Once they've evaluated you and don't sense a threat, it's pretty easy to slowly move into their world and create magic. (*Note:* When using a macro lens, you can get even closer by adding extension tubes, stacking macro lenses, applying a doubler, or even flipping the lens. Push your options to see just how far you can go!)

***Take Time to Train***

For the first few weeks of your training you should remember that you're *training*, not expecting to capture amazing pictures. You don't prepare for a marathon by running a full marathon. Too many people want to skip the whole experience part. They want this to be simple when it's anything but. Take your time when learning. Make sure you know how to get close first—before you start complicating the situation by adding light with your flash.

The absolute best part of owning a macro lens is that many models offer the photographer very small apertures—meaning more depth of field. For instance, our favorite macro lens (an inexpensive Nikon 60mm) actually affords the use of f/57 when the lens is focused at its minimum focal distance. This is a serious advantage when you want to get very small things in crisp focus!

## CLOSE-UP FILTERS

Close-up filters have been around for ages and offer a closer view of your subject. It's akin to putting a magnifying lens in front of your camera. They come in various degrees of power and most work well. For those looking to only dabble in close-up photography, these may be all you need . . . although the magnification (and sometimes filter quality) will soften most images. Many photographers find this softness a bit much and

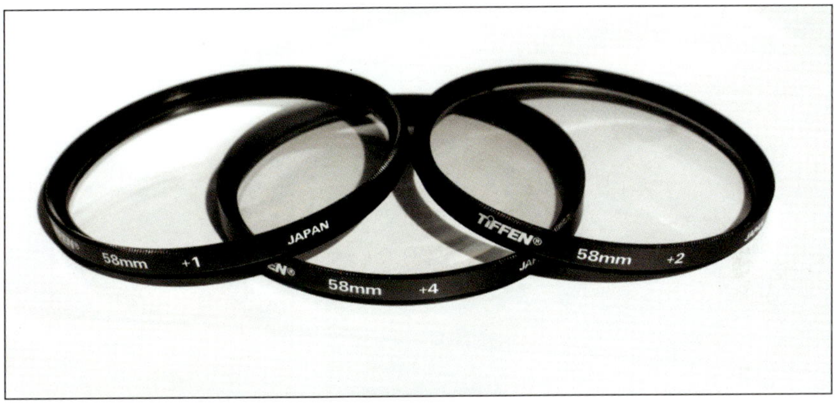


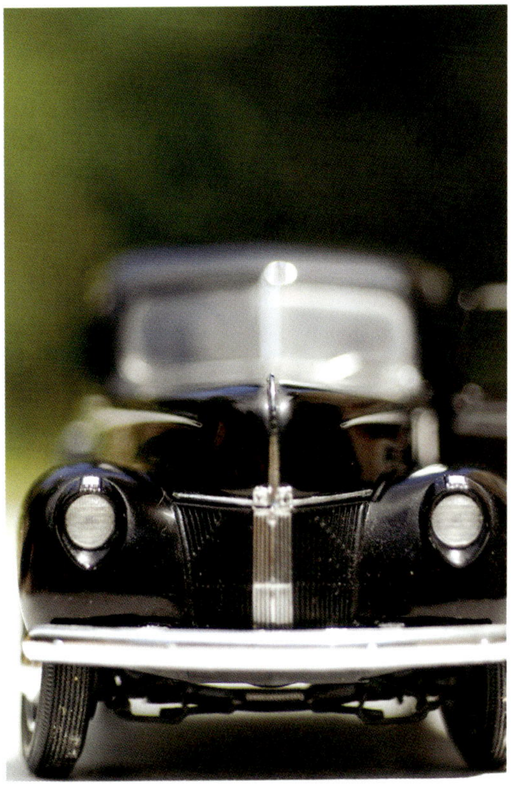

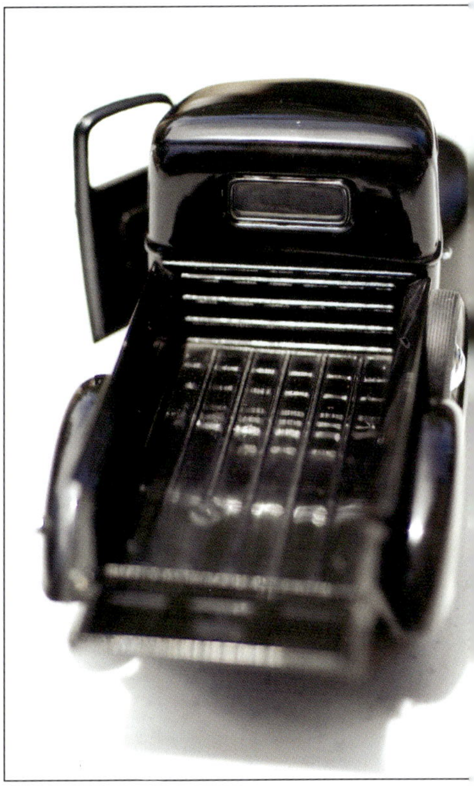

Inexpensive close-up filters (top image) allow you to create close-up images with any lens. There is a quality issue associated with close-up filters, however; most tend to soften an image. Still, for the options they afford, these are not bad tools to keep in your camera bag. When used well, close-up filters can also help you produce some amazing macro images.

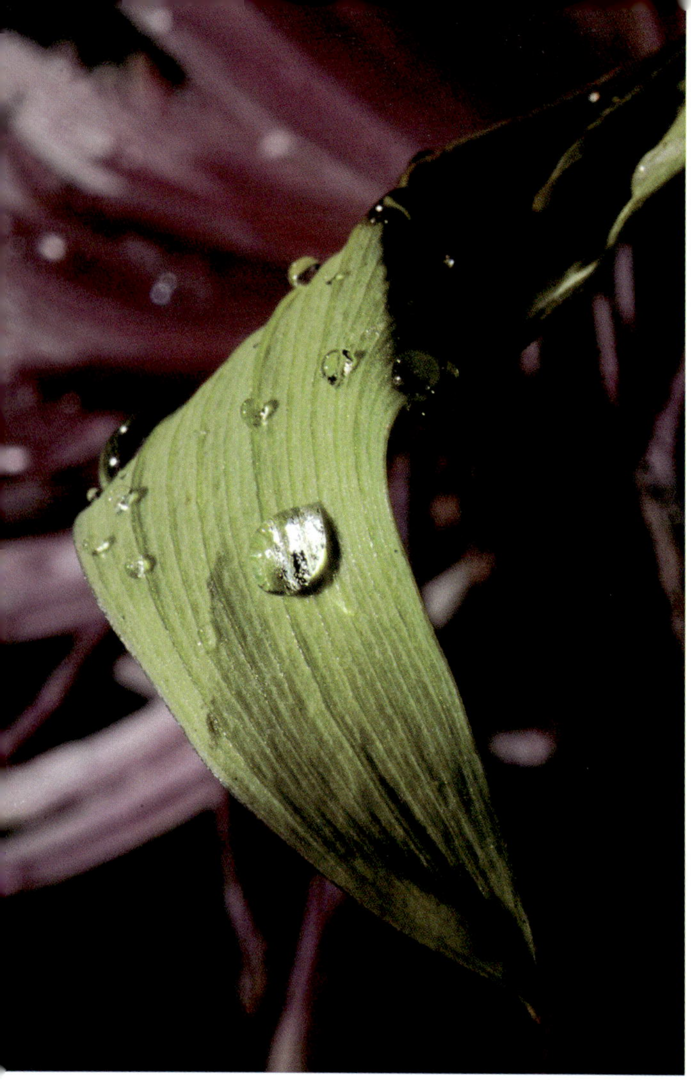

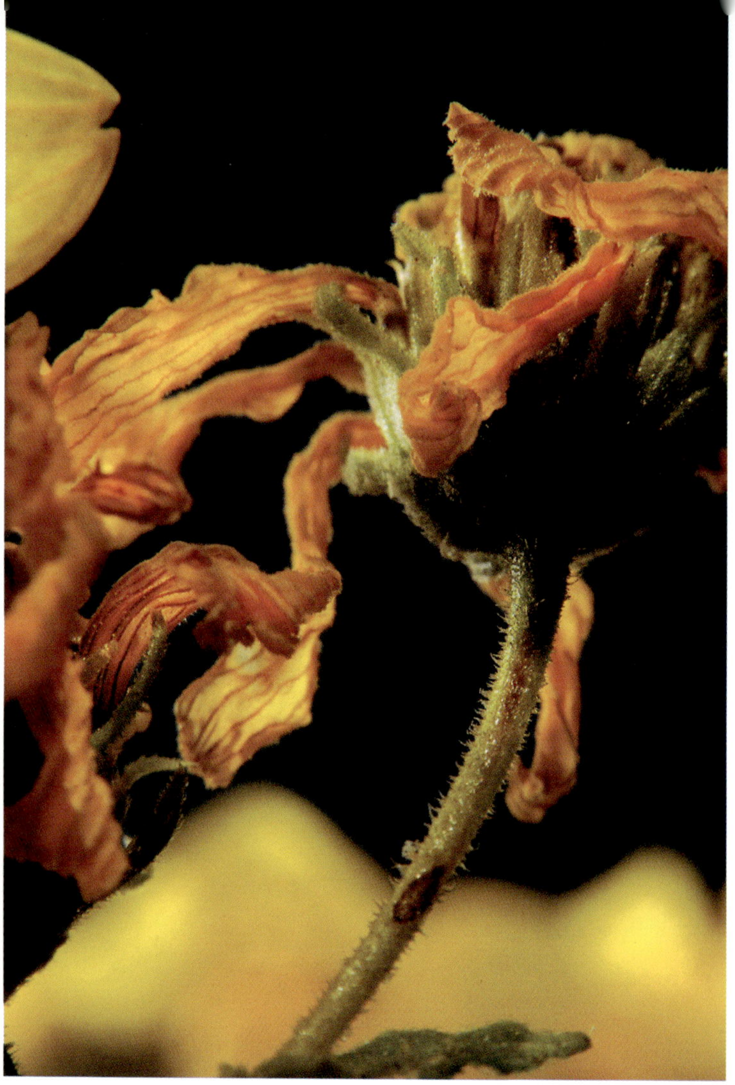

**Left**—Adding light with an off-camera flash is one of the most liberating experiences a close-up or macro artist will ever have. Gone are the days of motion blur; depth-of-field control becomes the norm, not a distant dream. In short, if you've got an inclination for shooting things close-up, you're going to want to add some light with an off-camera flash. **Right**—Once you get very, very close to a subject, you'll probably find some need to light it with a flash. Here, a tiny aperture (f/36) was needed to ensure the required depth of field. A shutter speed of $^1/_{100}$ second, an ISO setting of 400, and a polarizer were called into play to achieve the background exposure. A modified flash was then added to bring the subject into the light. Without the flash, this image would not have been possible.

choose another option. We, on the other hand, don't mind the softness if the image we are creating will handle it. There are plenty of times when sharpness is not the important factor—expression is. When that's the case, these simple and inexpensive filters will do the job.

## THE NEXT STEP: ADDING LIGHT

Once you've decided on your macro gear, it's time to think about the flash—which one you'll be using; what settings you'll choose; how you're going to communicate with it (since it will be used off-camera); what you're going to use to support it; what direction it needs to be coming from; and how in the world you'll be modifying it. Again, we suggest keeping things simple at first. Start with the gear you have. If you've got a flash—any flash—you're set. If not, then the next chapter will prove fun!

# 4. ADDING LIGHT

A flash simply adds light. It need not be special. It should not cost too much—and since it will be used off-camera, any flash (and we mean any flash) will do.

## WHAT YOU NEED TO KNOW ABOUT OFF-CAMERA FLASH

There are three things that are paramount in the mind of any off-camera flash shooter (whether he shoots close-up or not): communication, support, and modification. You will have to be able to trigger the flash in some manner, hold it steadily in position, and modify the light it is producing.

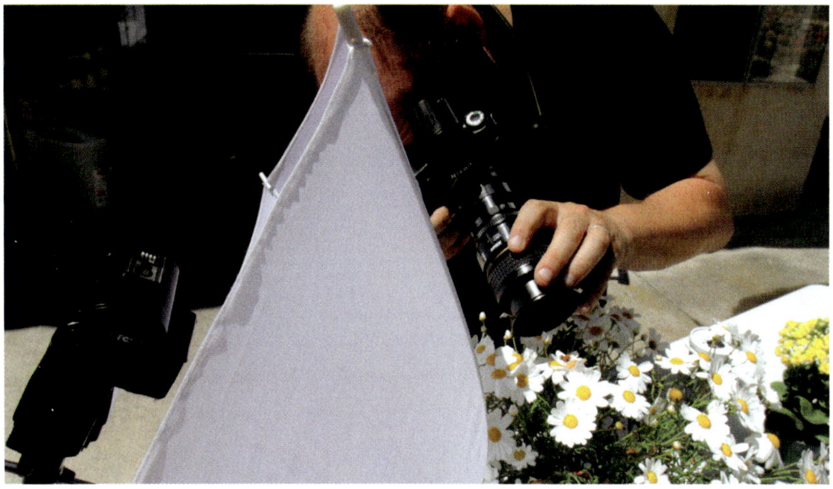

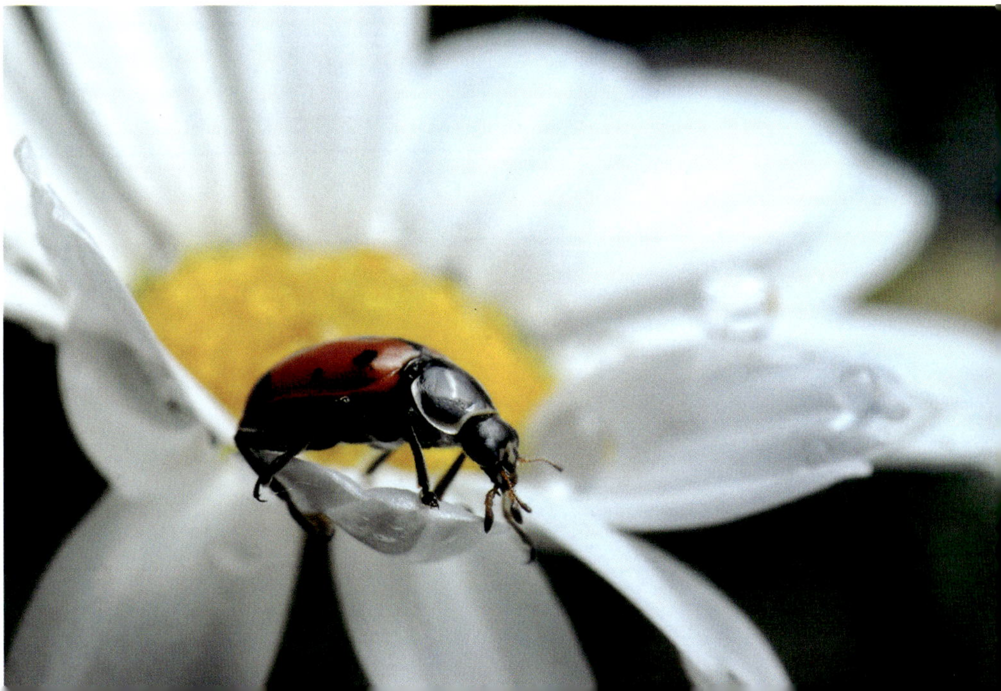

**Top**—Here, you see the three key pieces of off-camera flash photography (communication, support, and modification) at play. On top of the camera, you will notice an electronic device; this is a radio transmitter. On top of the flash, you can see the receiver. When the shutter is depressed, the transmitter sends out a radio signal to the receiver, which then fires the flash. You will also notice that the flash is being supported by a light stand (though you can hold it if you like). In front of the flash is a light modifier, in this case a studio shoot-through umbrella. This modifier enlarges and diffuses the light coming from the flash. **Bottom**—Creating amazing close-up images doesn't take expensive gear or luck—it just takes a flash, plus a way to trigger, support, and modify it. The rest is just you moving your body and lens back and forth to get your subjects in focus.

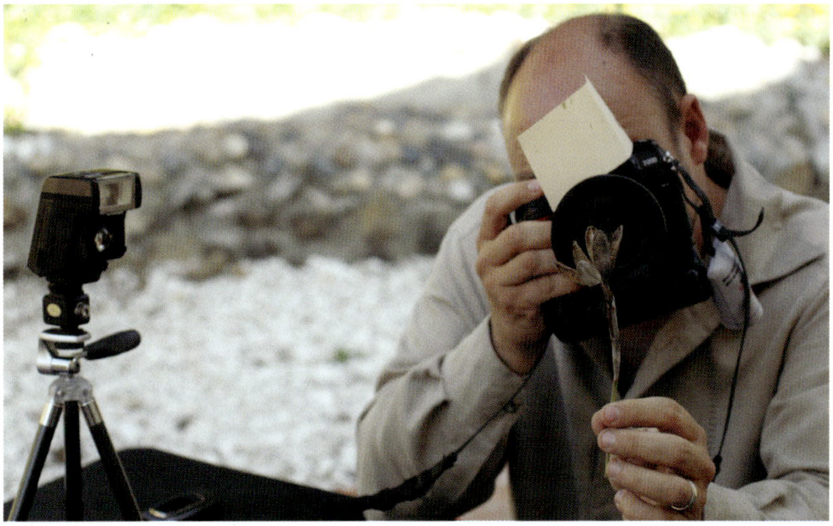

There is an inexpensive optical path toward off-camera expressionism—though it's not one we recommend. You could purchase an optical slave unit (seen on the bottom of the flash in the top image). With this system, firing the off-camera flash will require an optical triggering signal (your camera's pop-up flash will work just fine). This system requires a line-of-sight communication pathway between the trigger and the receiver. In the top photo, a piece of cardboard was taped in front of the pop-up flash to direct the light away from the twig and onto the receiver.

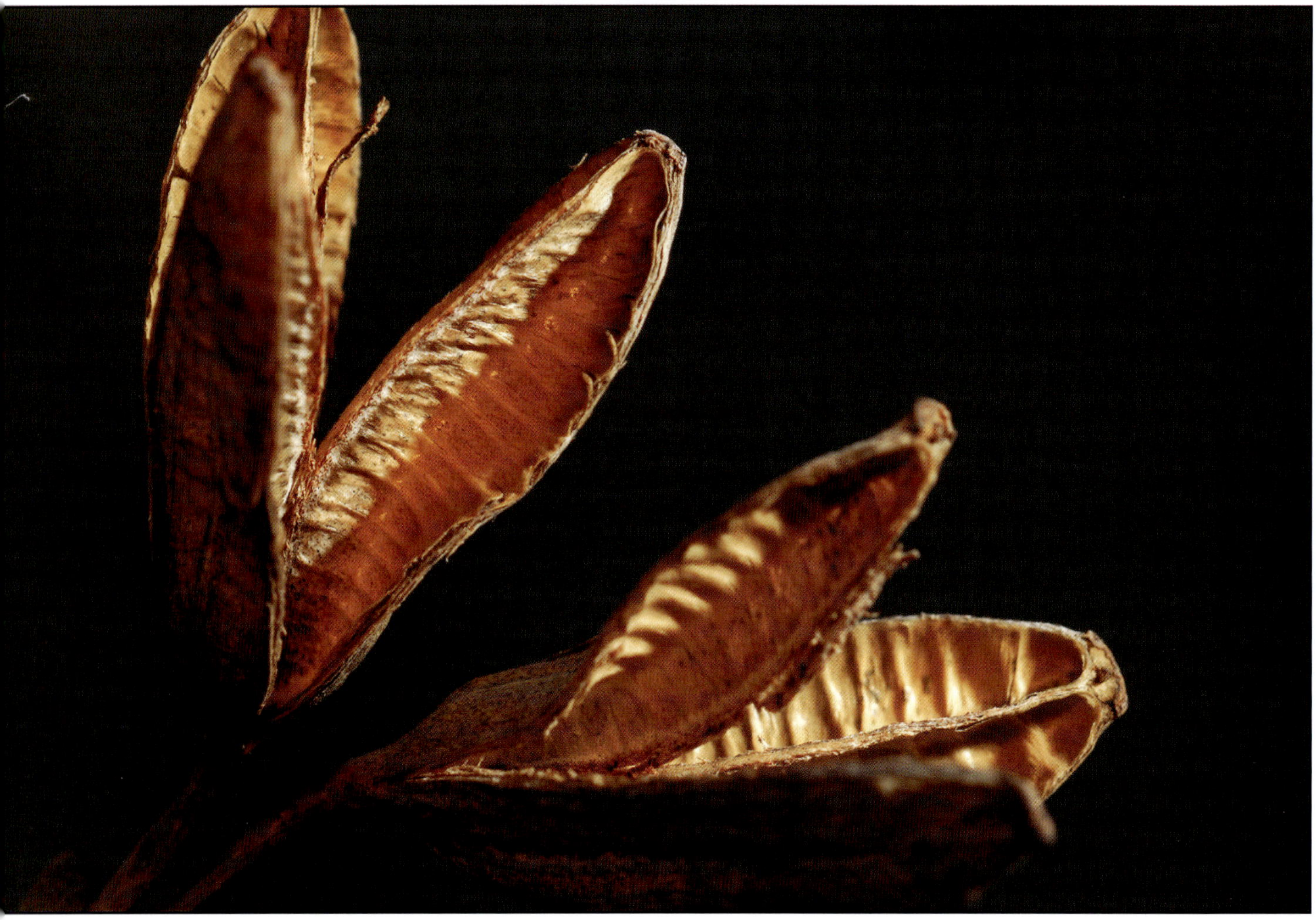

Each of these have a very real price—an actual dollar sign attached. Luckily, though, it doesn't have to be high. A brand new flash can be purchased for less than $90 (Vivitar 285HV), a radio transmitter and receiver is less than $40 (Cactus V4), and a simple homemade light modifier can be constructed from a potato-chip canister ($2)—plus you get to keep the chips (BBQ-flavored images are our favorites). If you've got a free hand, you can always hold the flash (this is our preferred method of deployment by the way), but a light stand can usually be purchased for less than $25.

In the previous chapter we showed you some very inexpensive ways of getting close with your existing lenses (techniques that don't require the purchase of a new macro lens). In this chapter, we'll explore other inexpensive options as we get in touch with the flash. Don't ever let expense get in the way of your creativity.

## ABOUT THE FLASH

Off-camera flash photography puts a unique spin on the message-building process. Since the flash is off-camera and coming from a direction a bit more natural-looking than when the flash is sitting atop a camera, any light produced will be quite striking—as long as it is controlled. Brand names, unit designators, and such really don't matter. Whatever flash you have is the best flash! Even if it's old, used, or archaic, if it pumps light, you can use it. For us, the flash of choice is often whichever flash unit has the freshest batteries. You'll always catch us using Canon flashes with Nikon cameras and vice versa.

The only caveat is this: if you're an auto shooter you're going to need the expensive stuff. (This is one of the big reasons you might want to abandon your auto settings; manual shooters have all the options but at a much lower cost. It doesn't get any better than that!) Automatic shooters

Does it really matter what flash produced the light in this image? Of course not. The greatest thing about flash photography, especially in the macro and close-up arena, is that it does not take a lot of money to get thoroughly involved. As a matter of fact, this image was shot using the camera's built-in pop-up flash (although highly modified).

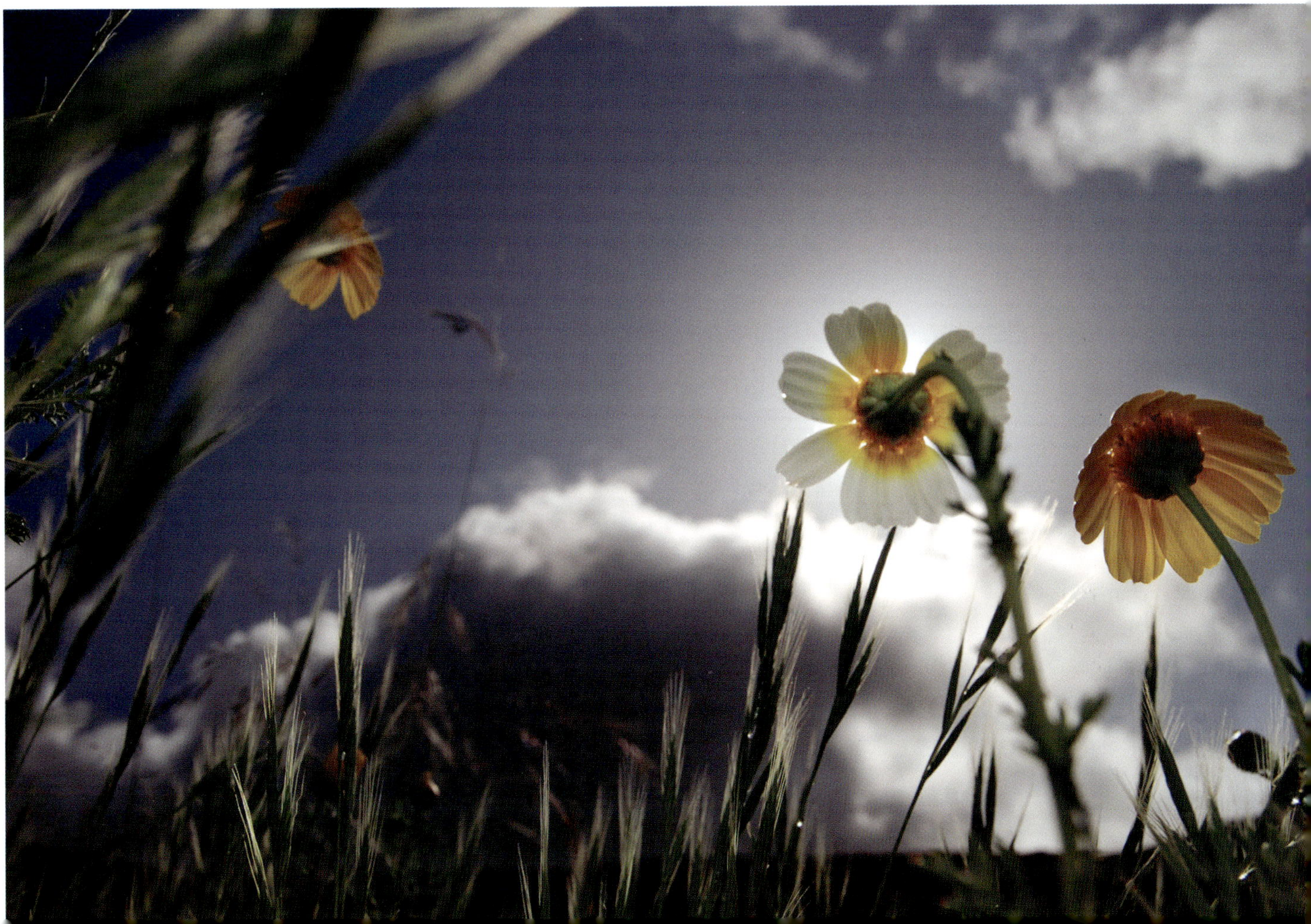

***For the Automatic Shooter Looking to Purchase a Flash***

Get the best flash your camera manufacturer makes. You can't settle for the less expensive versions of a flash. Power options vary drastically between models—and even though you will be close to your subjects, you're still going to need every ounce of power your flash can produce.

***For the Manual Shooter Looking to Purchase a Flash***

Use what you have got and buy a lot more. Keep it cheap and keep it coming. Don't stop at just one flash. Think about what would happen if you used more. Don't let your creativity wane because you don't have the gear. Shine a light on artistic expression—and never look back!

need to go with the manufacturer's recommended gear. We also suggest getting the best possible flash you can afford. This will give you the greatest amount of auto options and truly does offer the most "pop" for your buck. There is nothing worse than striving for perfection and then being held back by an inferior piece of machinery.

There are, admittedly, a few very cool advantages to having the latest and greatest flash—more power, specialized sync-speed solutions, built-in optical triggering systems, state-of-the-art electronics, and more—but there are also just as many reasons to not use them (expense, brand-name specificity, limited connection options, and more). If you have the resources, there is nothing wrong with purchasing a high-end flash unit—but don't think for an instant that you must. Dedication, spirit, and ingenuity can make up for any lack of advanced features. When you do away with the hype and concentrate on what you really need, you may already own everything you need.

## COMMUNICATION

When it comes to triggering your flash off-camera you have two options: wired and wireless. You can either use a cord (connected to the camera's hot shoe/PC port and running to the flash's foot/PC port) or you can employ an optical/radio transmitter on your camera with the appropriate receiver on your flash. Both work gloriously when shooting close-up.

Before you start purchasing communication gear, make sure you know what you already have. Many digital camera systems today offer their own version of wireless communication. Typically, these use the camera's pop-up flash (or an extra flash/infrared unit) as a triggering device. Certain flashes, those made by the same manufacturer, then see this triggering flash and fire.

If you already have this feature you can begin off-camera flash work right away—but don't worry if you don't. These systems can be quite limiting and can get expensive. First, you have to have the right camera and the right flash for this to work; it's a very brand-specific way of shooting. Second, these "advanced" or "creative" lighting systems, as they are called, are limited because they require line-of-sight to work. This means that the off-camera flash needs to *see* the triggering flash (or signal) to be activated. Often, when shooting macro or close-up photography, the flash will be far from the camera (or triggering unit)—or hidden behind an umbrella, plant, tree, flower, etc. It may be placed far to the right or left of the triggering unit or can sometimes be positioned behind the camera itself and, hence, behind the triggering signal. When shooting a close-up image, you can't be limited as to where you are putting your flashes. We recommend staying away from this in-camera option, as well as any other optical transmission system.

A better and much more reliable form of communication is achieved through the use of flash cord or PC wire. A flash cord runs straight from the camera's hot shoe and attaches directly to the bottom of the flash. This offers 100 percent reliability no matter where the flash is positioned. A PC wire (a cheaper alternative) can be used when both the camera and the flash have PC ports—though its effectiveness can be strained if the wires are frayed or the connection is loose. Either, though, provides a brilliant option.

Our favorite form of communication for close-up/macro photography is through the use of simple radio transmitters/receivers. Cheaper than a cord and not limited by a cord's length, radio transmitters and receivers offer alternatives no other type of communication does. We use the Cactus V4; a set (both transmitter and receiver) costs less than $40. If you

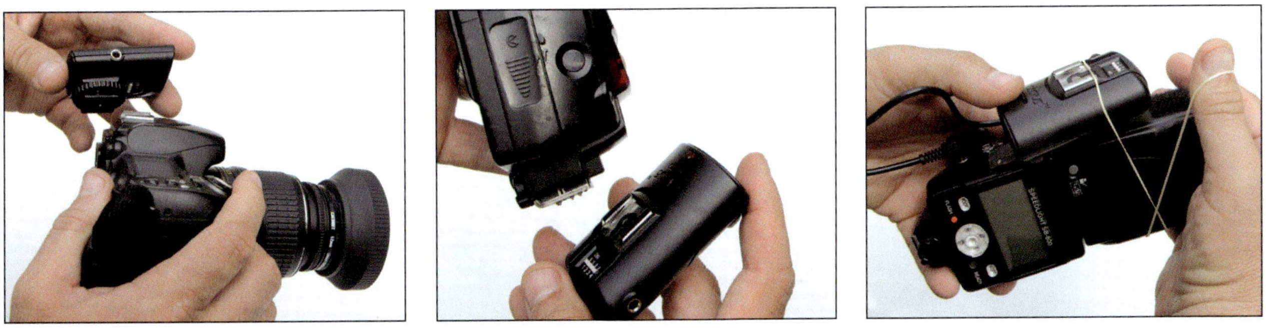

Our favorite brand of radio transmitter/receiver is the Cactus V4 made by Harvest One. For less than $40, you can get a transmitter and receiver and be shooting in no time. As this series of images shows, they are not the most complicated of devices to add to your camera of flash. The transmitter sits atop the camera on the hot shoe, while the receiver can either sit on the bottom of the flash (center image) or be attached with the included PC wire. (We use a rubber band to attach it to the flash when using this method, as the right-hand photo shows.)

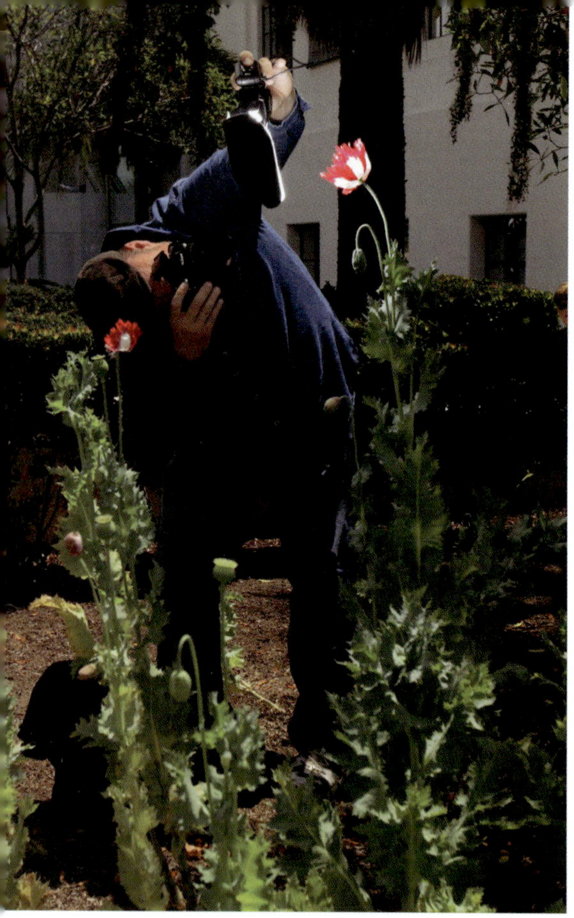

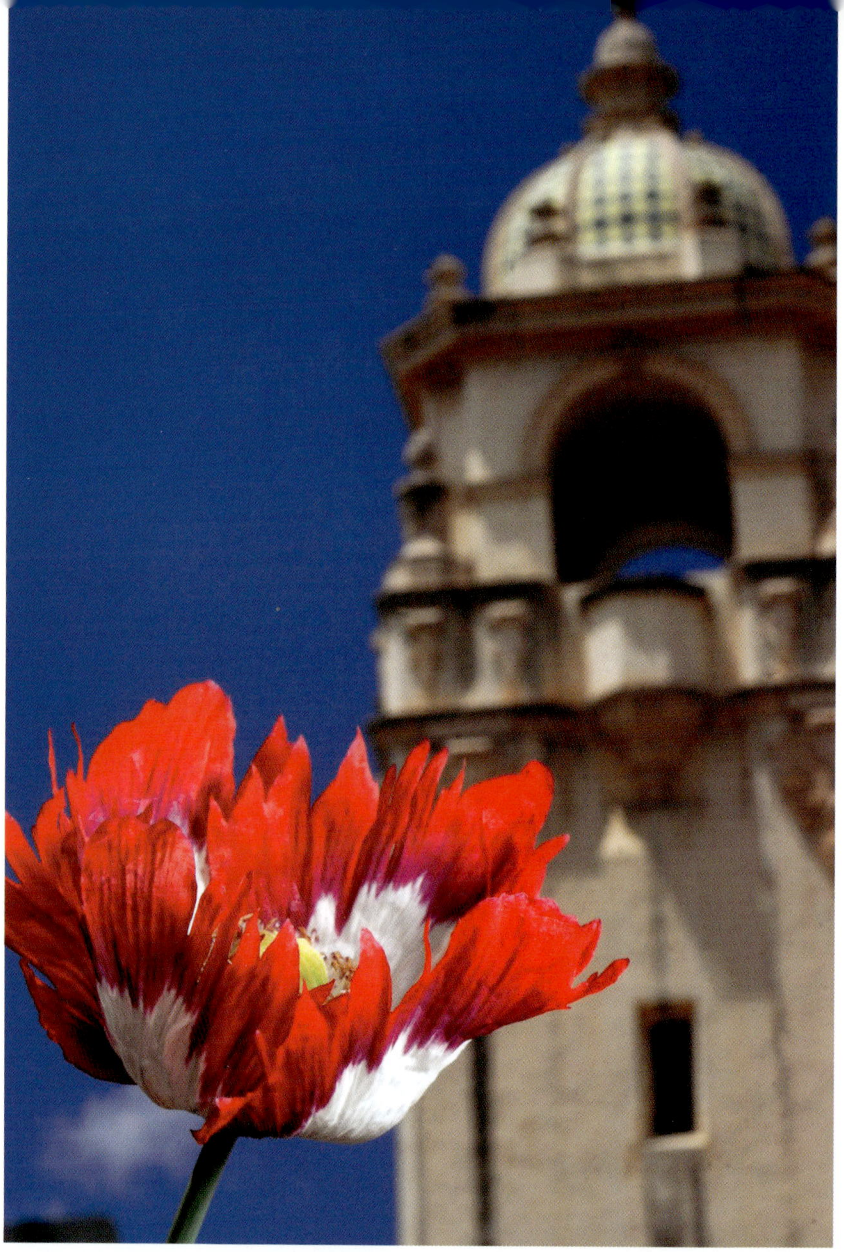

The addition of light from a flash is important in close-up photography—even when shooting under the blazing afternoon sun. To achieve the desired depth of field in this photo, a very small aperture (f/29) was needed. A shutter speed of $^1/_{60}$ second was then chosen, along with an ISO of 400. These helped the photographer achieve the perfect lighting for his background and maintain a shutter speed that froze the flower. Then it was simply a matter of modifying the light source (making it bigger and softer) and choosing a power setting on the flash that would illuminate the flower perfectly. The contrast, saturation, sharpening, and hue options were also chosen in-camera before the image was shot. This eliminated the need for any post-processing corrections in the computer.

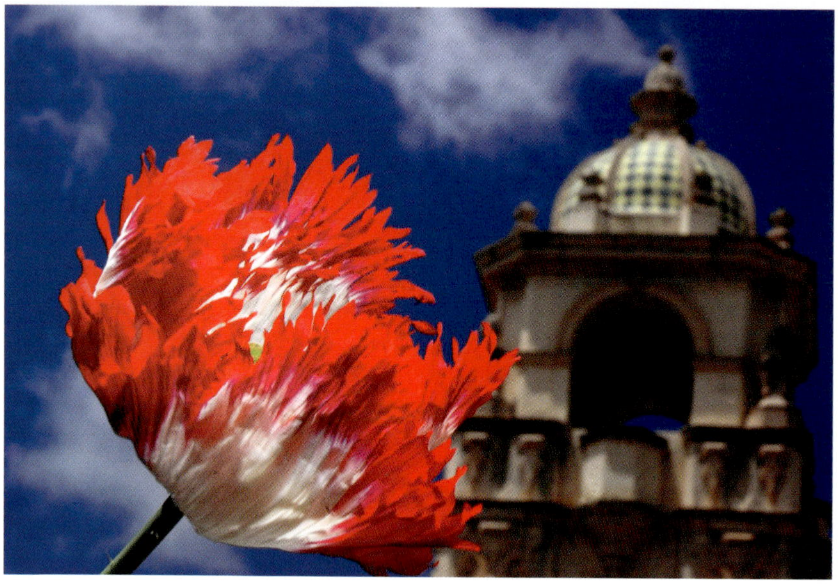

want to use more flashes, each additional receiver is only about $20. Pure creativity, no limitations—and cheap. Simply spectacular!

Keep in mind, though, that you do have to be a manual shooter for all of this "keepin' it cheap" stuff to work. If you're not, your close-up/macro dreams are going to cost you dearly. To maintain automatic connectivity between a camera and flash means staying in the family of manufacturer-recommended options—expensive flash systems, expensive wireless transmitters and receivers, and more. It's not a pretty road. The upside though, when spending all that money, is that you won't have to worry about those pesky little options like mood, depth of field, true intent, meaning, or expression.

## MODIFICATION

There is an old saying in macro photography about the illumination offered by a flash: the bigger the light and the closer you can get it, the nicer it will be. Boy—that is *so* true. While you would think a standard flash would be big enough to shoot small things, sometimes it isn't. Often, it's wise to employ a modification tool to enlarge it; larger light sources offer a bigger playing field, which is important when shooting things close up.

**Left**—Macro and close-up photography with an off-camera flash can be a very solitary business. Often it's just you and your small subject. What you look like, what gear you carry, and what you carry it in make no difference. There is no need to play the part of a photographer here—focus, instead, on being an artist. Create an image that reflects who you are and how you feel about what's in front of you. **Right**—We call this a "scatterbox." It's a beautiful and easily made light modification tool for your camera's built-in pop-up flash. We simply fold a large piece of aluminum foil around the flash and then mold a hood of sorts to scatter the light onto anything in its path. It's a very inexpensive (and easy) way of adding the softest light you will ever see to your macro and close-up images.

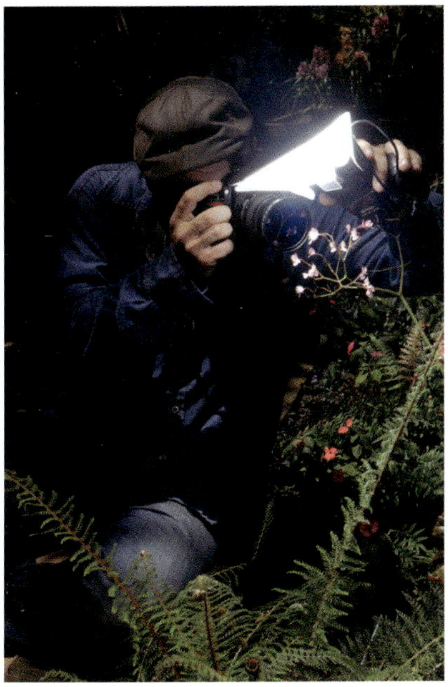

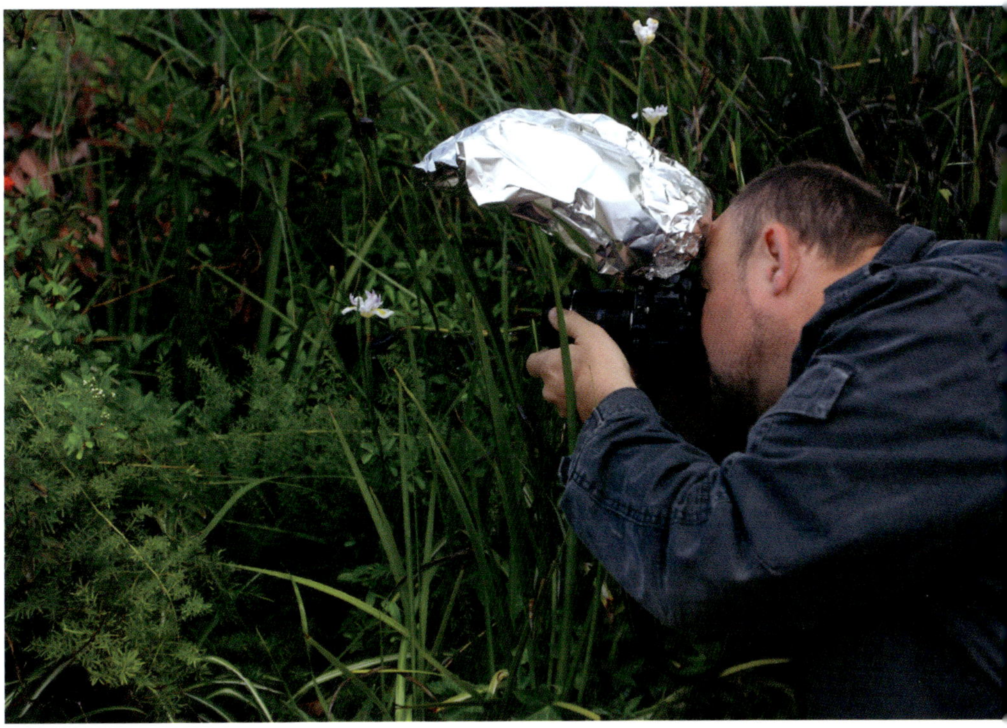

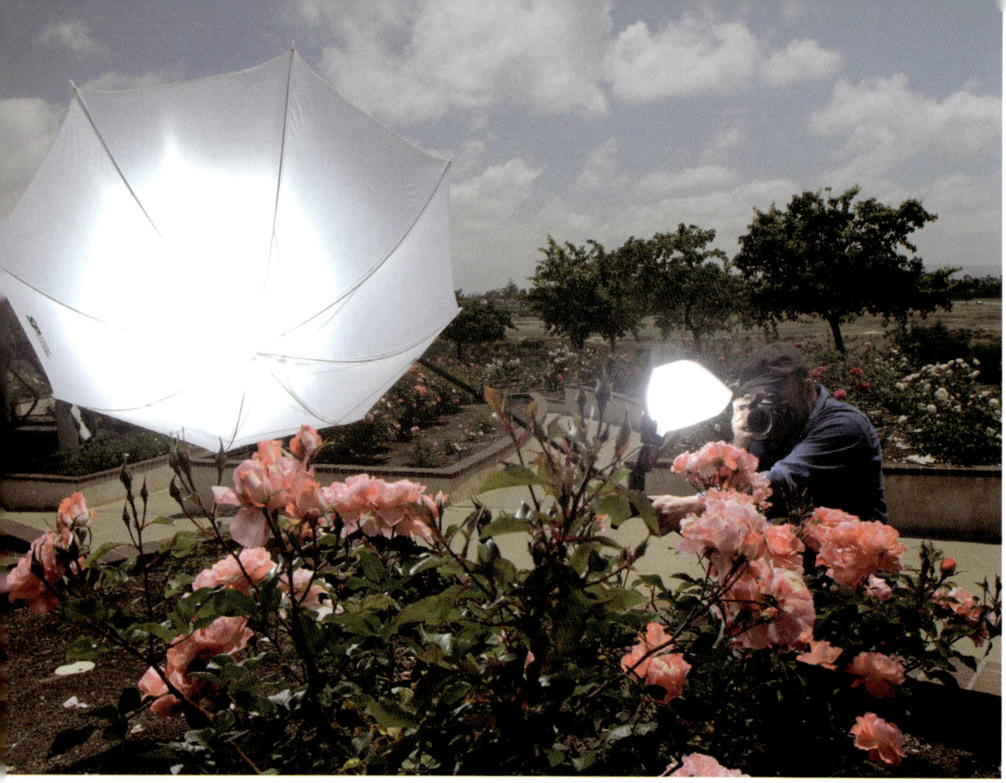

**Left**—Modification will be a factor—and sometimes you may need to employ the "big guns." Here, you see the photographer using two flashes attached to a flash stick (this is a modified light stand; we beat the legs off with a hammer). One modified flash is attached to the bottom of the stick (near the photographer's hand), while another is attached at the end of the light stand (modified with the help of a large shoot-through umbrella). Admittedly, this is a little odd to look at—but the options it provides to the single shooter are amazing. Imagine not only being able to light a front tier of graphic information with a flash, but also to be able to light a large background—without the aid of an assistant or light stands! The flash stick proves invaluable to us in nearly all of our photographic adventures.

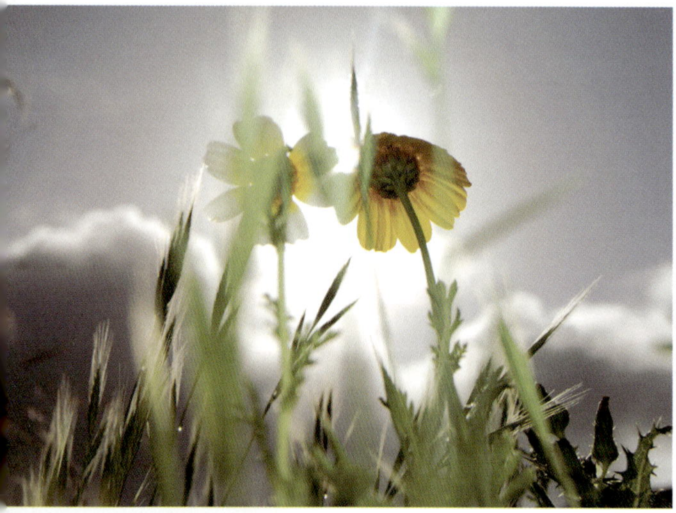

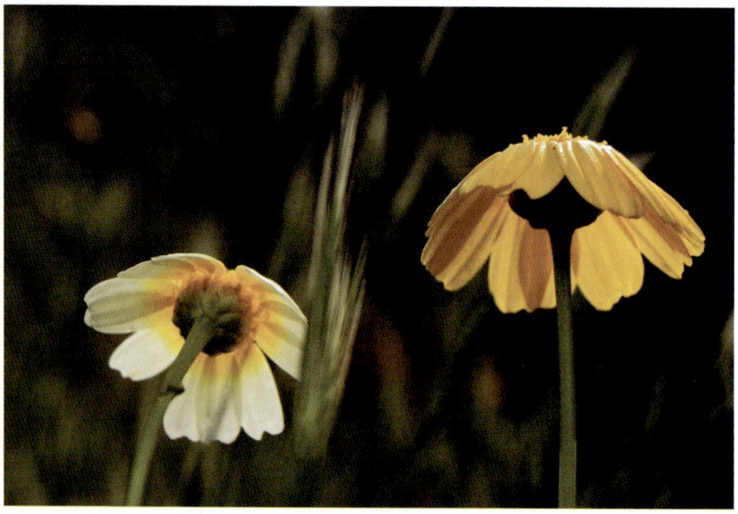

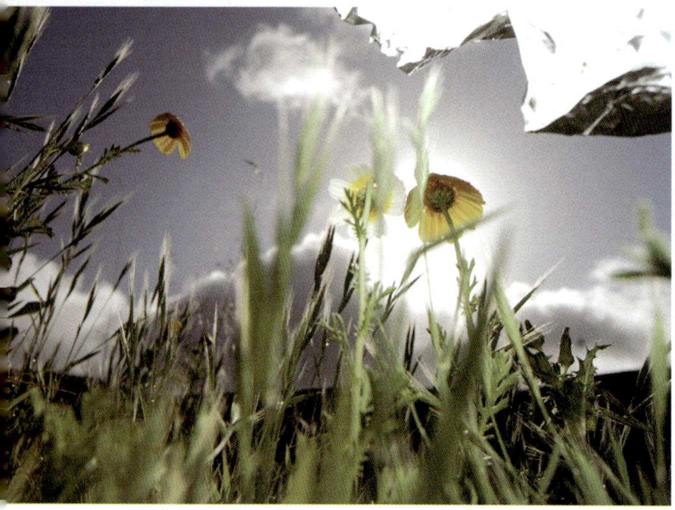

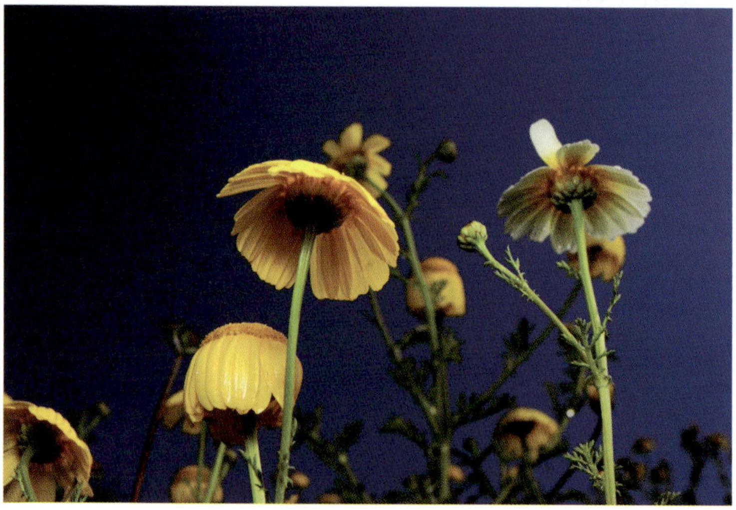

**Above**—These images would not have been possible without the addition of light from our pop-up flash. The in-camera flash was completely modified thanks to an aluminum foil scatterbox. In the top-left photo, we see that the scatterbox offered a very even light source that spread out not only to the flowers but also to the grass and weeds in front. In the top-right image, we see how a shift in perspective did not alter in the least the softness of the light. In the bottom-left image, you can see a bit of extra aluminum foil enter the scene—and the bottom-right image again proves that's not about the expense or type of your flash—it's all about how you use it.

We use a variety of modification tools (some purchased and some homemade) in our close-up activities. They range from a simple strip cut from a manila folder, which we attach to a flash with a rubber band, all the way up to a 3-foot wide (or larger) umbrella.

If a tool enlarges, softens, scatters, diffuses, pushes, shoves, corrals, or funnels light, it's an awesome and usable thing for your macro and close-up photography. And—here's the best part—if you need something specific, if there is a situation that demands something specialized, you can make it yourself. There are plenty of amazing garage-bound photo-engineers out there who do this all the time. Just search for "flash modifica-

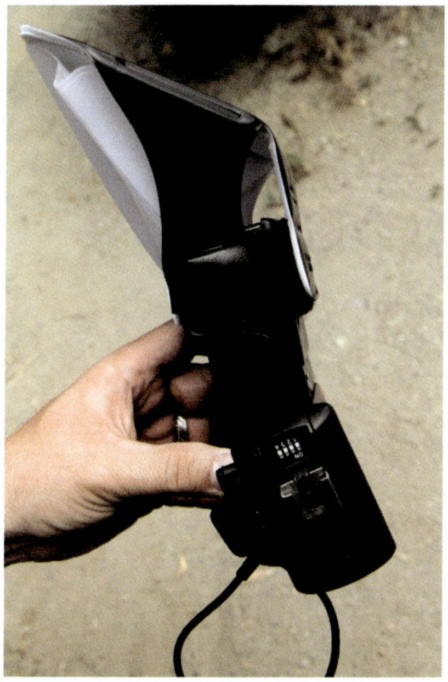

**Above**—This image shows an off-camera flash. A Cactus V4 receiver is attached via a PC sync wire, and the flash is being modified with a LumiQuest soft bounce.

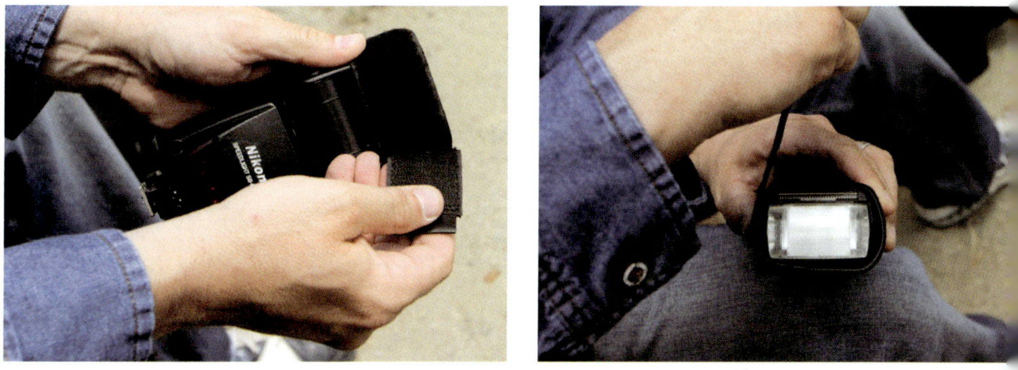


A Velcro cinch strap is attached to the flash. It provides the adhesive base for the flash modification tool.

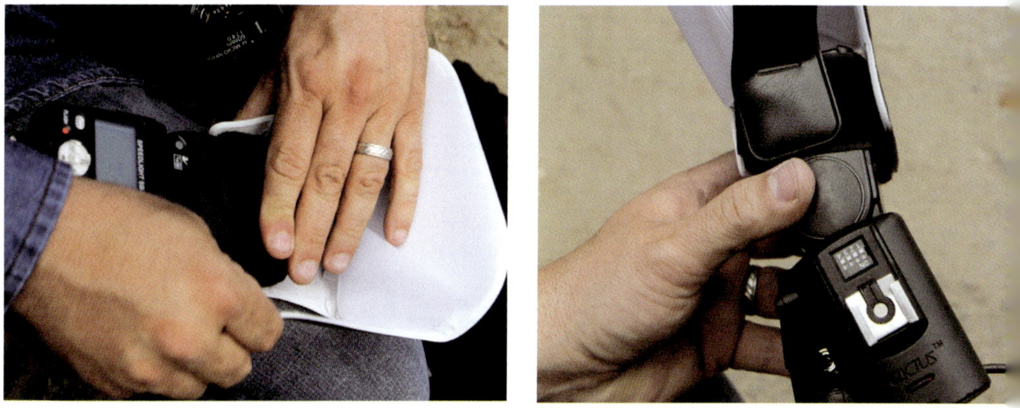

Here, a LumiQuest bounce is attached to the flash.

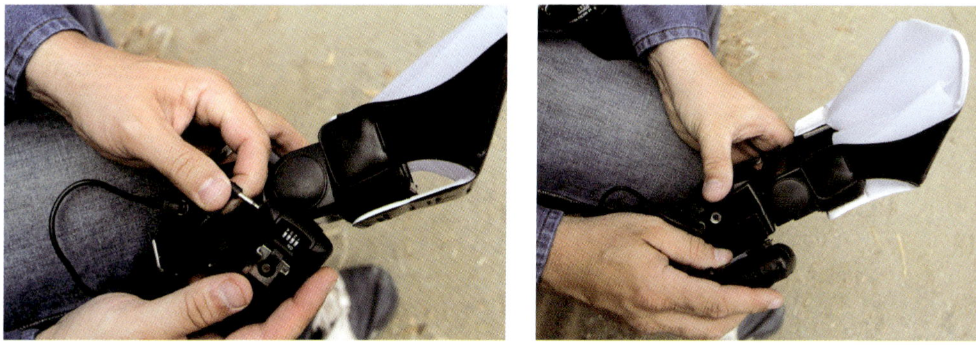

The wireless receiver is attached to the flash with a PC cord and is held in place with Velcro.

tion options" on the Internet and you'll see what we mean. (And while visiting their site to borrow some ideas, make sure to drop them a thank-you e-mail—it will make their day!)

## SUPPORT

**Hand-Holding.** Start by holding the flash. Just get it away from the camera. Connect it however you wish, stretch that arm out, and shoot away. Move the light to adjust its angle of coverage. Try to enlarge it to a point where it covers exactly what it needs to. If you want a whole graphic tier lit, enlarge your light and make it happen. Try lighting your subject from various angles—this is one of the greatest things about having your flash off-camera.

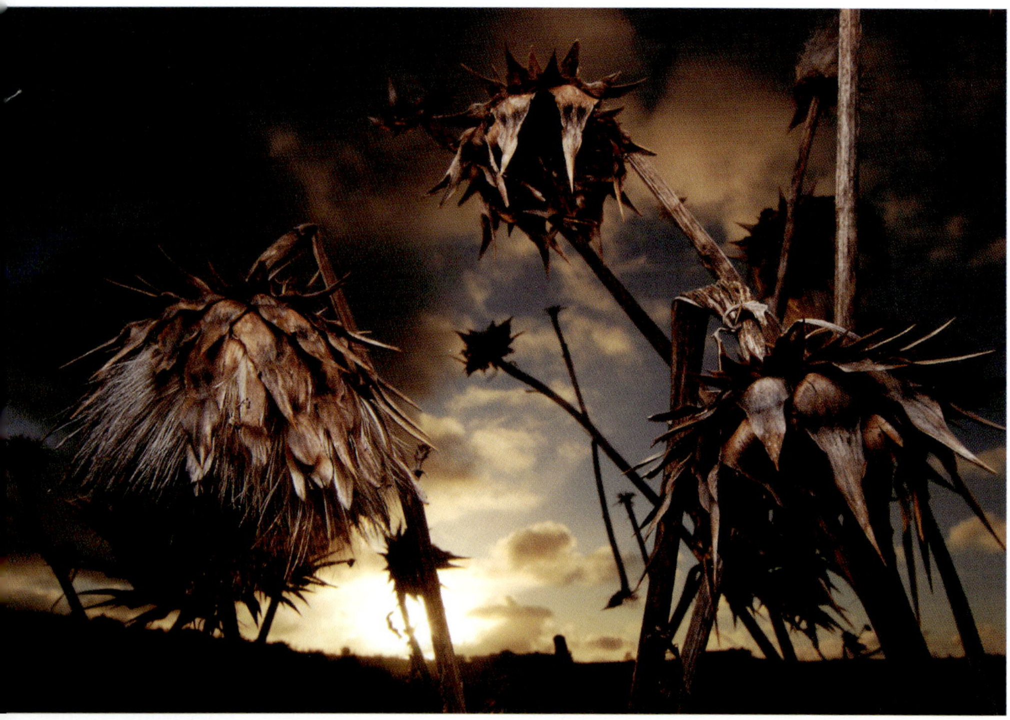

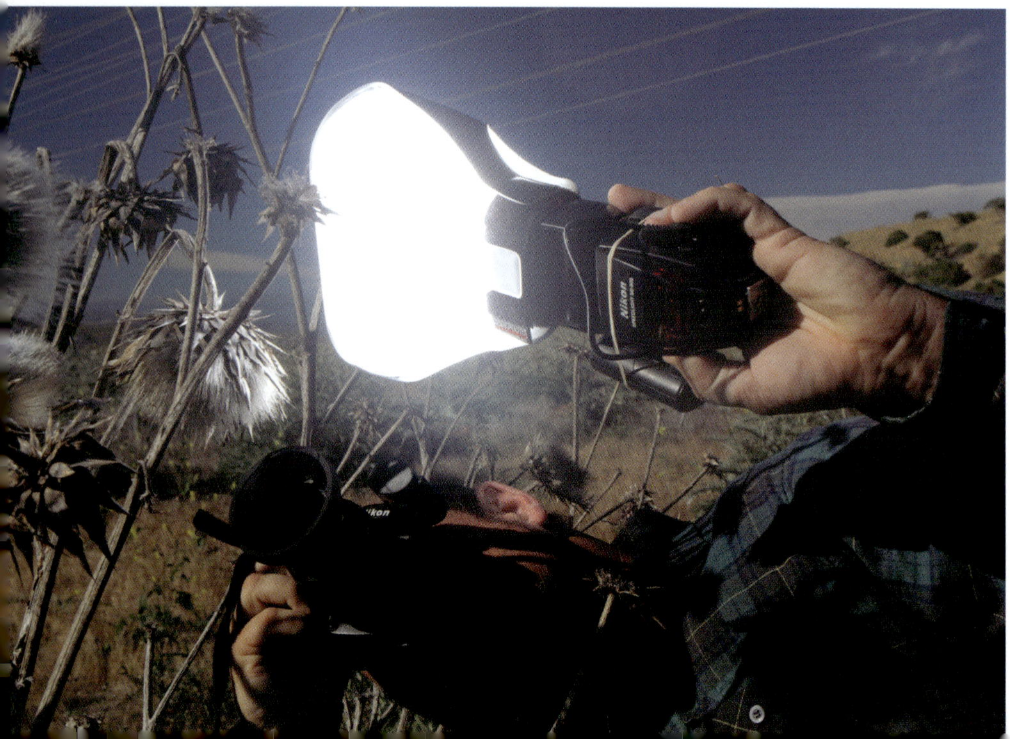

**Top**—As you are seeking growth, it's important to learn how to capture something as it feels, not just as it appears. Learning to dial in a background (in this case, to save a sunset) is important and needs to become something you can do instantaneously. Then and only then will you know how much light needs to be added and how it should be modified. **Bottom**—A photographer using the LumiQuest Big Bounce to modify his light source.

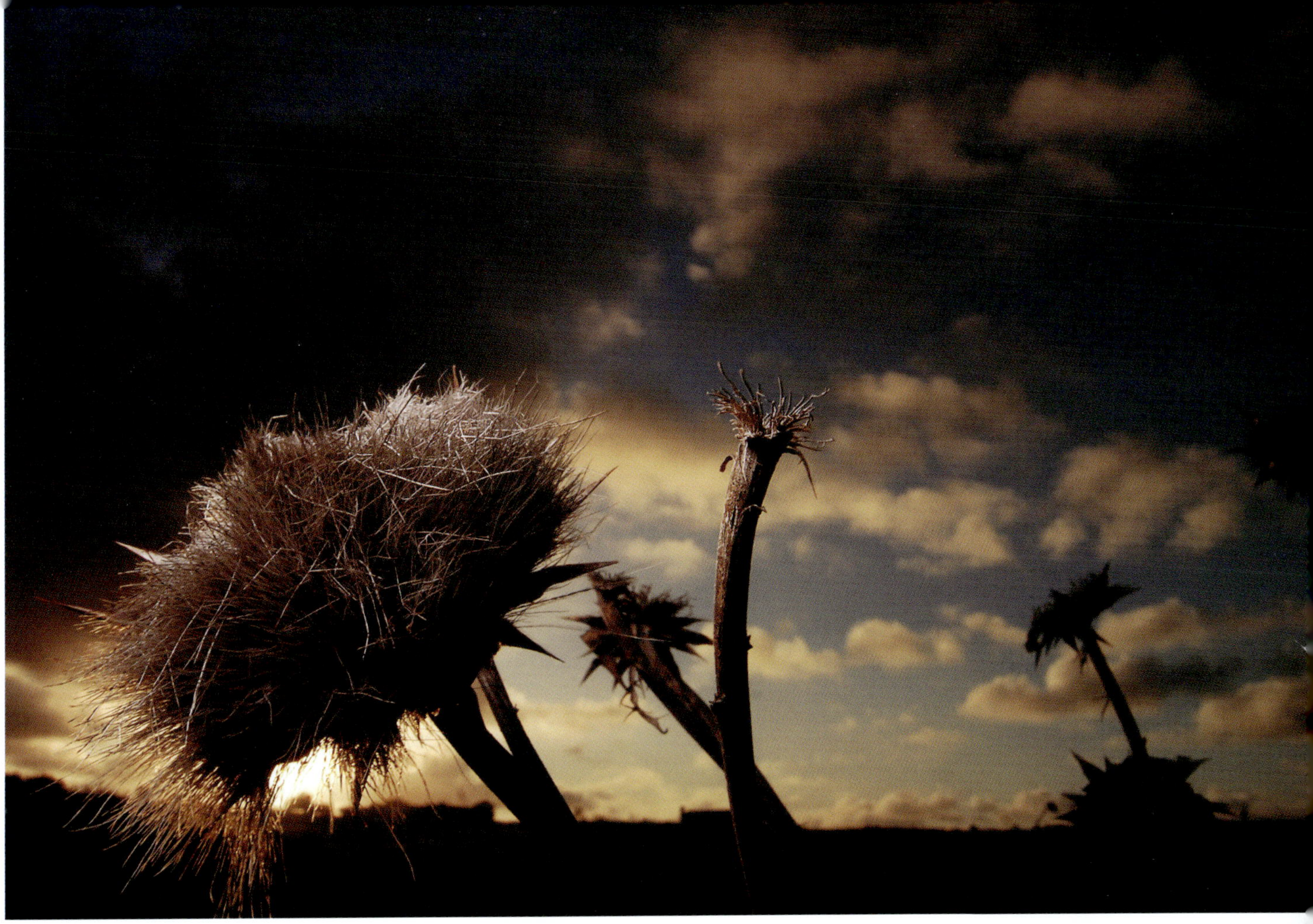

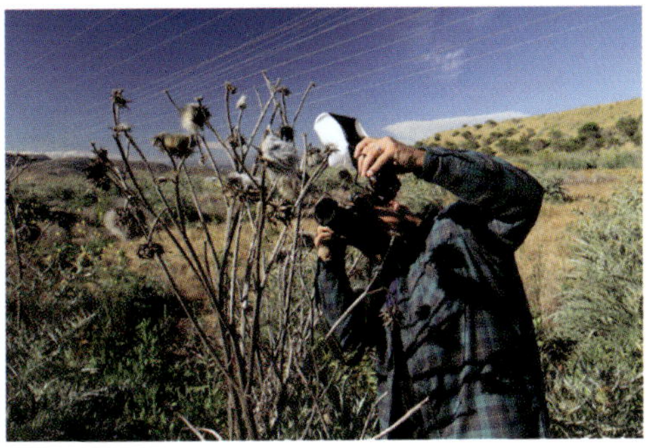

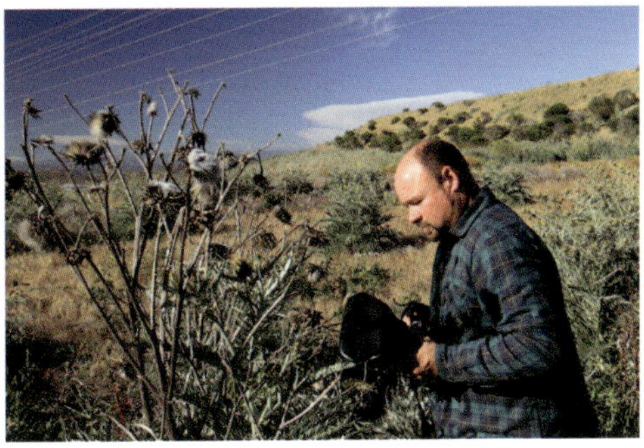

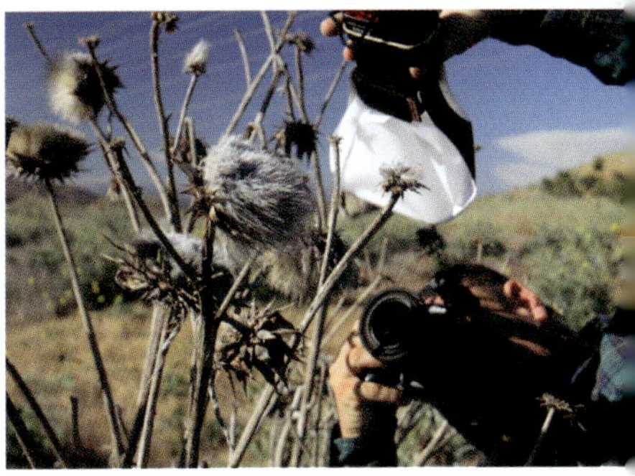

Variations will always help. Once you've got your perfect close-up image, don't stop. Move around, change angles, and find similar subject matter. Change the power of the flash or adjust some camera settings. You may be surprised at what can develop.

Now that you've got both hands occupied, it will be harder to focus manually, but don't give in; autofocus will fail you over and over again in macro and close-up photography. Don't bother with it. Set your depth of field, pre-focus, then move your body and your camera forward and back until you hit your focus point. Activate your depth-of-field preview button to ensure perfect coverage, then shoot.

Try to garner as much experience as you can with hand-holding your equipment; it is the most common situation you will find yourself in when you're out in the field. While light stands, extending handles, and such

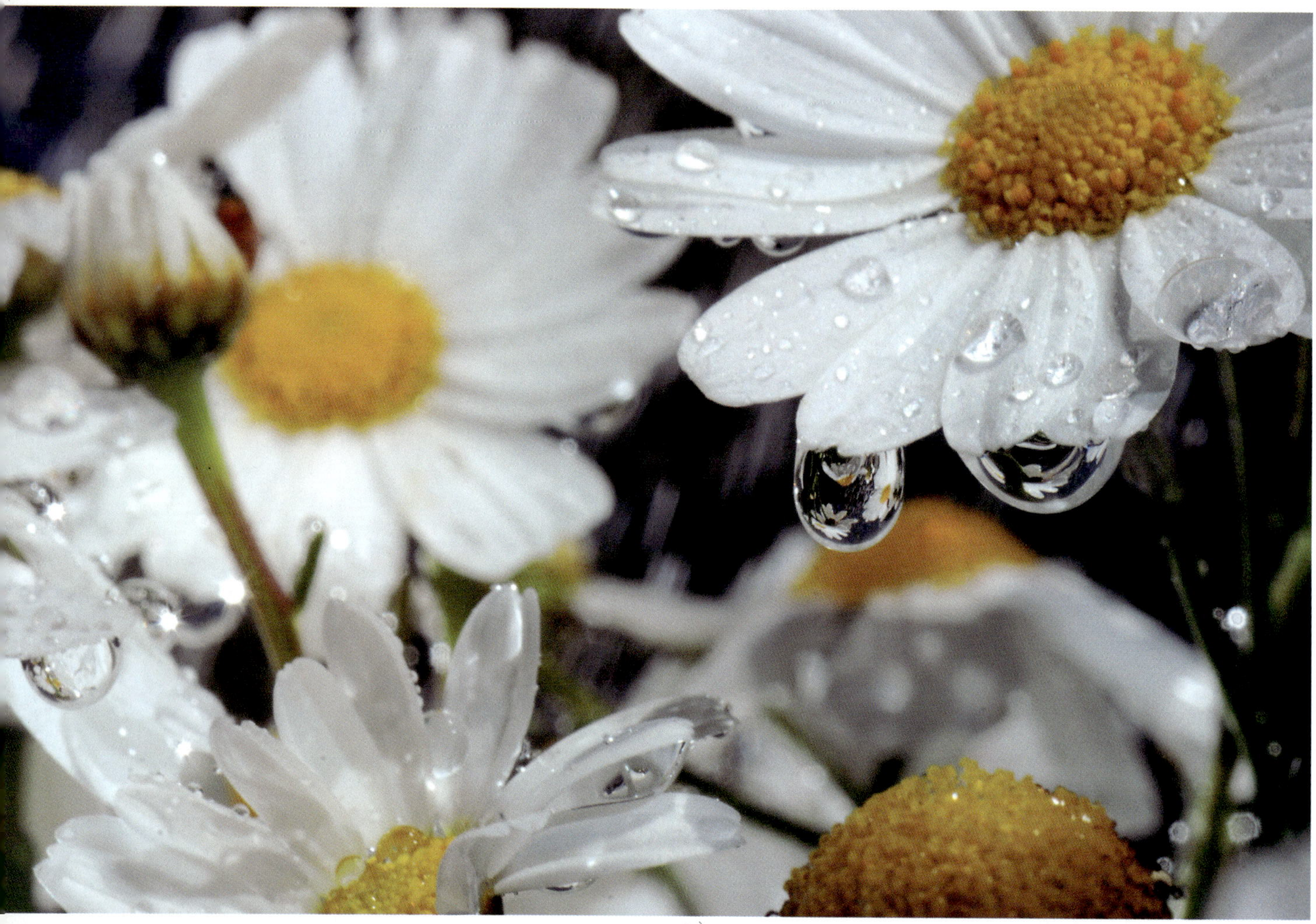

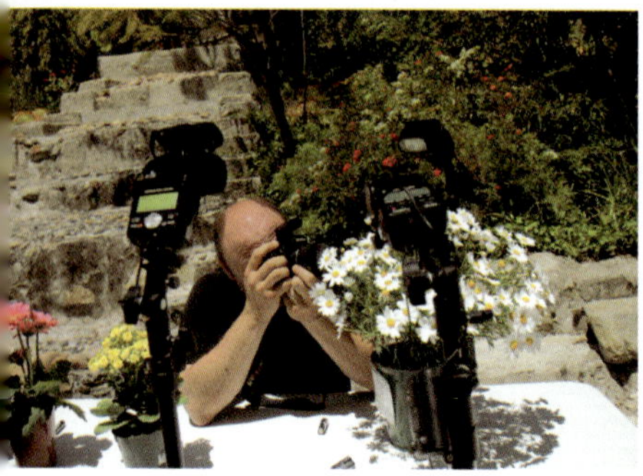

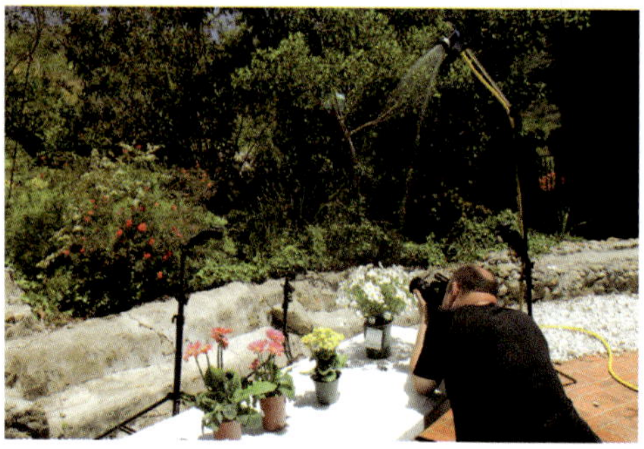

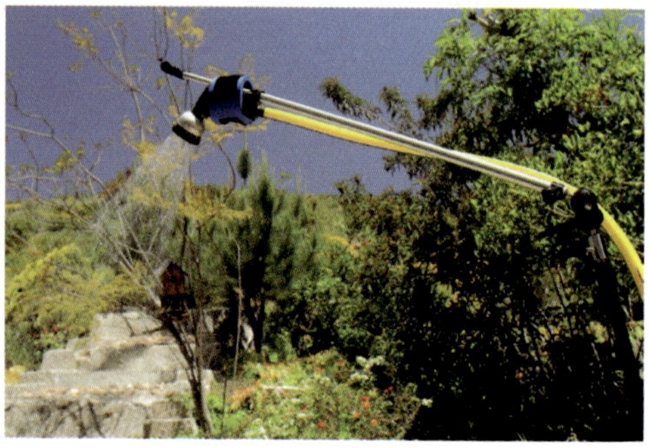

**Above**—Three flashes were placed around the subject (a pot of flowers) to ensure even lighting. A macro lens made it possible to get close from any perspective. We used inexpensive light stands to stabilize the flashes and our rain-making hose. After a few test shots, and the corresponding in-camera and flash corrections, we could easily move around the subject, firing at will without worrying about the light (although we did keep track of the water). To keep the costs down, we used an inexpensive wireless radio transmitter/receiver system (the Cactus V4), with each piece costing roughly $20 ($80 total). Using an automated wireless communication system to do the same could easily have cost $800 (with each wireless radio unit running nearly $200). If it costs that much just to fire three flashes off-camera, we doubt many people (who live on a reasonable budget) would try this—never mind the even more radical setups that require more flashes. If this price tag doesn't dim the lights on creativity, we don't know what will. **Facing page**—Many people are truly afraid to play in or near water with their expensive digital equipment, but we find that a little common sense goes a long way. Here, you can see that we were in full control of the water and could easily move the camera out of the way if needed.

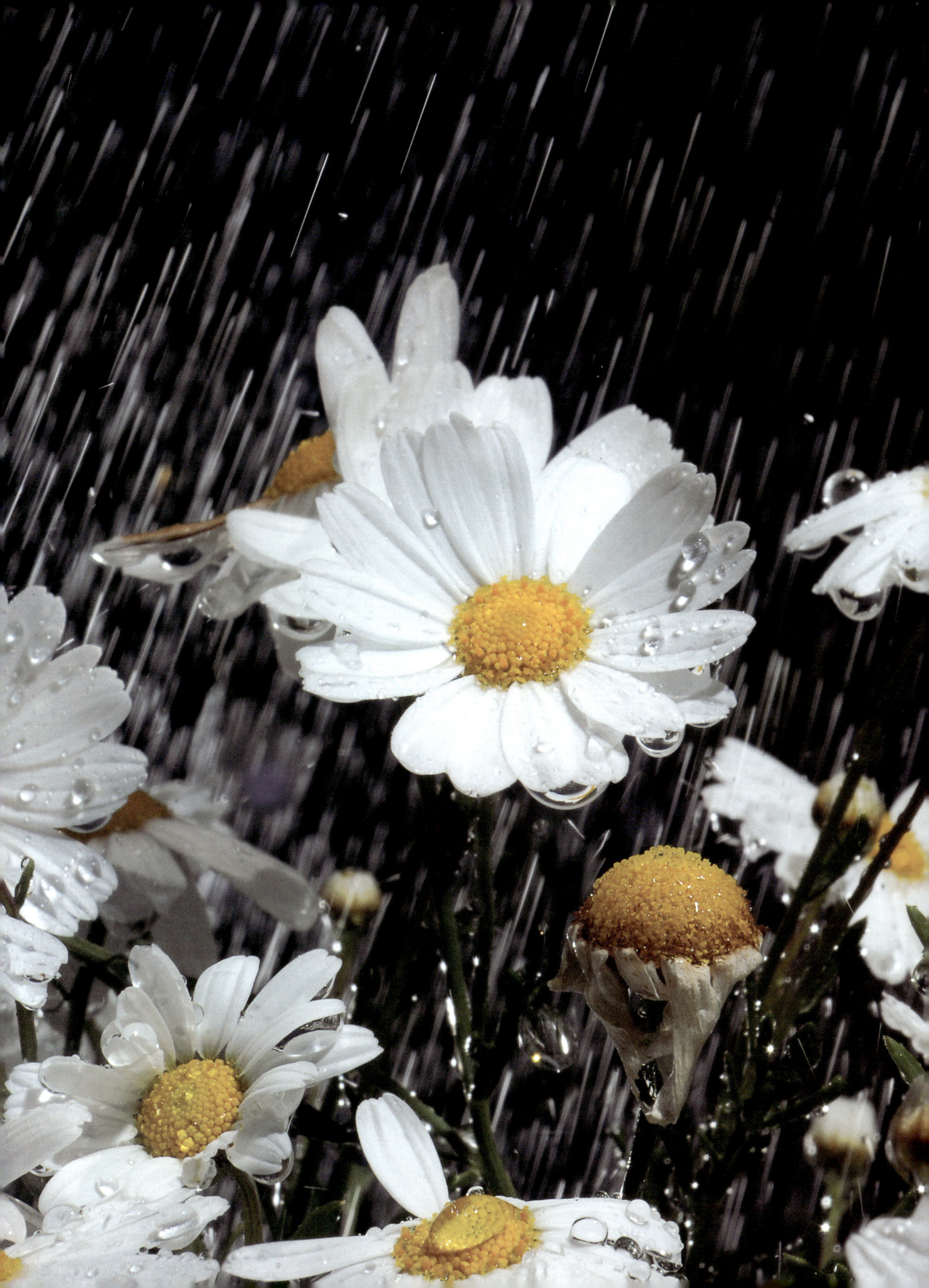

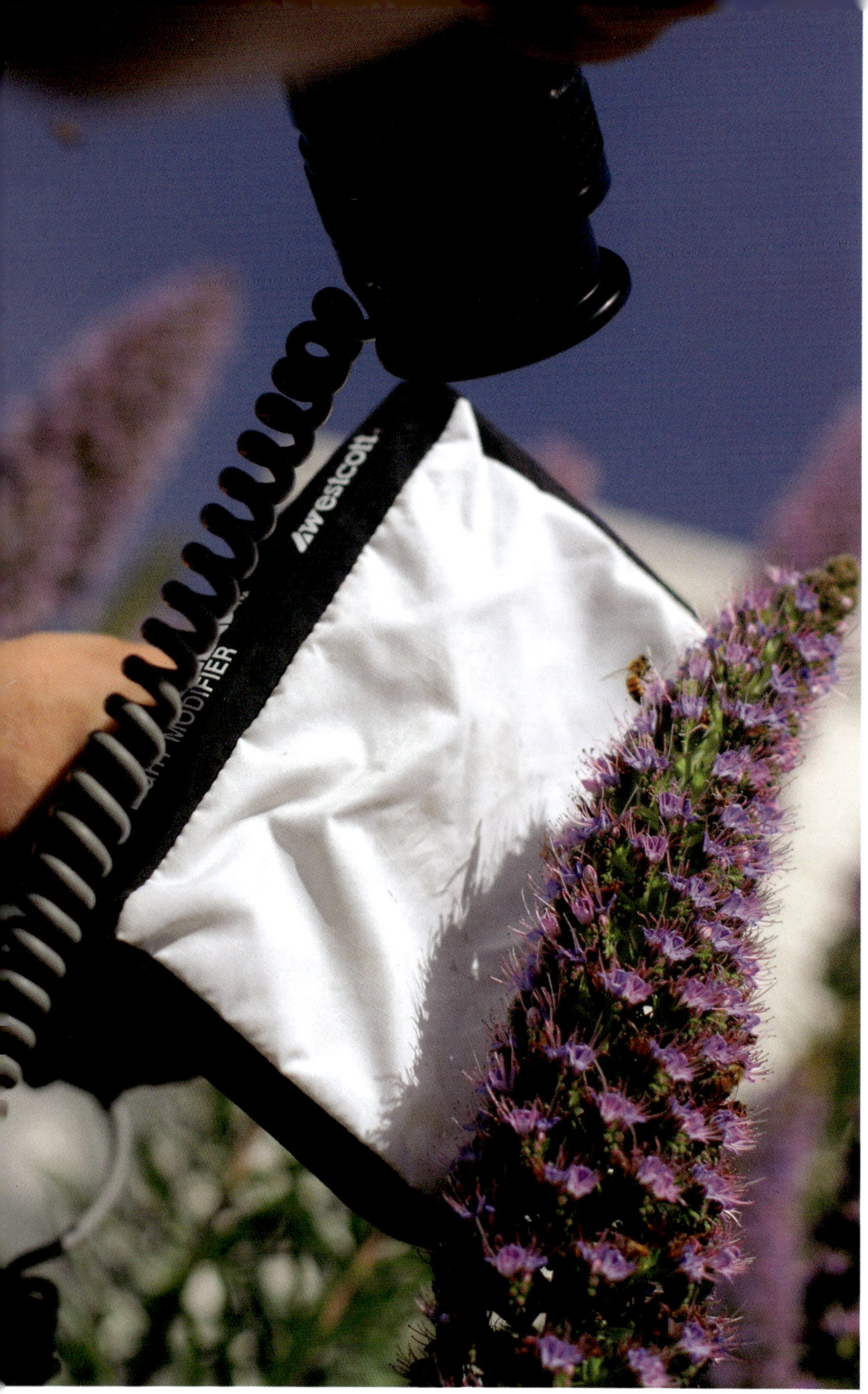


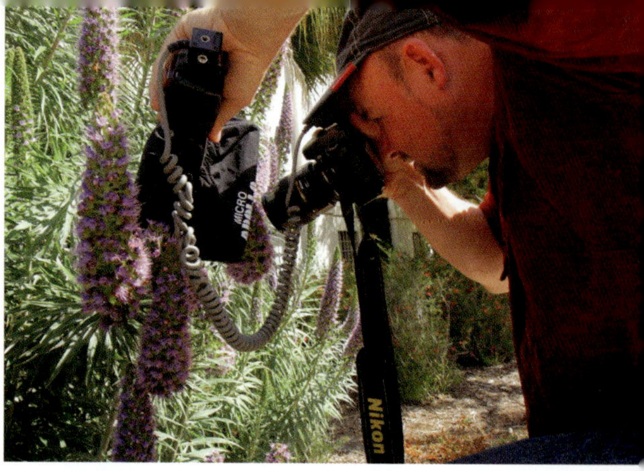


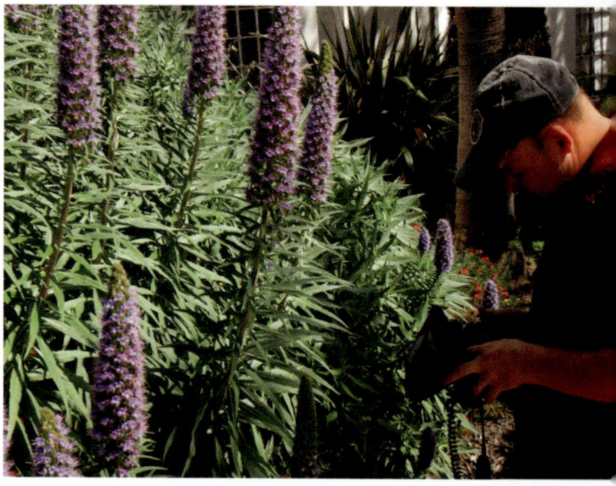

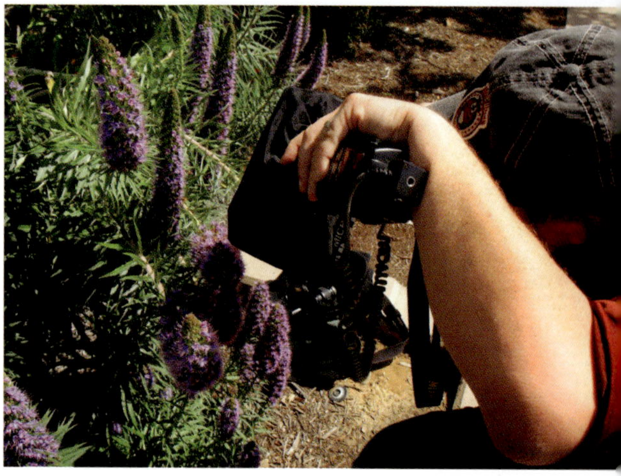

**Above**—Insect photography (here, we worked with bees) is no further than a cord and small light modifier away. It simply takes patience, perseverance, and a little courage to get up close and personal. The secret is moving slowly and allowing the insect to come to you. Always manually focus (we have yet to see any autofocus system that can keep up with a moving bee!). Watch their patterns; they will usually return to a favorite flower or location, so be ready. Dial in an appropriate aperture and check it with your depth-of-field preview button. Choose a shutter speed that illuminates your background the way you want it lit. Then let the bee come to you and start shooting. **Facing page**—The amazing depth of field seen here was acquired through the use a very small aperture (f/57). Luckily, the bee and the background were both within striking range of our modified flash. Without the flash and aforementioned modification, this image would not have been possible.

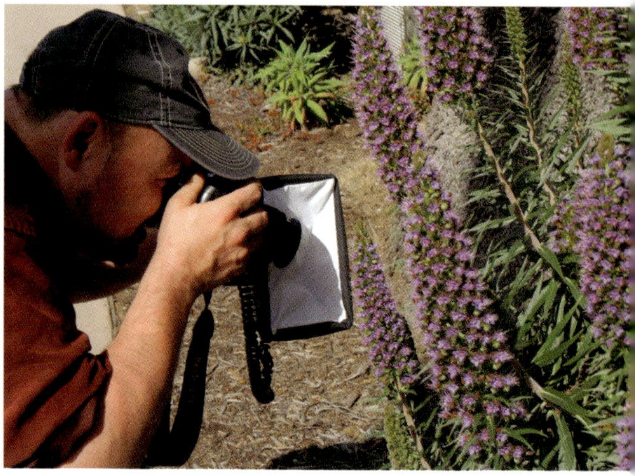

are nice, you're probably not going to bring them *everywhere* you go. Get used to doing things on your own. Learn to be quick, efficient, and accurate. This is how it's done.

You'll also want to practice something we call "crossing over" with your hand-held flash. After all, while you'll probably be holding the flash with your left hand, you might not always want the light coming from the left side of the scene. To cross over, simply move your left arm under your camera and point your light source at your subject from the right side. This will take some getting used to, but it works like a charm.

**Tripods, Light Stands, and More.** Once you've got the one-handed approach down and are adept at using various modification tools with it, it's time to push your vision—and your flash—even further. Tripods, light stands, bean bags, and even extending handles can be used to hold the flash away from your camera. All of this equipment may sound odd at the moment, since we're talking about close-up and macro photography, but there is a real need for this. Not all messages need the front tier of graphic information lit; often you'll need to light the background, use more than one flash, or even employ an extremely large modification tool that you can't hand-hold.

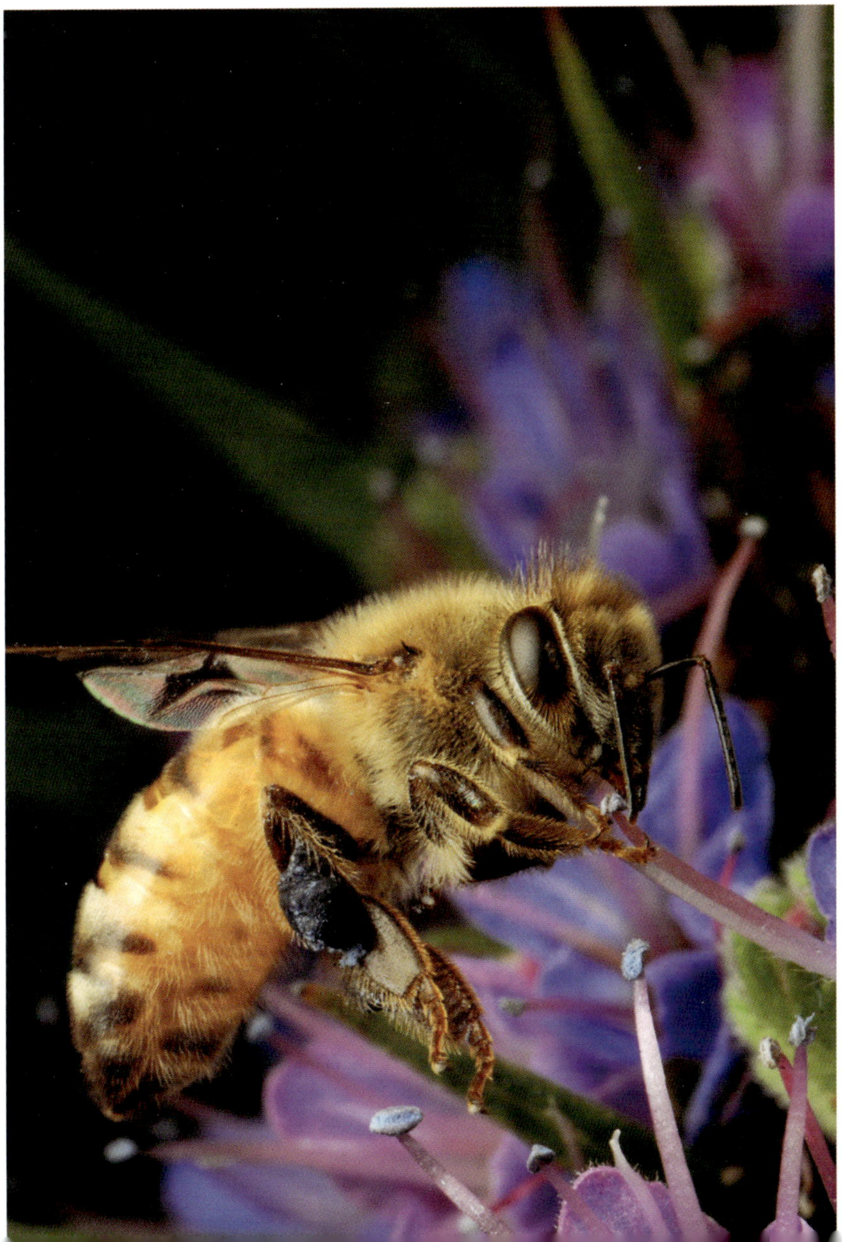

For all of these reasons, you'll need some type of support system besides your hands—but, again, it doesn't have to cost a lot. A simple light stand usually costs less than $25, bean bags are cheap when you make them yourself, and a willing assistant may only require a nice lunch or dinner once your shoot is over.

Using your chosen support system is pretty self-explanatory. Set it up, aim it at what needs light, and start shooting. If you choose the light stand route, you may want to purchase a few hefty sand bags, as well. The last thing you want is for your flash and its associated equipment to fall over. That can definitely ruin a good photography outing.

One of our favorite support tools is the flash stick. It's simply a light stand with the legs knocked off (literally—we just bang them off

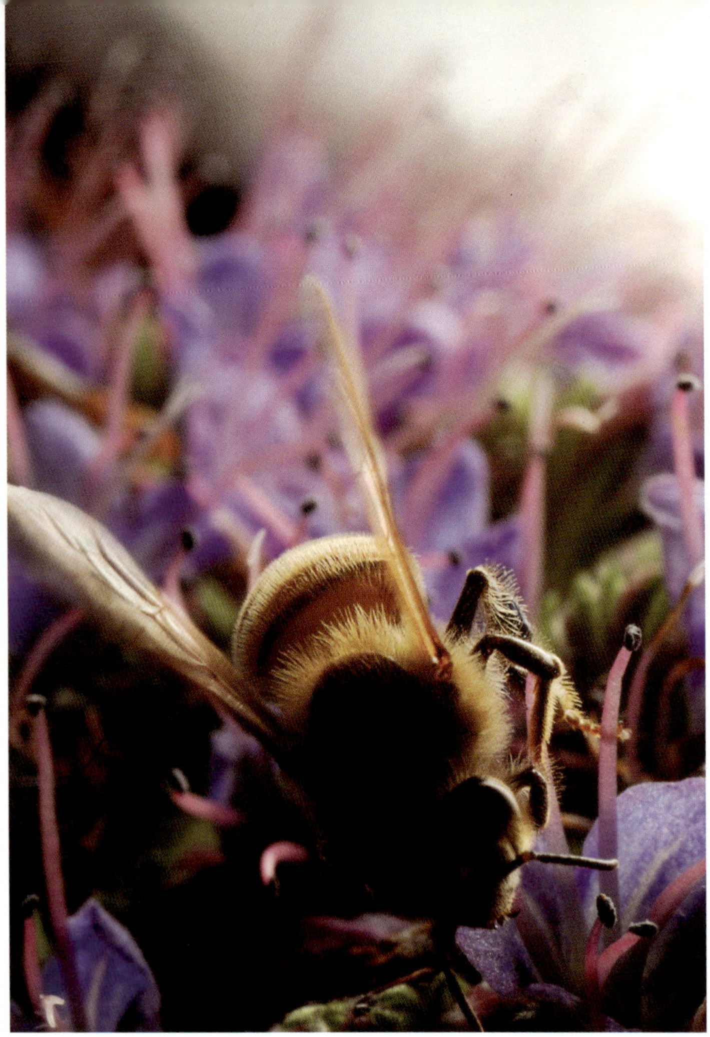
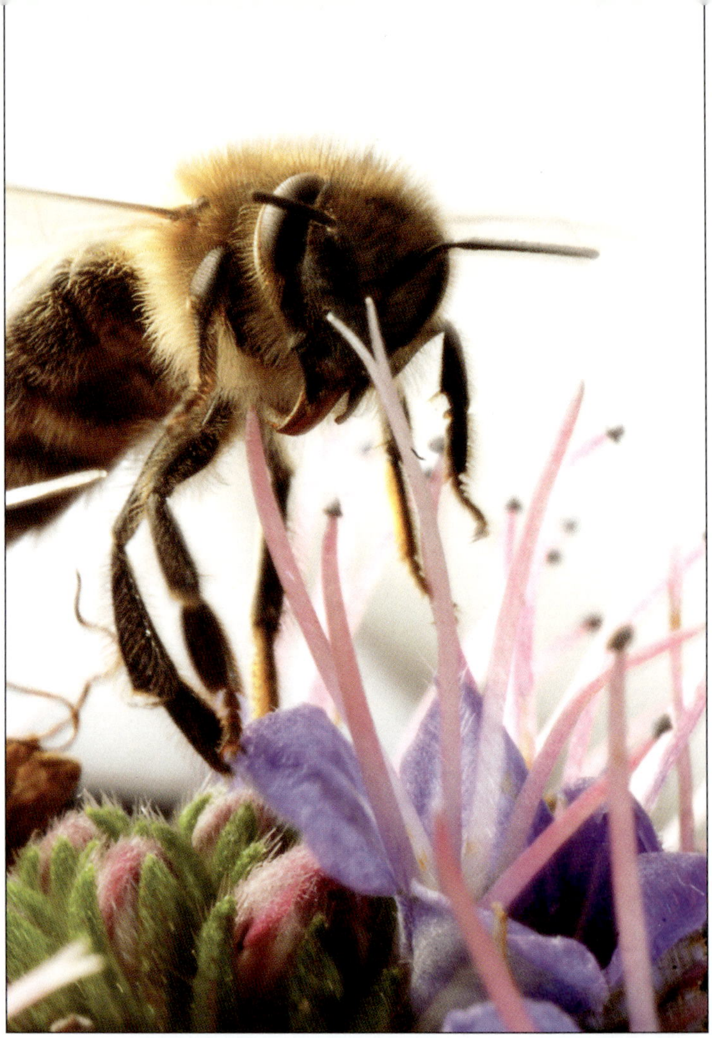
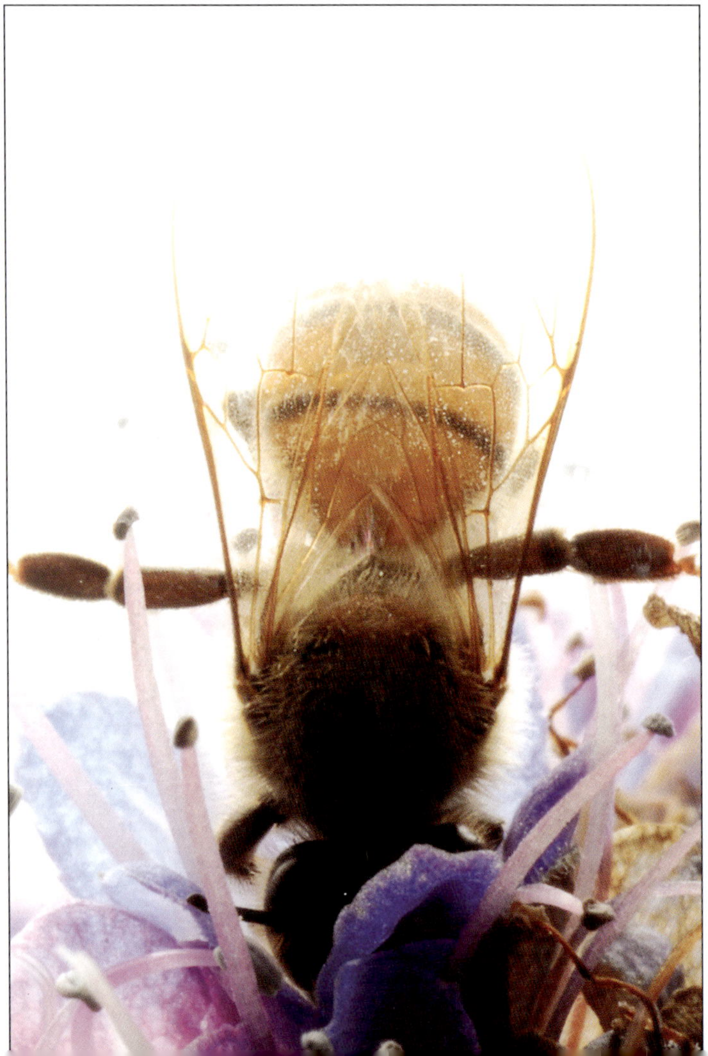
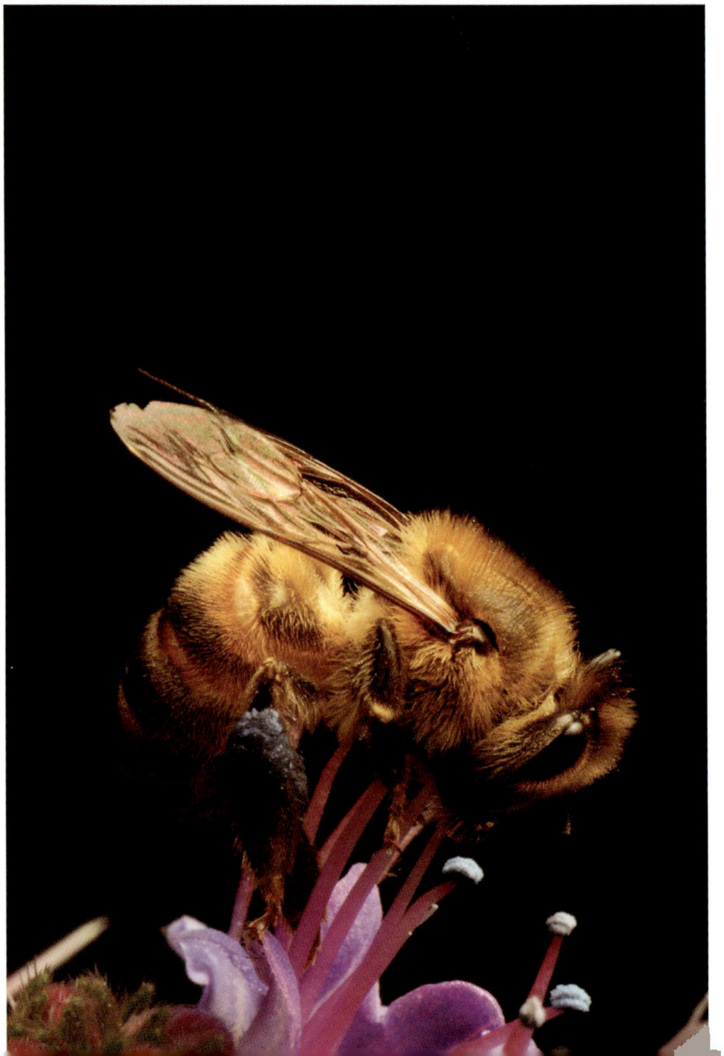

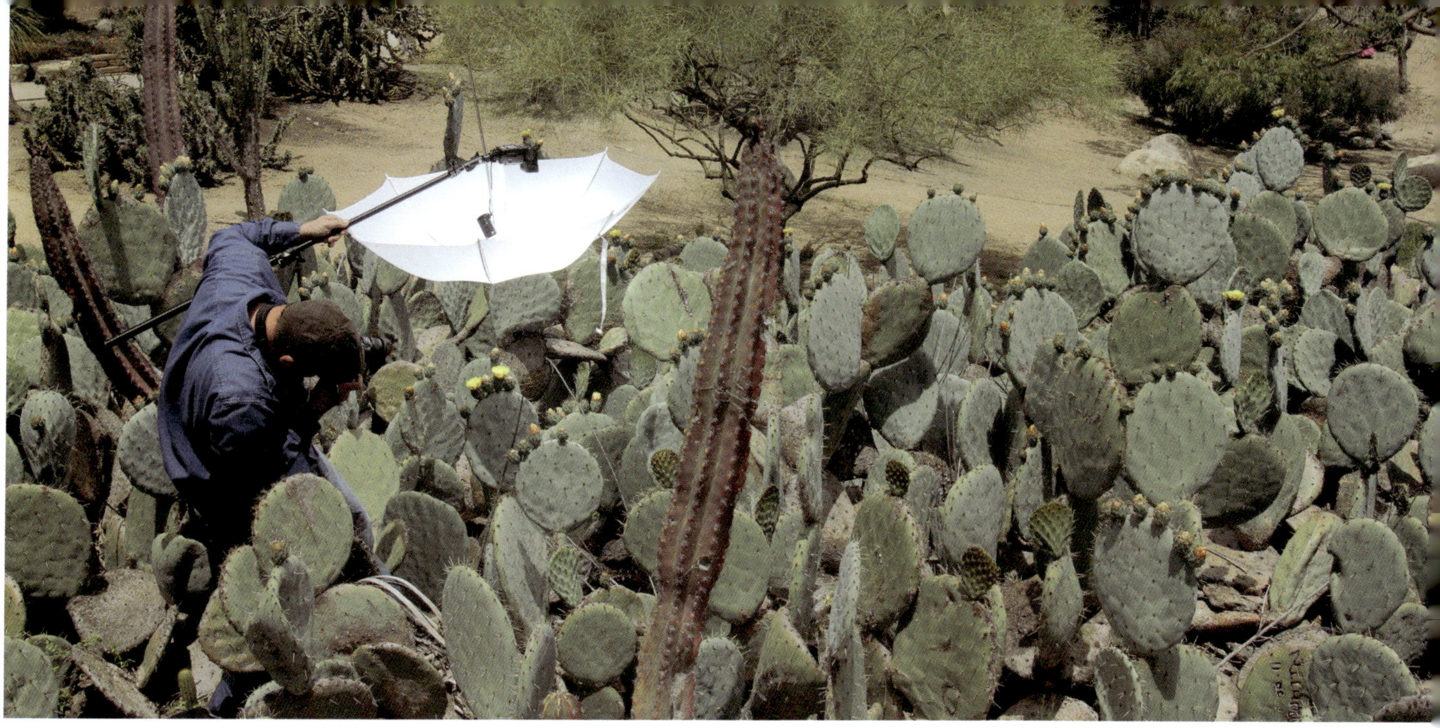

**Facing page**—When you think you have the perfect image, shoot some more. Never waste an opportunity to explore and gain experience. Change something. Adjust the power setting of the flash, change lenses, put an extension tube on, modify the flash—do something else and keep shooting. It's not just about the pretty pictures, it's about garnering the experience needed to better yourself. Build your skill level, not just your portfolio. **Above**—Sometimes the reach of a flash stick comes in handy. Here, the terrain made getting physically closer with the flash an impossibility. A very modified single flash (attached to the end of a flash stick) was used.

with a hammer!). With a light stick, we take the idea of hand-holding your flash to a whole new level. It solves so many problems that we feel every serious photographer should consider it. You can enlarge your light source, manage its position, and employ more than one flash while using the light stick—and you can do it all by yourself without ever once asking for help. Now that's pretty cool!

## PUTTING IT ALL TOGETHER

Using communication, modification, and support tools effectively means getting familiar with them. Once you've made some kind of decision as to the gear you'll select, you should invest some time getting used to it. For the moment, make the process of gaining experience, rather than the quest for pretty pictures, your top priority. Get to know the weight issues and the balance options. Go through the motions. Adjust some settings, try different accessories—just get out there and shoot. The more experience you have, the easier it will be to create striking images.

# 5. A BASIC INDOOR WALK-THROUGH

Remember, a little practice goes a long way in strengthening your skills. Now that we understand the basics of flash, close-up, and macro photography, let's put it all together.

If you've never done close-up or macro work with an off-camera flash or are unsure of how to "do" all of this on manual, we've got a pretty easy walk-through for you. It's not going to make you an artist (only you can do that), but it will gently take you through the motions required—and you might just end up with a few pretty pictures, too.

Our goal as instructors is to encourage, guide, suggest, and inspire—not to tell you how to shoot every image you take. We'll begin with a simple lesson that will take you deep into the heart of off-camera flash photography. If you've never attempted to do this in full manual before, we suggest you give this chapter the time it deserves.

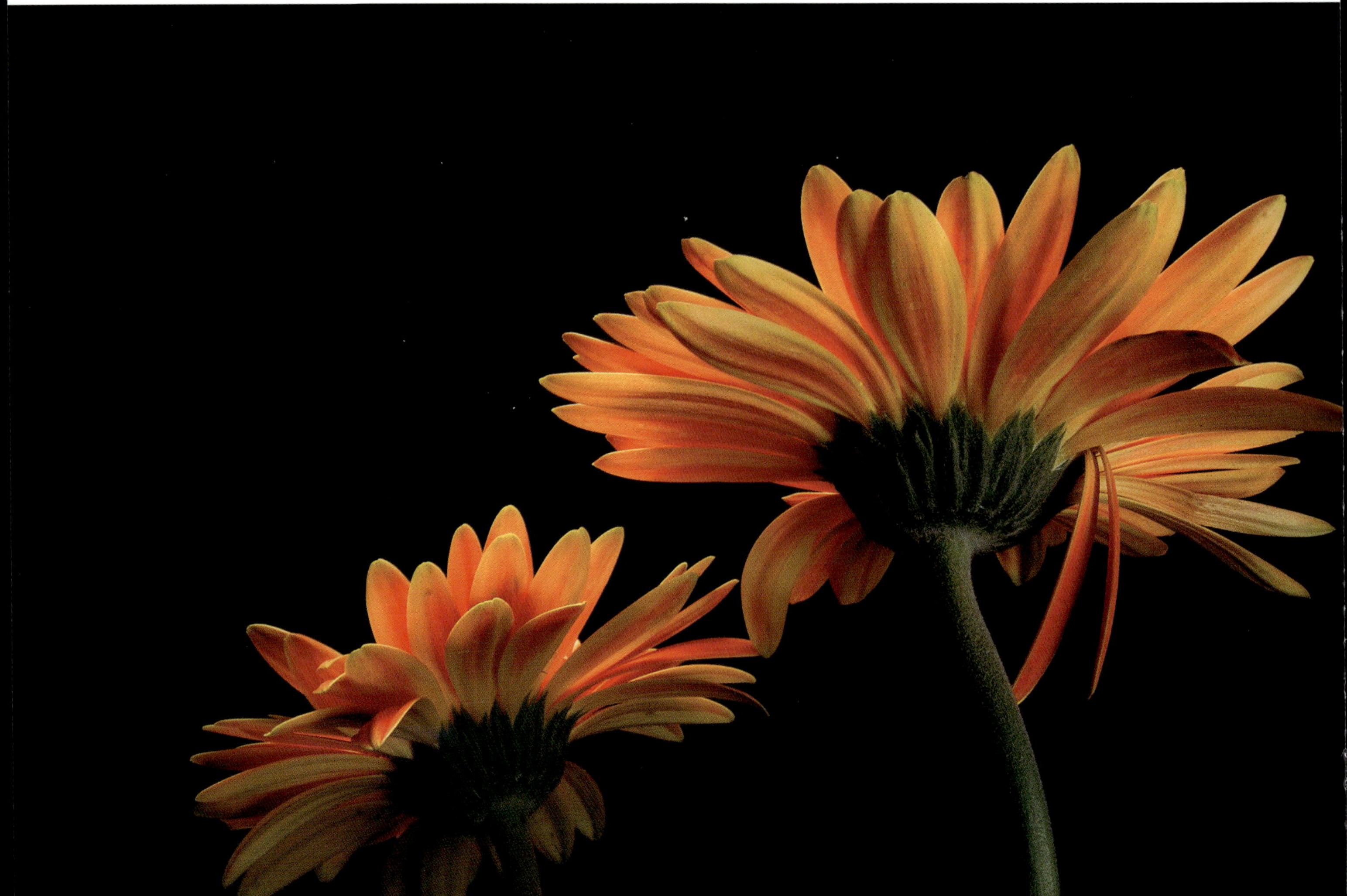

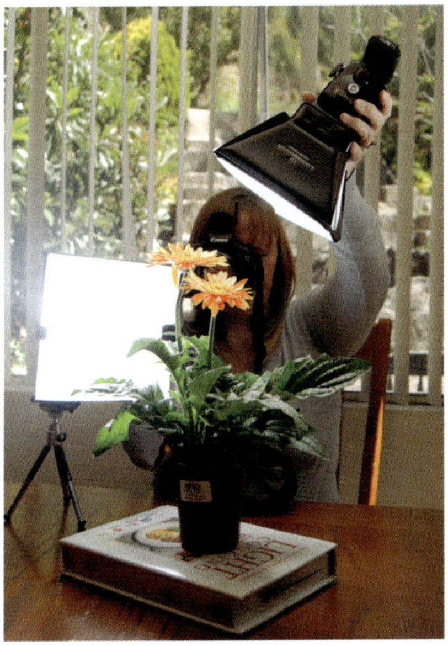

This is a simple lighting setup that anyone can do on their kitchen table. Two modified flashes are seen; one is supported by a small tripod, while the other is hand-held.

## PRELUDE

This entire exercise should be done in your home, on your dining room table. You want to do it when you're alone and there is nothing that will prove a distraction. Set aside at least 15–20 minutes (longer if you want to really get into this). Your goal is to learn how to create a black background with a close-up subject that is not only well lit, but completely in focus.

## YOUR SUBJECT

You will need some sort of item to shoot—something small that doesn't have a pulse is preferable. (It's best to keep things simple, and a moving target is a bit too hard to handle in the beginning.) We suggest using a flower (not too big, not too small). A quick trip to your local nursery will provide you with options. You will want to place the flower fairly close to you, turn the room lights on, and prefocus on the bloom. While it may be easier to use autofocus indoors under these controlled conditions, it won't be like that once you get outside—so you might as well start practicing now.

## YOUR GEAR AND THE SETTINGS

You'll need at least one flash (more if you've got them), a way to trigger it while off-camera, and a way to modify it. These choices are as much

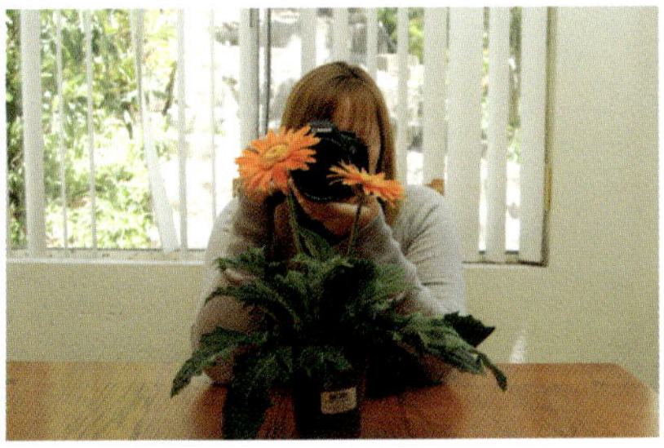

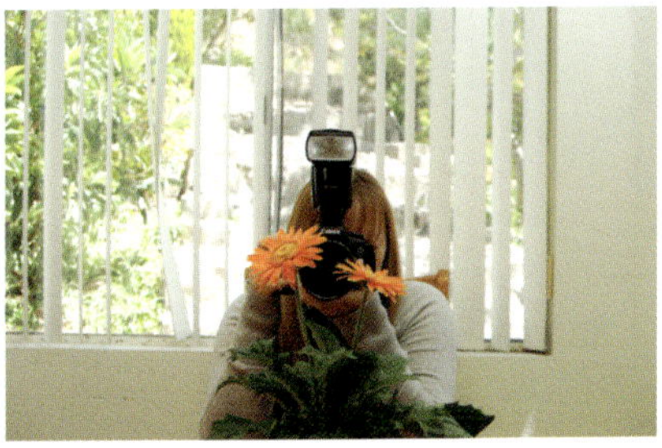

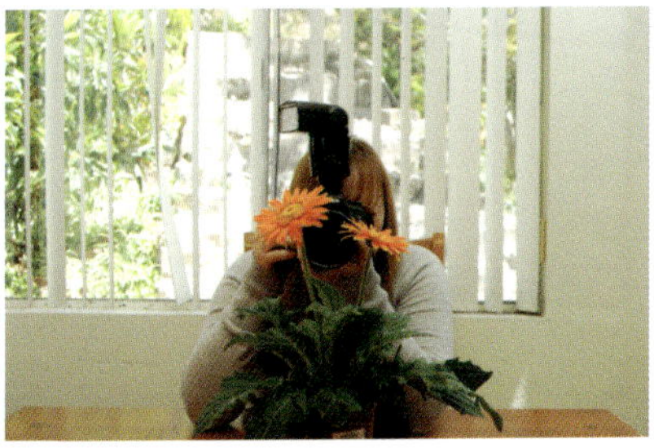

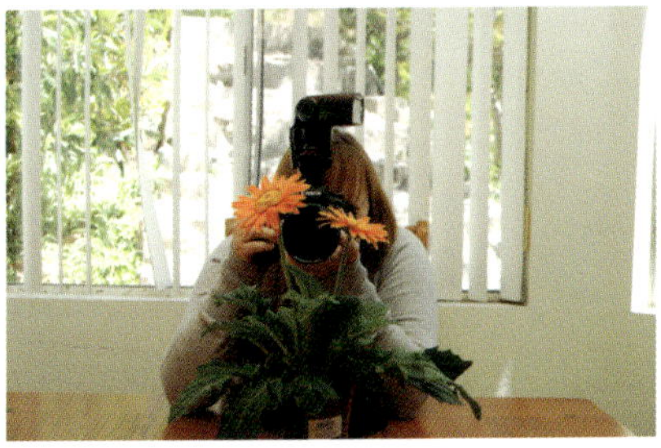

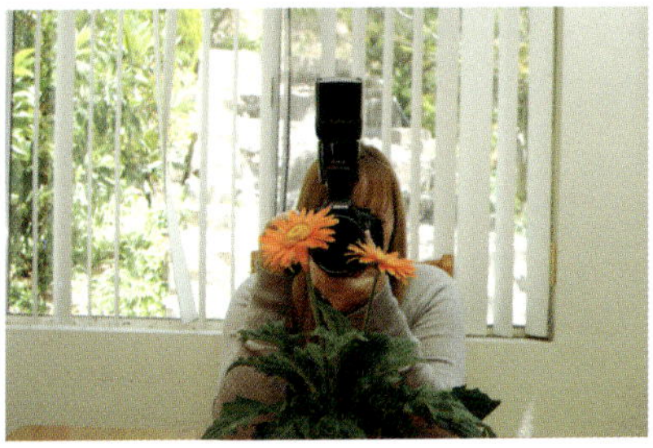

Oddly enough, we suggest you begin your journey into off-camera flash photography by shooting with your flash on-camera and testing the waters. As shown in this series, we suggest shooting the image in every conceivable fashion just so that you will appreciate the magic offered once the flash is taken off-camera.

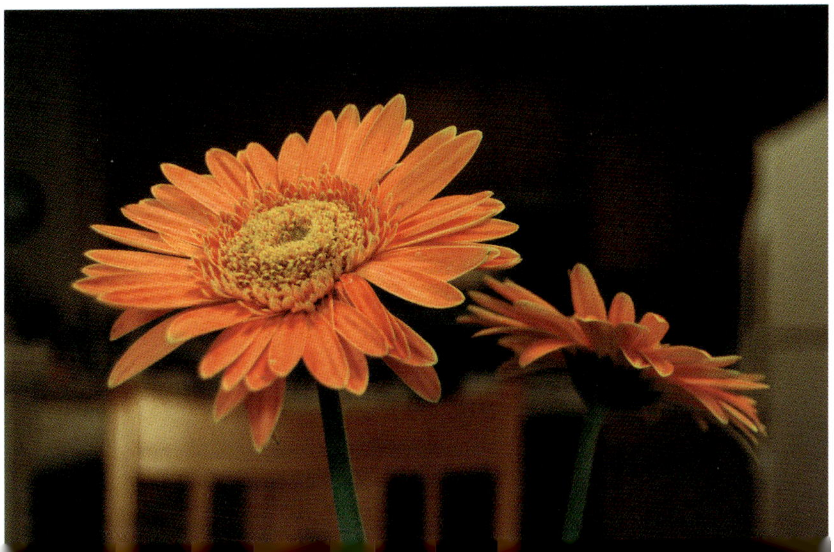

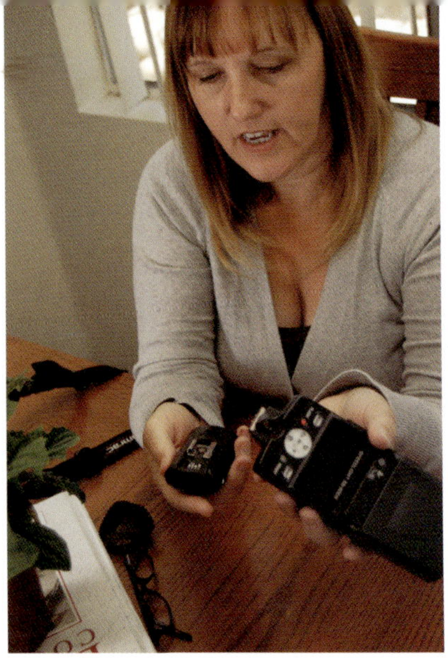
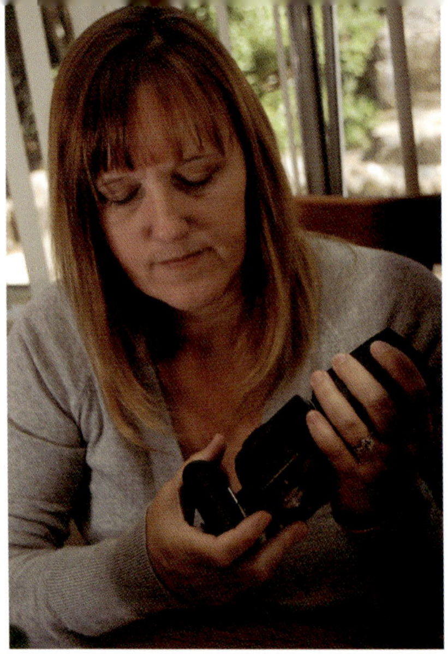
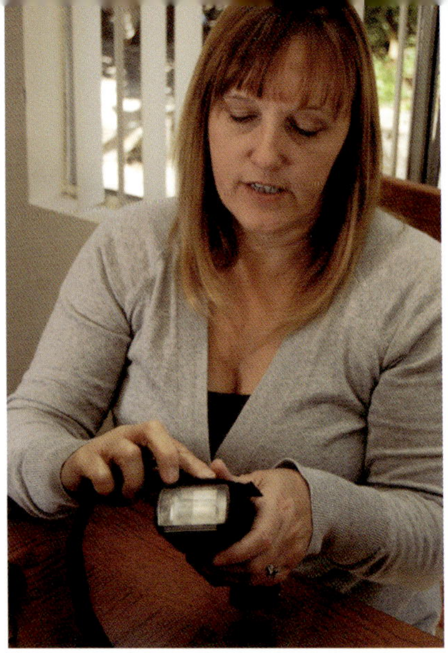
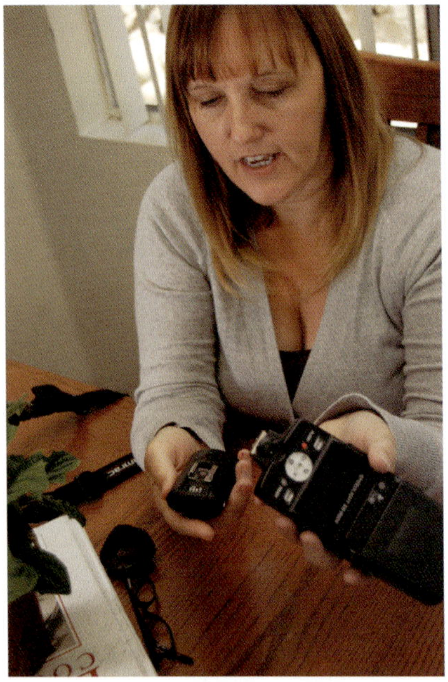
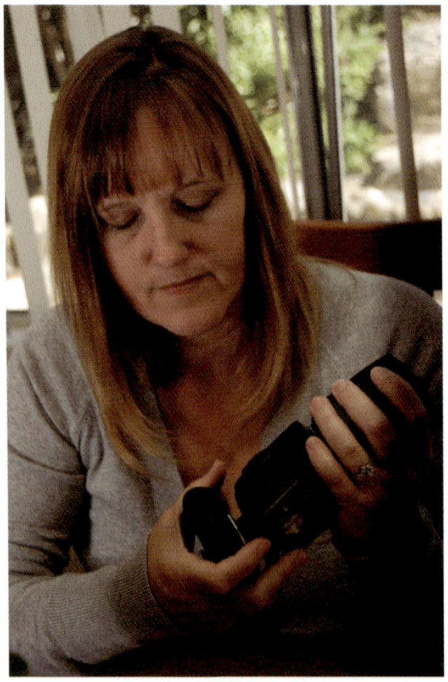
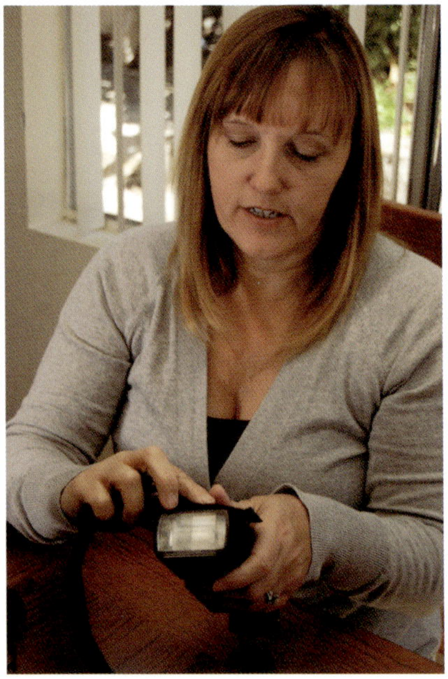
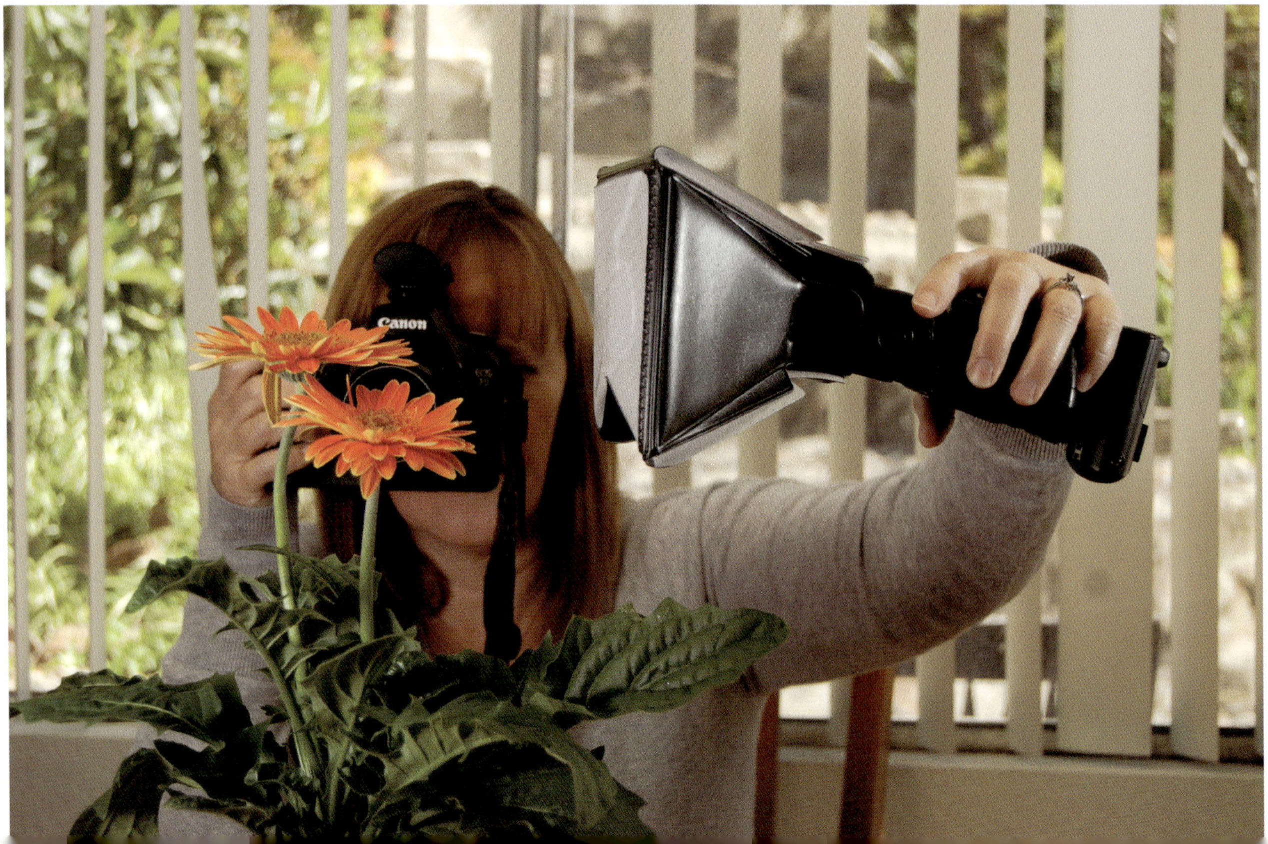
Canon

**Facing page**—Communication, modification and support—these are the words that should be going through your head each time you pick up a flash. In these images, we see a radio receiver being attached to a flash, a LumiQuest softbox being used, and an example of how our photographer chose to support her flash.

a personal decision as are the socks you're wearing right now. Whatever works for you, that's what is best.

Lens choice is next on the list. For this exercise we recommend a medium focal length lens—something between a 35mm and a 85mm. If you want to use a longer length lens, feel free . . . just be wary of space limitations when sitting at your table. Most importantly, know your lens's minimum focal distance. If you don't have enough space to work with a certain lens, then don't use that lens.

Next, dial-in the lowest possible ISO your camera affords, usually 100 or 200. You'll also want to manually adjust your camera's white balance setting to around 5300K (or to the flash preset). If you know how to adjust your contrast/saturation settings in your camera, we would suggest doing that as well (based on your taste).

Choose the smallest aperture your lens offers (remember, a small aperture is represented by a larger f-number). Then, set a shutter speed of $1/200$ second on the camera—or if your camera's flash-sync speed is higher or lower than $1/200$ second, dial in that number. If you are unsure of your camera's flash-sync speed, check the camera's manual. Alternately, you can activate your camera's pop-up flash and spin the shutter speed dial to the faster shutter speed possible; your camera will stop at the flash-sync speed. Having determined the flash-sync speed, deactivate your pop-up flash by pushing it back down or turning it off. (*Note:* If you are using a wireless

Physically, all you'll be doing is holding your flash and camera—but be prepared! If you're not used to juggling two pieces of somewhat weighty equipment, this may prove more of a strain than you think. This is another good reason to start by practicing at home. Once you have a knack for holding one flash and can visualize the results of your placement options, it's probably time to move on to two flashes.

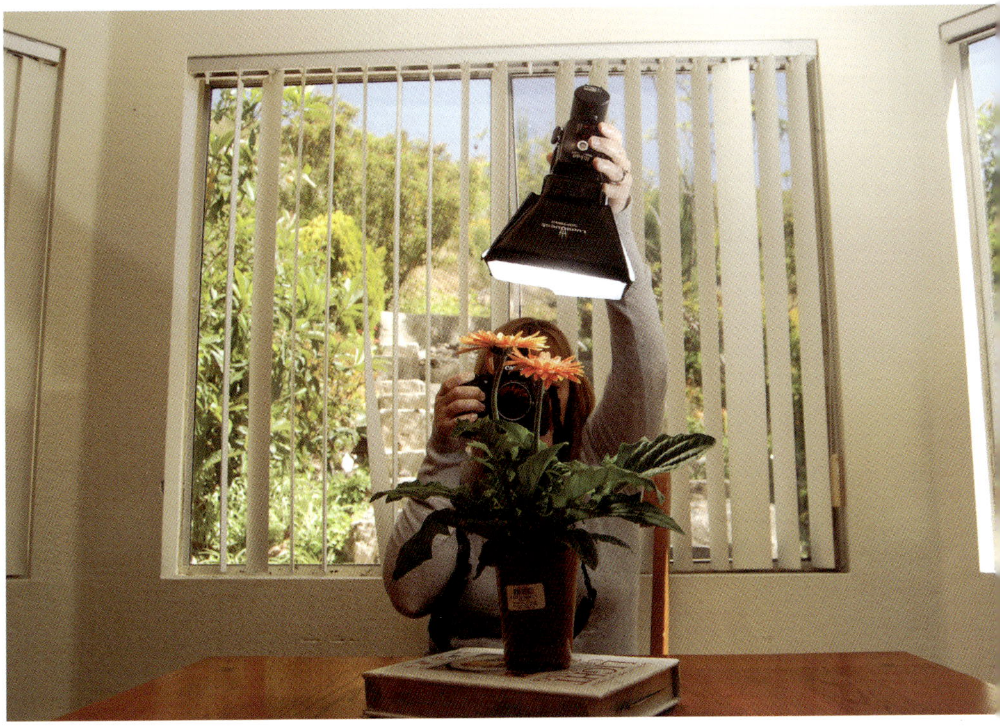

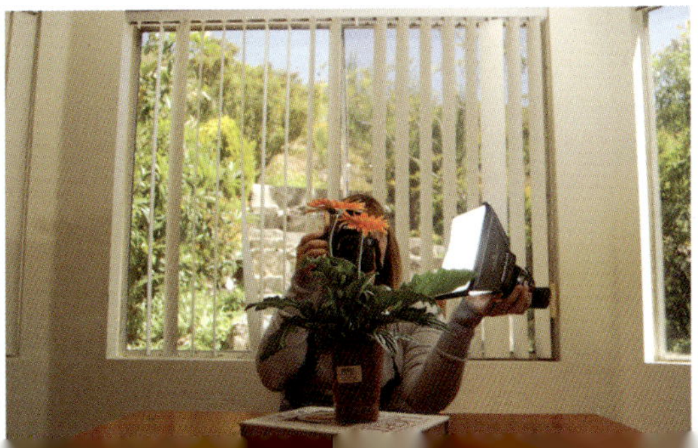

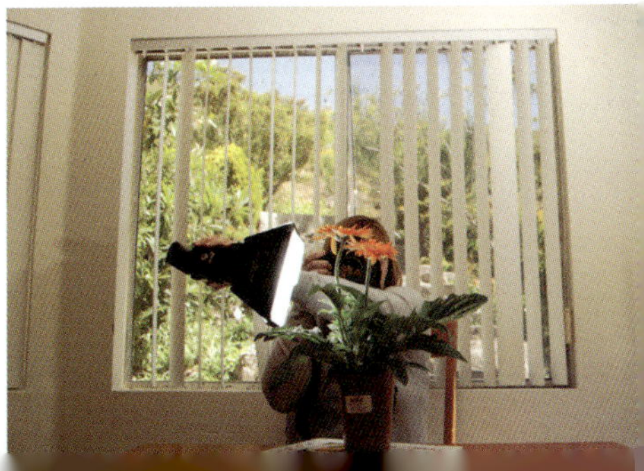

flash control system, you will have to remove your transmitter/cord before doing this test. Don't forget to put it back on.)

Take a test shot *without* your off-camera flash. If you've prefocused, you should just have to move your body/camera back and forth until the flower is in focus, then snap the image. That's it—don't make it any more complicated. You should see a very crisply focused black image staring back at you. Congratulations! You've got half of the image already: the black background.

Now, all you have to do is add light to your subject. Before you do that though, modify your off-camera flash. Enlarge it in some fashion. Larger light sources equal better light when you're shooting close-up and macro. Once you've got that accomplished, it's time to move on to actually creating the image.

### ONE FLASH

Set your flash to its highest power setting. Hold your camera steady in your right hand and your flash in your left hand. Position the flash directly above your subject. Make a mental note as to how far away the flash is from the subject; you'll be returning it to this spot. Move your body/camera forward and backward until your subject appears in focus, then shoot.

Examine your image. Depending on the power output of your flash, you may have just the image you want—or it may be too bright or too dark. (Chances are good that the image is too bright.) Simply lower the

You'll want to be in manual focus when you do this. Pre-focus when you're not holding the flash. Then, once you've got your flash in your hand, all you'll have to do is move your body/camera back and forth to achieve the desired focus point. This will take some practice, but you'll get it. Keeping your houselights on for this exercise will help when trying to find that focus point.

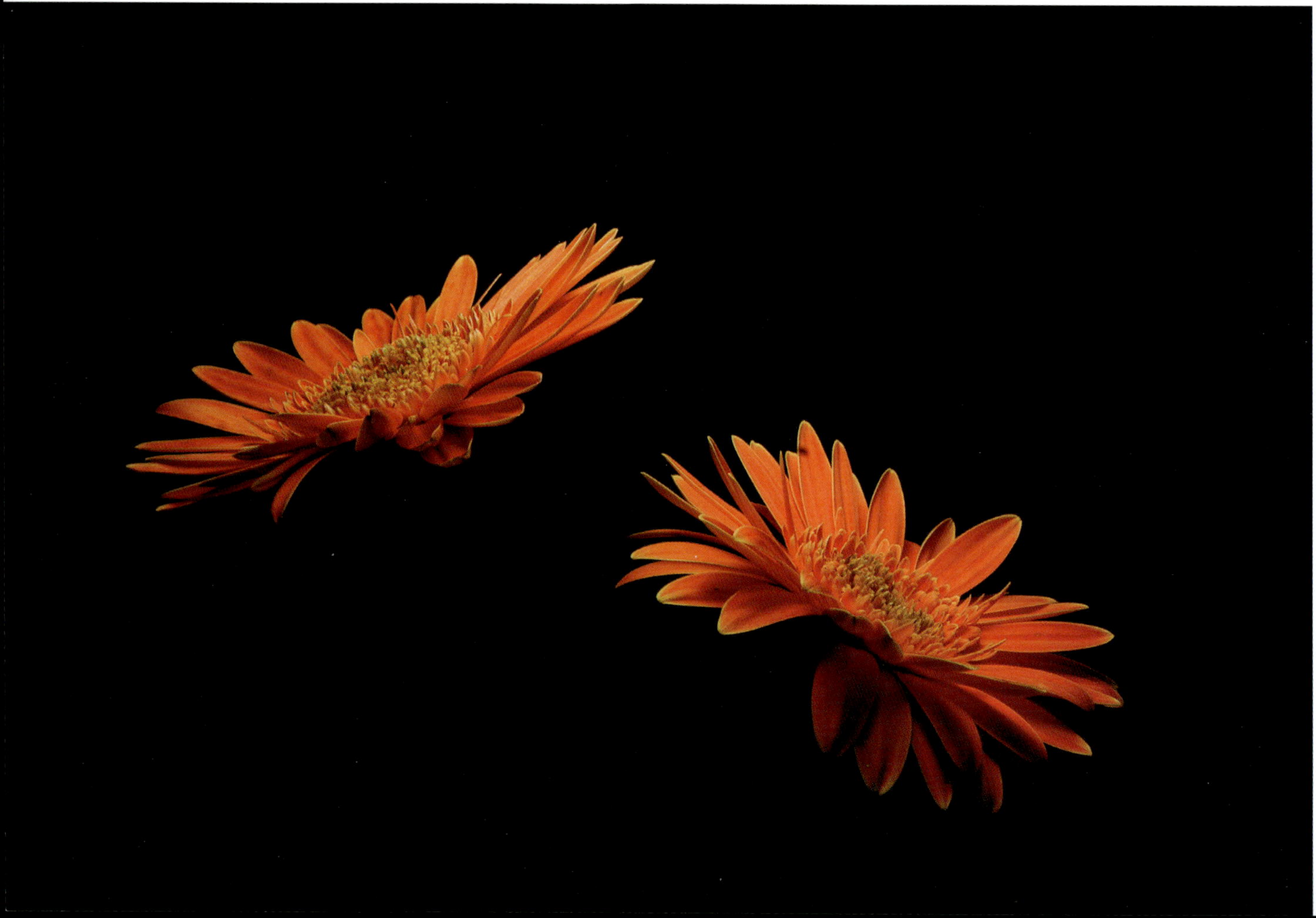

Here you see a photographer practicing her indoor techniques with the help of two flashes. Each flash is modified by a large LumiQuest softbox.

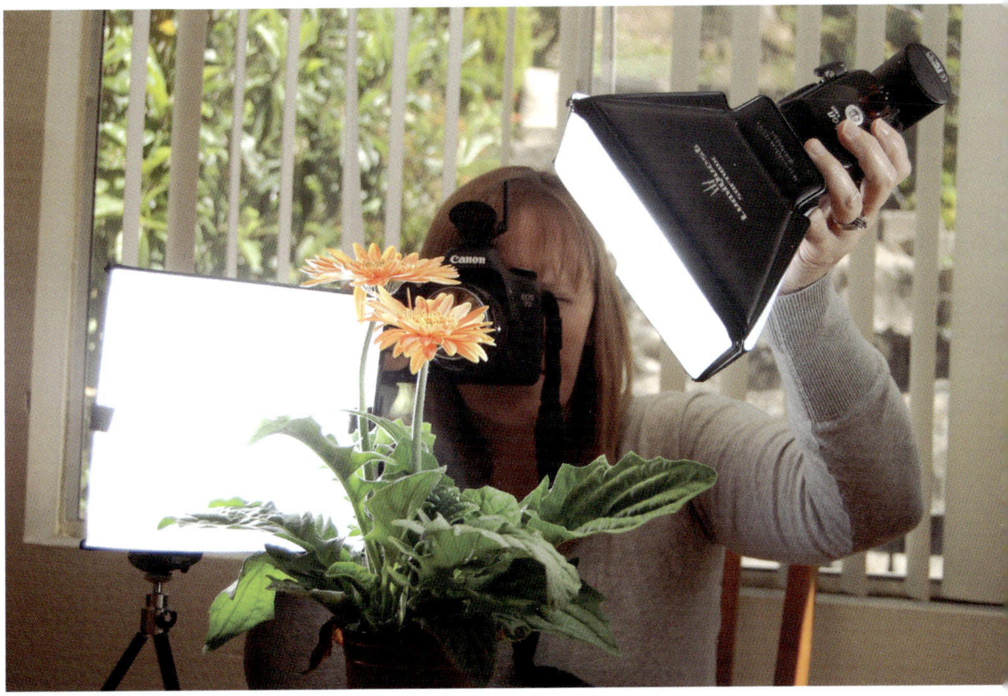

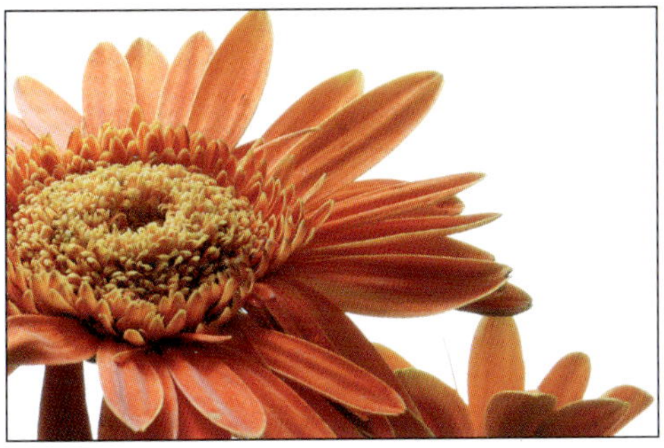

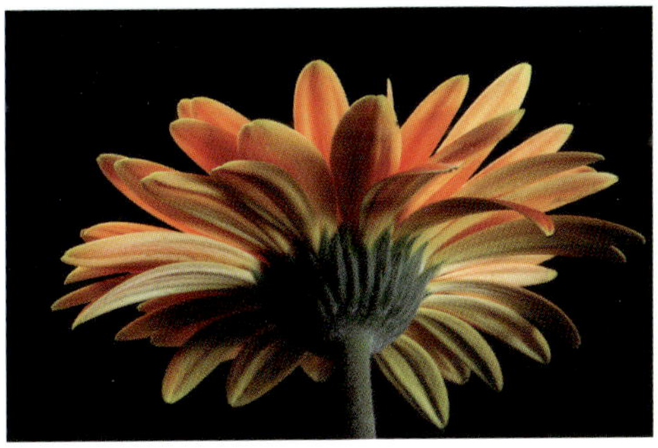

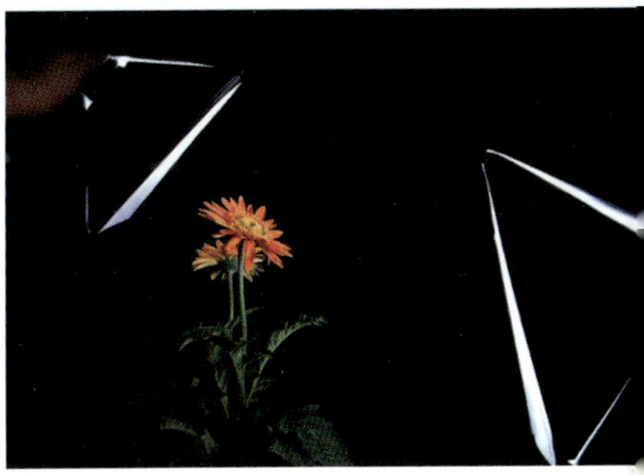

Once you've mastered one flash and have shot every conceivable image, add another flash. Modify it in exactly the same manner as your hand-held flash if you can. Place it to one side of your subject at first, then move it (and your other flash) around. Adjust the power settings on each flash, moving them closer to and further away from your subject. Do everything you can think of—then do some more. The more time you spend training like this, the better your reaction time and your visualization skills will be when you take it outside.

power setting, then shoot, check, adjust, and shoot again until you achieve the perfect light for your message.

Now, move your flash. Place it to the right of your subject, then to the left. Put it behind and in front. Explore the various angles of view your off-camera flash affords. Once you've mastered that, change your own angle of view. Shoot from below or from the side. Get lower or shoot from higher. Change your approach and grow from the experience.

Keep shooting until you have at least ten images that you love. Then, take a few moments and try to repeat them. Keep practicing until you can re-create these images very quickly.

### TWO FLASHES

If you're lucky enough to have more than one flash, use it. Repeat the previous process for the second flash, dialing in the perfect power setting, modifying it the best you can, and supporting it with whatever it takes. (Small table-top tripods prove a perfect support tool—as do beanbags, books, DVD cases, and boxes of cereal.) Once you've got your lighting

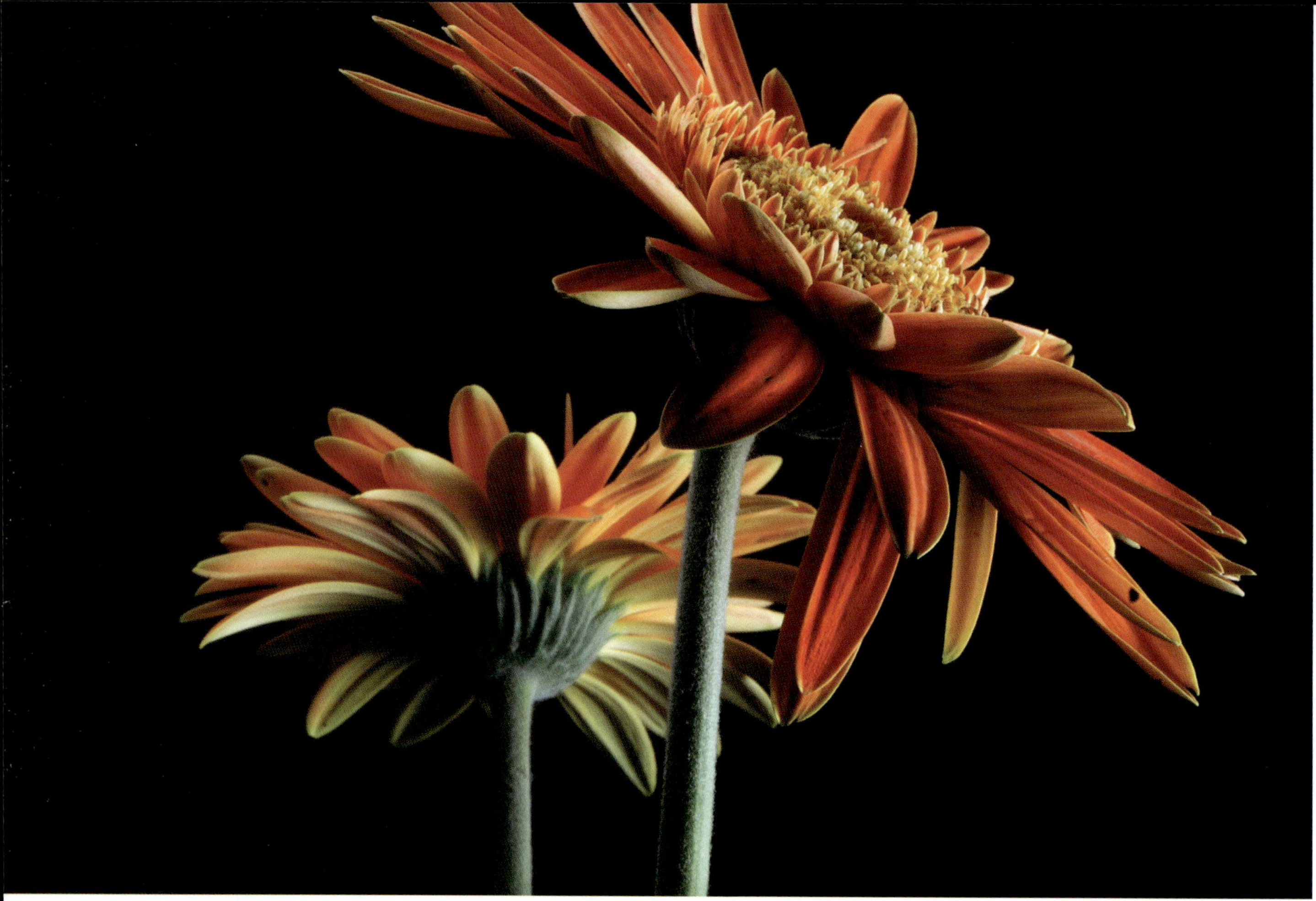

down, move the flash around your subject while it's on the support. Find a location that works great, lighting just one side beautifully, and leave your flash there. Now hand-hold your second flash and begin moving it around, lighting various other angles of your subject.

When you have more than one subject, or the area you wish to light is large (such as in this photo), a larger modification tool (such as the large LumiQuest softbox) will be needed. Here, two modified flashes were used.

Keep moving and adjusting your hand-held flash while the second flash remains stationary. It's important at this point to observe the variations in shadows that can occur. Watch how each flash illuminates different portions of the flower.

Now, start moving the second mounted flash around, as well. Explore the possibilities of what two lights afford. Lighting your subject from various angles, adjust the power settings of the flashes to vary the results. Try backlighting, side-lighting, and even front lighting—always moving your free flash and the stationary one to different locations.

Experimentation and experience are the keys to great photography. This isn't costing you anything but time, and you are worth the time. And keep this in mind: the only thing you are actually doing is learning how to position and adjust the locations of your flashes. The camera settings haven't changed a bit!

## THREE FLASHES

If two flashes opened up the flood gates to creative freedom, imagine what three flashes will do. If you've got three, use them. (If not, borrow and beg until you get them!) Really start experimenting with all of the options.

When you've tried every possible combination, rethink the assignment. Forget about the black background part. For a white background, you could purchase a tabletop light tent built for close-up/macro work. To use this, you place your subjects inside, then light the translucent sides with your flashes. This works, but it's extremely limiting and doesn't really give you a lot of usable experience—unless you're going to light *all* of your subjects while they stand in a white tent.

A quick trip to your local hardware or craft store will provide a cheaper a more versatile solution. For about $6, you can purchase an amazing white backdrop: a tri-fold display board. You will want to keep this a good distance from your subjects at first. Otherwise, you may run into a problem with flare or bounced light coming back from your board to your subject. Simply set the board up at one end of your table and keep your subject on the other. Keep your camera settings where they are and concentrate, at first, on lighting your background. Use one flash—or two, if you have

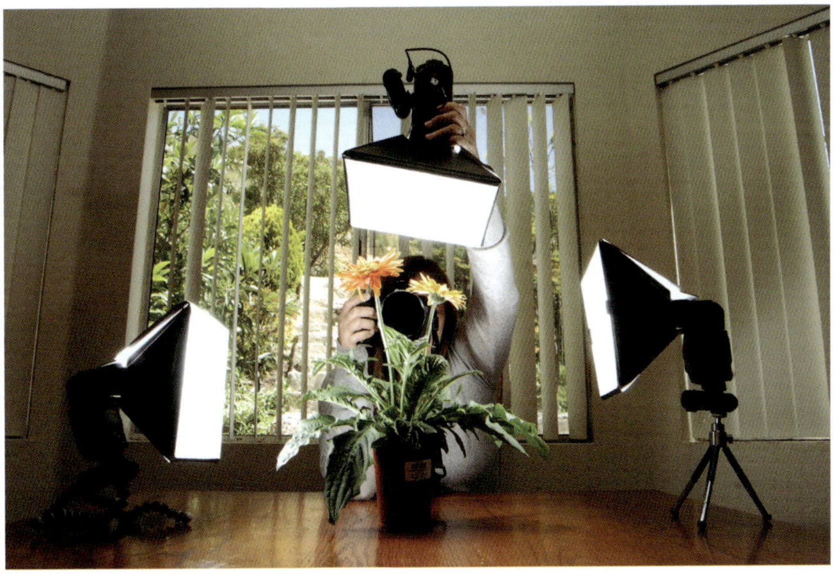

If you've got more lights, use them. Work on each independently. Start with your first light, working on its power setting, support, communication needs, and angle of coverage. Then work methodically, adding the second light, and the third (usually a hand-held one). Take several test shots as you place each light and aim it at your subject.

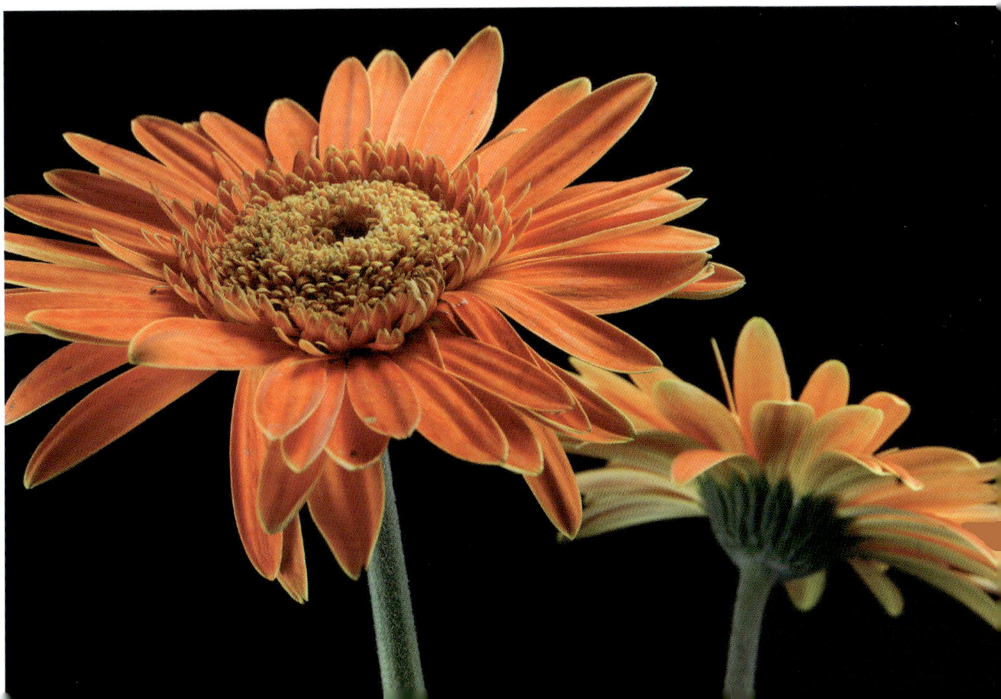

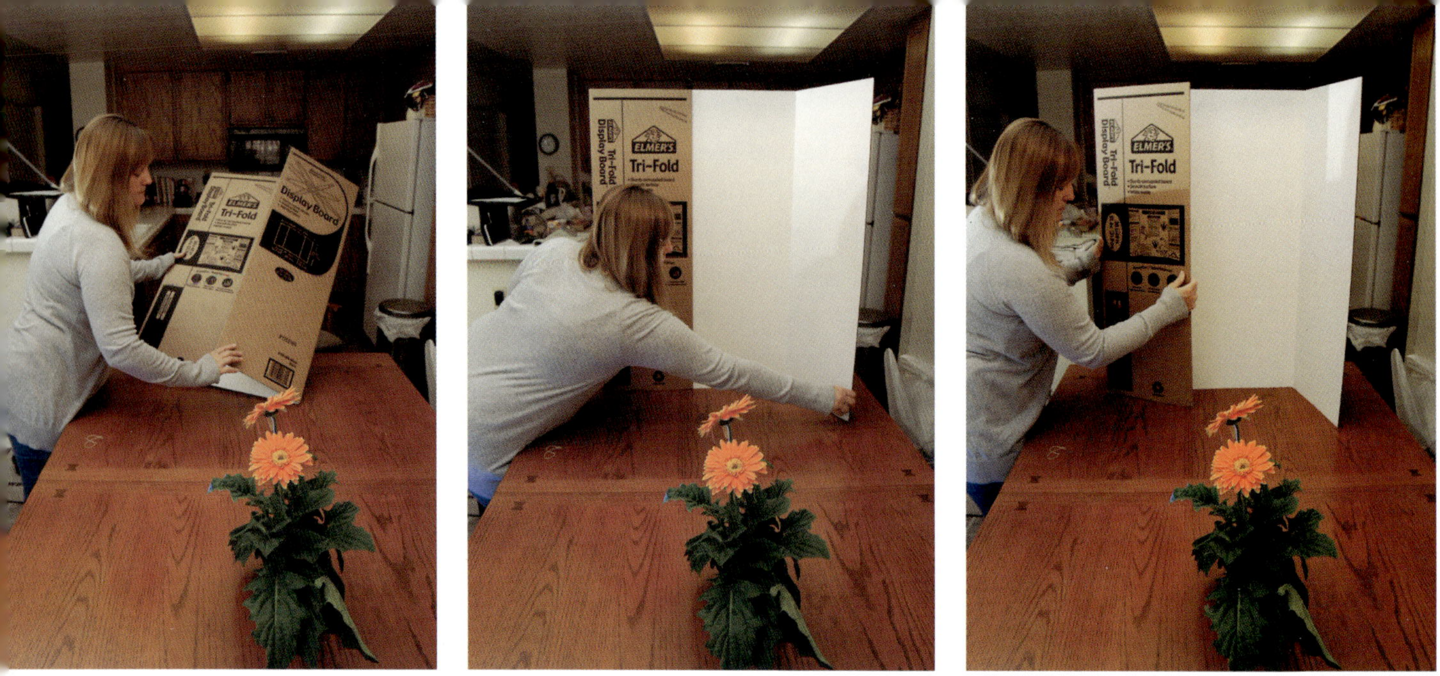


With three flashes, any location becomes a studio. Here, an inexpensive tri-fold project board was used to create a white background—without a few flashes pointed at it, the board was not going to be white.

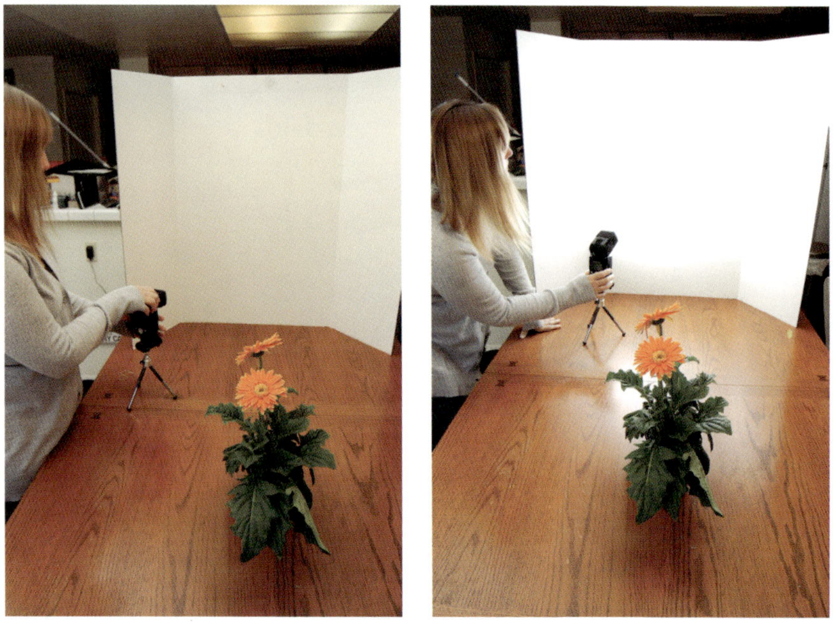

It takes the addition of a flash pointed at the tri-fold background to really brighten things up behind the flower. Take note that some extra illumination did fall on the table. This glare can be eliminated with the aid of a polarizer.

them—to light the board. It's best to take any modification tools off these lights; simply point your flashes directly at the board. It will probably take several attempts to get the board lit just the way you like it—but have some faith. It will happen. Once you've got your board lit the way you want it, go back and light your flower with your hand-held flash according to taste. You will be shocked at how easy this all is.

Once you've explored your white background, change things up a bit by adding some color to it. Instead of enlarging your flash with modification, try changing its color by adding a gel. Gels are relatively inexpensive and open up an even more exciting world of in-home studio options.

When working with gelled flashes, we recommend lowering the power setting. With gels, it's not the intensity of light you're looking for, it's just the color. We suggest using just one colored flash on the background at first, aiming the remaining flashes on the subject. The options are simply amazing and have to be played with to be believed.

Once you've got the whole tabletop studio figured out, it's time to move the idea outside, where it belongs.

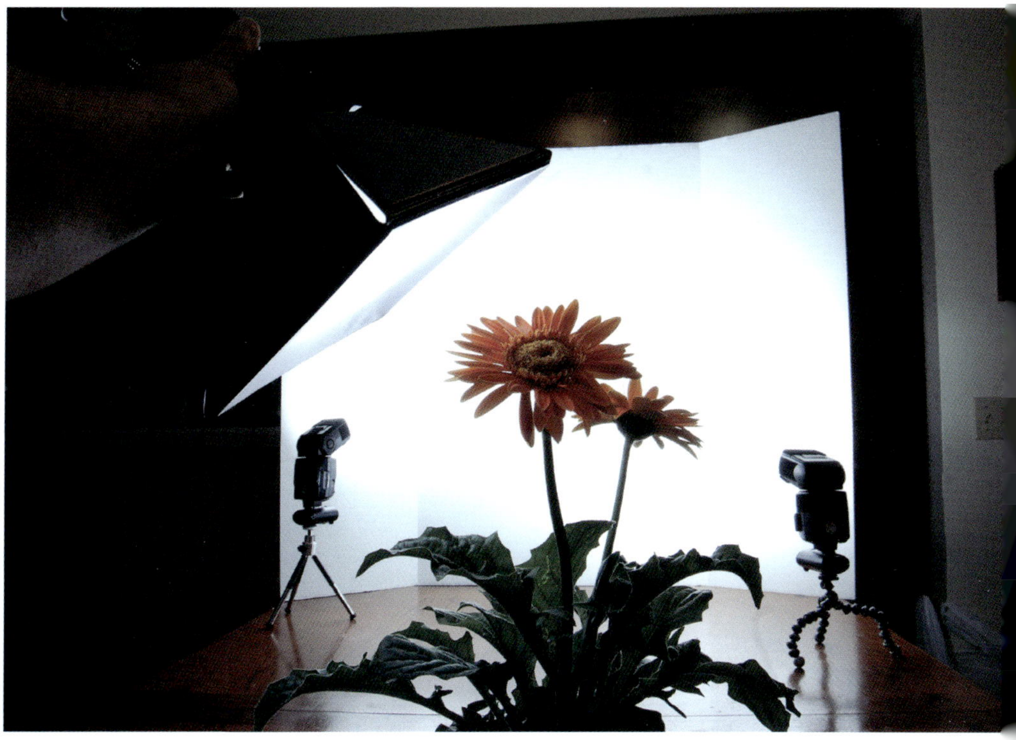

Our impromptu studio is beginning to look more like a studio with the inclusion of yet another light on our background and one hand-held flash pointed at our subject. A longer focal length lens was used to crop into our image, leaving nothing but white in the background.

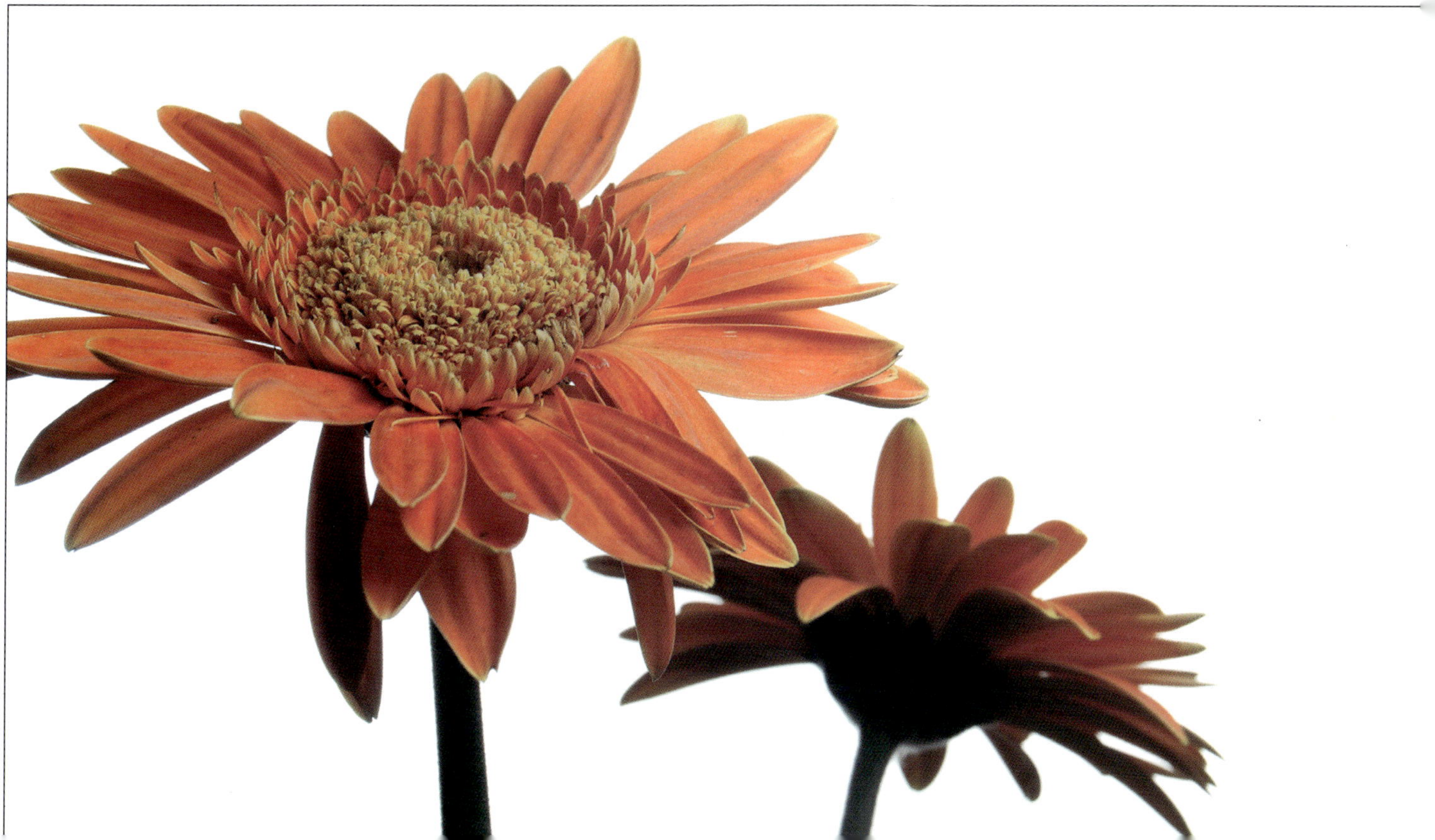

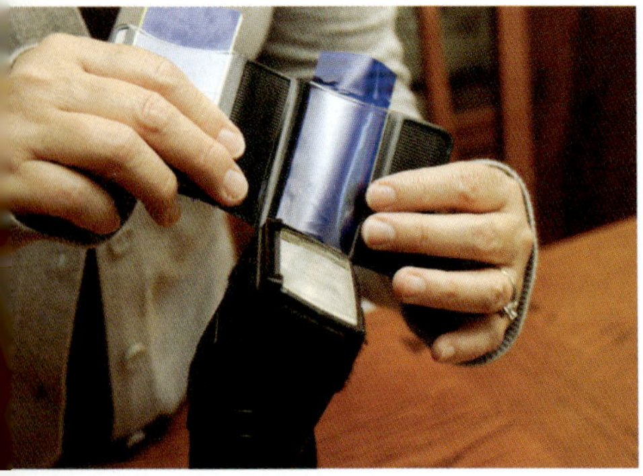

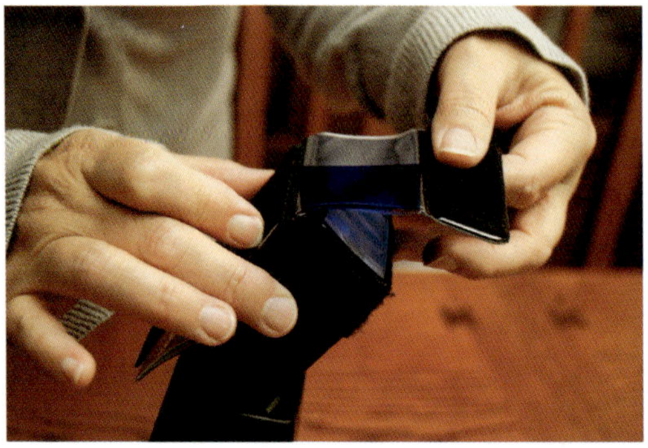

A blue gel was added to one of our background flashes and the power setting was turned down low. The second flash was turned to face the subjects and the hand-held unit was positioned to give the plants some nice top-lighting. Let your imagination run free here. Think of this as your chance to explore the options that off-camera flash affords when there are no problems or distractions—no reasons to fail. Shoot, learn, experiment, and then push yourself and your vision. See just how creative you can be!

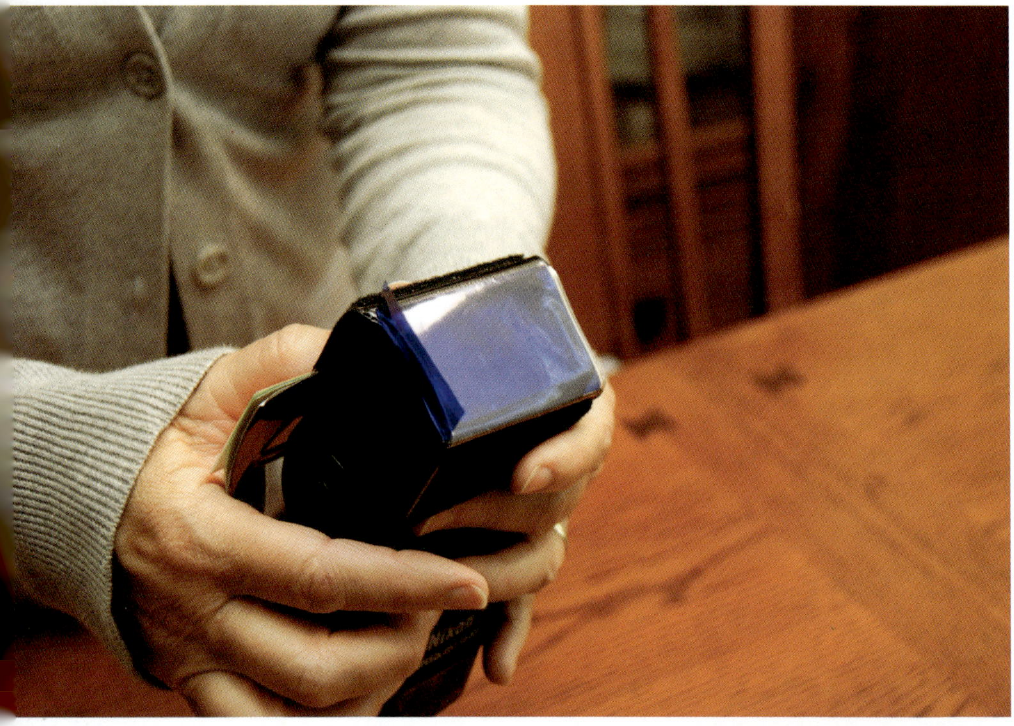

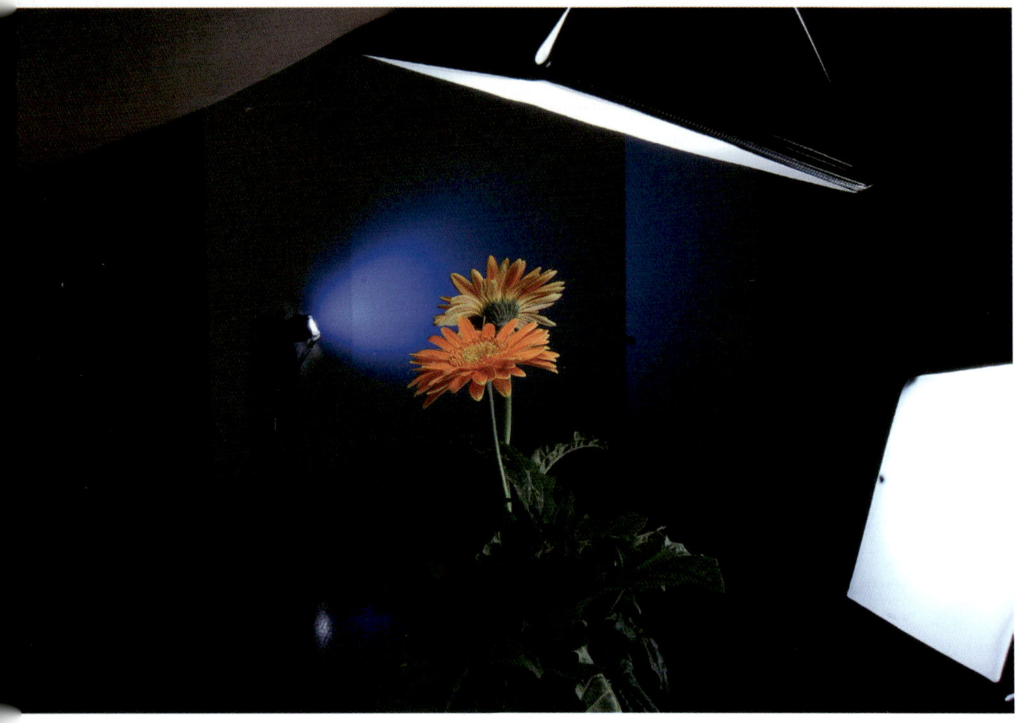

**Left and facing page**—Once you've satisfactorily completed this exercise, repeat it with different settings, more lights, different colors, and so on. You'll love the differences these choices offer. The only hard part will be choosing which one you like most.

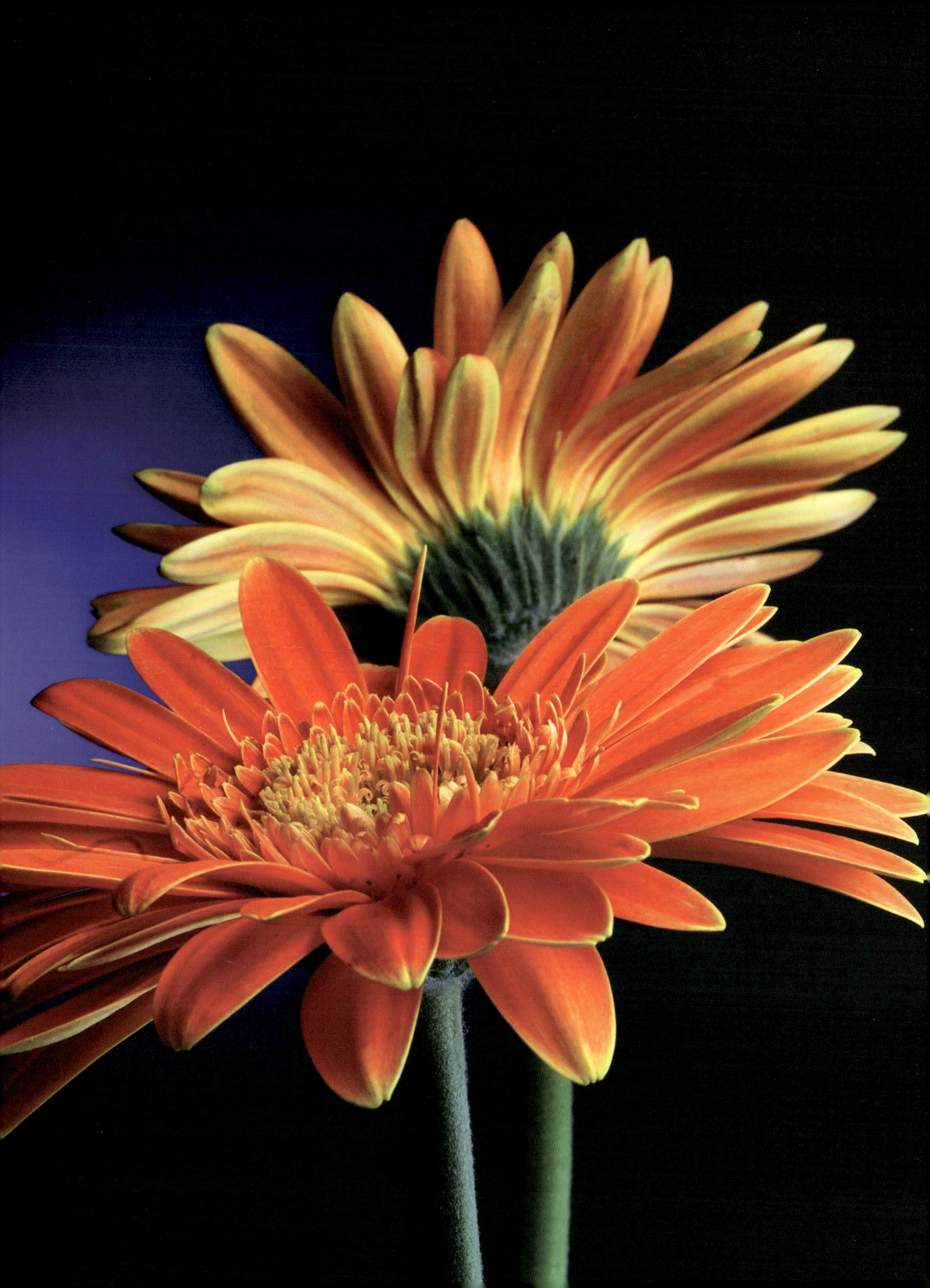

# 6. TAKING IT OUTSIDE

Light is light and choices are choices. When it comes to off-camera flash photography they are endless. The lessons learned from the last chapter will help prove that—especially when we take it all outside!

## ANOTHER EXERCISE

Let's re-examine our indoor studio challenge in the light of day. In the last chapter, we learned that if you choose a fast enough shutter speed and shoot with a small enough aperture, you can achieve a black background, sharp focus on your close-up/macro subject, and (with the help of your flash) nice illumination on your subject. So let's try it outside.

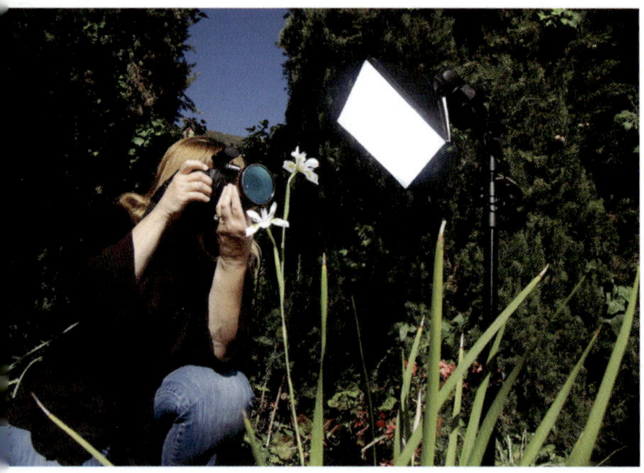

Find a flower or some other small subject to shoot in your backyard. Feel free to bring a light stand if you wish. Dial-in your settings as in the last chapter, setting your shutter speed to your camera's flash sync speed and your aperture as small as it will get (the largest f/number). You'll also want to modify your flash substantially—again, a larger light source makes

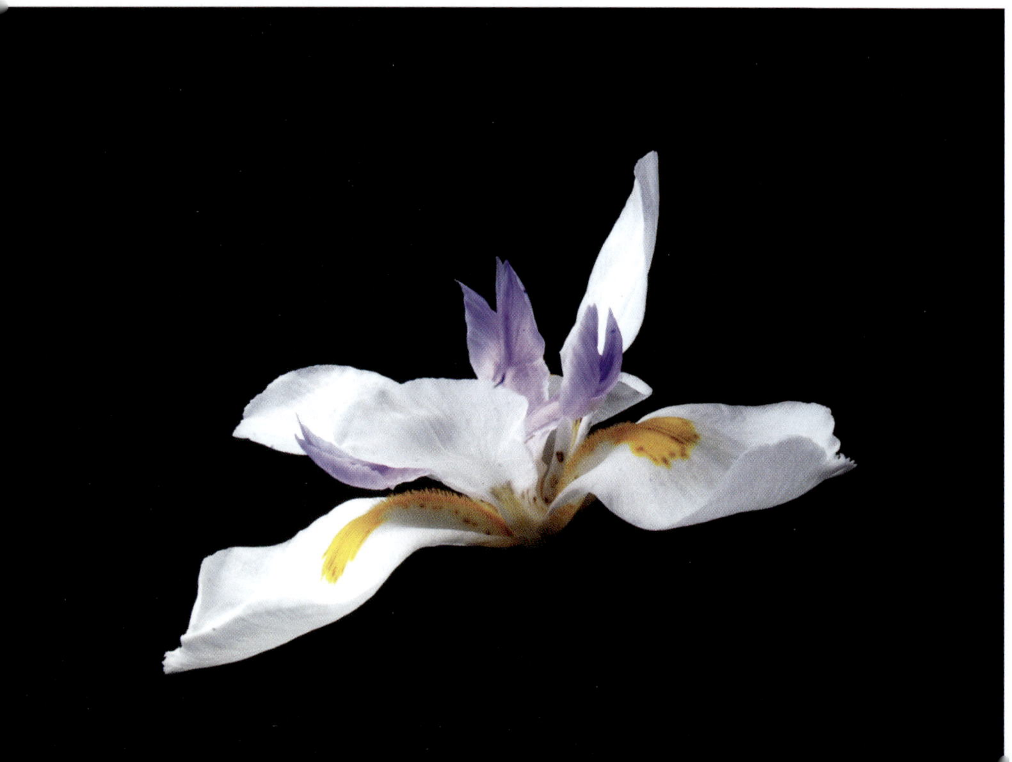

In the beginning, do what you know how to do. Practice creating some amazing black background images outside. Use exactly the same techniques you learned in the previous chapter to isolate your small subjects. What you'll garner from this outside exercise will be pride and experience—and you may even end up with a few amazing photos! Once you're capable of shooting amazing indoor macro and close-up images, move the techniques outside. Start small, practicing on flowers, twigs, and plants in your backyard. Employ a light stand if you wish (as seen here), and remember to modify that light source.

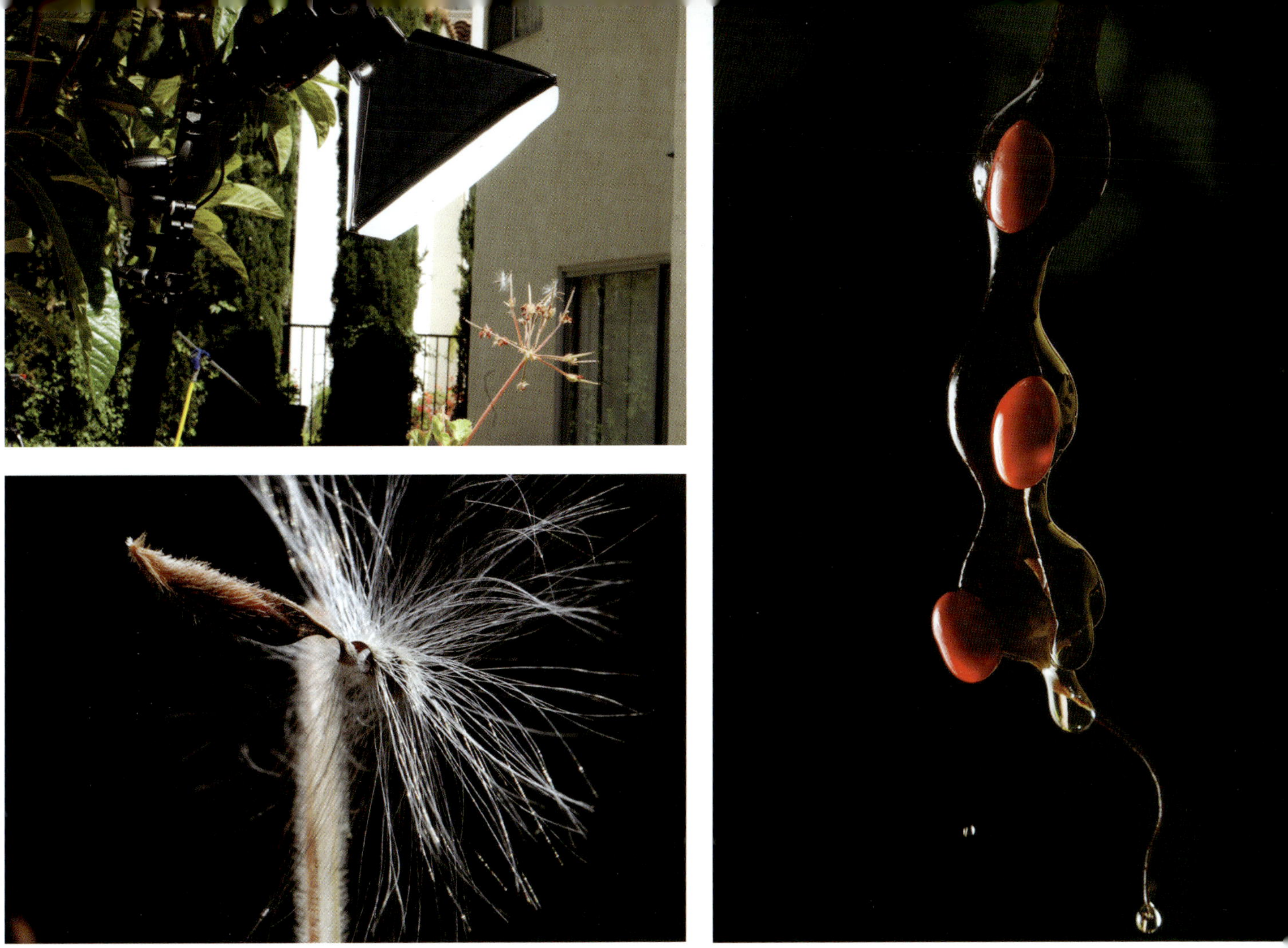

When we say start small, we mean it. One very small "model" can provide hours of practice time. Look for the simple things in your yard; don't overlook the obvious. As evidenced in these photos, we used one modified flash set atop a light stand to achieve the perfect lighting for our subject.

for better macro pictures. Take a quick test image without your flash and try to get that nice black background. Don't pay too much attention to your subject; that comes next.

Immediately, you may notice a striking difference between shooting inside and out: there is a lot more light outside. It may actually prove difficult to achieve a completely black background. There are solutions for an excess light problem as you'll recall. You could employ a lens that affords smaller apertures. You could also use neutral density filters or cross polarize to eliminate the excess light. You could even change your composition a bit, filling your frame with a background that is hidden in shadow.

Once your background is as dark as you can make it, work on lighting your subject with your flash and keeping it in focus. Remember to check the focal depth with your depth-of-field preview button. (Yes, the image you see through the viewfinder will get dark, but at least you will be able to see what will be in focus.)

Begin with your flash at full power; then, if needed, adjust the setting accordingly. If you brought a light stand, move your flash into the "perfect" position and really start practicing. If you have other modification tools—such as umbrellas and softboxes—use them as well. If you have more lighting equipment, start adding more lights. Modify them, too, repositioning them often and practicing just as you did when indoors.

Shoot and shoot some more, making the proper adjustments to both the lights and their placement when needed. The goal is to repeat the type of image you shot indoors, creating a very sharply focused image of a small object with a completely black background. Once you have accomplished your mission, move on to another object and create yet another black background. Keep repeating the process until it becomes easy.

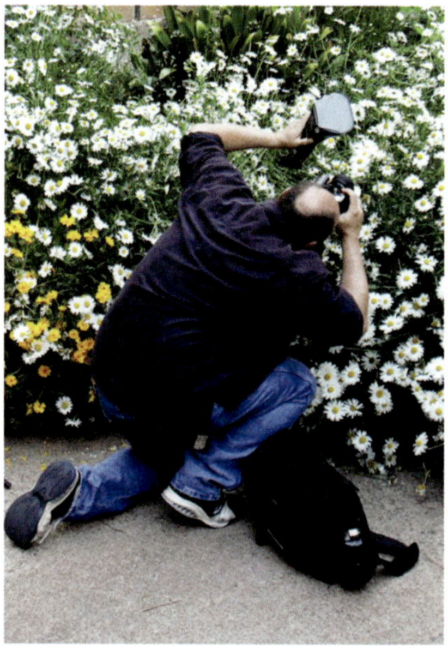

## THE WHITE BACKGROUND

Once you've mastered the black background outside, go the opposite route and try to create a white one. Position your lighting in such a way as to create your own white background, using your modification tool itself as the backdrop.

The trick is not allowing an excessive amount of glare (or flare) from your flash to enter your camera. We usually angle our flash behind and very near our subject and only use the sides of our modification tool as

The graduated white/blue background seen in the image below was created with the help of a very large light modifier: a LumiQuest Bounce attachment. The flash modifier is the background. We simply moved the flash directly behind the flower and shot from below (as seen in the top-right image).

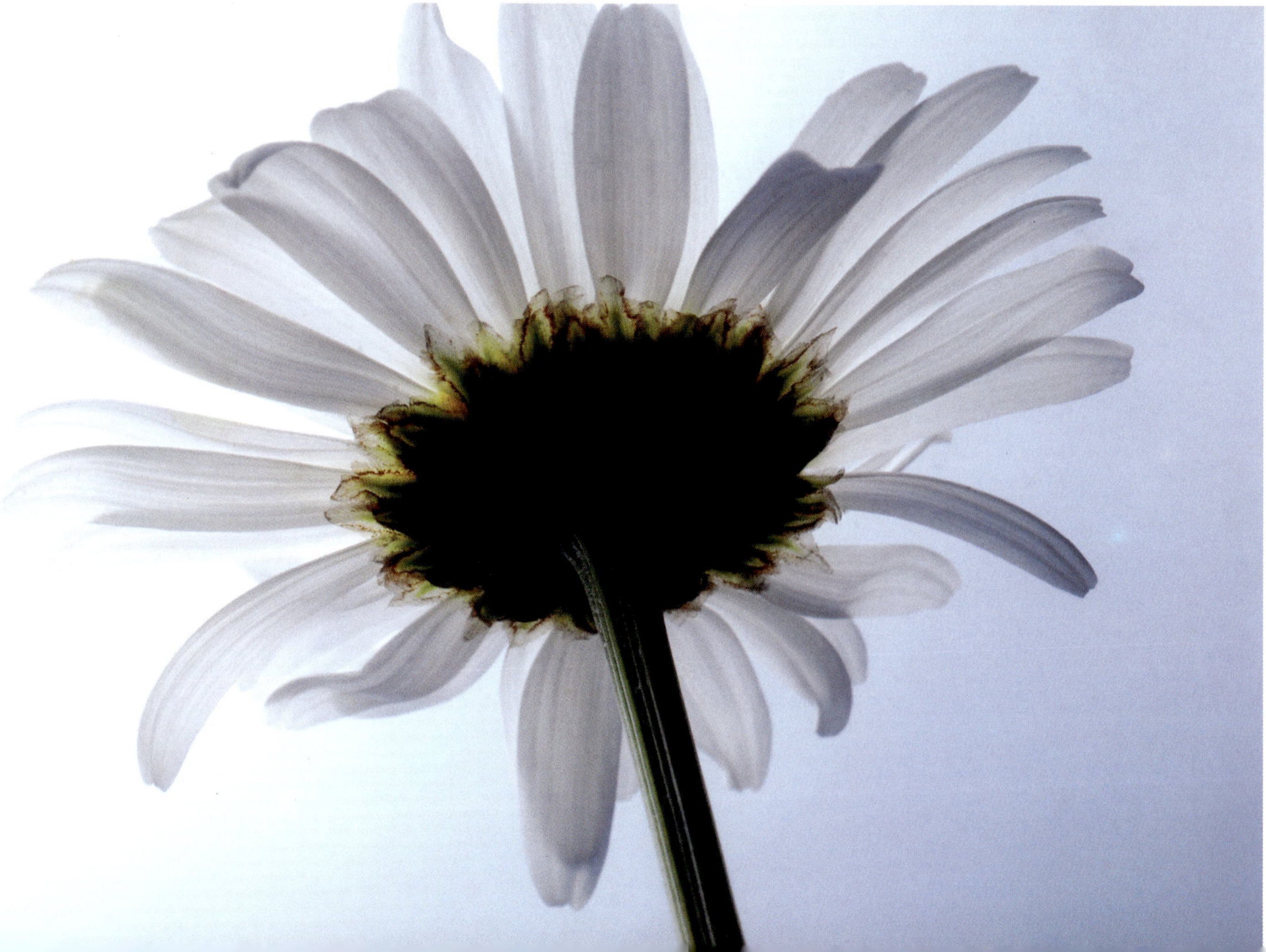

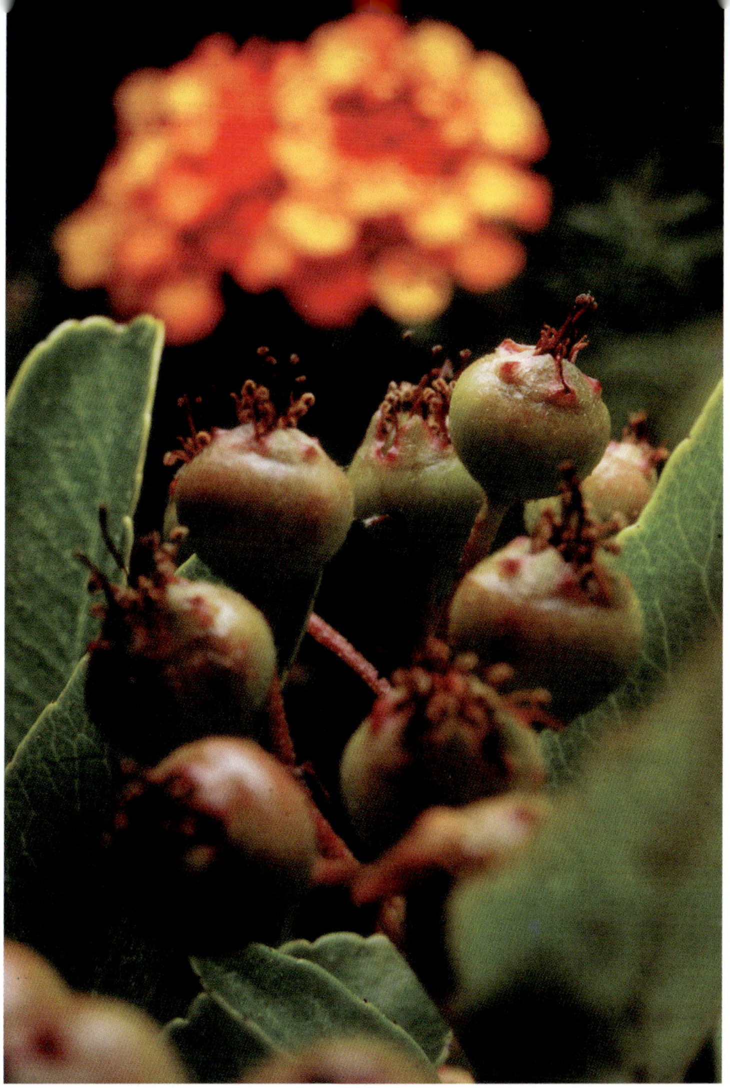

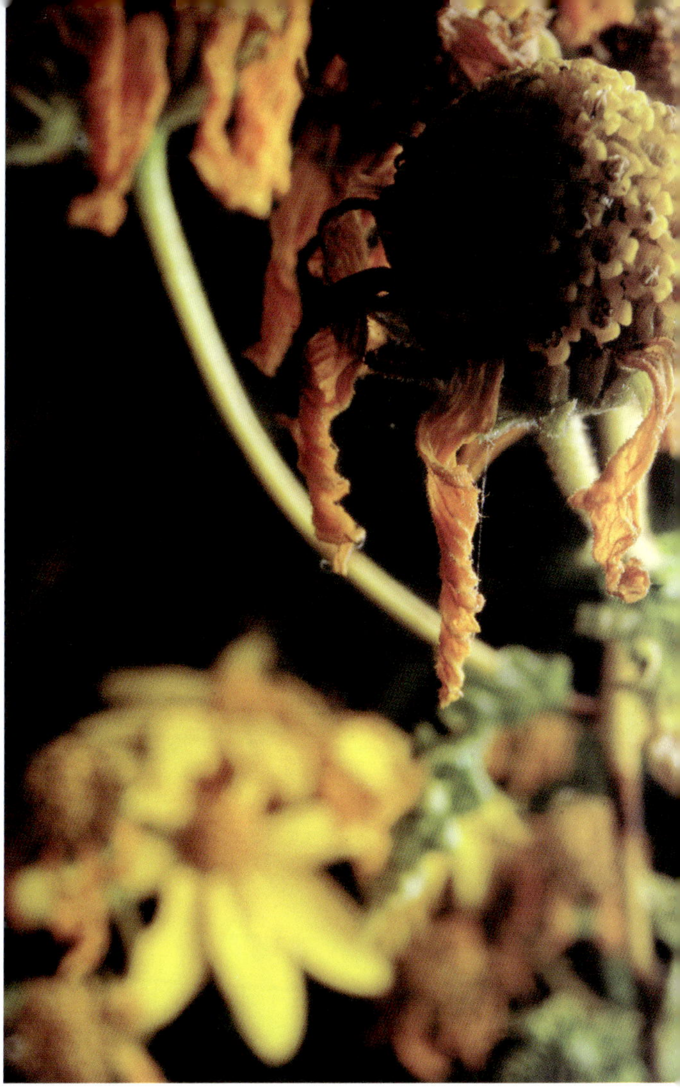

When shooting close-up images with an off-camera flash, don't forget the background. By spreading the wealth of your flash you can begin telling stories of not just a subject, but of that subject within its environment, as well. Notice in these images how the flash was put in between a subject and its background to show more than just a subject.

the background. It doesn't take many practice sessions until you'll find the perfect position for your flash(es). You will, however, need a very large modification device to pull this off. Something that is about ten to twenty times the size of your subject should do very nicely.

### LIGHTING MULTIPLE TIERS

You will also want to practice lighting several tiers of graphic information at a time with your single flash. Make sure your flash is enlarged with a modifier; instead of using it to light just one subject, you're going to be spreading the wealth a bit. Look for opportunities where several small subjects can use some light. Don't focus your attention on lighting just one thing now, light more than that. Direct the flash in between graphic elements, allowing the light to push from one direction but still hit several pieces of your graphic puzzle. You will be shocked at how much more "realistic" your off-camera lighting will look when you start thinking about your message instead of just your subject. No longer will they look like

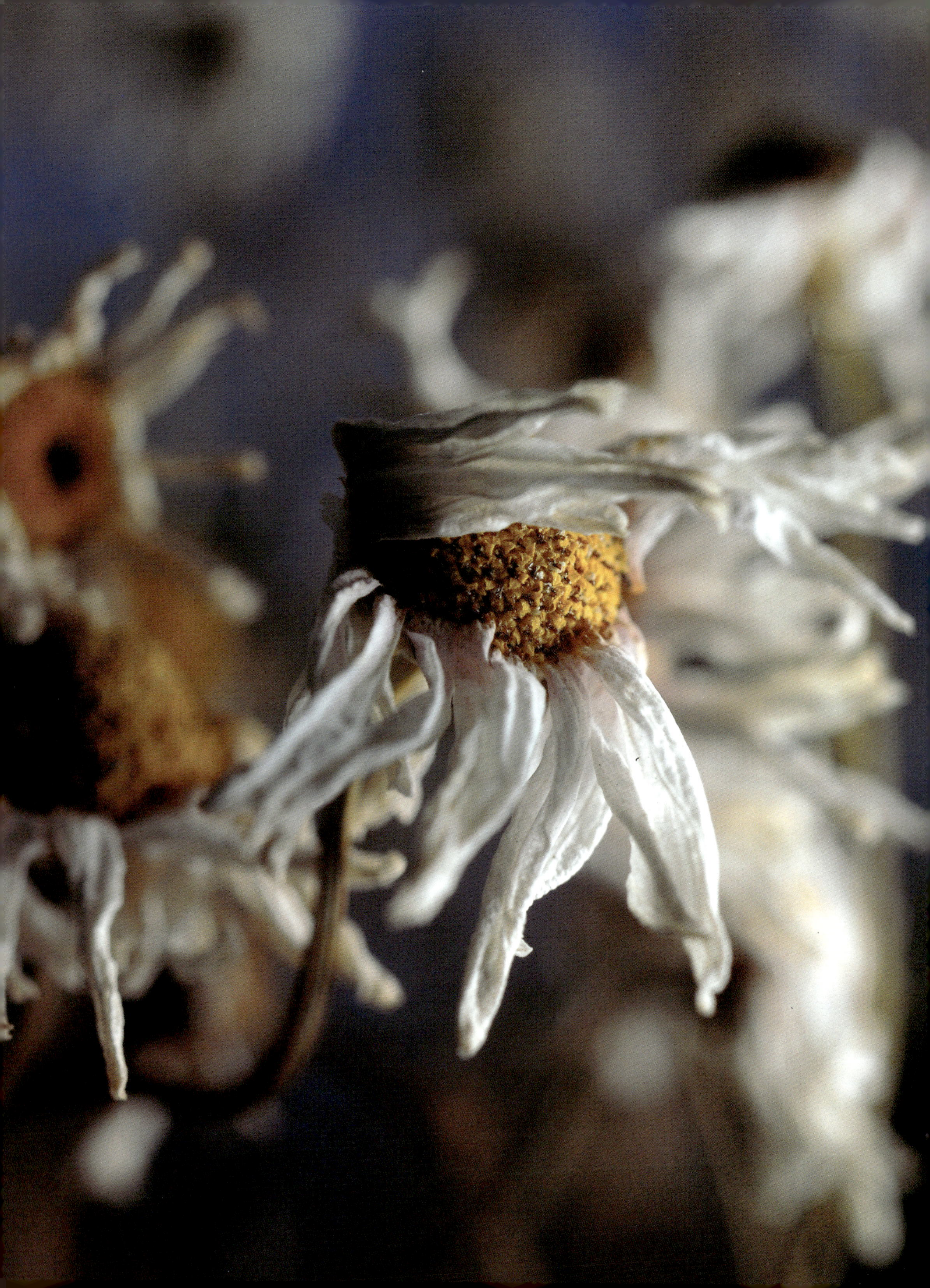

**Facing page**—Make sure the light coming from your flash is perfect. If it's not, fix it—adjust your modifier, vary the power setting, move the flash closer or farther away, or change its angle of coverage. Do whatever it takes and do not leave the spot until you have the image lit and as in focus as you want it to be. Too many great photos were never created simply because the photographer didn't have the heart or the patience to finish what he started. Artfully mixing ambient and man-made light takes skill, perseverance, and dedication. Practice is the best possible "tool" you have. The more you practice, the better you get.

There is no tougher test for the photographer than to create an image with mixed sources of light and still remain true to his initial vision. Here, the photographer tries to find a happy balance between the two—a balance in which his rather fanciful flower can shine.

***Trial and Error***

The harder you make the situation, the more challenging the assignment and the more you'll learn. Trial and error is an amazing thing—and keep in mind that this isn't costing you a dime. In the past, garnering this much experience would have cost you a bundle in film processing.

flash pictures; they will appear to have been shot at the most "perfect" time of day.

Admittedly, this will take some work—and if your current modification tool doesn't afford you the "proper" light spread, you'll need to buy or make another (much larger) one. Keep practicing and make sure to challenge yourself as you go. Don't settle for anything less than spectacular. You are in full control of the light and the situation, so change whatever needs to be changed and just make it happen.

## COMBINING FLASH AND AMBIENT LIGHT

Up until now, if you've followed along with the exercises, you have been in total control of the lighting elements, forcing an image to happen and making it look the way you want. When you start mixing the

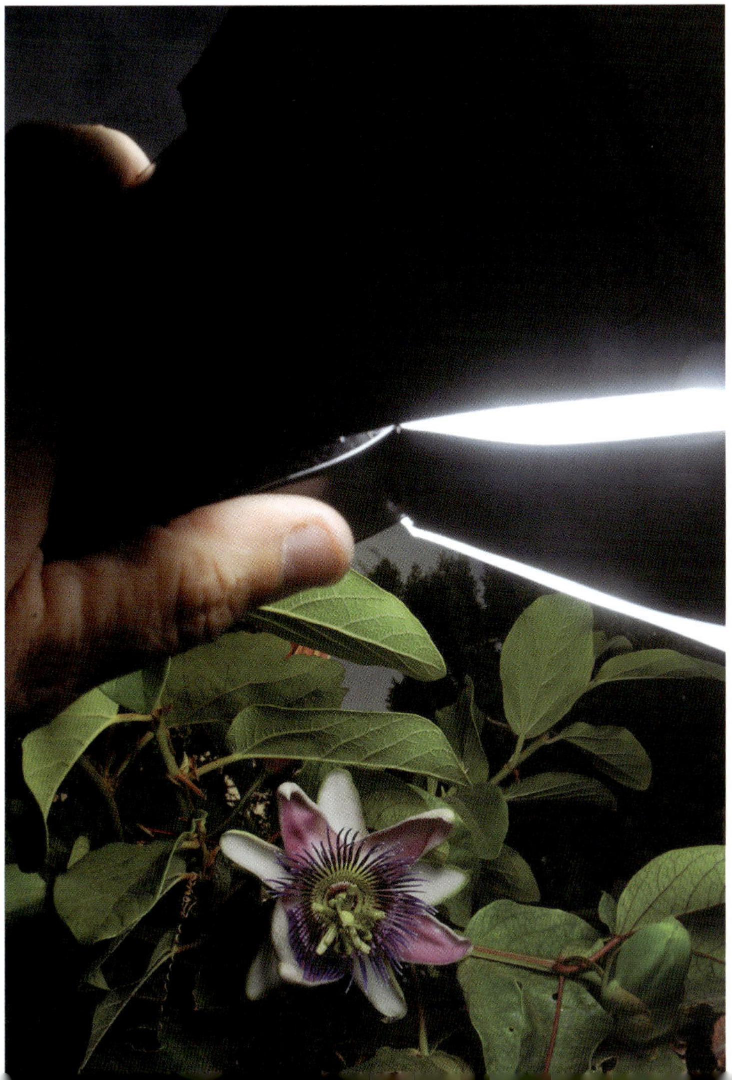

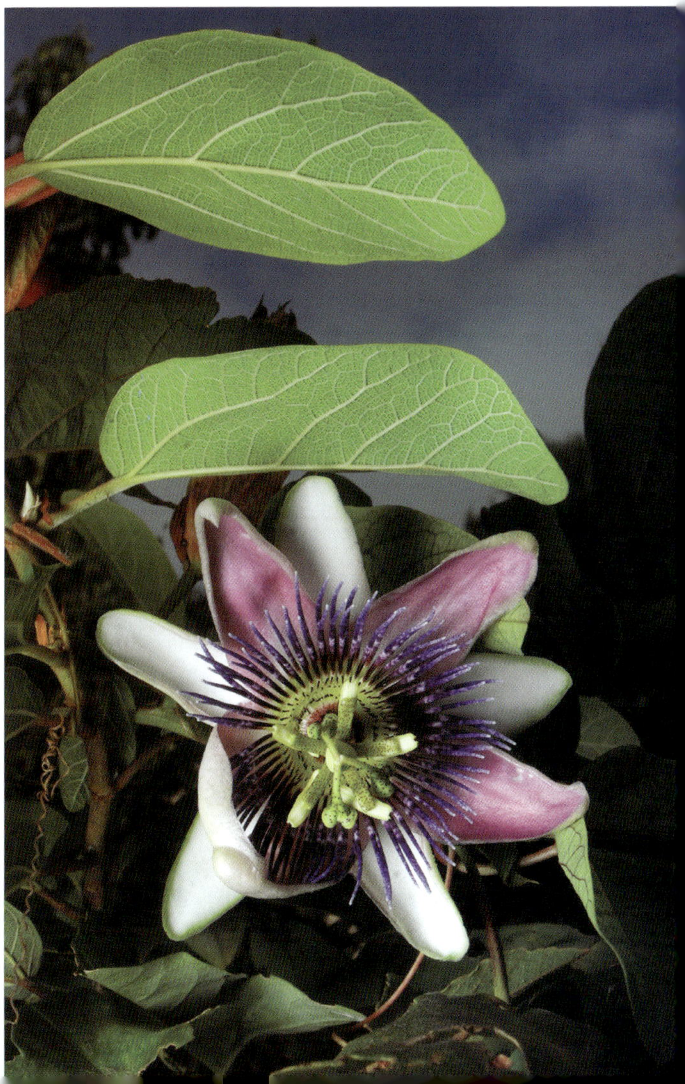

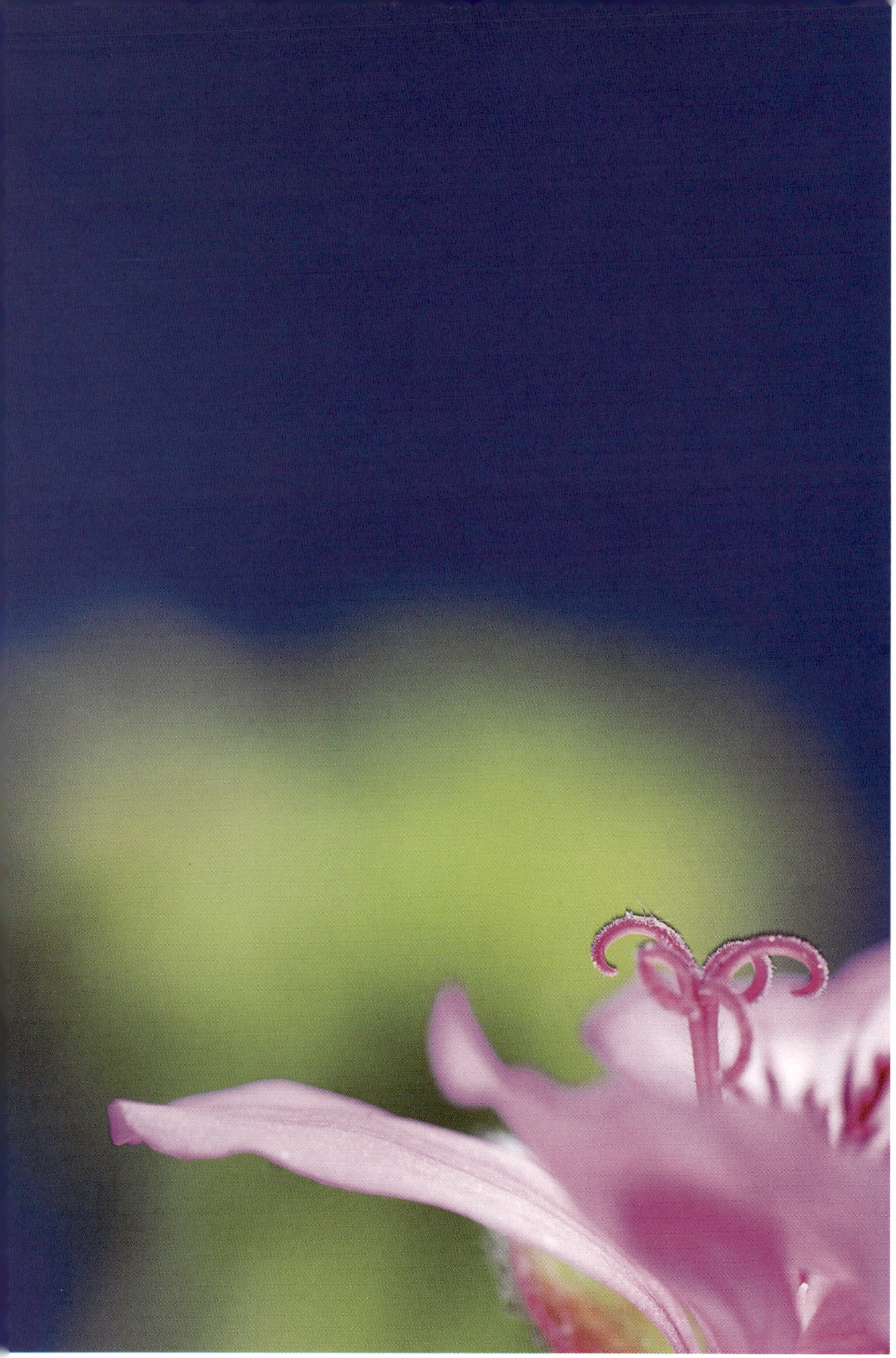

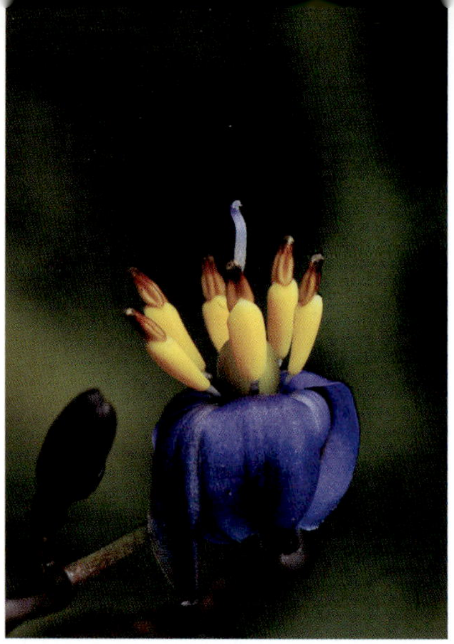

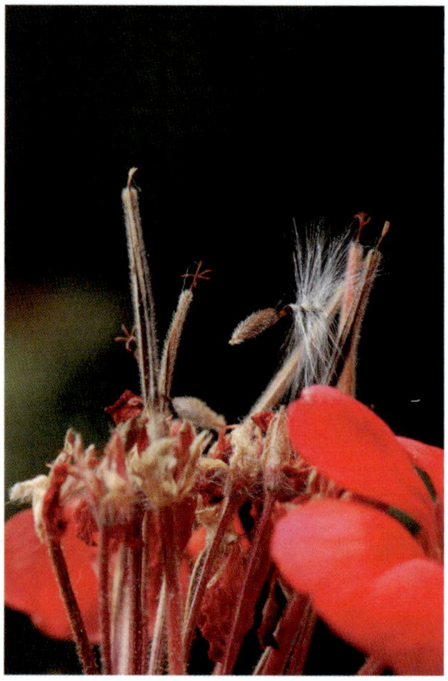

Amazing backgrounds are possible with your flash work. With the proper control of your shutter speed, aperture size, and ISO setting, you can literally dial in just about any background you can imagine—and still employ a flash to help freeze and illuminate a subject.

ingredients—especially those you can't control—things can get a bit more complicated.

**Exercise 1.** Dial in your camera's flash sync speed and set your aperture to f/16 (rather than the smaller aperture setting we were using previously). Make sure the camera's ISO is at its lowest possible numbered setting (either 100 or 200). Adjust your flash's power setting to full, then take a picture to ensure proper flash modification size and power settings, adjusting them as necessary based on your results.

***Mixing It Well***

When mixing ambient light with that of your flash, keep track of your real goals and make some sound choices.

1. Decide how much depth of field you want, then choose an aperture that ensures it (checking it with your depth-of-field preview button).
2. Think about shutter speed. Do you want to minimize camera shake or background motion? If you do, then choose a shutter speed that is twice your current focal length or faster. (Be sure not to exceed your flash-sync speed.)
3. If your background is still too dark after employing your slowest "acceptable" shutter speed, adjust your ISO. Raise it higher to garner any remaining background light required.
4. If you don't like the consequences of raising the ISO, then start adding extra flashes to the background—you don't really have any other choice if you want to remain true to your vision.
5. Add light with your flash.

You may notice that your flash seems to be pumping out more light than before—but it's not. The larger aperture (f/16) you are shooting with now gives you an apparent boost of power. Remember: larger apertures increase the apparent power of your flash, smaller ones reduce it.

Once you've got your flash power set properly, take note of your background. How is it lit? Is it too bright? Is it too dark? Is it black? By setting the aperture to f/16, you let in much more light than in our previous exercise. The background, however, should still be fairly dark. If you find the background to be too bright, simply decrease the size of the aperture (making the f/number larger), employ a neutral density filter, or use the cross polarization technique. Make any appropriate flash power changes for your subject. Once you have your subject lit well with your flash and the background is fairly dark, it's time to play.

First, let's try to add light to the background the old-fashioned way. Begin by slowing your shutter speed. Slower shutter speeds add light by allowing more ambient light to reach the sensor. Keep slowing your shutter speed and checking your images until the background is just slightly darker than your subject. (The best part of this approach is that your subject will most defiantly stand-out against the background, since it will be

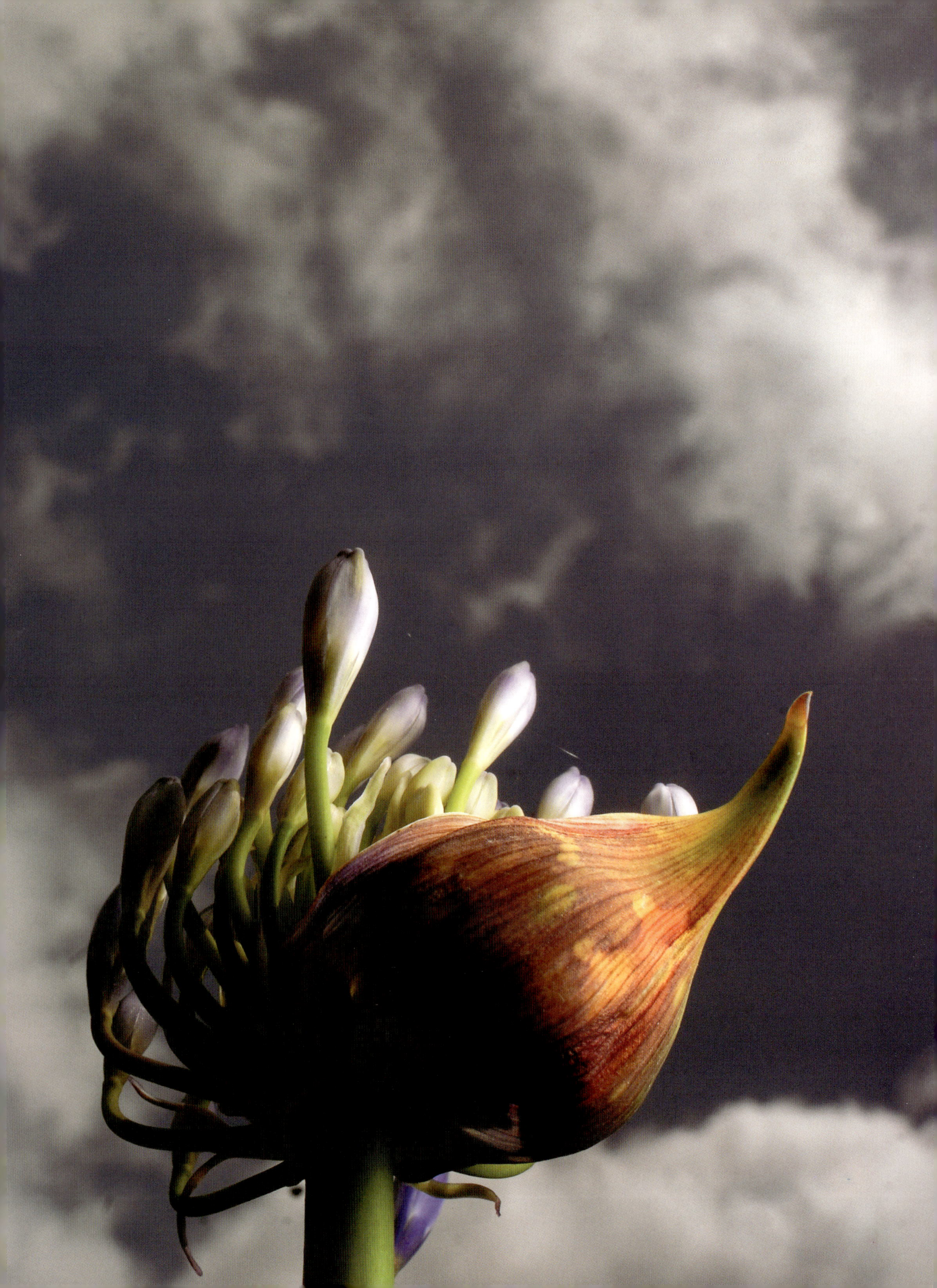

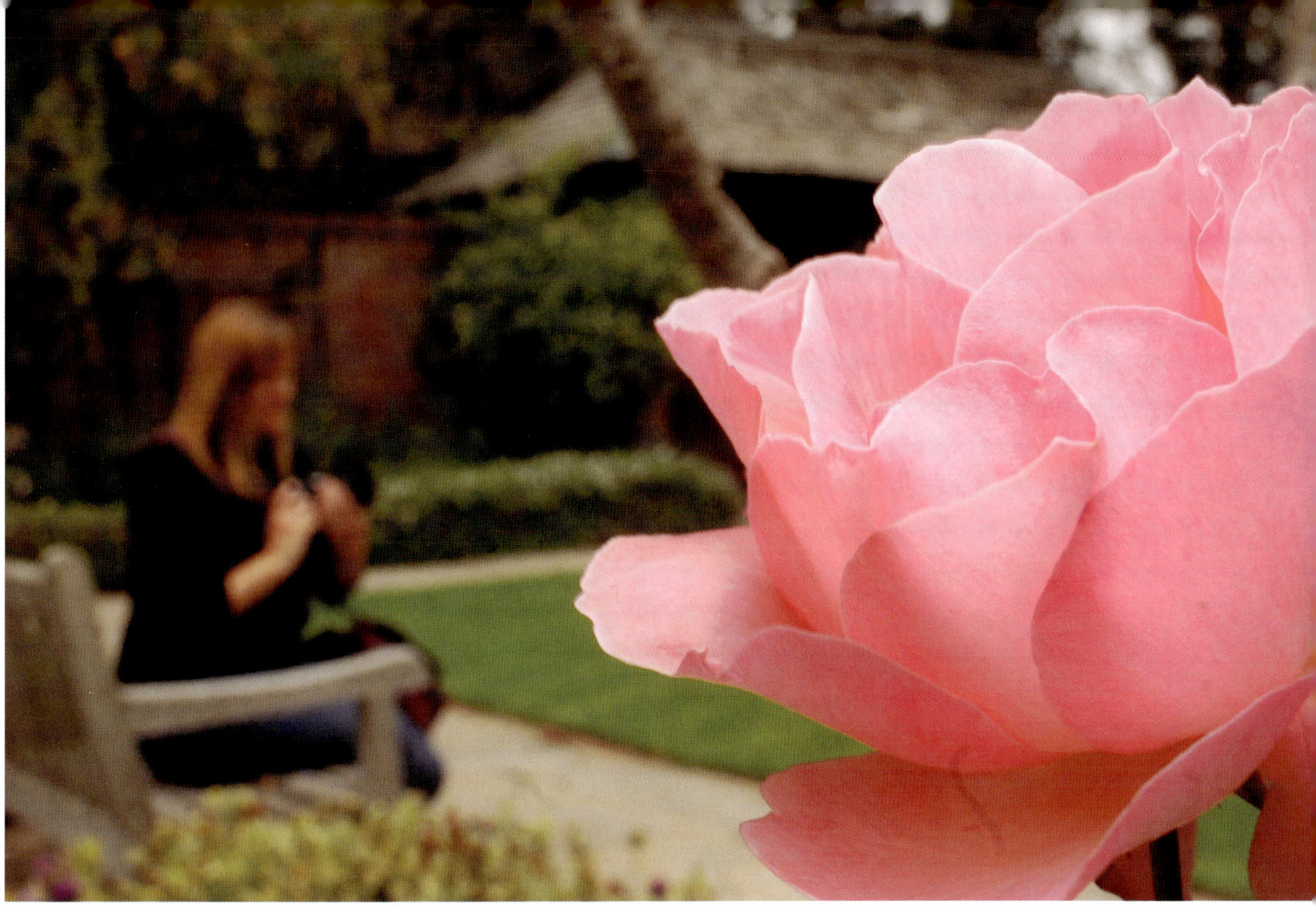

**Facing page**—Try to go with the grain of the natural light, positioning your light source at the same (or close to the same) angle from which the sun is hitting your subject. This way, any shadows seen in the background (or clouds, as in this image) will appear more natural. **Above**—There is a difference between motion blur and the blur created by a limited depth of field. Here, a flash was used to illuminate the foreground flower and ensure an amazing depth of field. To be specific, the photographer guessed at an aperture of f/16. He then checked his depth of field preview button to see how good his guess was—and it was right on target. He then dialed in a shutter speed of $^1/_{60}$ second (double his current focal length of 28mm). To pull his background up from the shadows, he adjusted his ISO to 250. The rest was simple—just add some light to the flower, to delicately bring it out into the open, and to nail the focus. Bam! The flash is an amazing thing!

just a bit brighter than everything else. Plus it will be in razor-sharp focus because of the smaller aperture. You can't lose!)

Be careful not to dip too slow with your shutter speed. While a physical blur in the background is fine, a motion blur can wreak havoc with your message, confusing your audience more than pleasing them. To solve this issue, we suggest following the old double-your-focal-length-and-that's-your-shutter-speed rule. This will usually eliminate the worry of motion blur. To make that happen, you may have to adjust your ISO to achieve the needed illumination.

**Exercise 2.** Choose your aperture settings based on the needed depth of field. Dial in a shutter speed that is at least double your current focal length. Adjust the ISO to attain the "proper" lighting for your background and hit your subject with whatever flash power is required. This approach actually makes things quite simple—and it works like a charm.

Keep in mind that any adjustments to the ISO will also affect the apparent flash output—so, again, you'll have to make the appropriate corrections to your flash's power settings. There will be times when adjusting the ISO will not be an acceptable option. In that case, you can always add more light to the background—just grab a few more flashes and set them up facing your background, not your subject. Of course, all of the same modification, communication, and support issues will need to be taken care of for these flashes, as well—just as you would for your hand-held flash.

You do have other more creative options to explore when it comes to slow-shutter macro shooting with an off-camera flash. Let's take a moment to look at those.

### WORKING WITH SLOW SHUTTER SPEEDS

Motion blur, for most photographers, is a bad thing, however for the free-thinking macro artist using an off-camera flash, it opens up a world of possibilities. Instead of shooting with a shutter speed fast enough to freeze a background, why not let it blur? Since the flash will virtually freeze anything that is fully lit with it (usually your subject), why not play with the two ideas and see what happens?

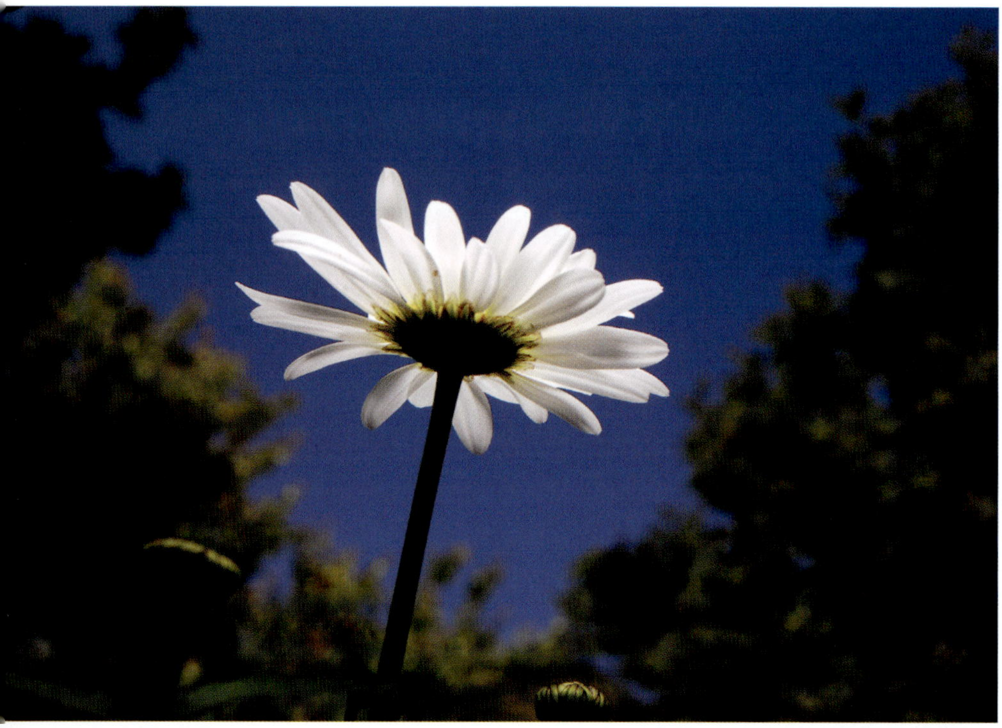

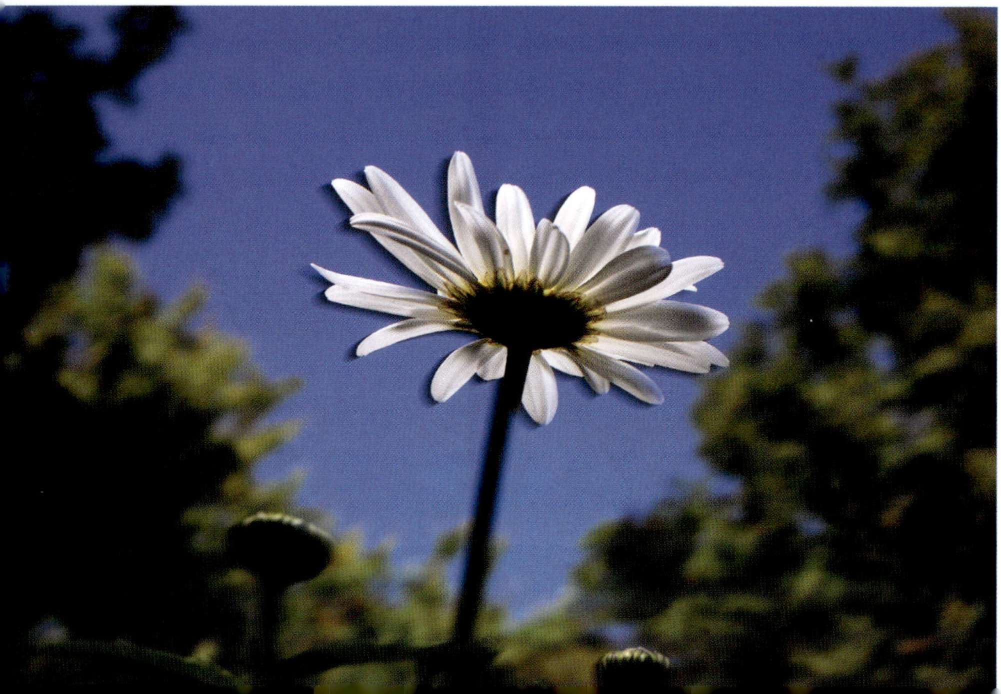

The top photo illustrates the use of an off-camera flash when a fast shutter is employed. The bottom photo shows the effects of a slower shutter speed. Notice the motion blur directly behind the flower—it looks very similar to a shadow effect/filter offered in photo-editing software.

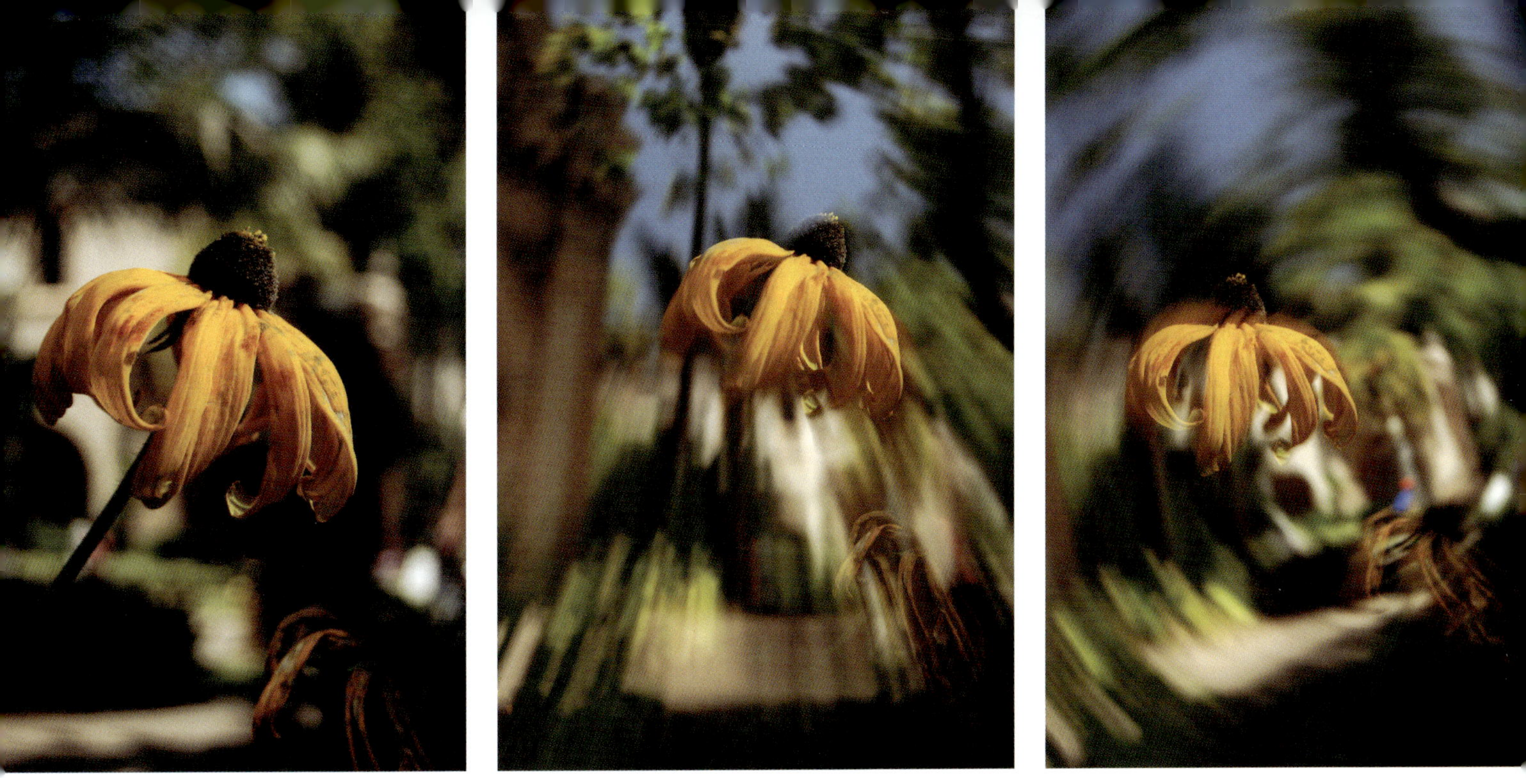

These photos demonstrate the effects offered by using the slow shutter speed technique. In the left-hand image, we hand-held the camera and dialed in a slower shutter speed to light the background well. We also lit the flower (which was hidden in shadow) with a flash. In the center image, we moved the camera upward during the exposure. In the right-hand image, we rotated the camera. Notice how the flash froze the subject, despite the fact the camera was moving.

**Exercise.** Find a subject in full shadow. This is vital, because you'll want to light the subject fully with your flash. Make sure that the background behind your subject is well lit—much brighter than your subject. (You have to get these two pieces right or the technique will not work well.)

Now, go through the regular motions of creating a dramatic close-up/macro image—one in which the background is lit well and your subject is stunning. Take your time to create a magnificent image.

Then, change your shutter speed to 1/15 second and make any necessary adjustments to your ISO or aperture to keep the background from blowing out. If you have to employ a neutral density filter or use cross polarization, then do so. The goal is to create a perfectly lit image using the 1/15 second shutter speed and a flash.

Take the image and examine it closely. You may see what seems to be a shadow behind your subject. It's not, it's actually your subject. This happens because there are two distinct things happening here—all within a fraction of a second. First, you are capturing an image using the ambient light. This image includes your subject hidden in shadow—a silhouette of sorts. Next is the flash-frozen image, which includes whatever your flash hits when it fires. Since this well-lit, frozen graphic tier is "near" the same location as its silhouetted doppleganger, you will see what appears to be a shadow surrounding your subject. The "shadow" stems from the fact that the camera (or subject) moved slightly away from the shadowed doppleganger during the longer exposure.

Try the shot again. This time, physically move the camera slightly while taking the photo. You'll notice that the subject remains intact while that background shadow blurs even more. You will also see the background itself blurring just as much as the shadow.

Now, have some fun! Really be aggressive with your camera movements. Spin the camera or zoom-in while you shoot. Since you're using such a small aperture, don't be too worried about focus (the available depth of field will help out quite a bit).

Of course, this can only be attempted if you are a manual shooter. Auto-anything will not produce these amazing special effects (we've never seen a "spin-my-camera mode," after all). Sadly, even the most basic of outdoor shoots, where our background is slightly darker than our subject, are something that auto settings will not allow. If you plan on being creative, if you plan on having fun, stick to manual—and never go back.

## INSECT PHOTOGRAPHY

**Butterflies.** There are a few iconic subjects that always attract a lot of attention in macro and close-up photography—and butterflies easily top the list. For the novice, photographing these amazing and beautiful creatures can be a painful experience, filled with failure upon failure and only a few images worth sharing.

Butterfly photography becomes simpler and more rewarding when you pair a modified off-camera flash with a little patience and understanding.

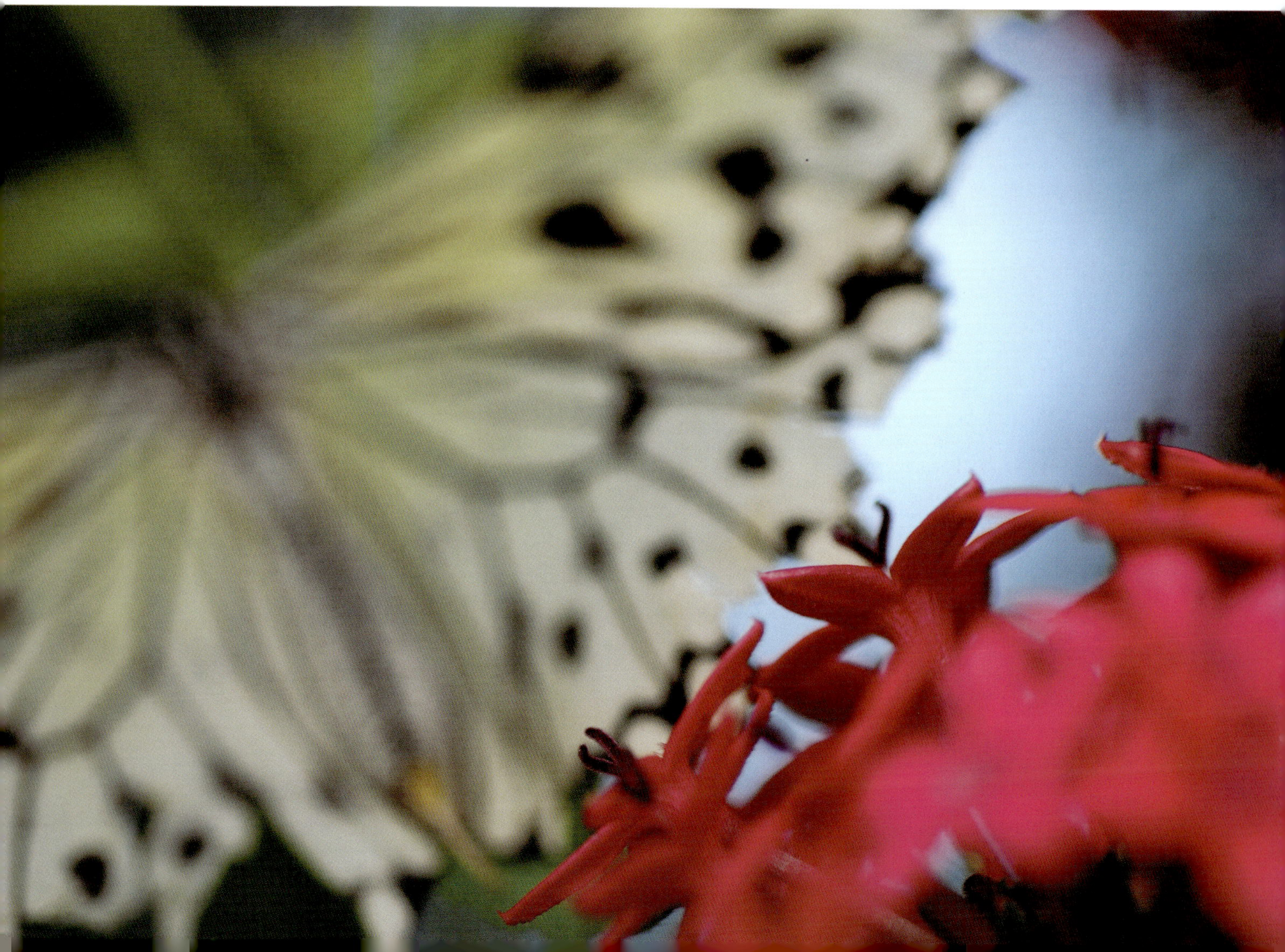

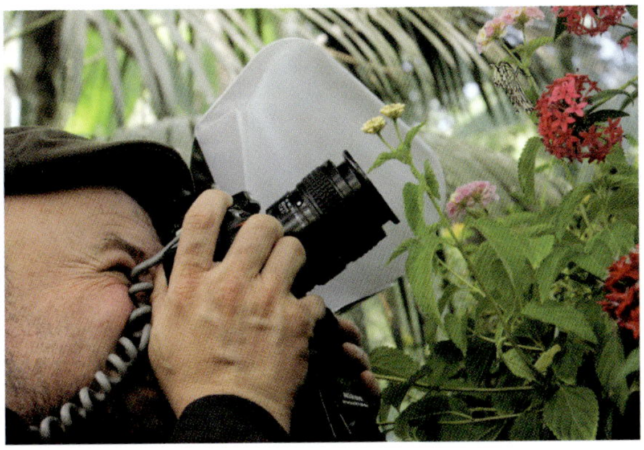

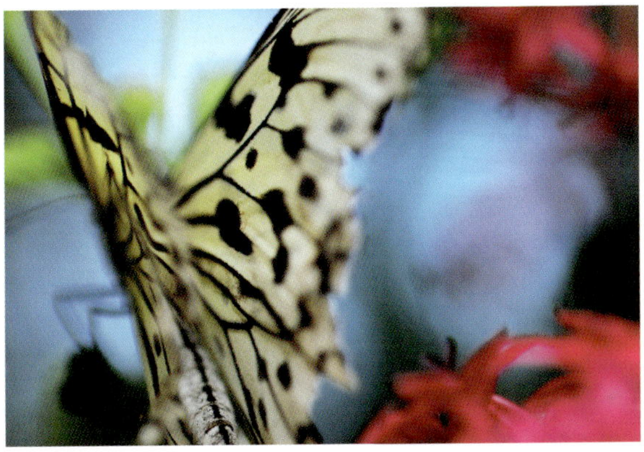

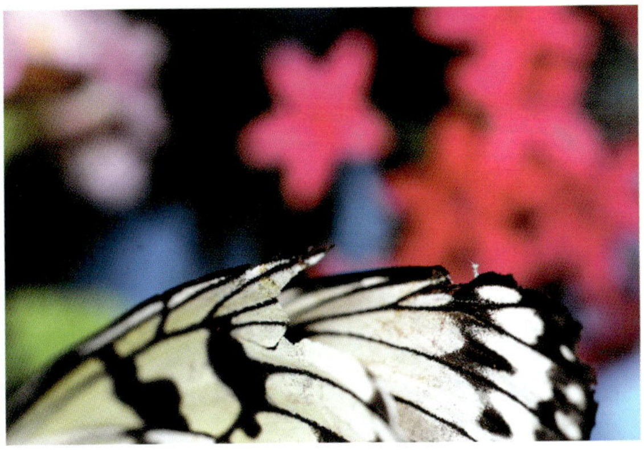

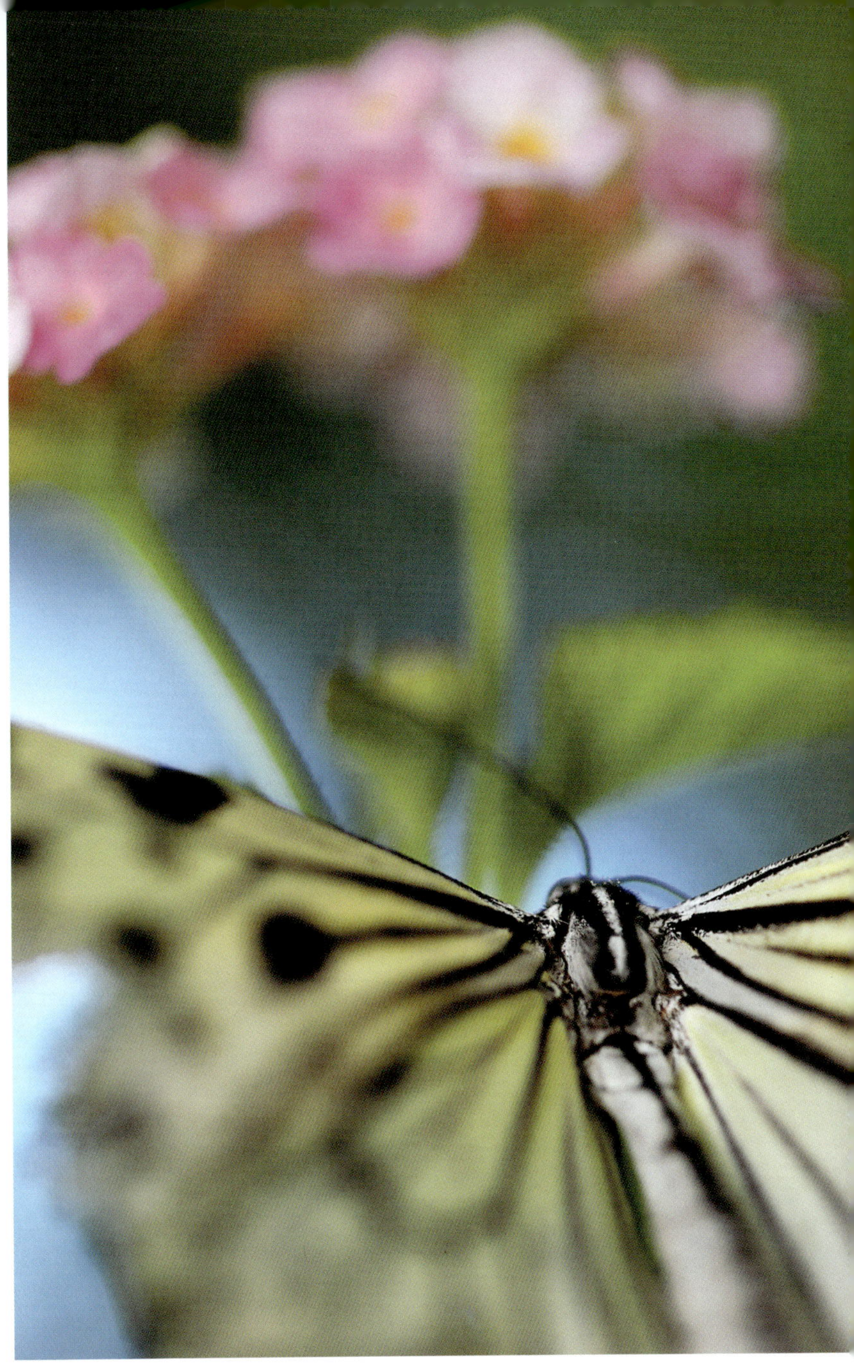

All of the images seen here were shot within moments of each other. Because of the photographer's experience, settings could be changed, lighting could be adjusted, and depth of field determined in the blink of an eye. He knew what he wanted and had done it all before with other subjects, so he could move quickly and accurately—and be confident in his results. Don't discount the value of experience.

The secret to capturing amazing close-up or macro images of butterflies is allowing them to act and react naturally. To be successful, you need to learn to anticipate these creatures' movements—not chase them around with expensive gear.

The tools required for butterfly photography are pretty simple and should look familiar by now: an off-camera flash, a large light modifier, a camera, and a lens. The techniques and reasons for using them, as you've learned, are as personal as individual expression. What proves difficult for most, though, is the speed at which all of these must come together when shooting insects.

When photographing insects, the most important part of the equation will be your reaction time—there is no doubt about it. You have to be fast,

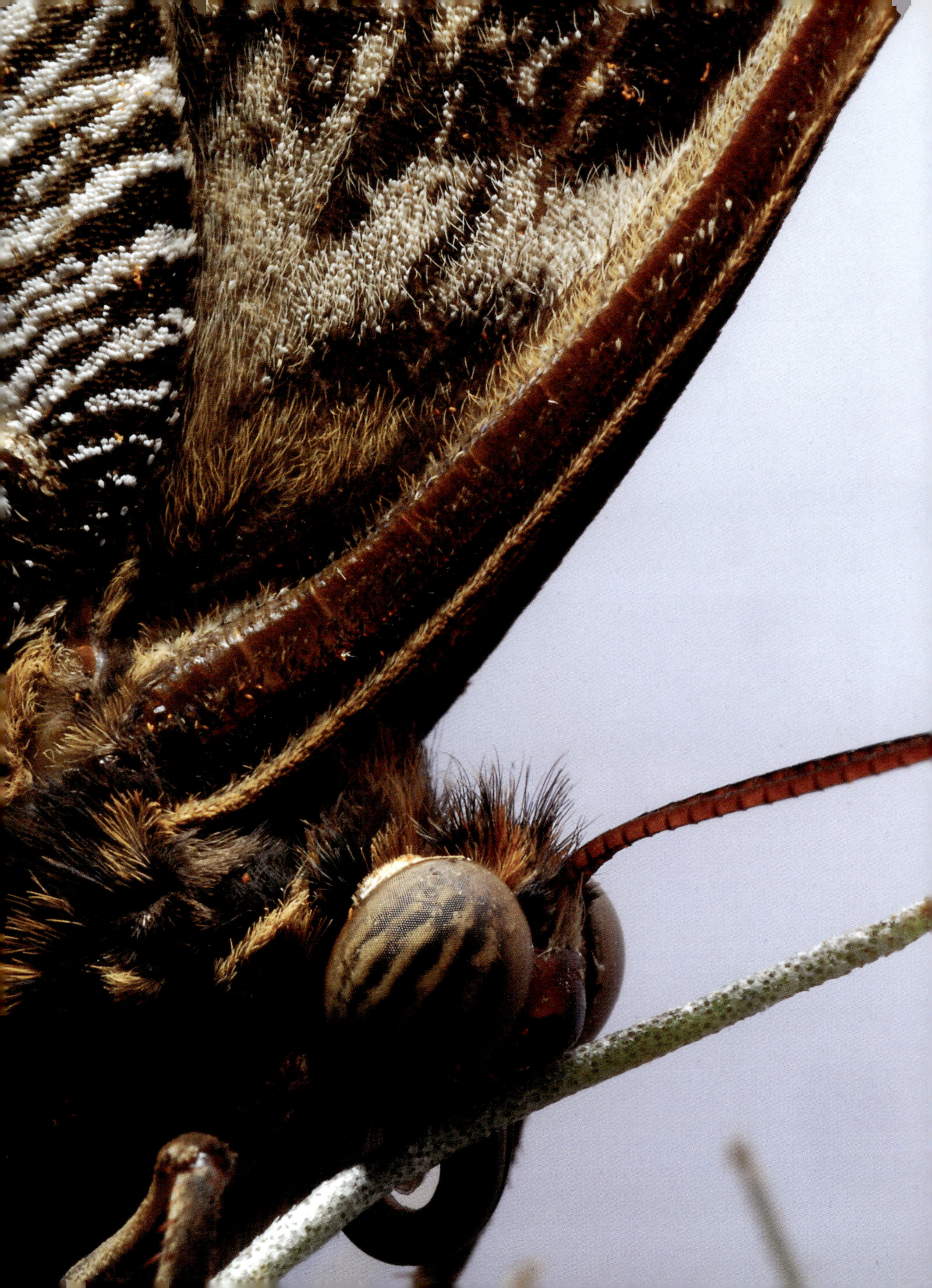

**Facing page**—In this image, a very small aperture helped ensure our depth of field, while the flash modification tool provided the background. **Below**—Working in an area where there are hundreds of models raises the odds in your favor.

confident, and focused. A fair amount of practice in your backyard should get you ready. The goal is to blend in with the scenery, to become one with what's around you. You don't need to go as far as to camouflage yourself, just move slowly and with purpose. Get to a point where the butterfly (or other insect) simply accepts you and your equipment as part of its world. If you go into this with an aggressive attitude, you will lose—that's a promise. When it comes to photographing insects, the secret lies inside the artist; it has nothing to do with what gear he uses and everything to do with how much time he's spent using it.

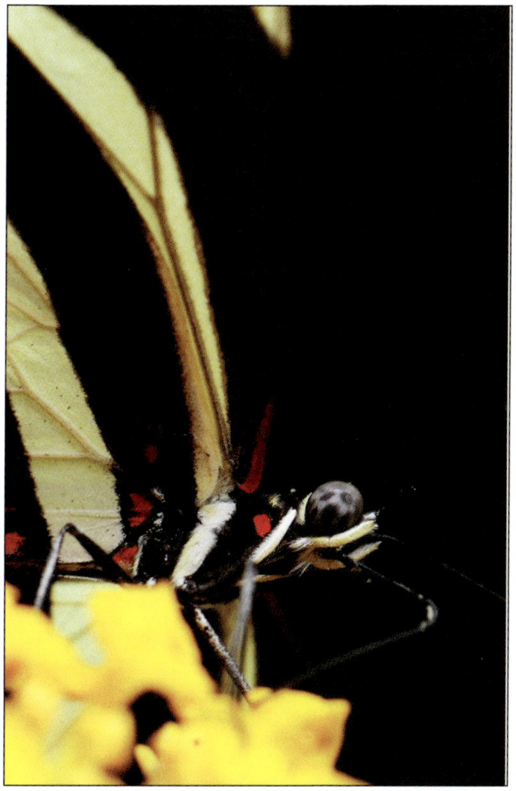

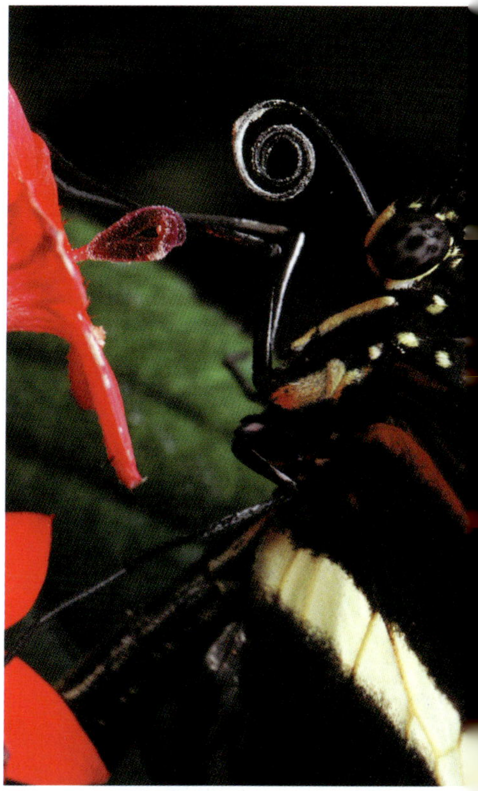

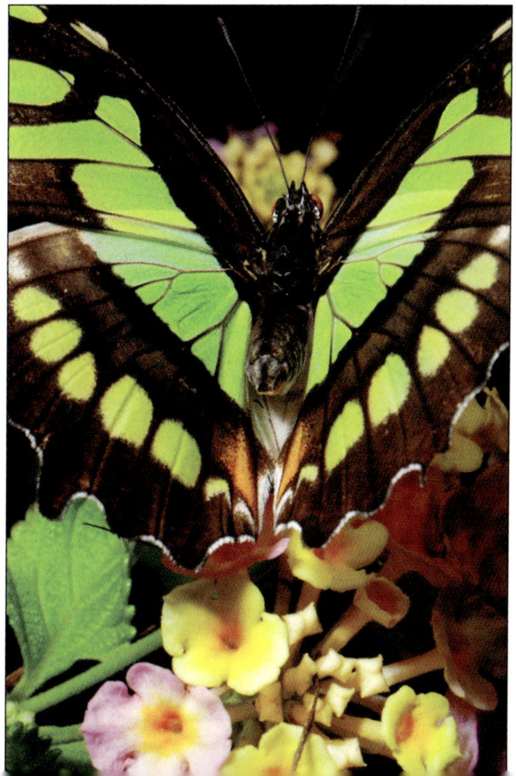

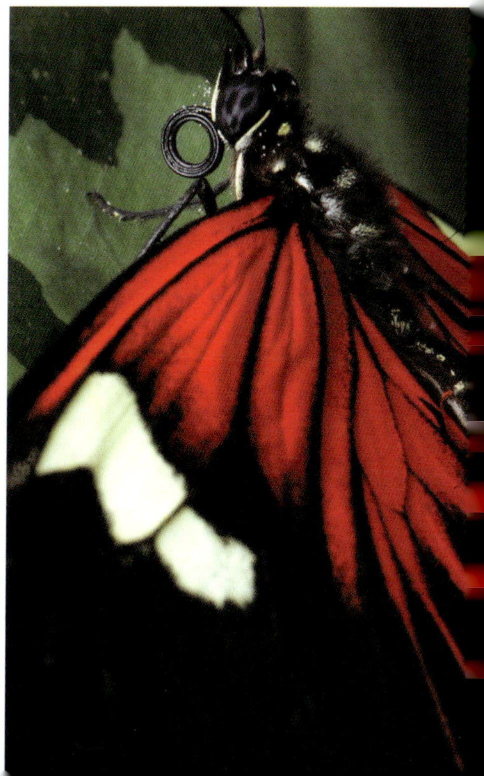

In addition to getting ample practice, we recommend going somewhere where there are plenty of models. Chasing a solitary butterfly in a field of flowers is quite difficult—if not impossible. However, if you are in a field where there are hundreds of models, the odds raise quite a bit in your favor. You may also want to take advantage of local garden clubs, zoos, or parks. Sometimes, these centers offer a butterfly day, weekend, or month when they bring in hundreds of the insects. These trips can make for a fascinating journey and the photographic lessons learned will stay with you for a lifetime.

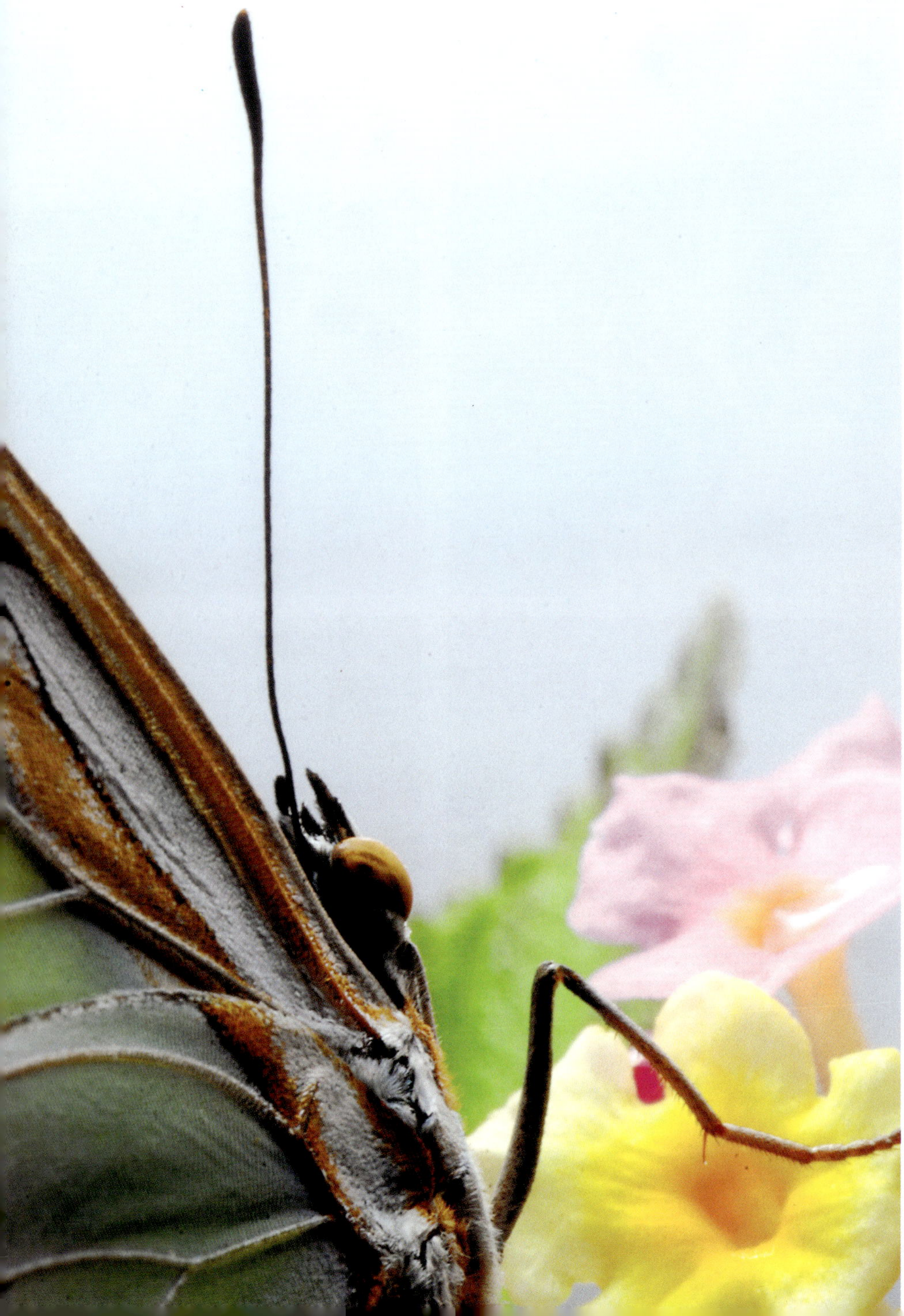

Yes, they move quickly—but butterflies do not spend every second doing that. If you can react quickly, you will have chances to capture anything you can imagine while they sit still. Draw upon your artistic side and play with blur, or lock up the details by stretching out the depth of field throughout the entire image. It's your choice—and it's an important one.

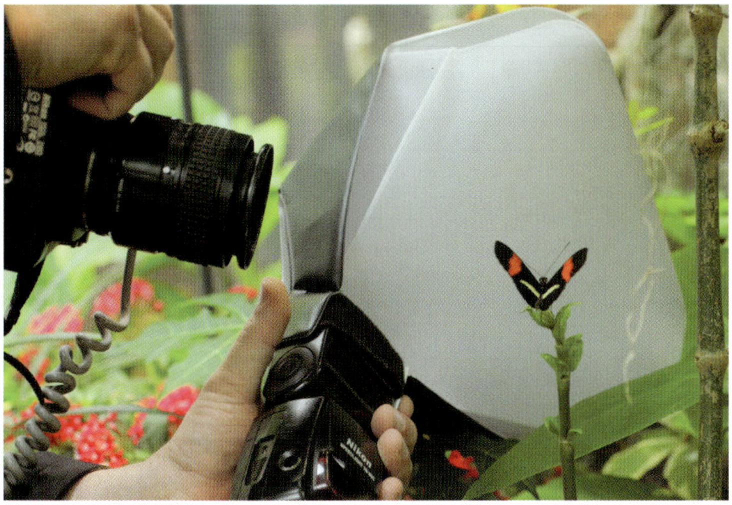

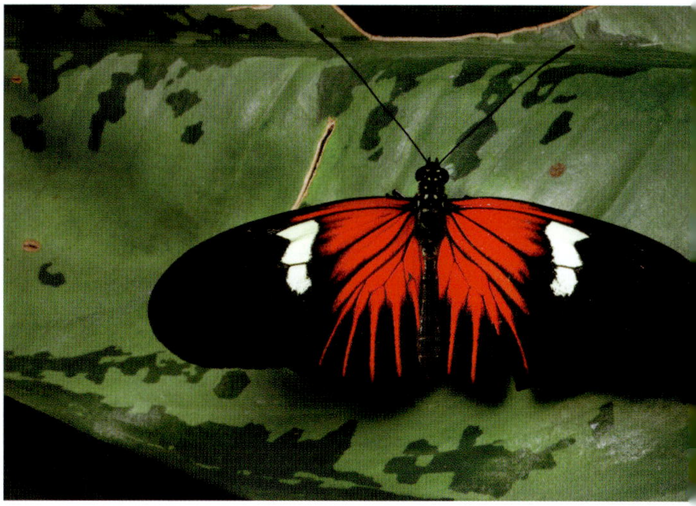

It's not right to injure a creature just because you want to take a photo of it. If you feel compelled to corral, harm, stun, or shock your models, maybe you're not ready to photograph them. Instead of looking for shortcuts to make it easier on yourself, why not simply learn how to make things work? Why not learn what your camera affords, practice, build your skill level—and *then* create the image. Trust us—with that kind of experience, there is no need to ever harm your subjects.

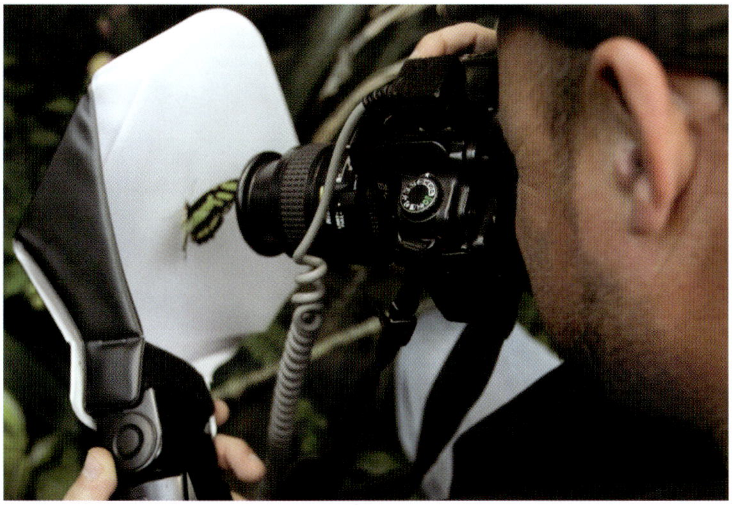

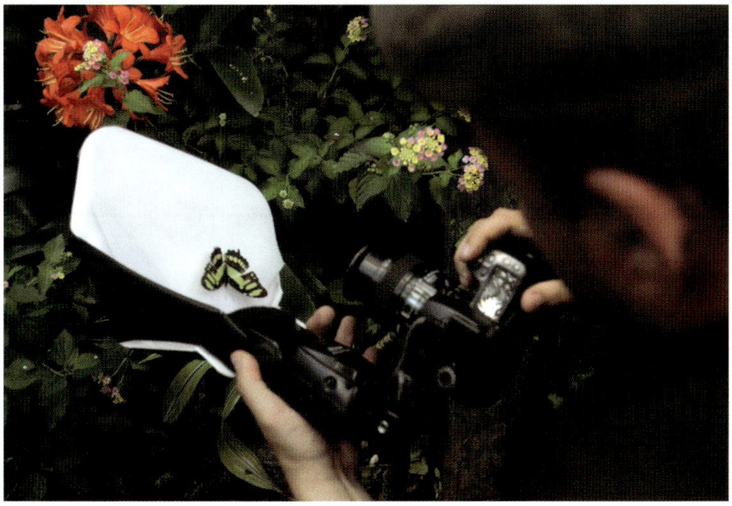

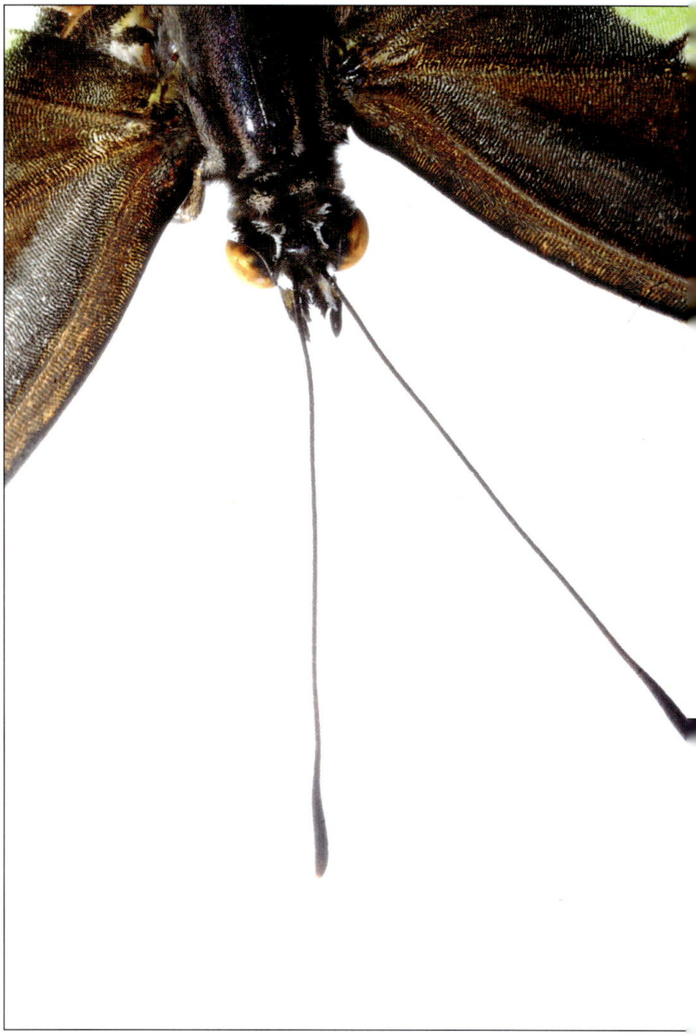

Over the last few years, we've noticed a disturbing trend spreading through the close-up/macro community—that of using "kill jars" and treating animals like toys. There is no need for this barbaric behavior. Stop looking for shortcuts and learn your craft. As these images prove, with some patience and understanding your models will often come to you.

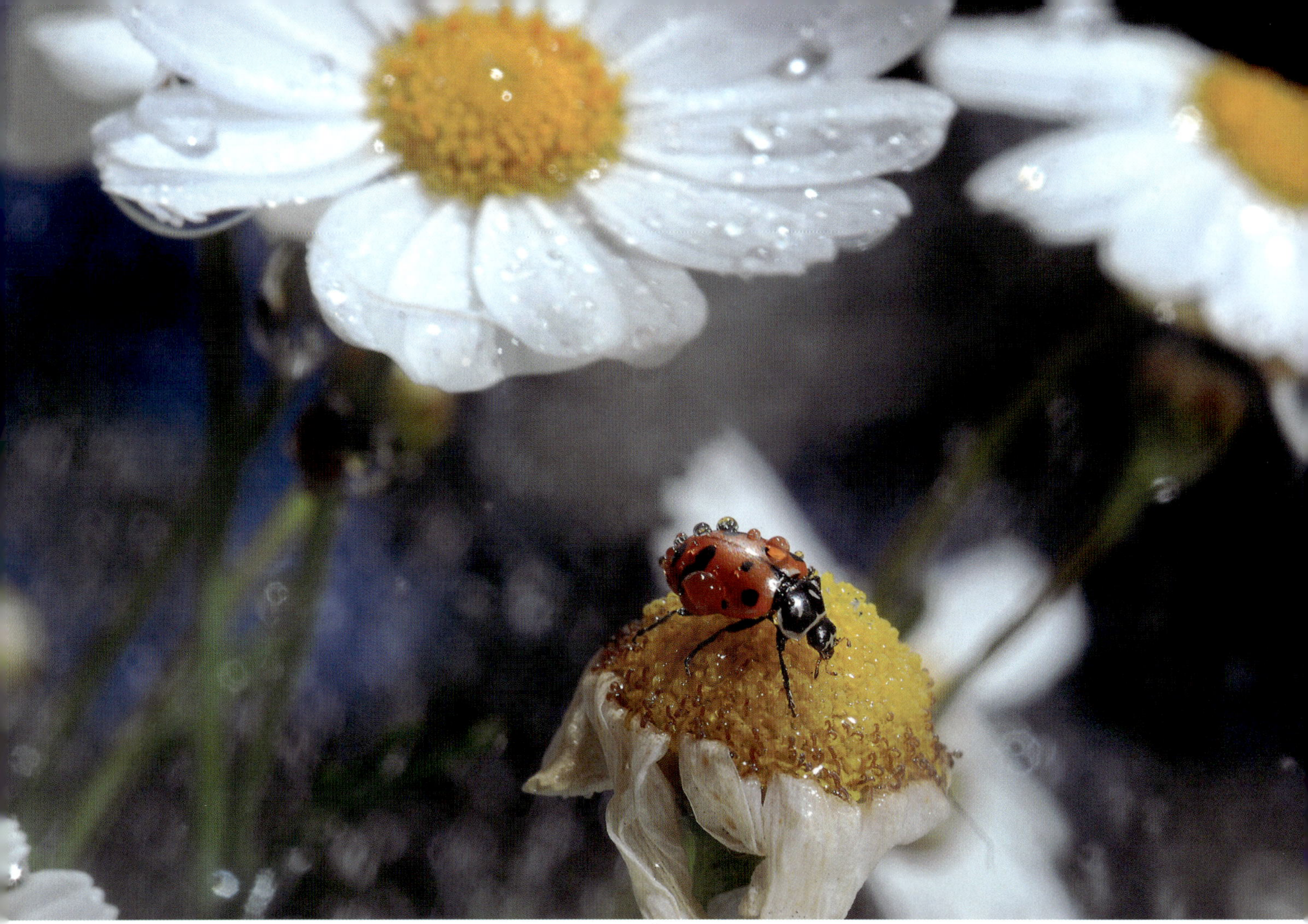

A small container of ladybugs (more than 1,500) can be purchased at your local gardening center or even online—usually for less than $15.

**The Ladybug Dilemma.** Colorful, patient, and focused on the job at hand, ladybugs make great subjects for the macro and close-up photographer. When hunting, they are focused like you wouldn't believe—and quite oblivious to your shooting technique.

The problem, of course, is finding them. Generally, the ladybug (or ladybird) is considered a useful insect, as its diet consists mainly of plant-destroying aphids and scale insects (though there are some ladybugs that are herbivores as well). They are prevalent in the early spring, when their dormancy period ends. They are voracious beetles, constantly on the move looking for food, so if you find a flower-filled hill, you might just find ladybugs. We've found them mostly near dandelions, geraniums, and cosmos—although they certainly aren't restricted to any particular plant type.

In the last few years, however, we have noticed fewer and fewer ladybug patches around our home. Old tried-and-true photography locations just don't work any longer. It seems the beetles in our area have migrated to greener (or more brightly colored) pastures. To help, we've taken a bold step: we've brought the ladybugs to us. A small container of ladybugs (more than 1,500) can be purchased at your local gardening center or even online—usually for less than $15. This not only provides you with plenty of willing models to photograph, but also helps your environment—especially if you are a gardener or have plants you want to protect. (*Tip:* If you water the plants down before the release, we find the ladybugs stick around longer.)

Ladybugs can also live for several years and lay many eggs. If your surrounding area is hospitable to them, you may just be setting the stage for many years of wonderful shooting!

Photographing recently released insects means creating a conducive environment for both the ladybugs and you. The last thing you want is for them to take off the instant you open the container. We set up a large table in the backyard, purchase several different types of plants, then slowly release the insects, shooting as we go along.

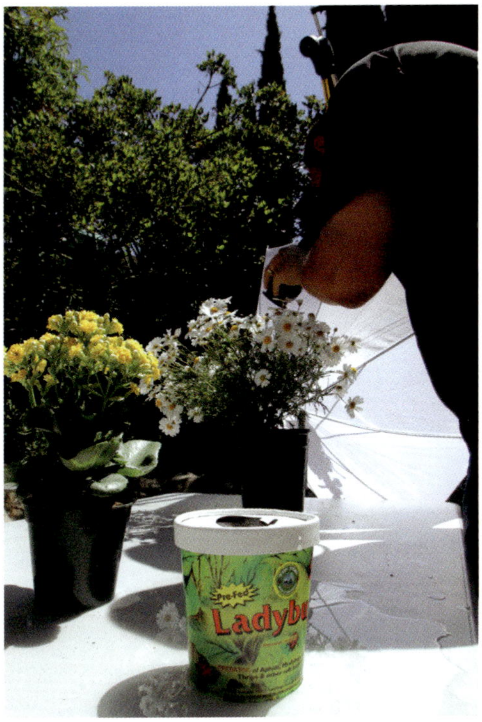

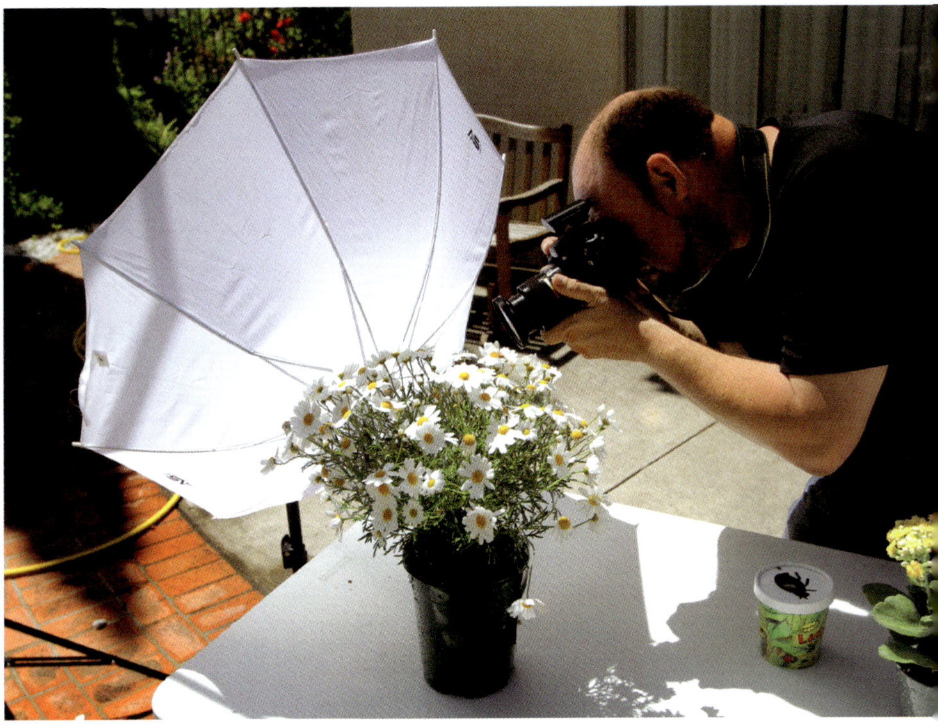

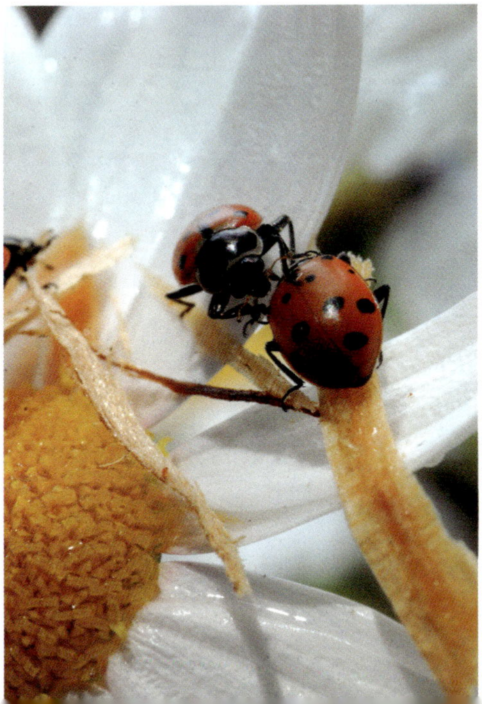

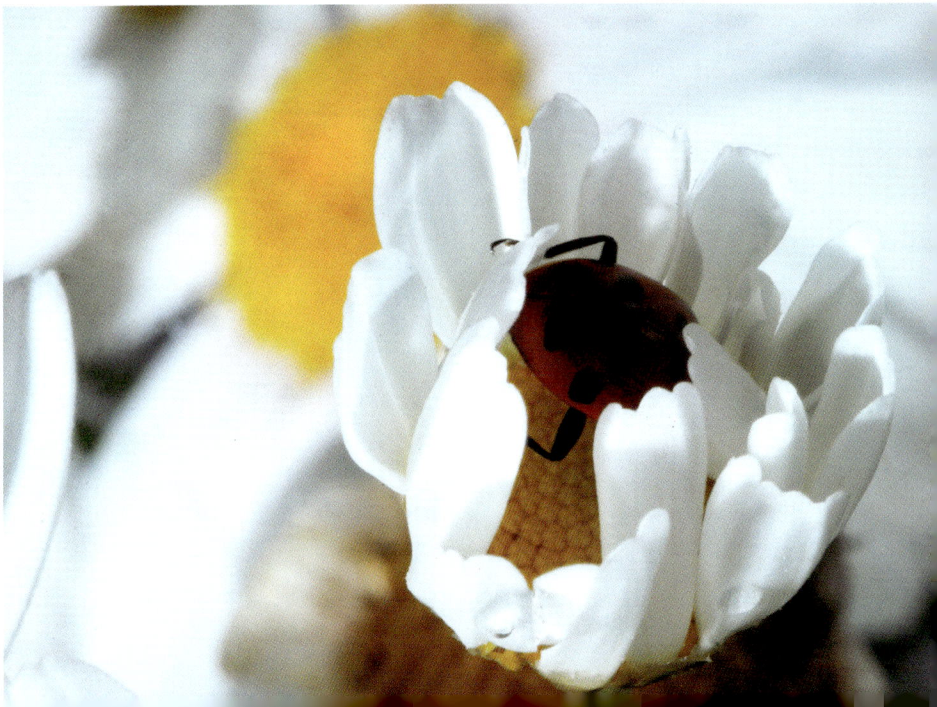

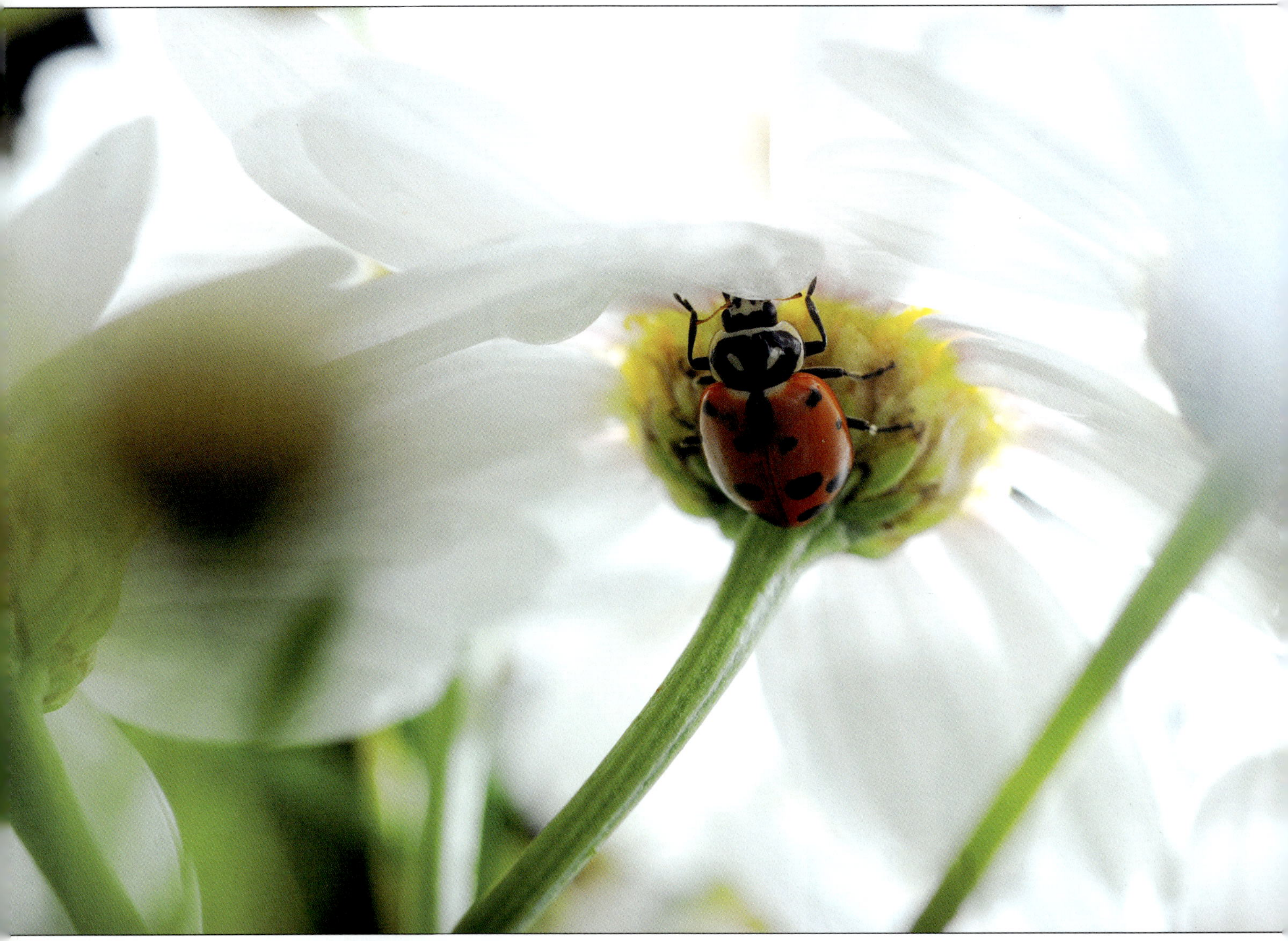

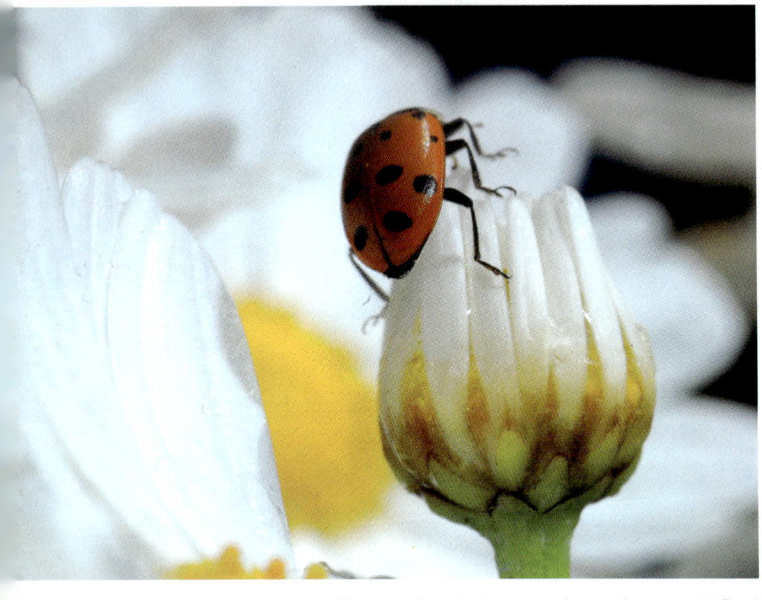

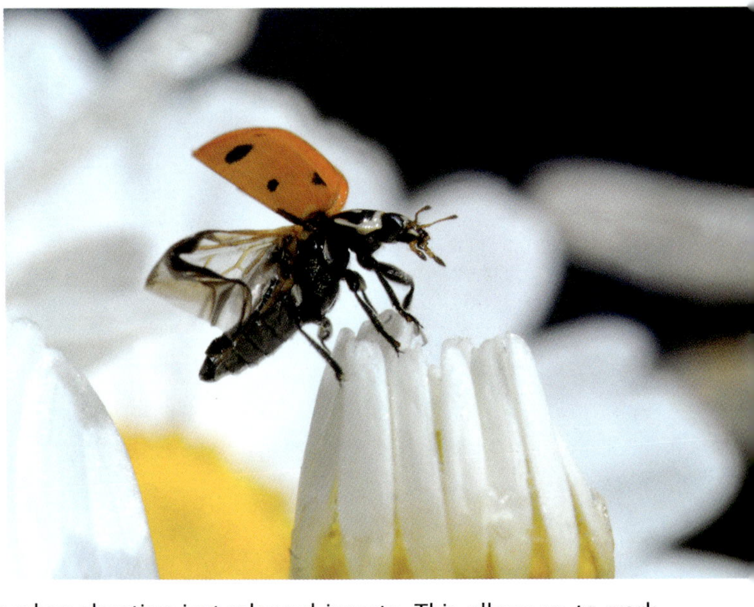

**Top**—We usually employ light stands and several flashes when shooting just-released insects. This allows us to work freely, moving around our subjects and shooting from locations that would just be impossible in the wild. **Bottom left and right**—Think of the whole setup as an outdoor studio in which you can employ any trick, lighting setup, or technique you wish. Since you've got complete control over the environment and your models love the freedom, why not take advantage of it? Why not pull out all the stops?

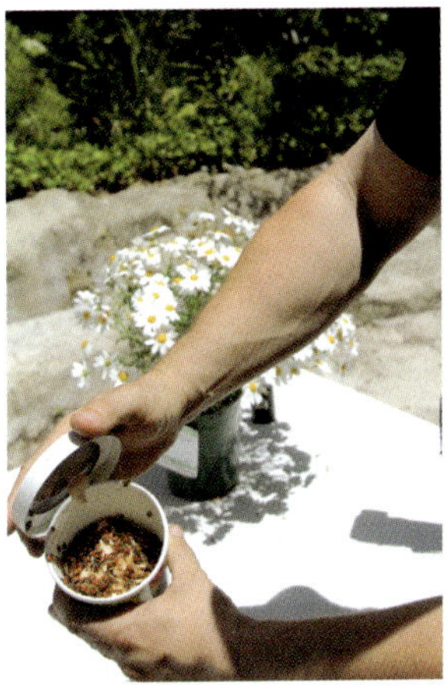

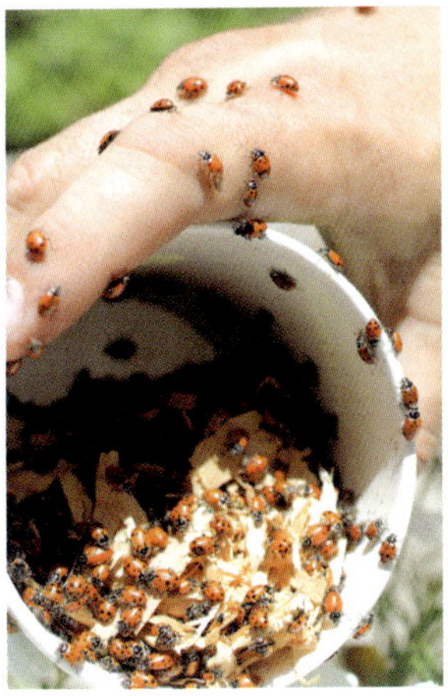

**Above**—We release our ladybugs in stages, gently spilling one small group at a time out onto our flowers. Sure, many immediately fly away—you would too if you'd been trapped in a box!—but just as many stick around. If you water the plants down first, before the release, we find they stick around for quite a long time. **Right**—We sometimes use a hose mounted to a light stand to simulate a gentle rain. We mist the plants and insects, offering up a drizzle no more aggressive than a slight rain. Then, we turn off the water and begin shooting once again—this time paying attention to the glare and adjusting our polarizers if need be. The ladybugs seem to love this shower, as most stay for repeated shoots.

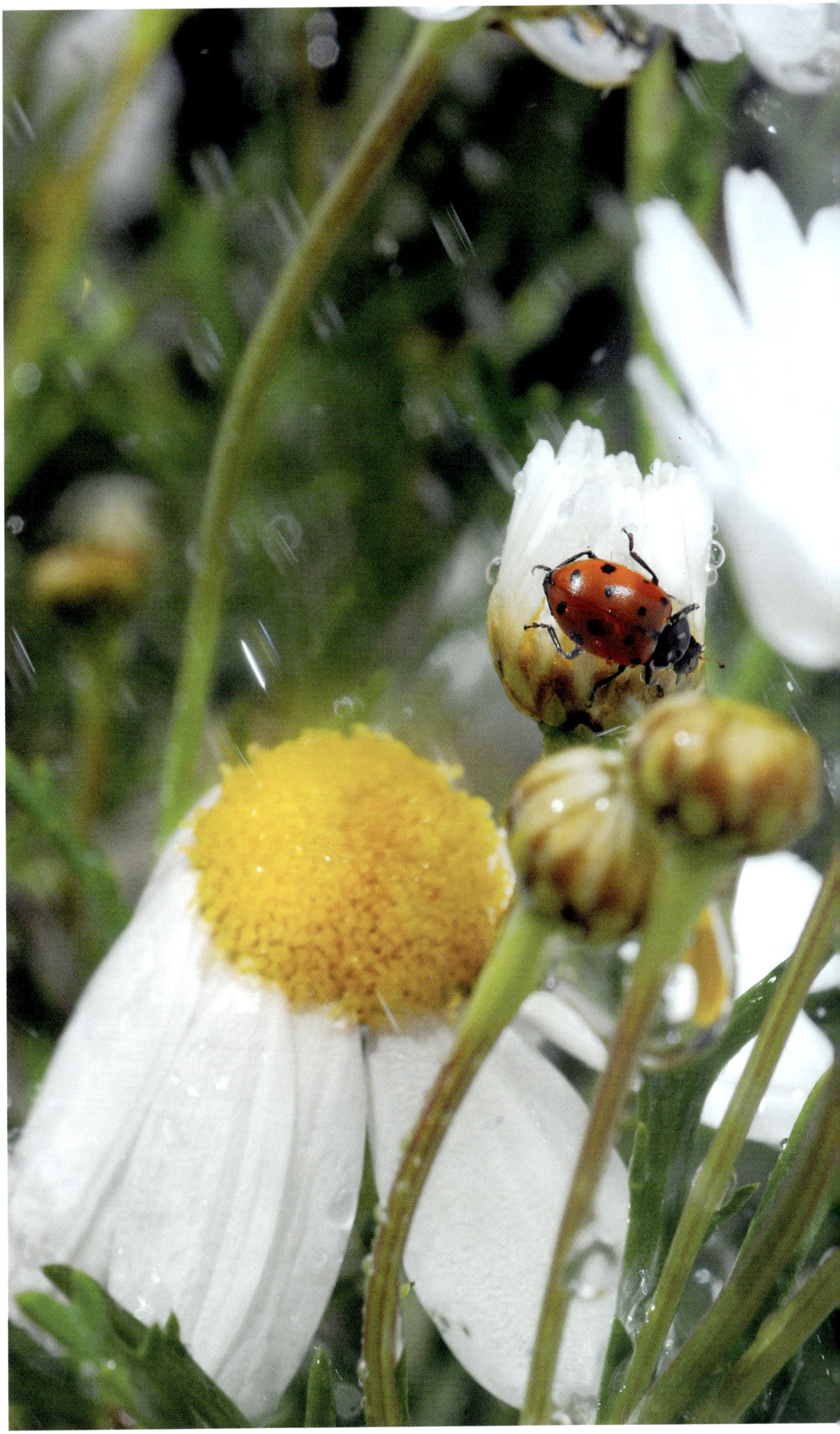

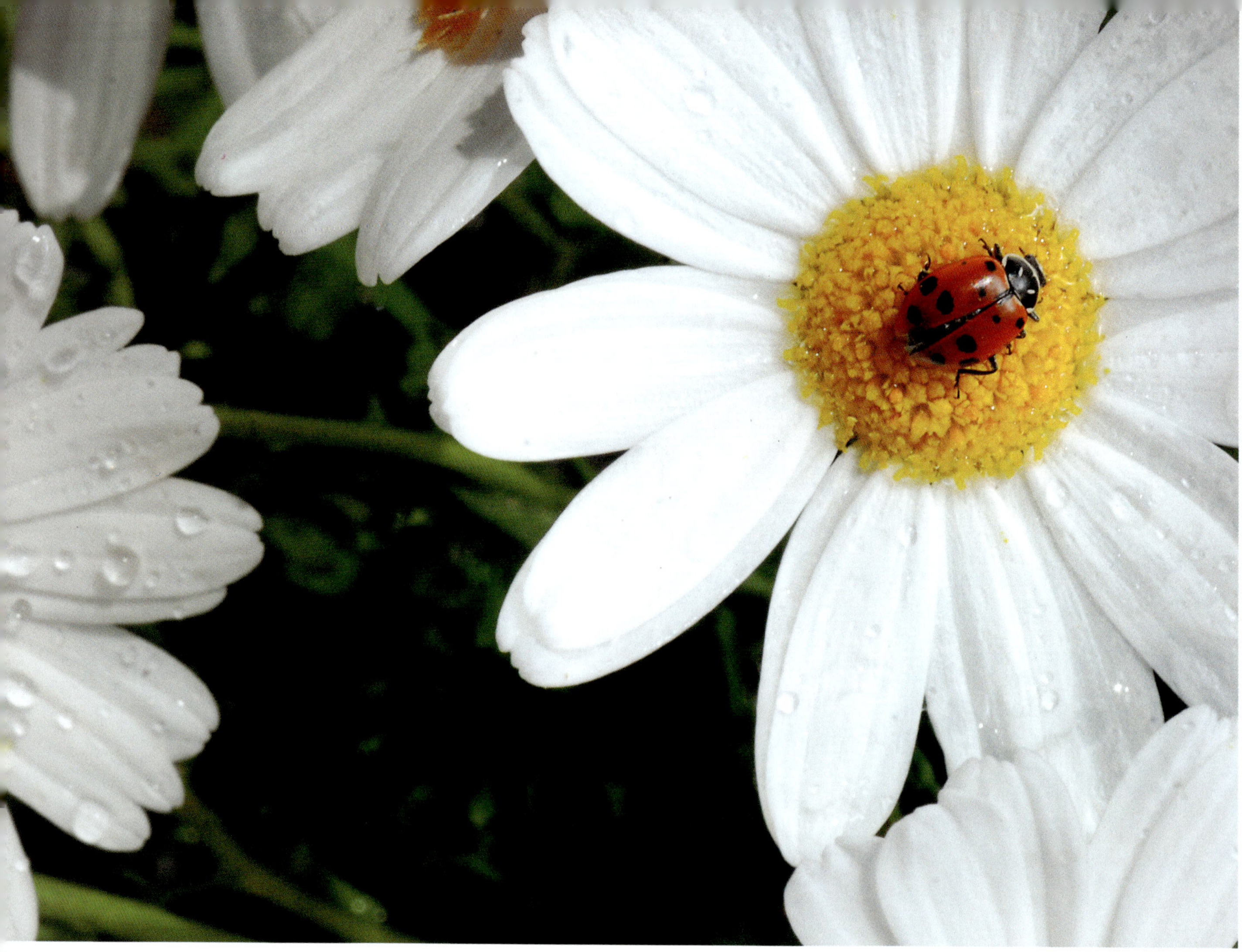

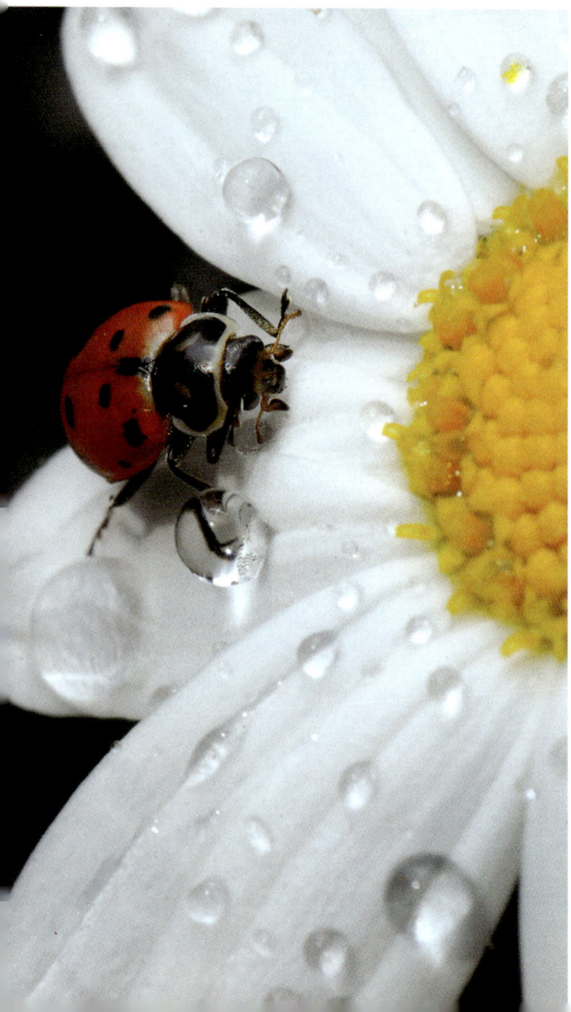

**Above**—Even though this image was shot in full daylight under the most perfect conditions, we still employed several off-camera flashes, producing the needed depth of field. **Left**—Releasing your own ladybugs can make for some rather dramatic images and will allow you plenty of practice time.

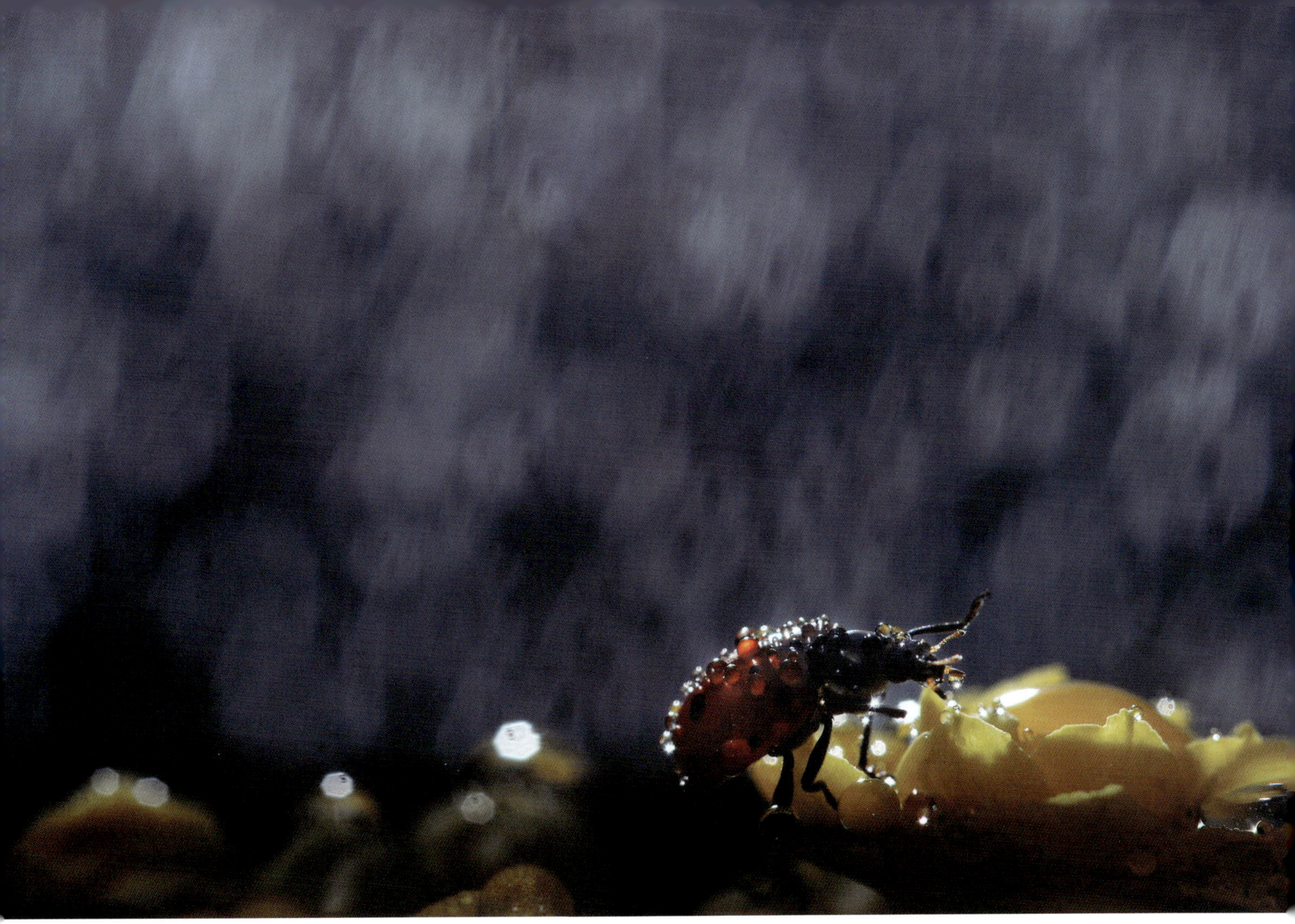

Several flashes were needed to not only illuminate the ladybugs but also to light to our “rainy” background and to ensure the perfect depth of field. A very small aperture (f/29) was used. Higher-than-usual contrast and saturation settings were also chosen, based solely on how the artist felt about his subjects. Close-up and macro photography is quite a personal journey. Isn’t it time your images showed that?

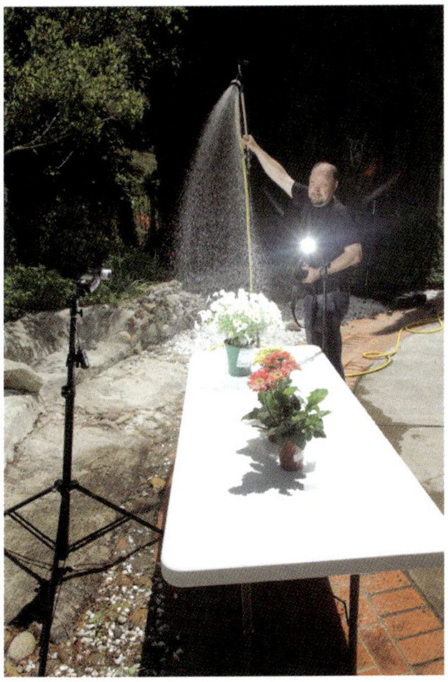

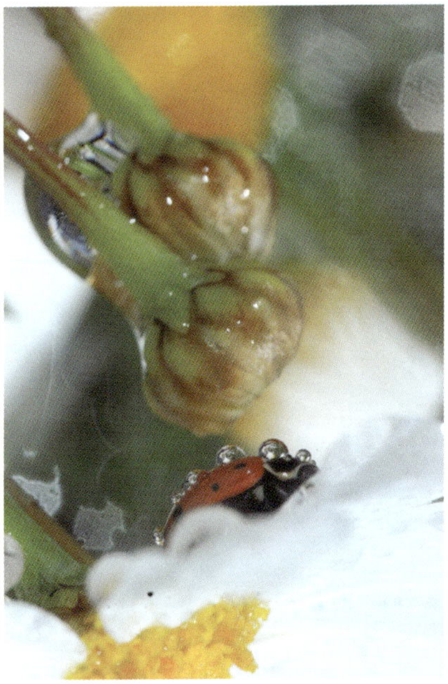

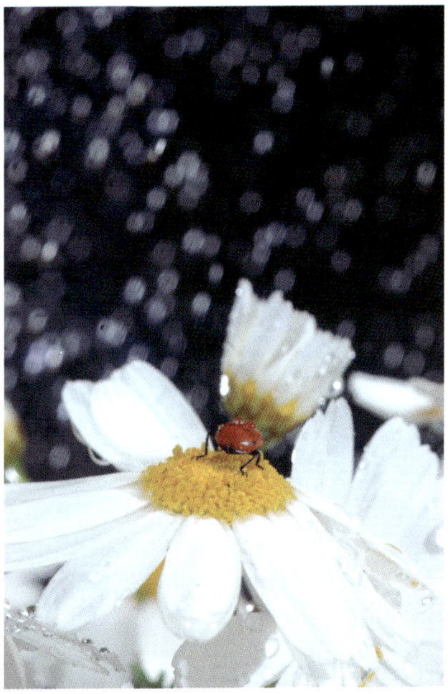

The image on the left shows a typical outdoor studio, with several flashes, several plants, and even a water hose. The total control offered by a setup such as this can make your journey into macro and close-up art an enjoyable, exciting, and rewarding experience.

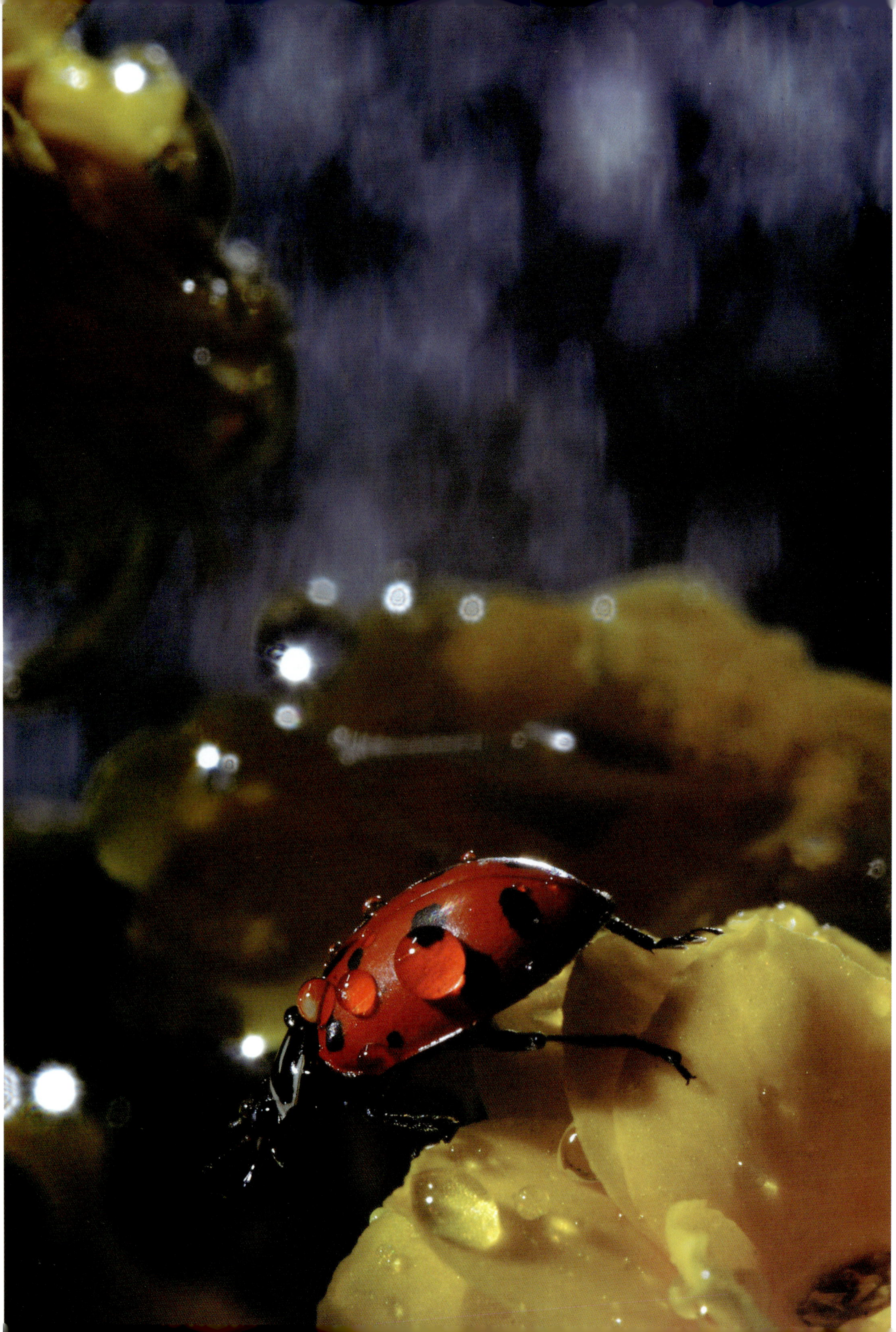

# 7. ARTISTRY

Now that you've got the basics, don't fall prey to the hype or the biases. Think for yourself and be the artist you know you can be!

## FREEING THE MACRO ARTIST WITHIN

You are playing in a world uncharted—one that doesn't require a certain look to be deemed "correct." Free your imagination to explore, unhindered by preconceptions. The lines, shapes, colors, and tones found in your backyard can truly only be found in *your* backyard—no one has shot them before and it's okay to make them look however you like.

This is why we, as artists and instructors, love macro and close-up photography so much. You can shoot something totally crazy, make it look however you like, and people will still be fascinated by it—even though it may break every compositional, mechanical, and sociological "rule" there is. You can keep the whole thing out of focus, you can keep your subject in a shadow. You can light your background instead of your subject. You can increase the amount of grain (or digital noise) in your image.

**Facing page**—Color, contrast, saturation, depth of field, shutter speed, angle of view, and our own memories and expectations can often be combined (in-camera) in ways natural vision just can't afford. When out in the world (no matter where), think about these options, think about what could be . . . not just what is. There is magic out there . . . and believe me when I tell you that it's not in your camera bag. Be an artist, create a memory. There are too many photographers in the world taking pictures of things. Be different, be unique, be in focus. **Right**—Many photographers believe that to achieve a "correct" macro image, a huge depth of field is needed. That's just not true. Blur is a powerful tool, as illustrated in this image. We know this is a flower; it does not have to be in crisp focus for that recognition to happen, nor does it have to be in the center of the frame to be meaningfully captured. Its ambiguous appearance only adds to the graphic puzzle laid out to the viewer. Mechanically, it still took depth-of-field control and an off-camera flash to create the image. Artistically, it required that the photographer give up a few of society's biases and create something he wanted—not what everyone else expected.

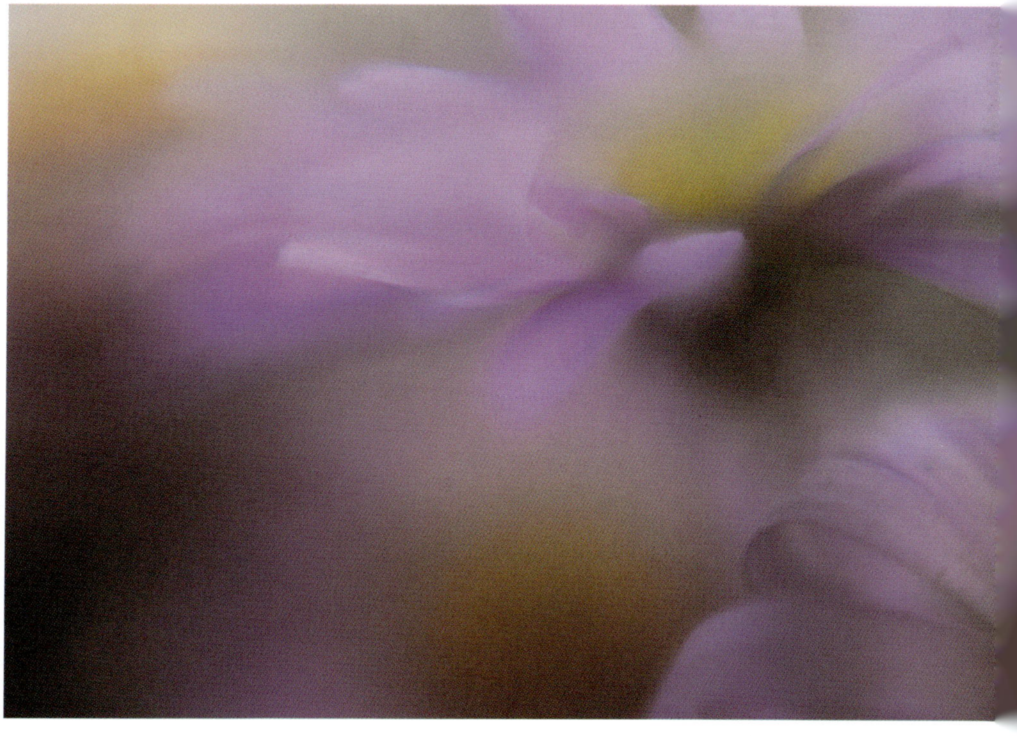

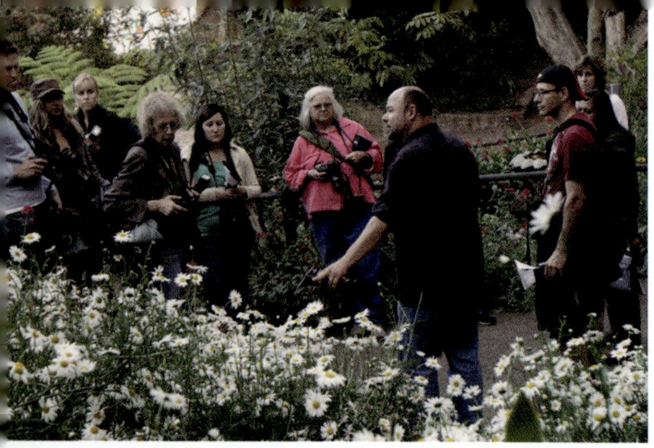

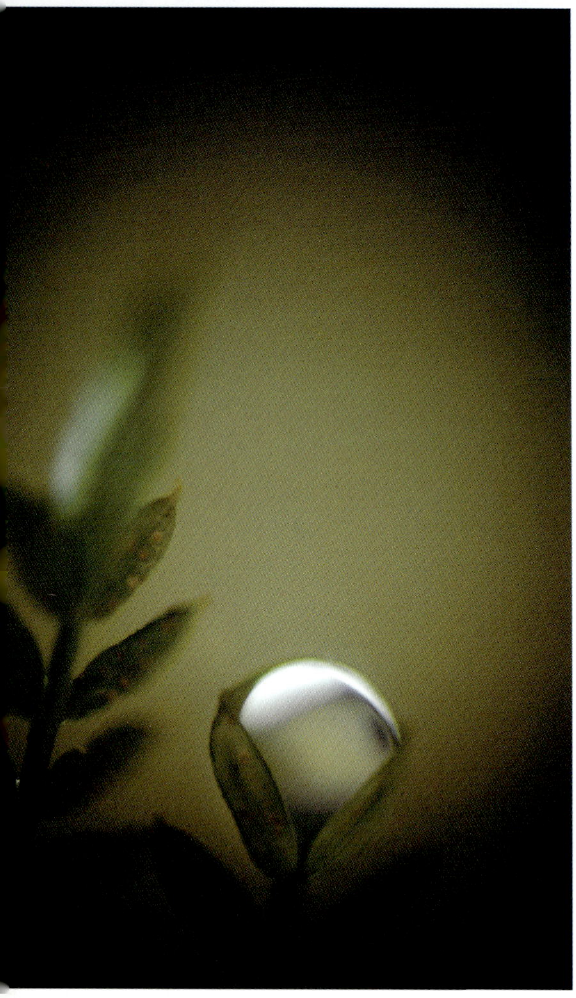

**Top**—Creating amazing macro images with off-camera flash means leaving the world of "normal" behind. It means thinking about how something makes you feel and sharing that with an audience. It means striving for excellence within yourself and being okay with occasional failures. Here, a group of photographers gather to test their powers of observation, visualization, and mechanical skills as they create images that are outside of society's "box." **Bottom**—Even though a shallow depth of field can be achieved without a flash, one was used in this photo to illuminate the background.

You can use chromatic and spacial aberrations—and no one cares. If the image moves them, they love it. They don't react because they think they have to. They don't compare it to other images (since there aren't any). They just feel. The very rhythm of the message sings, the colors engulf, and the shapes entrance. It's real expressionism—it's real art.

This, in and of itself, is quite novel. Too often, photographers measure the quality of their own images by how they look when compared to someone else's—not by asking whether or not the image in question expresses how they felt. This might be an acceptable strategy for the masses, but not for an artist. What you produce *should* be different—not something that begs comparison to seven million other photographs. Your vision and how you present it should be a true reflection of who you are as an artist.

Now, whether or not *you* like what you see in your photographs is something you're going to have to deal with. If you want to improve that look, think more carefully about what you're doing. Have a firm idea of what you want to say before you take that picture. If it helps, remember that you are not just shooting pretty pictures of little things—you are making a statement about who you are as an artist. You are trying to share with others how something makes you feel.

## BREAKING THE BIASES

You can start exploring this fanciful and artful world by allowing some of that blur back into your photos. Many people start their odyssey through macro and close-up photography complaining about the excessive amount of blur. Then, when they learn to incorporate a flash and eliminate this blur, they never bring it back. Blur is an amazing tool; it can (and should) be used often. Sure, you can choose an aperture to dial in your depth of field, but who says it has to be deep? This is *your* choice, and if your image really does just need color and tones to make it sing, why not just shoot that? Why does it all have to be in focus? Who said that's how it's supposed to be? No one did. So don't!

Make up your own mind. What was it that made you stop and point your camera at that flower, twig, or insect? Was it the object? Or was it the fact that it affected you in some way? Was it the colors, the lines, the shapes? Once you've got that figured out, adjust your in-camera options (white balance, contrast, saturation, sharpness, and hue) to match your

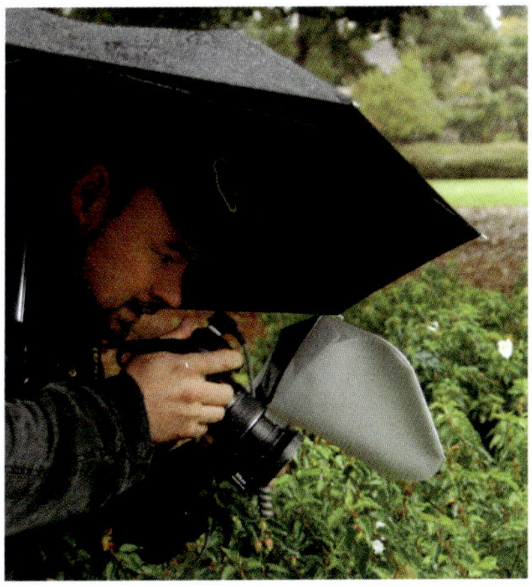

Your images should be yours and do not need to reflect how the scene "actually" looked before you started creating the image. Remember: it's not about capturing how something looks, it's about sharing with others how it made you feel.

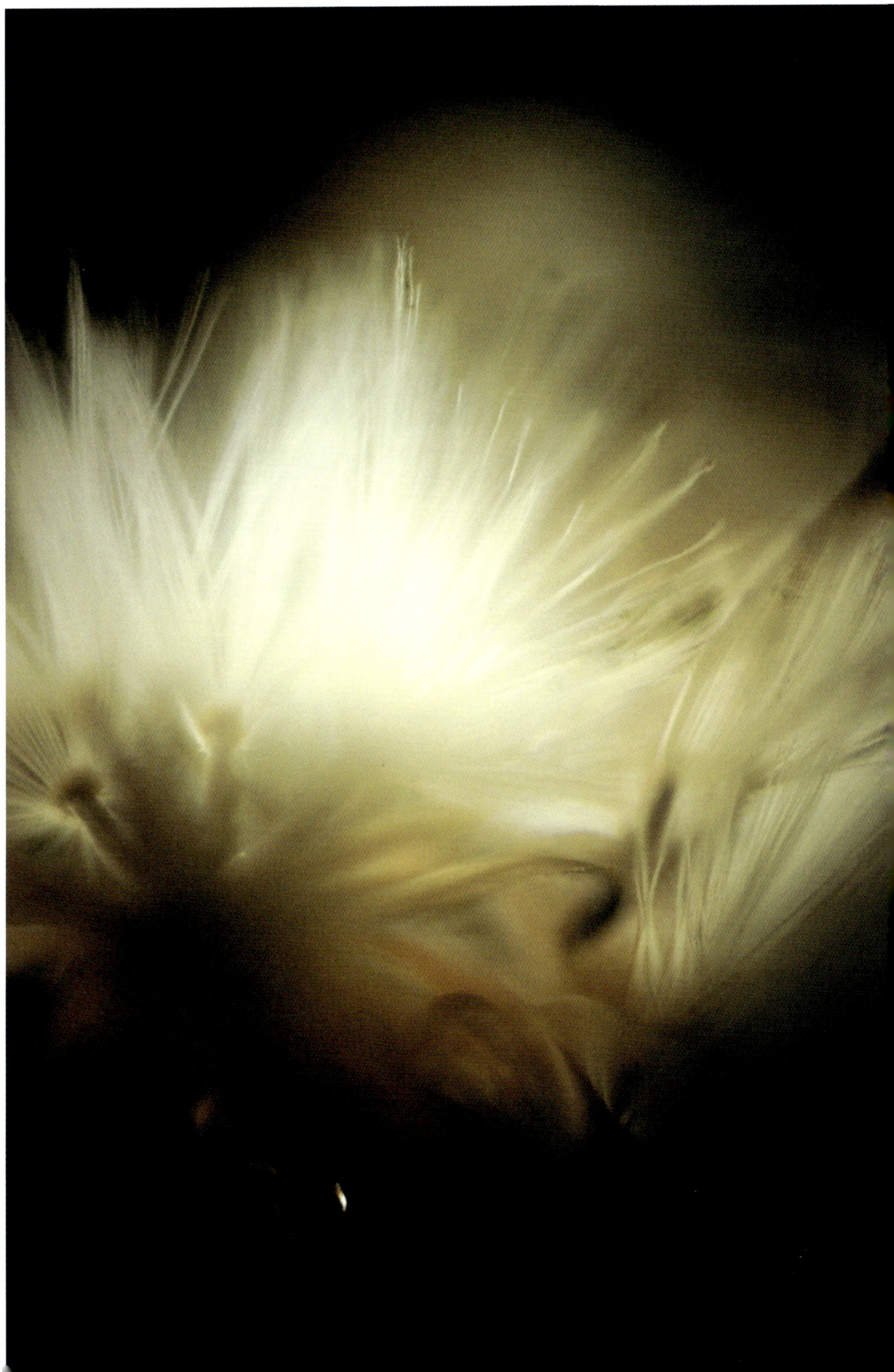

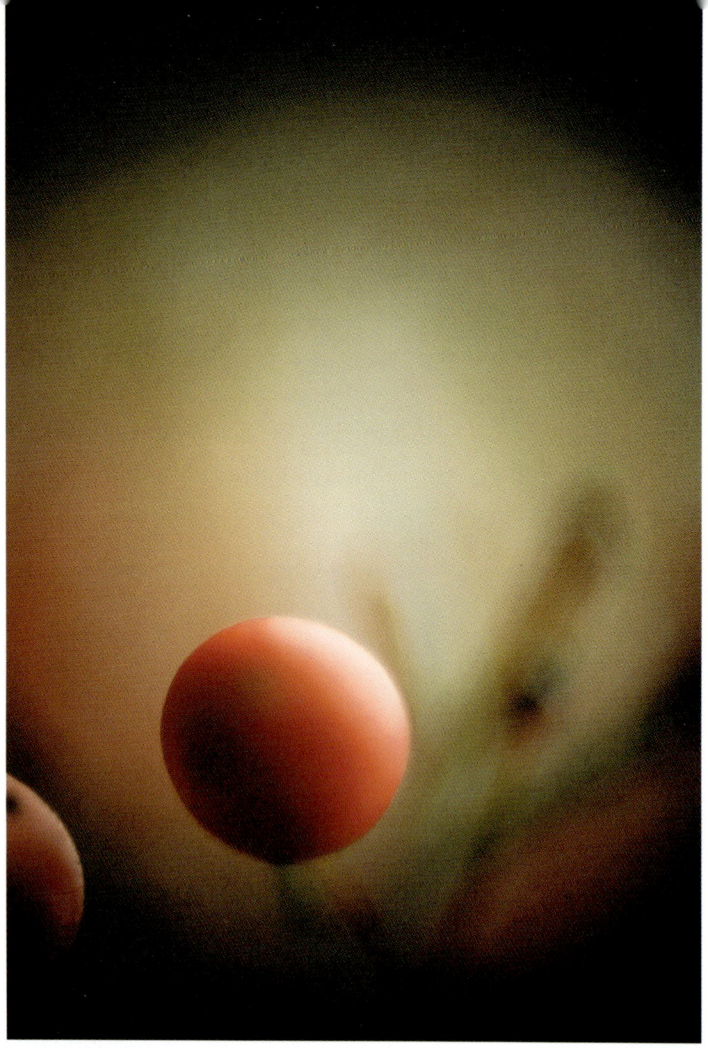
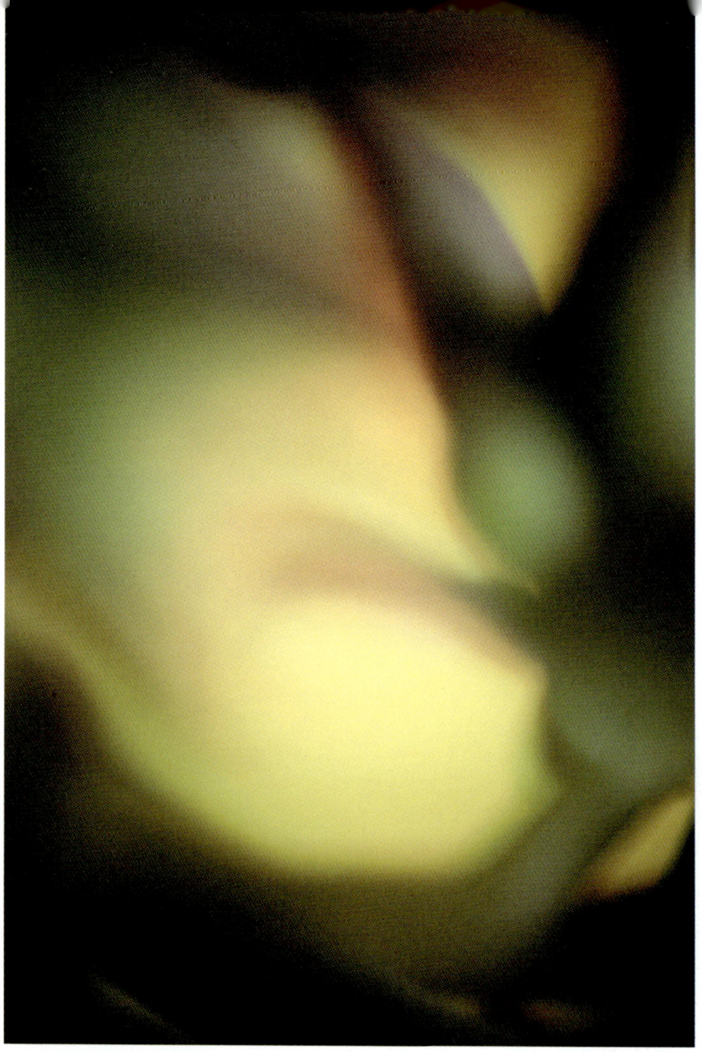
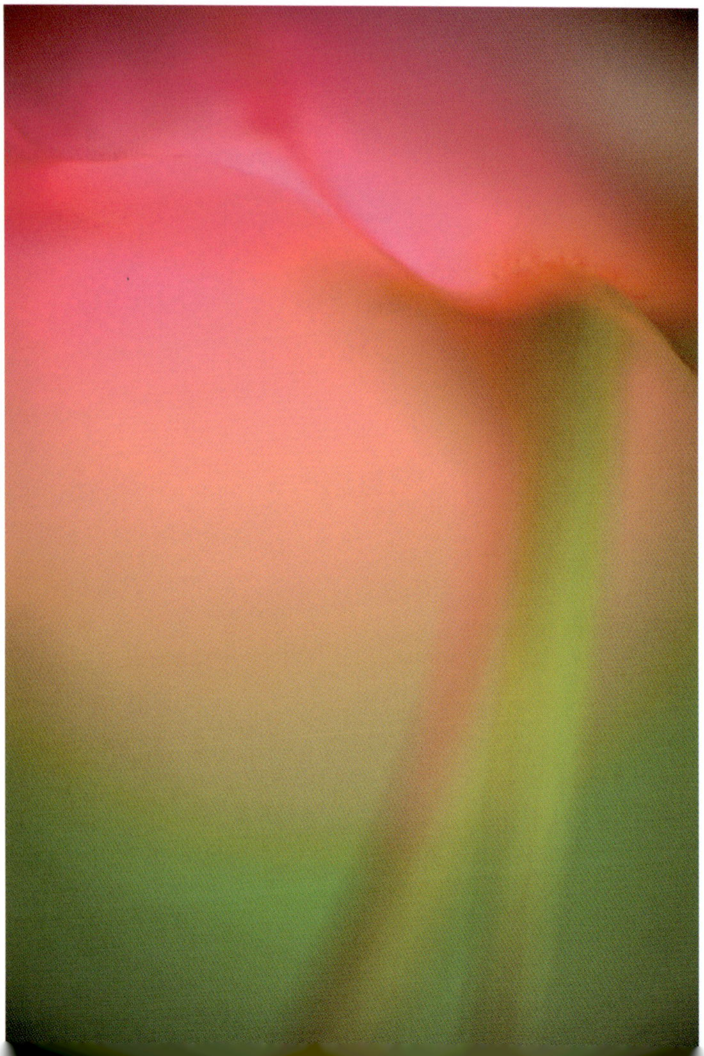
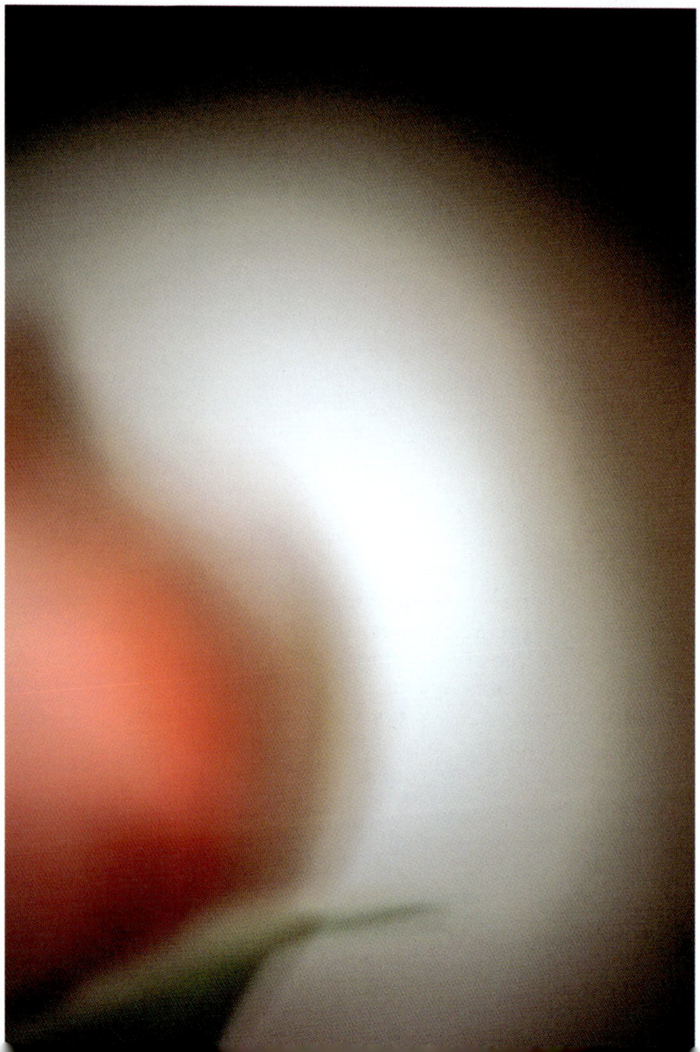

vision. It's now when these feelings are most powerful—not later, when you're sitting behind a computer. Next, seriously choose that depth of field for a reason. Dial in an aperture setting that truly allows your feelings to come forth. What you may discover is that sometimes you really don't need everything in focus. Sometimes, a blurry image actually says more than one that is in focus. Then just adjust your shutter and ISO to make your background perfect and add light with your flash (or flashes) to whatever needs it. (Don't make this too complicated—you're just adding light, after all.)

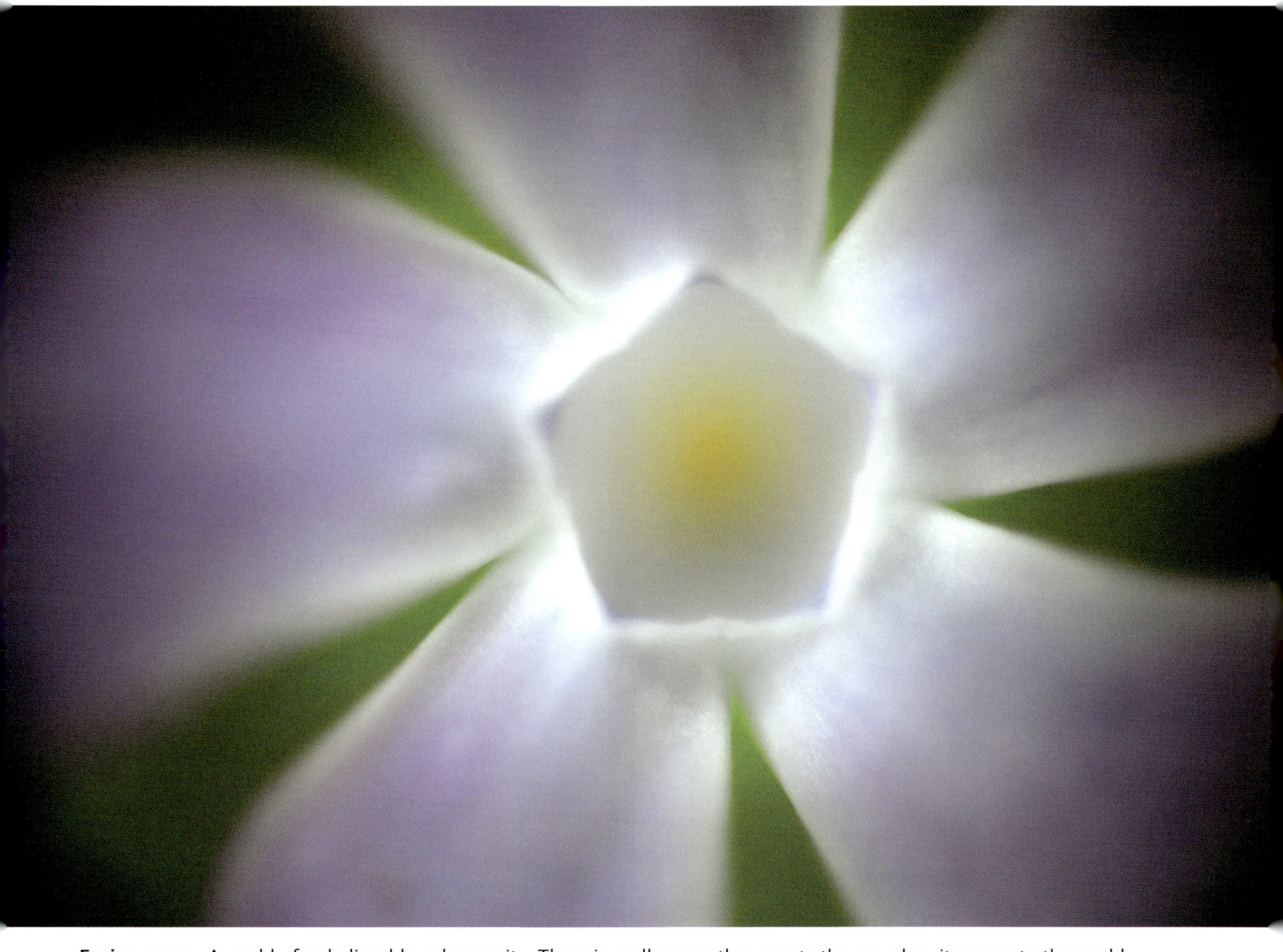

**Facing page**—A world of unbelievable color awaits. There is really more than meets the eye when it comes to the world near our feet. Sometimes, all you have to do is look down, point your camera, add some light, and smile. **Above**—When shooting true macro images, you will be faced with a pretty important decision: "Do I use the blur that is now running rampant through my image, or do I get rid of it?" The answer will affect not only the how the image looks but also dictates what extra equipment you'll need. The extreme blur seen in this image is caused by a larger aperture. We could have chosen a much smaller aperture and forced the flower to come into focus, but then we would have needed an off-camera flash to light it. (And, in fact, a flash *was* used in this image—but we used it to light the blur we created!) Without purpose, gear is useless.

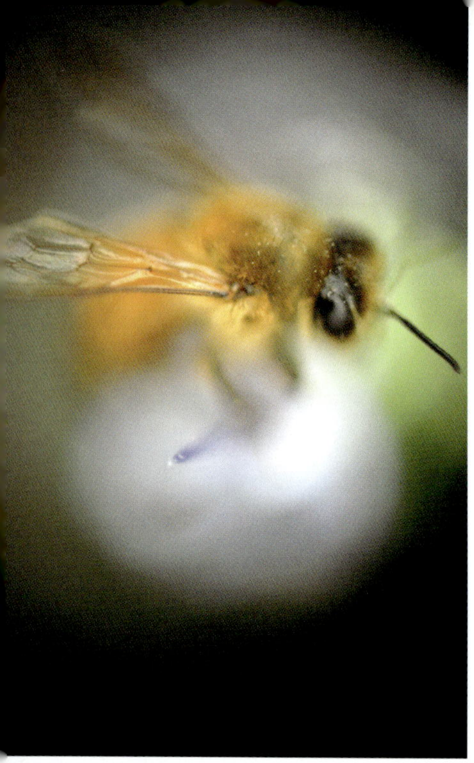

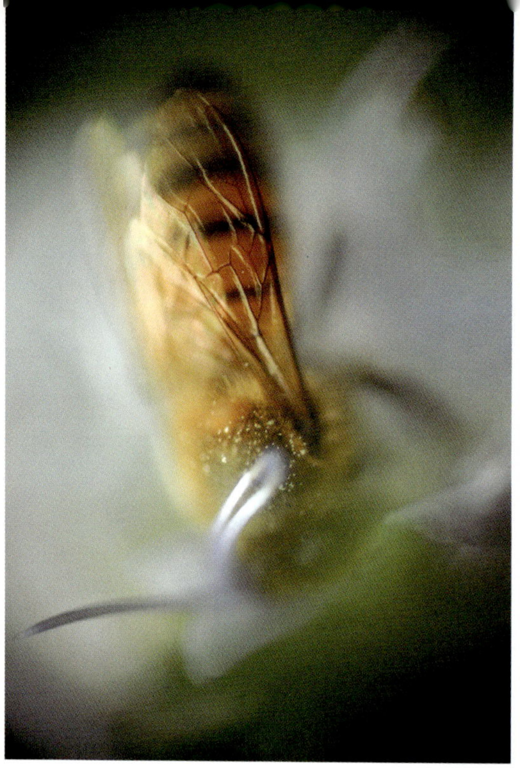

**This page**—You do not always have to make everything crisp and in-focus to tell a story. Throughout this book you've seen macro and close-up images that were super crisp, thanks to a very deep depth of field, but it does not have to be that way. The images here are just a few more examples of how you can shoot bee images. Just because an off-camera flash affords you opportunity to capture detail and achieve crisp focus, doesn't mean you have to do it. **Facing page**—For us, the power of this shot comes from the colors and the shapes. We know it's a bee, but we didn't have to make the bee in focus for that to come forth. Think about what it is about your message that you love and focus your attention on that—not just your lens.

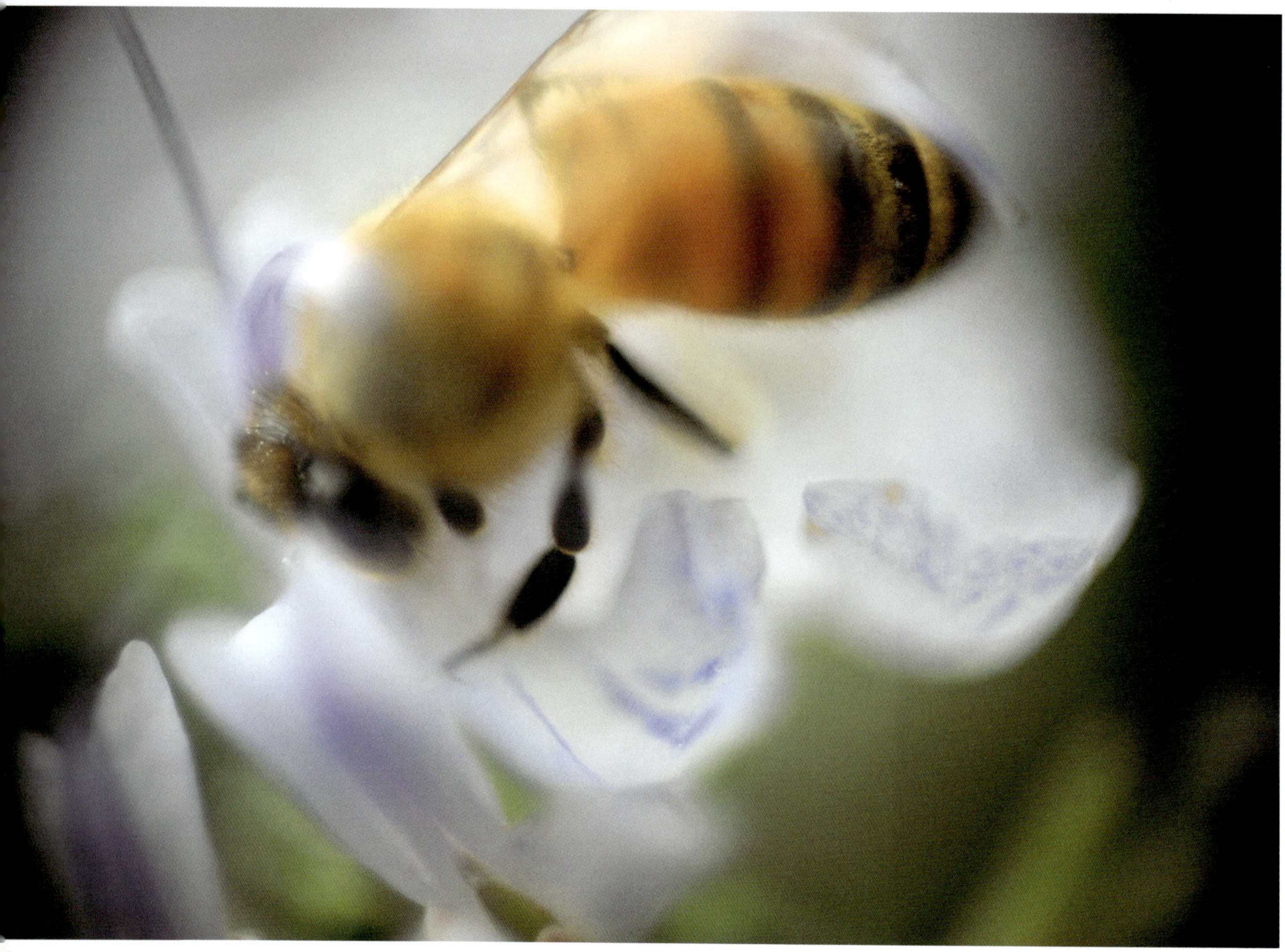

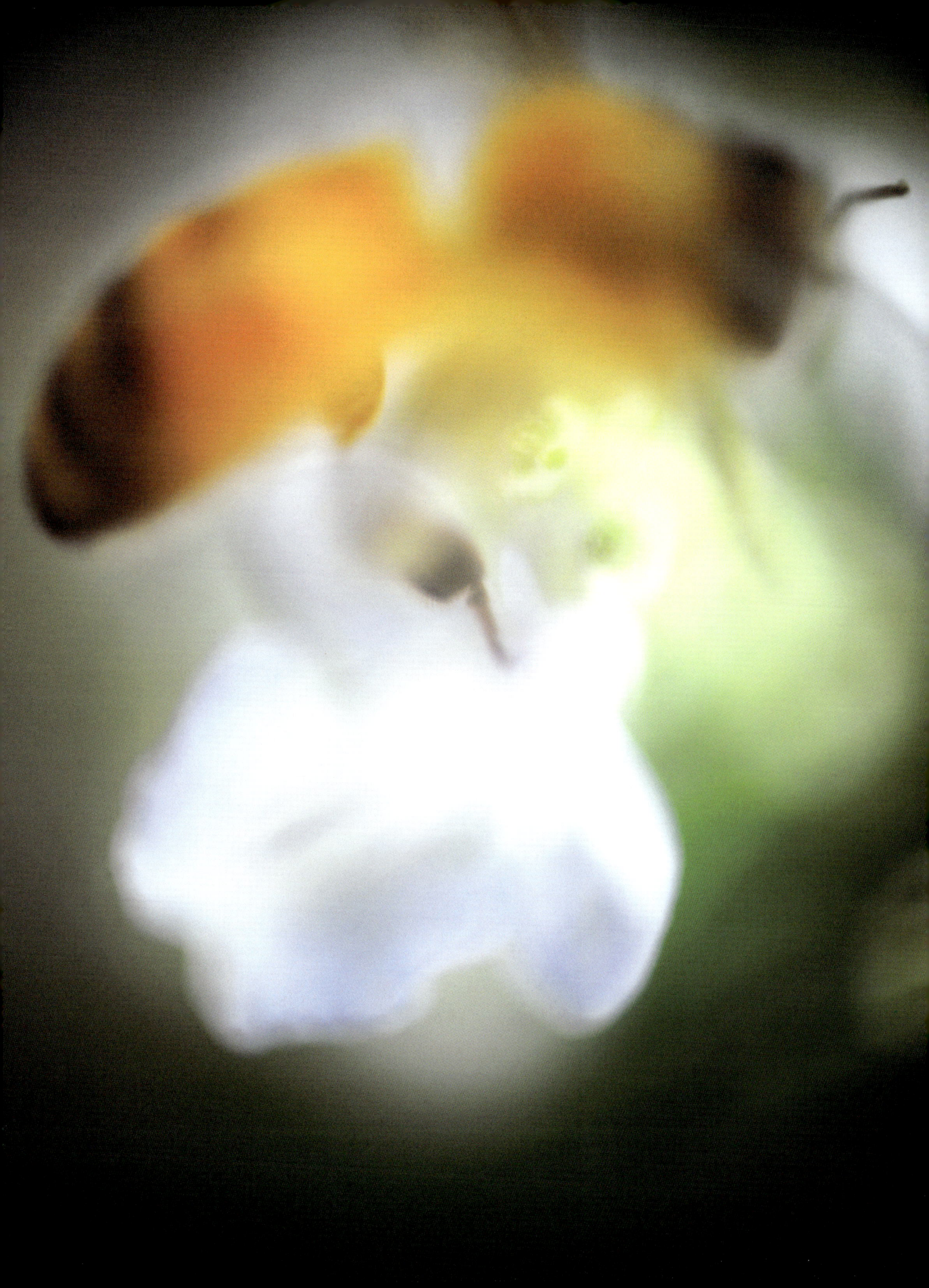

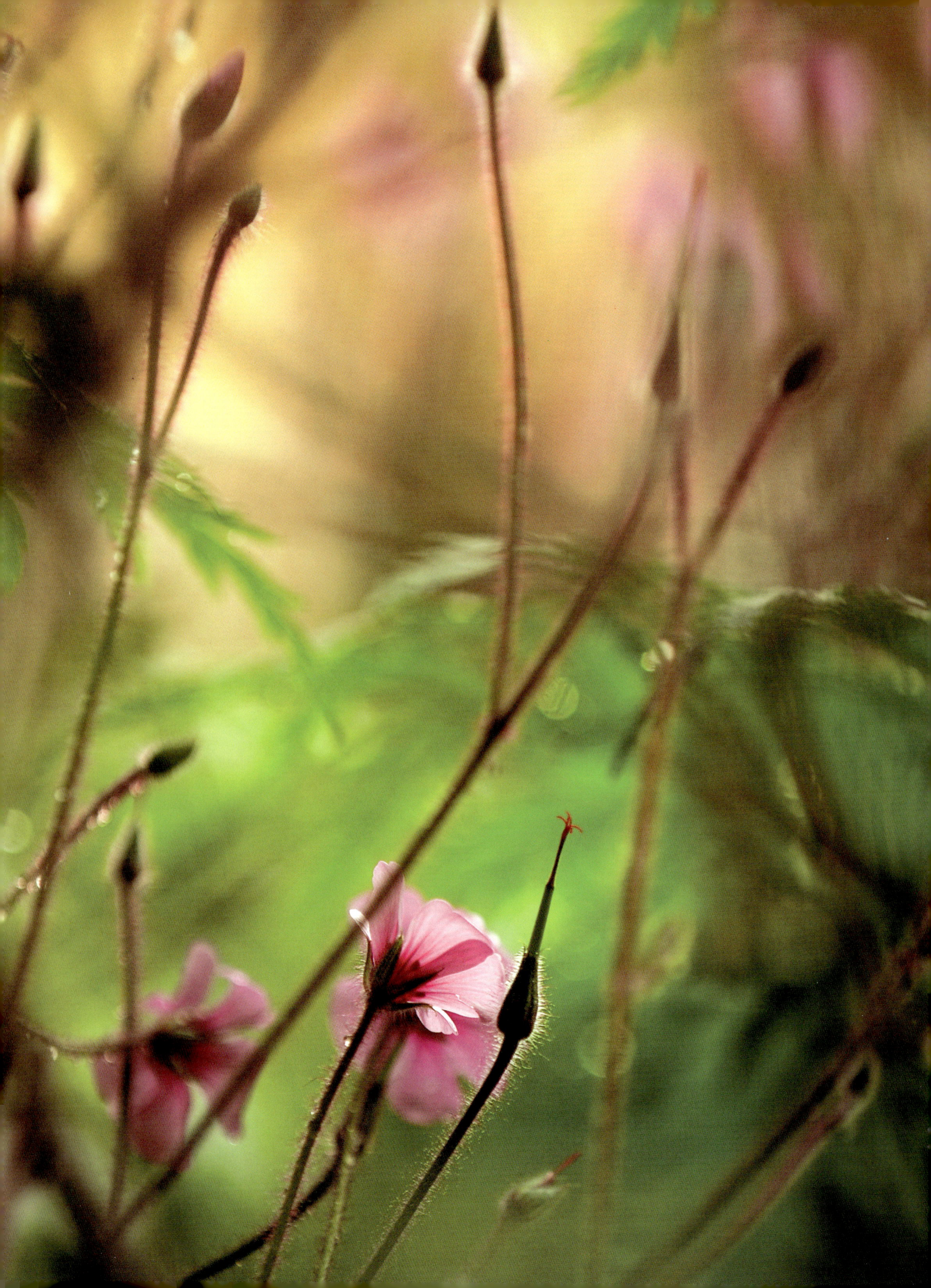

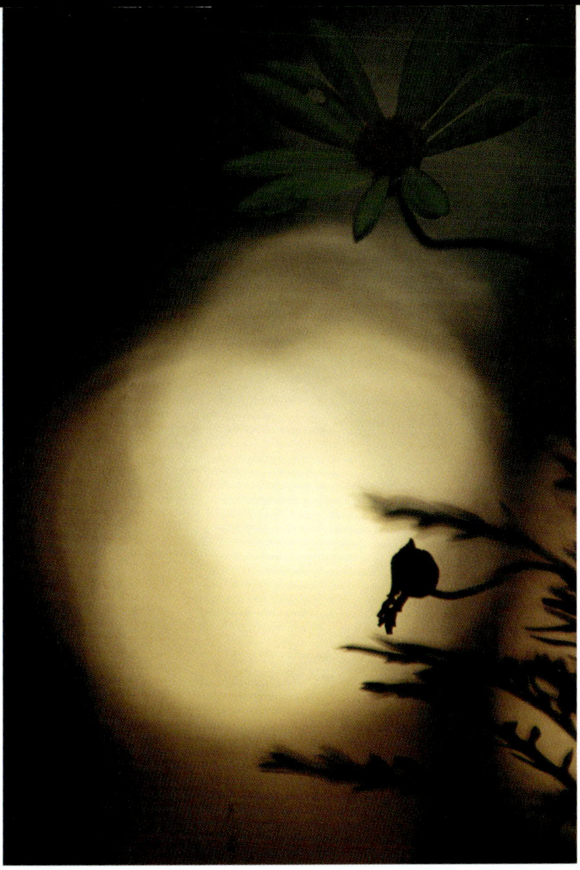
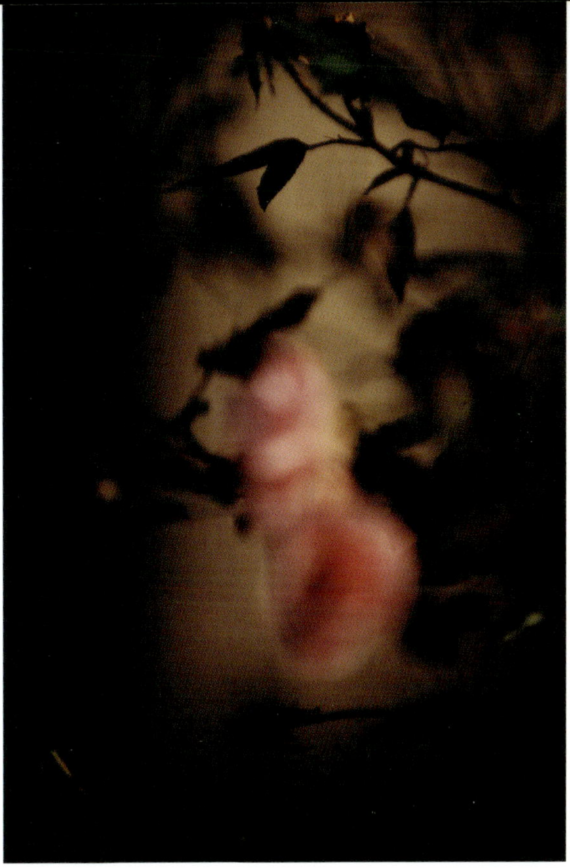
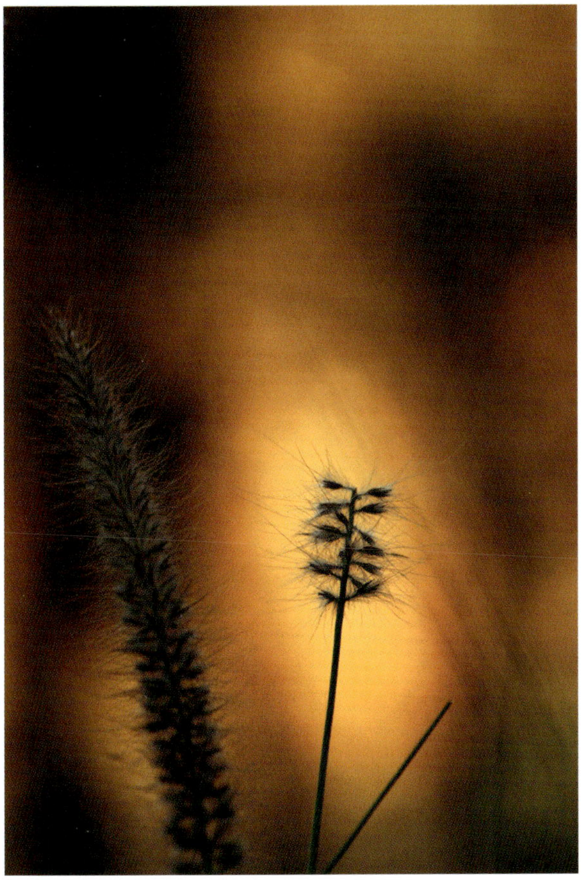
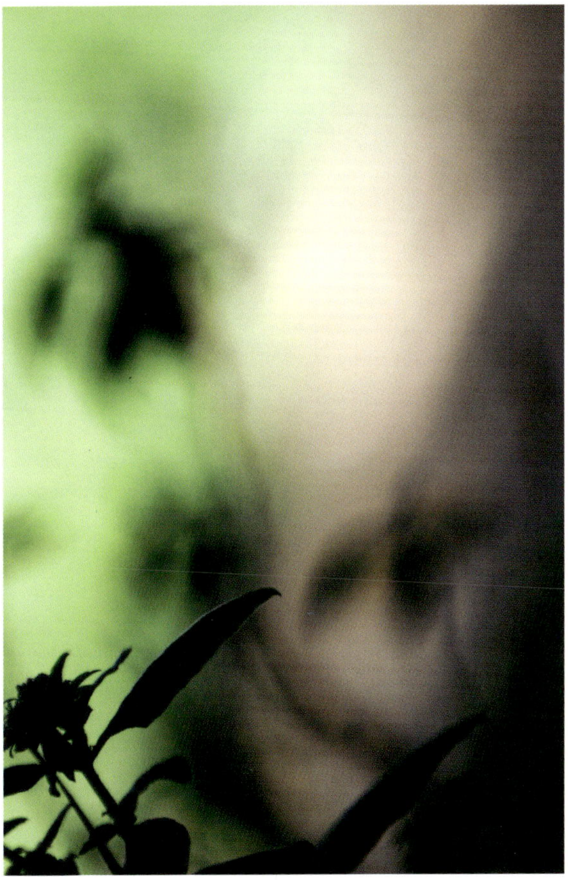

**Facing page**—You could even combine every technique into one masterful play of light, color, texture, and movement. In this image, three flashes were used. One was used to light the middle tier of graphic information (our in-focus flower). The other two were used to light the background; one was directed at a patch of green, while the other was pointed further back toward the side of a building (both of which were blurred fully). **Above**—Here, our off-camera flashes were used to light the background while allowing what would typically be considered a "subject" to drift off into darkness or blur.

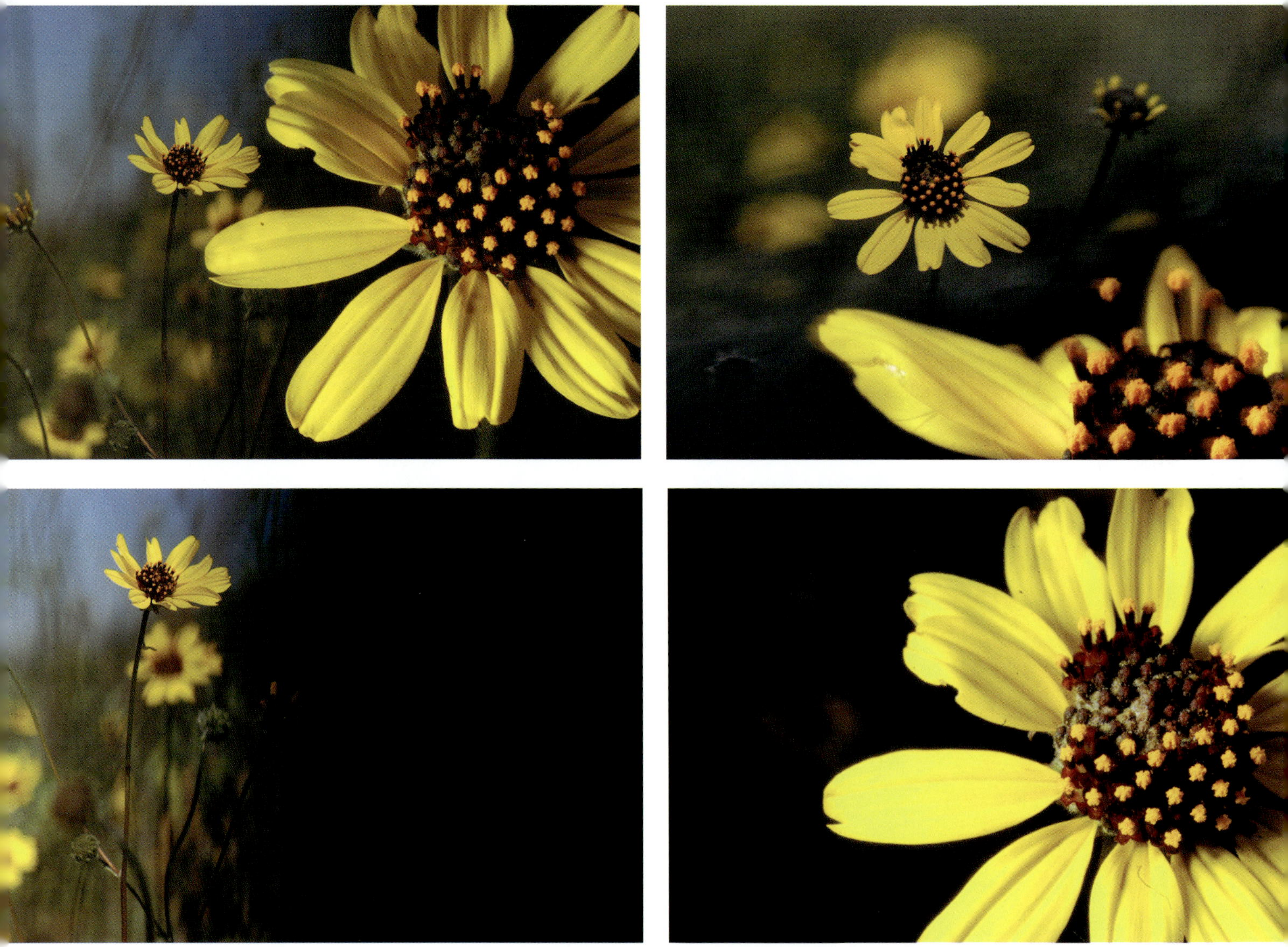

**Top row**—If you are lucky enough to have a system that offers in-camera multiple exposures, you can push the artistic envelope as never before! These photos illustrate the typical results of a simple double exposure. **Bottom row**—The images at the bottom of the page show the pieces. (Hint: When using this feature you may want to hide certain portions of the scene with your hand, as was done here.) **Facing page**—Instead of simply taking pretty close-up pictures, focus on becoming an artist who makes them happen. If you make that your goal—if you concentrate on bettering yourself, improving your skill, and seeing the world in a different light, then you will succeed. That's a guarantee!

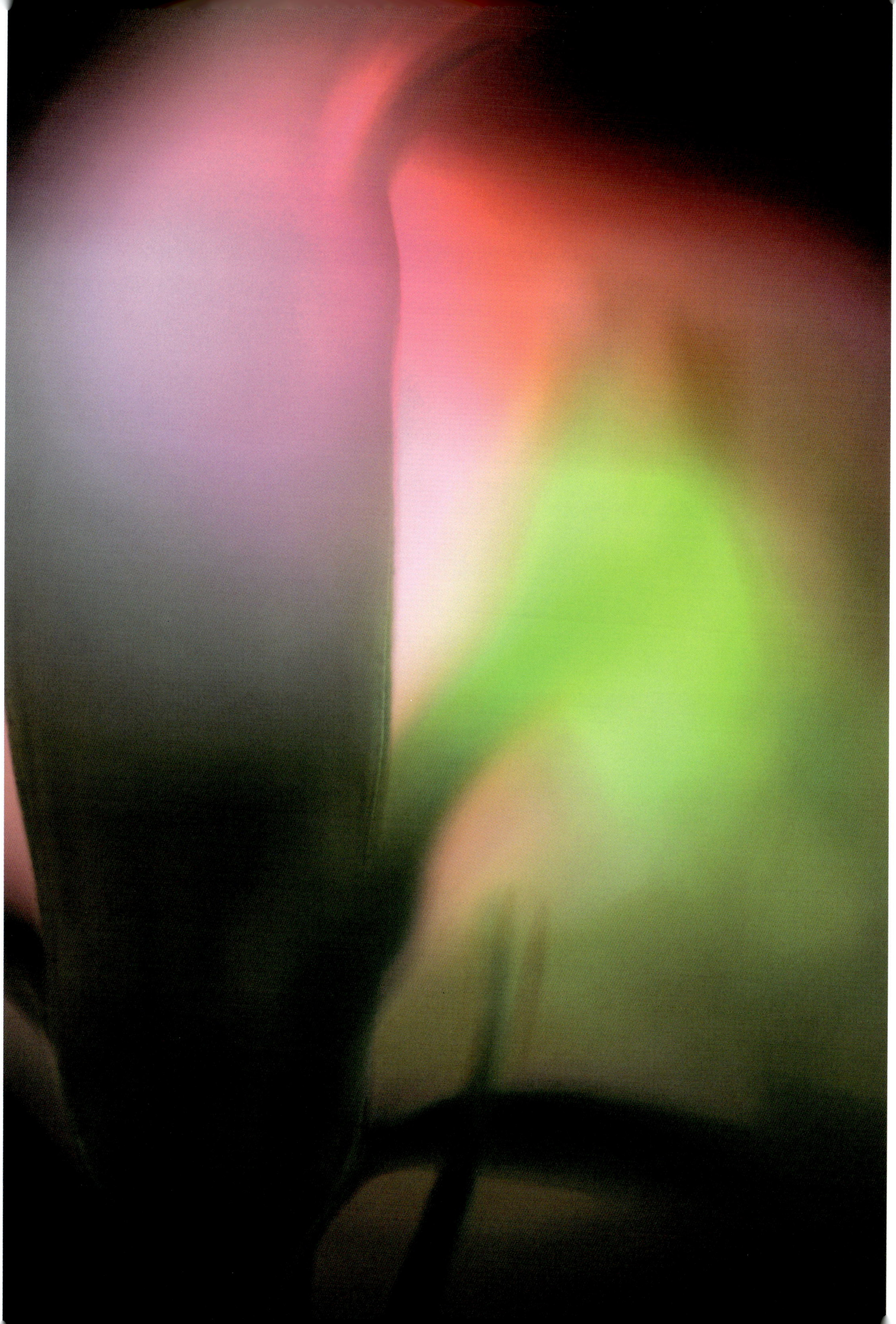

# CONCLUSION

It's not just about getting your small subjects in focus; it's about what you're trying to share with others, and what you're feeling and trying to express. That's what it means to be a macro artist. Does your message ring true?

An off-camera flash produces shadows that the eye (and brain) is accustomed to. You can't take that lightly. If you add light with a camera-mounted flash (even one that has been modified), you run a high risk of flattening out these shadows or, worse yet, destroying them completely. Remember a flash is there to illuminate ideas . . . not eliminate shadows.

When you come armed with an off-camera flash you can achieve that incredibly small aperture that guarantees image sharpness. But, as discussed in the last chapter, that's not what makes a close image (or any image for that manner) wonderful. It's all in how you use that light, where you put it and what type of shadows you end up creating. In this image it's all about the shadows. You'll notice how depth and meaning are being added not by the light, but by the shadows created. When adding light with an off-camera flash, you are trying to create unique shadows not just light simple subjects.

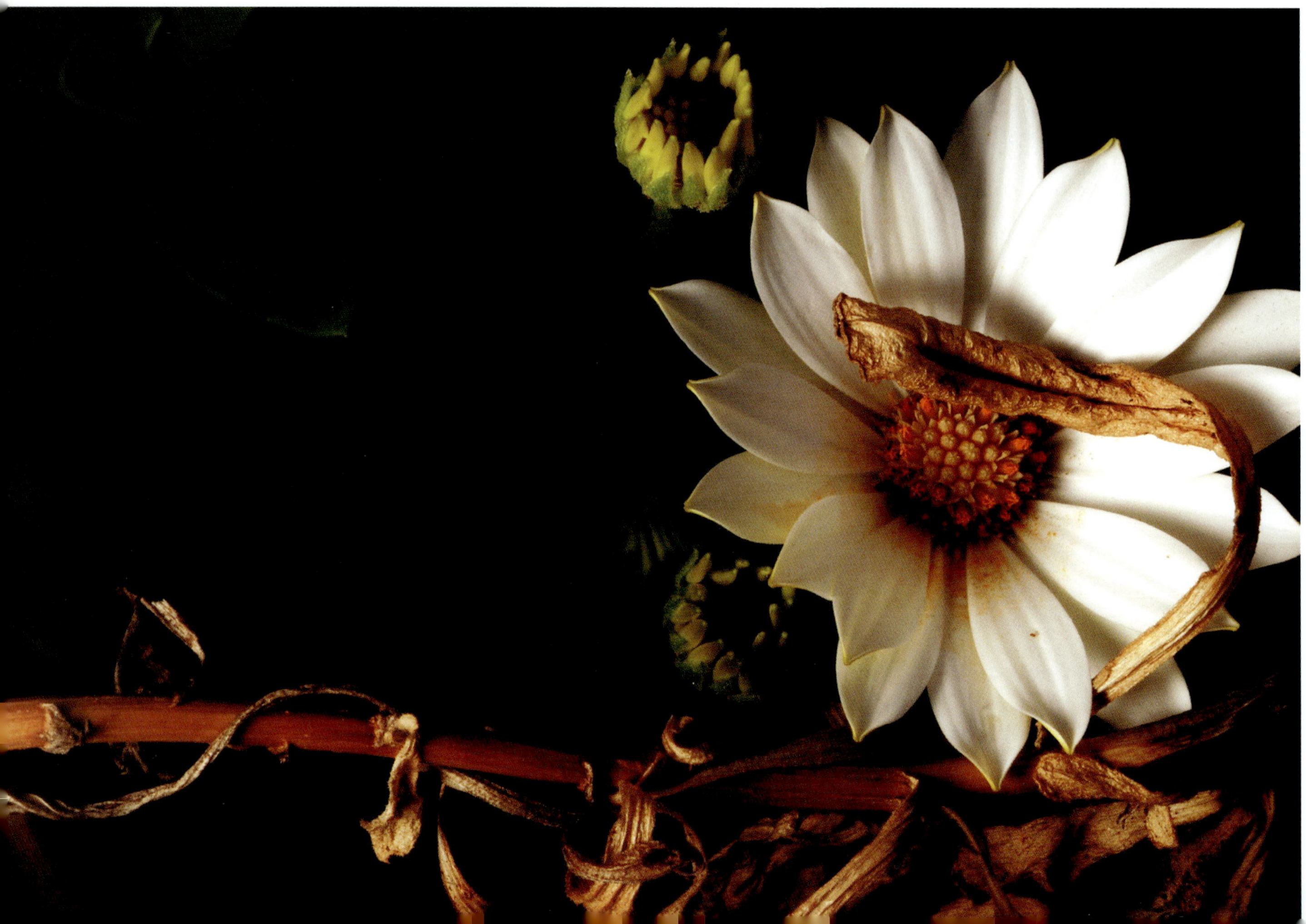

When shooting in-camera black & white images, even more options prevail. You could dial-in a red filter setting in the camera and then cover the flash with a red filter. This creates an even brighter light source, allowing you to keep your background much darker. Couple this with your internal contrast option and those amazing black backgrounds are just a few button presses away. The texture seen in this image comes from the angle of the flash and the depth of field from the very small aperture chosen (f/18).

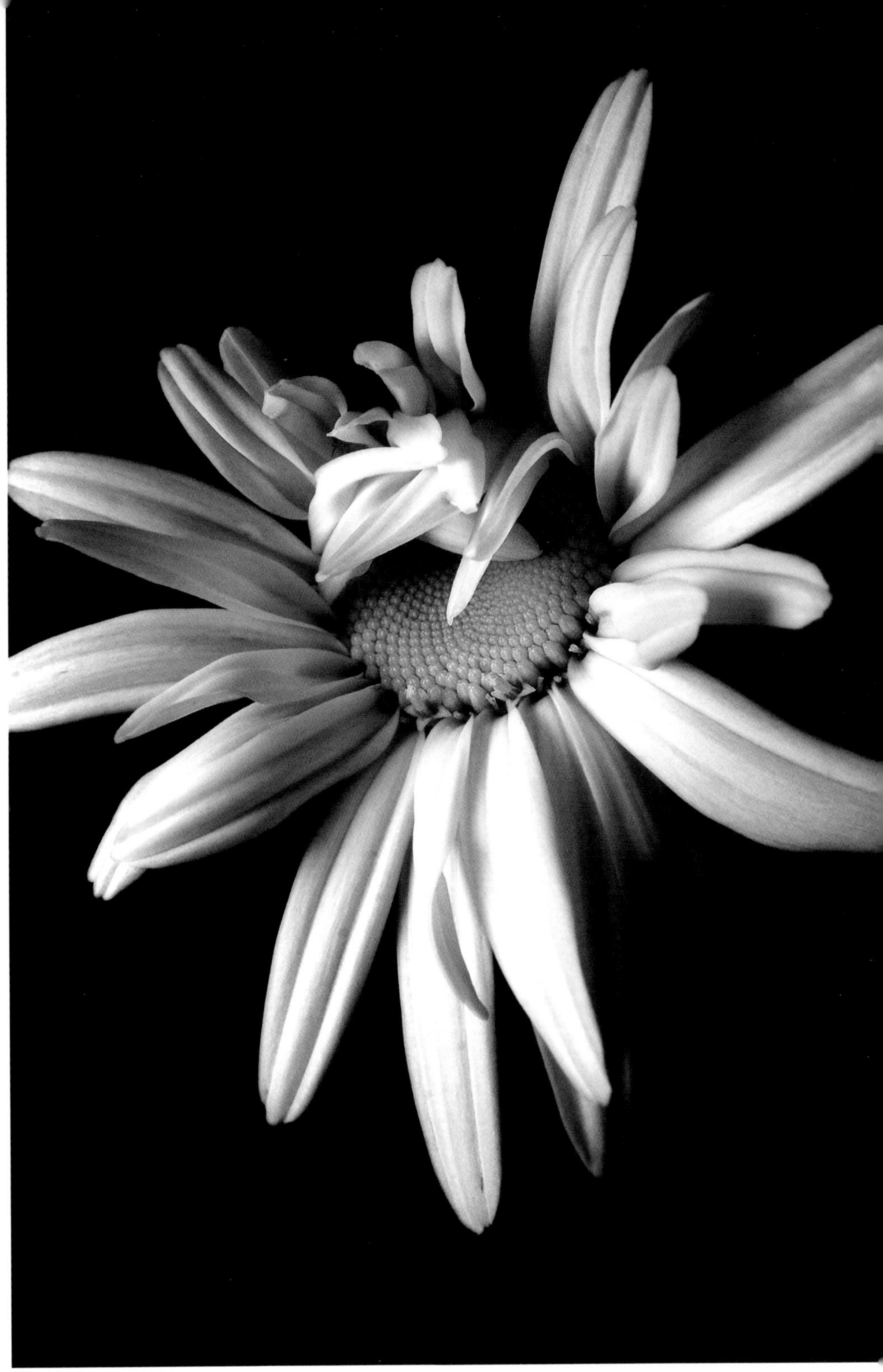

Shadows are a real part of life. They make things special. Without shadows life would be boring, flat, and quite textureless. Keep this in mind when creating close-up and macro images with your flash. Your goal is not just illumination or great depth of field, it's to create something that truly reflects how you feel—and (hopefully) that's never flat and boring.

To do this requires you to think beyond subjects and build a unique message. Placement of your flash will be critical, as each inch changes the

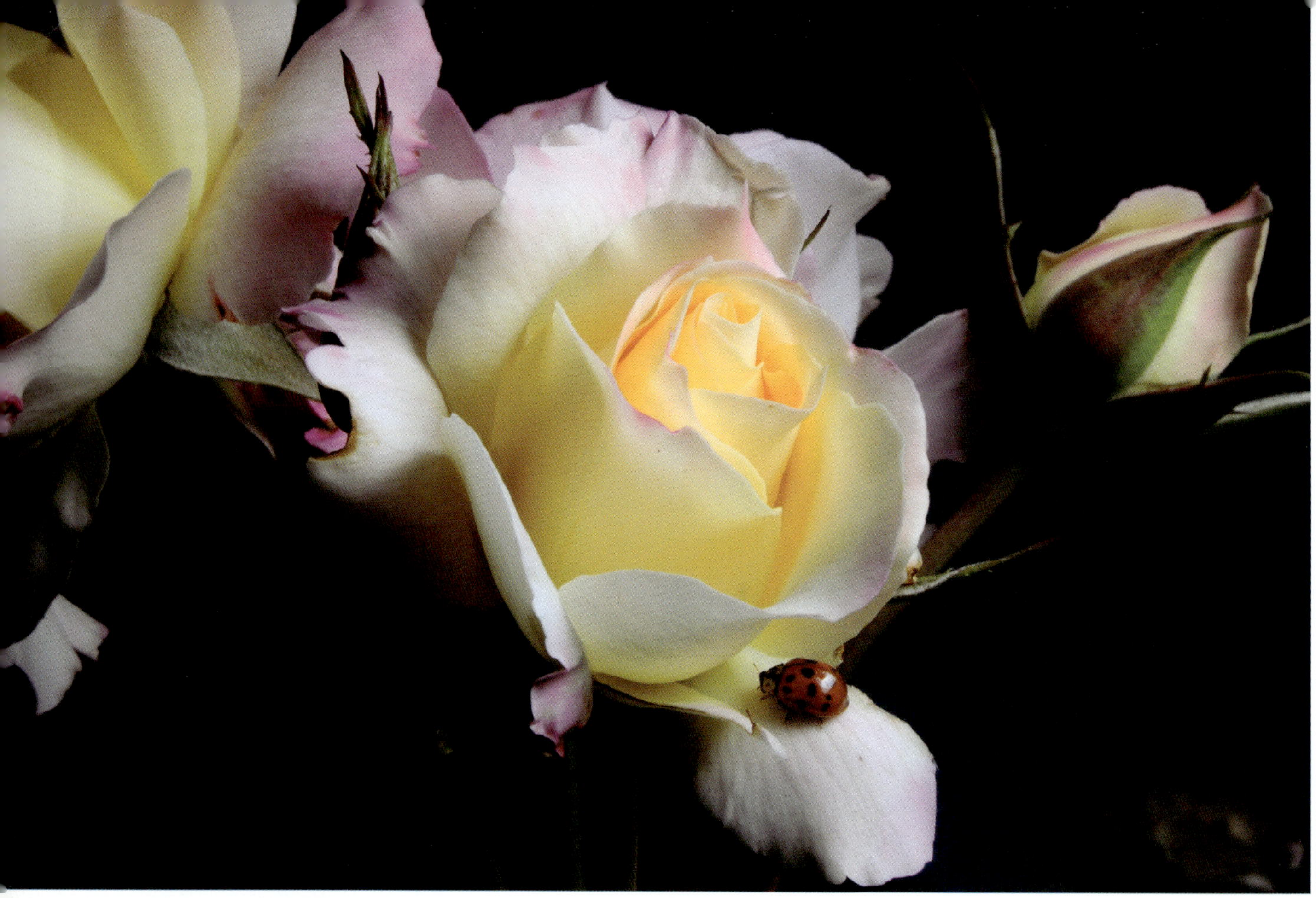

As seen in this image, a very large light source (a modified off-camera flash) placed high creates a wonderful array of textures (shadows) throughout the image. A smaller aperture (f/36) ensured the required depth of field. Shutter speed proved inconsequential as it was the flash that provided all the illumination. Any shutter speed (except one too slow that allowed ambient light to enter the image or one that was faster than the camera's sync speed [$^1/_{200}$]) would have provided the exact same image.

direction of light and hence affects the direction of your shadows. With the most gentle of motions, angle of the wrist, or turn of the hand/flash your image can be utterly fantastic or monstrously dull.

Getting it right will take practice—tons of practice. At first, you'll be tempted to simply light your subjects well—and this is good. But you will have to grow a bit and be more adventurous if you intend to create magic. You'll need to push your light from odder-than-usual angles, modify it differently, stick your flash, and more.

Start simple. Move the flash slightly beyond your subject—just an inch or so in back or to the side. Take a shot and examine the image, not just for illumination but for texture. Look at the shadows you're creating and then imagine what would happen if you moved the flash, if you changed the angle of flash coverage. Think about the shadows. Now shoot again. Keep repeating the process until you're well versed in what your flash can do, what type of shadows you will create. Get to know which angle produces what type of shadows. Play with your flash. Create something different, something unique.

Whatever it takes, an artist will do. It's in his message and its clarity that his intention is focused, nothing else. If his image needs light, then he adds lights the best he can. He learns, he pushes, he explores. This is not just about pretty pictures of flowers, twigs, or insects; it's about becoming the best artist-with-a-camera you can be. It's about *you*—not just your pictures—being in focus.

Stay in full manual control of your camera and flash. Don't use auto focus, don't use aperture or shutter speed priority. Dial-in your own white balance, contrast, and saturation settings. Think about how something makes you feel and try to share that with us. Seriously, we already know what a bee looks like. What we don't know is how you feel about the bee or what your imagination can come up with. Be unique, be an artist. Let your images speak for you. Just because your flower is in focus doesn't mean anything other than you know how to work your equipment. Now comes the hard part. Now you have to put all of that mechanical knowledge to use. Create something. Think before you shoot. Feel. Explore.

Be the artist you know you can be.

Anything is possible once you free your vision and become an artist. You will be fast, you will be focused, and your images (just as this one) will be brilliant. Good luck all, and stay in focus.

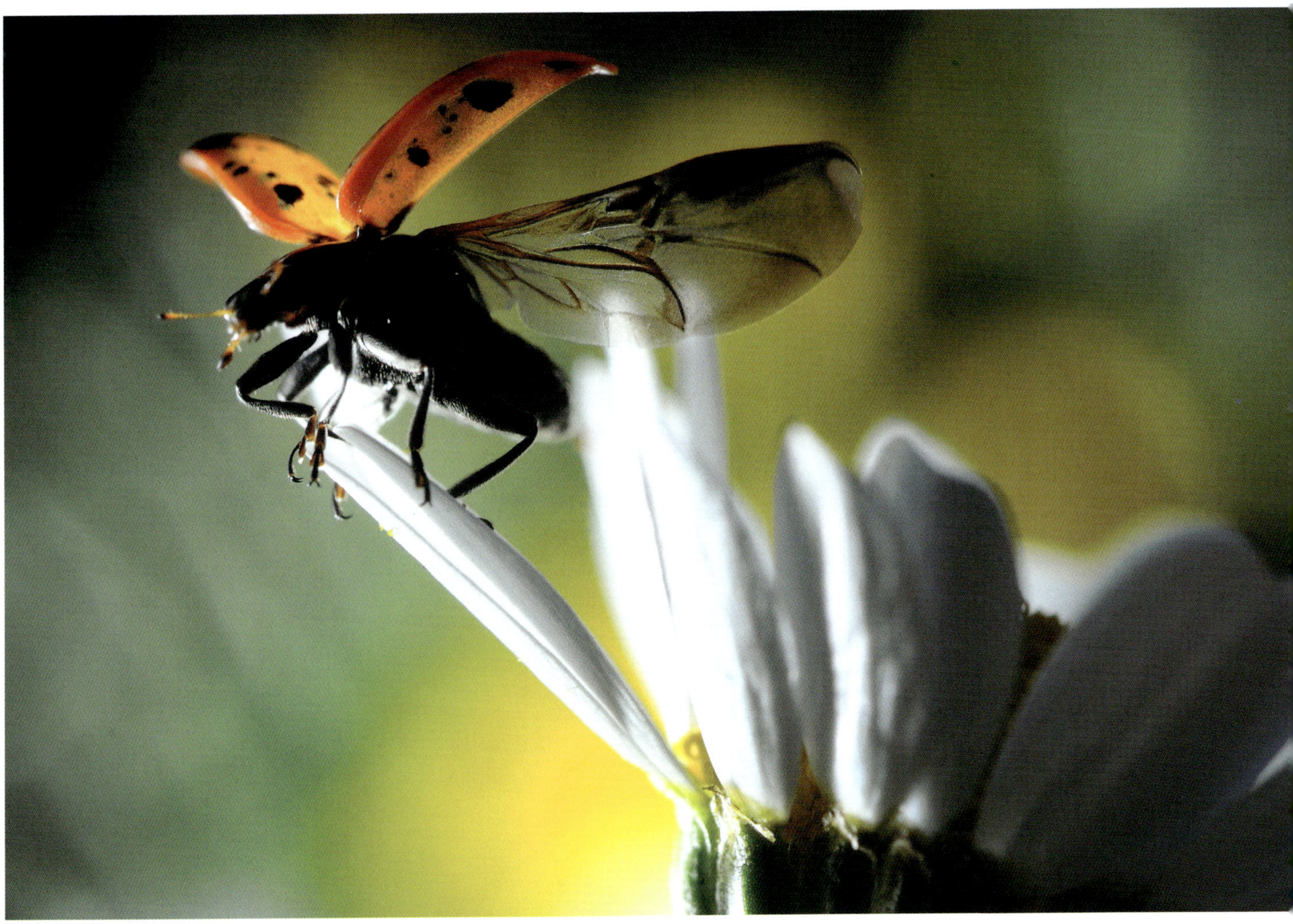

# THE GEAR

Every photographer has his favorite tools and accessories. As off-camera flash and macro photographers, we'd like to give you a look at some of our favorites. The images in this book wouldn't have been possible without their help.

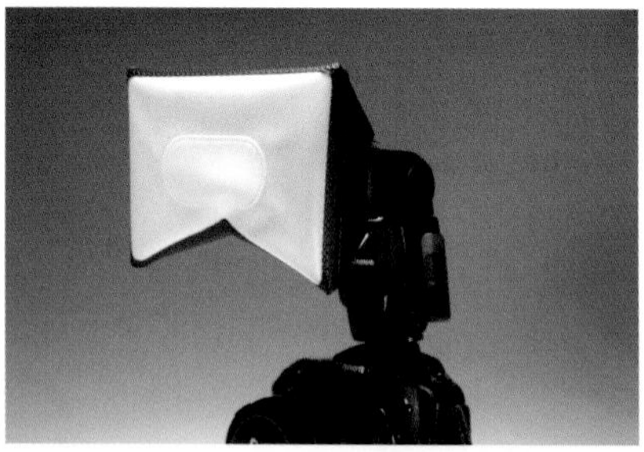

**SoftBox (LQ-107)**

The SoftBox enlarges and diffuses the light with the flash in the direct flash position. The light is softened and more evenly distributed as it passes through a center-weighted frosted diffuser. Available at www.lumiquest.com.

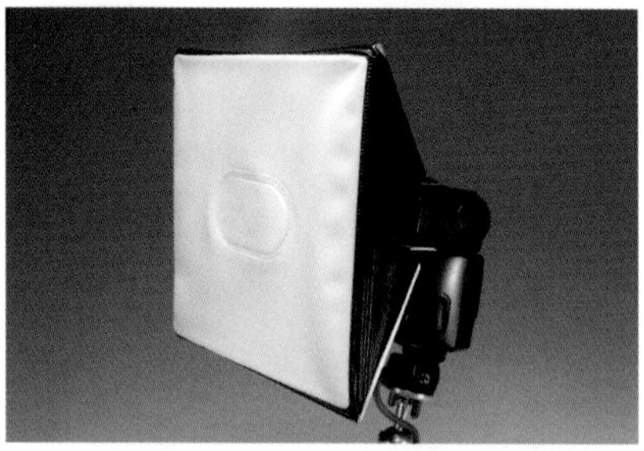

**Softbox III (LQ-119)**

The SoftBox III is roughly twice the size of the original SoftBox, thereby producing considerably softer shadows. It fits conventional flashes (Nikon, Canon, Sunpak, Vivitar, etc.). Available at www.lumiquest.com.

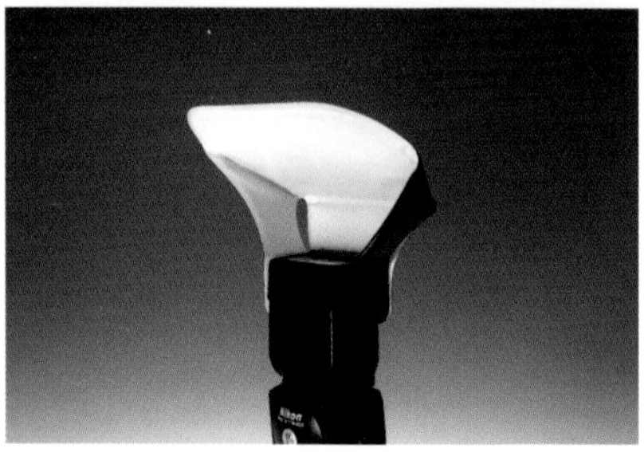

**Pocket Bouncer (LQ-101)**

The Pocket Bouncer enlarges and redirects light at a 90-degree angle from the flash to soften the quality of light and distribute it over a wider area. While no exposure compensation is necessary with automatic flashes, operating distances are somewhat reduced. Available at www.lumiquest.com.

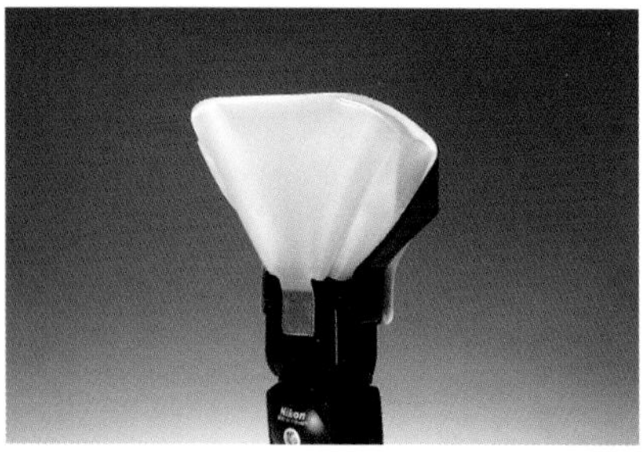

**UltraSoft (LQ-103)**

The UltraSoft enlarges and redirects light at a 90-degree angle from the flash and then further softens the light by passing it through a frosted diffuser. Available at www.lumiquest.com.

### Big Bounce (LQ-104)

The LumiQuest Big Bounce enlarges, redirects, and softens the light. Available at www.lumiquest.com.

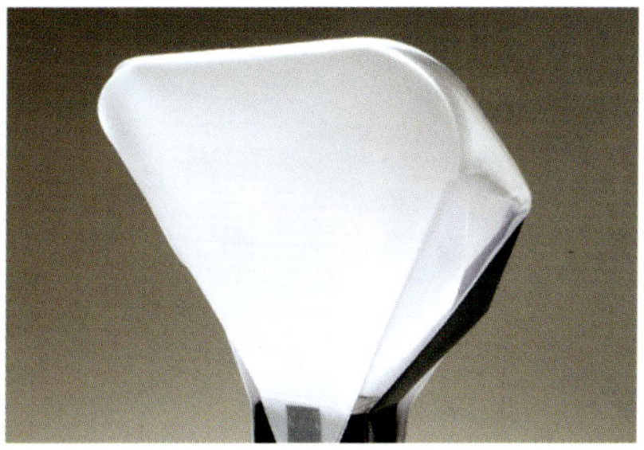

### Cinch Strap (LQ-117)

The LumiQuest Cinch Strap enables the photographer to attach LumiQuest accessories without installing a self-adhesive loop to their flash. In addition, wrap-around velcro attaches LumiQuest accessories for a more secure attachment. Available at www.lumiquest.com.

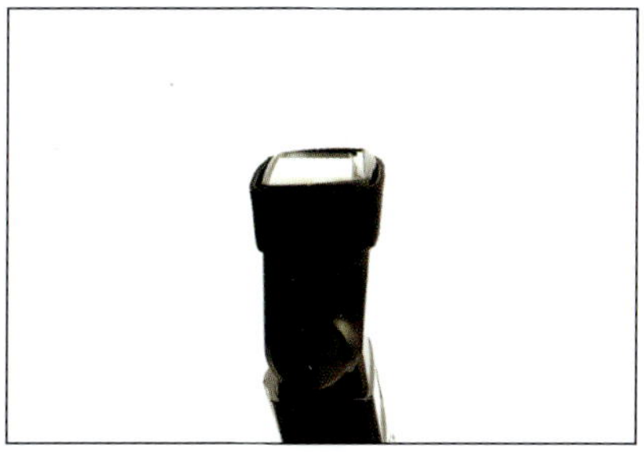

### FXtra (LQ-121)

The FXtra is a compact gel holder that facilitates a quick installation and removal of colored gels. Eight Rosco gels are included. Available at www.lumiquest.com.

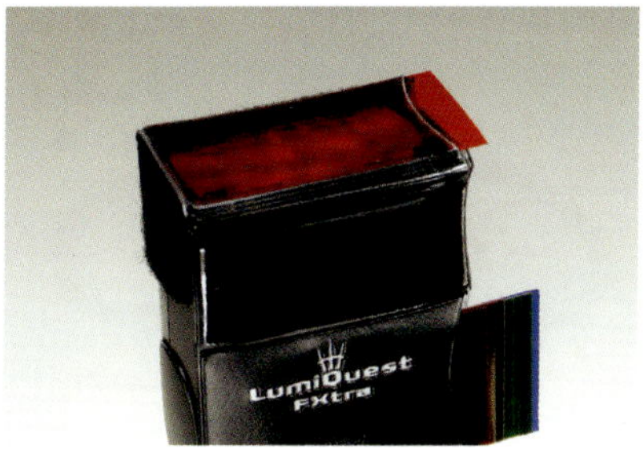


### Teleconverter (Tele-extender)

Teleconverters mount between camera and lens. The optics make it essentially a secondary lens, which increases the overall focal length. Available online and at most camera stores.

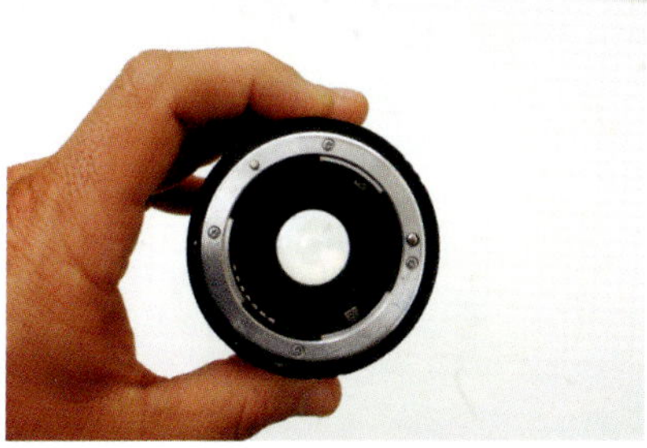

### Extension Tubes

Extension tubes mount between camera body and lens, shortening the minimum focal distance of the lens, resulting in the magnification of the subject. Auto extension tubes maintain electrical connection between camera and lens, while the lesser expensive non-electrical tubes do not. Available online and at most camera stores.

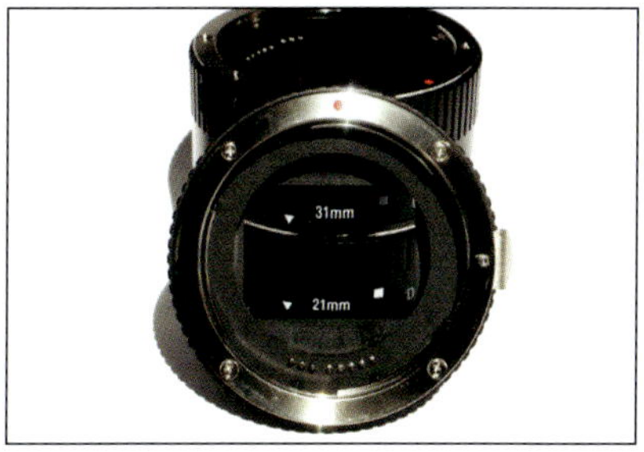

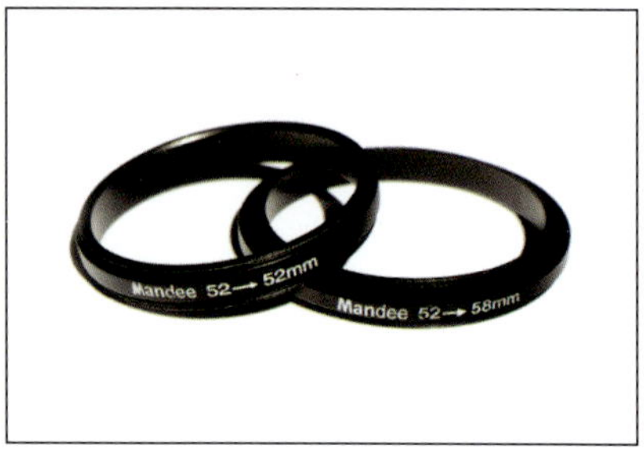


## Macro Coupler

Couplers mount two lenses face to face, shortening the minimum focal distance of the lens, resulting in the magnification of the subject. Available online and at most camera stores.

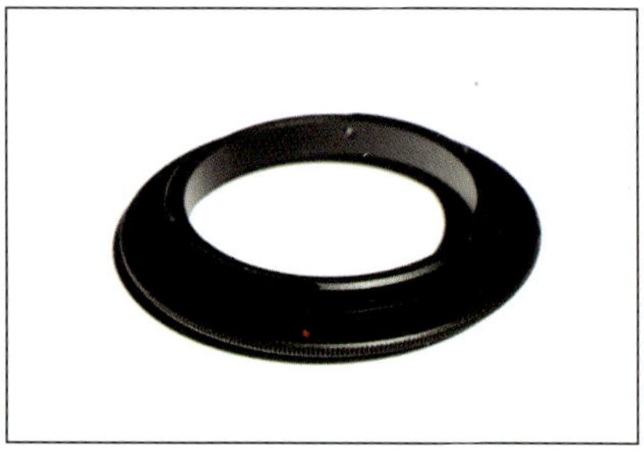

## Reversing Ring

Reversing rings mount the face of a lens to the camera body, shortening the minimum focal distance of the lens, resulting in the magnification of the subject. Available online and at most camera stores.

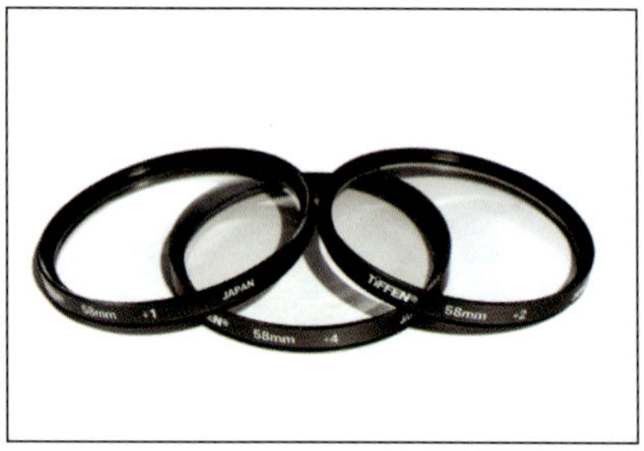

## Close-up Filters

Close-up filters attach to the front of the lens, shortening the close-focus distance and optically magnifying the subject. Available online and at most camera stores.

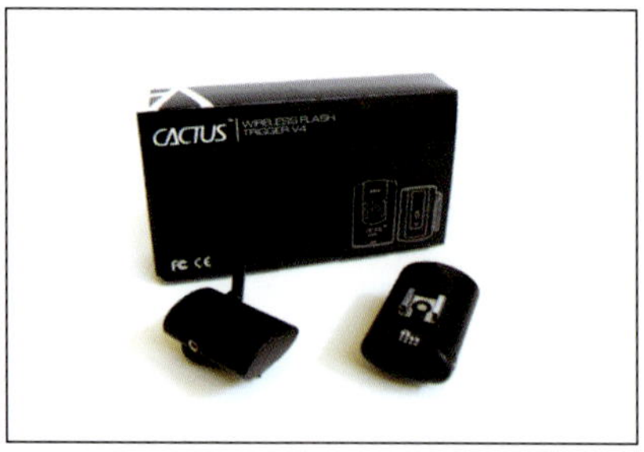


## Cactus Wireless Flash Trigger Set V4

With the new Cactus Wireless Flash Trigger System V4, you can place multiple flashes at various angles and distances from your subject. Each receiver works with one flash. You can use as many receivers as you wish, all receiving their signal from one transmitter. Available at www.gadgetinfinity.com.

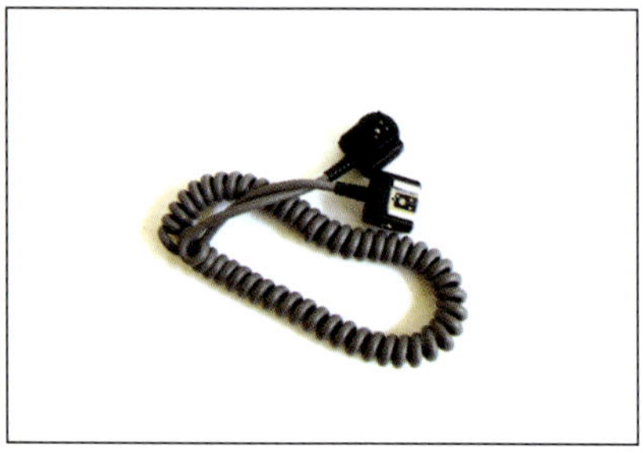

## Dedicated (TTL) Flash Cords

Connects the off-camera flash to the hot shoe of the camera, allowing exposure and distance data to travel between gear. Flash fires as shutter is pressed. Available online and at most camera stores.

**Sync Cords**

Connects between the flash and camera allowing camera to "talk" to the flash for firing. Available online and at most camera stores.

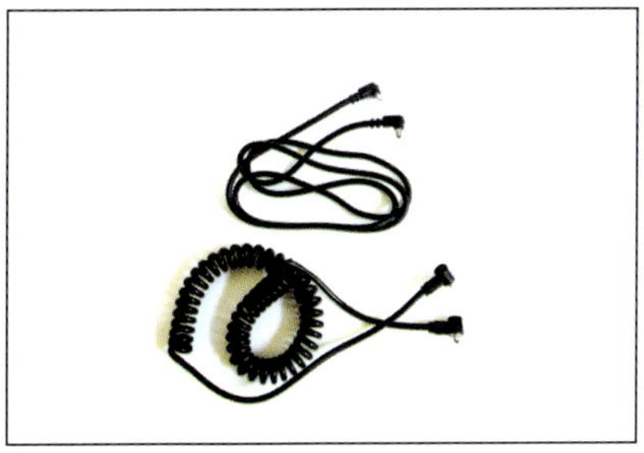

**Connectors and Adaptors**

Connects various sync cords between flashes for multiple flash work. Available online and at most camera stores.

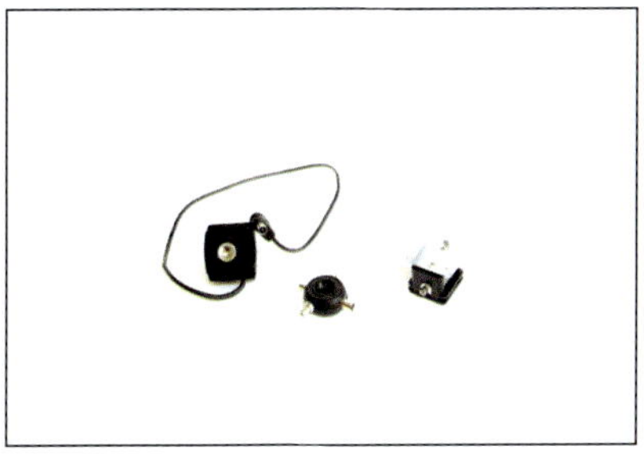

**White Umbrella**

White, shoot-through umbrellas enlarge and diffuse the light coming from the flash. Available online and at most camera stores.

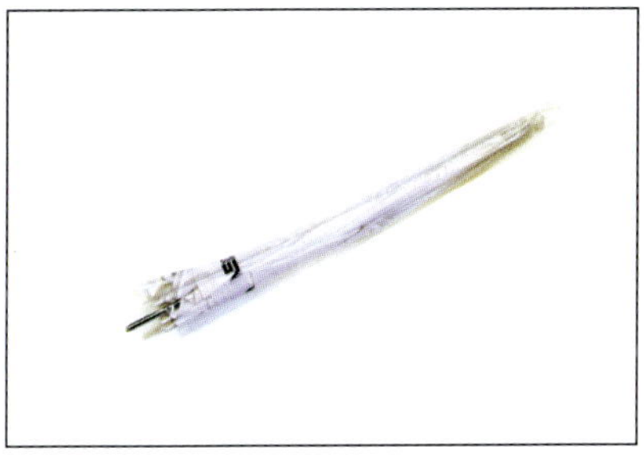

**Umbrella Bracket with Flash Shoe**

Connects to light stand and securely holds both flash and shoot-through umbrella. Available online and at most camera stores.

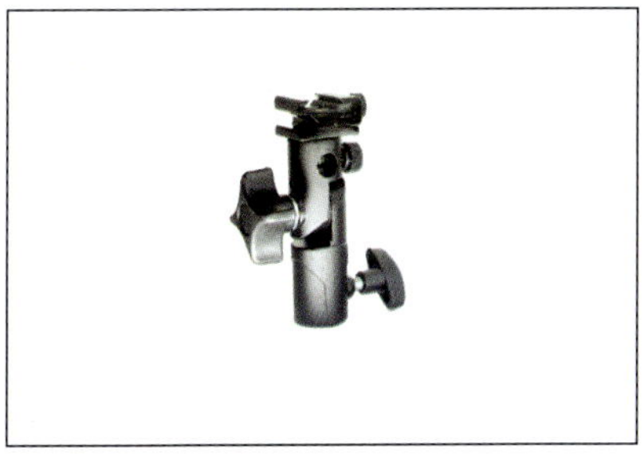

**Spring Clamp with Flash Shoe (175F)**

Clamps onto bars up to a diameter of 40mm. Supplied with a positionable miniature ball head with a flash shoe attachment to allow it to clip and position a flash unit wherever it is needed. Available at www.lastolite.com.

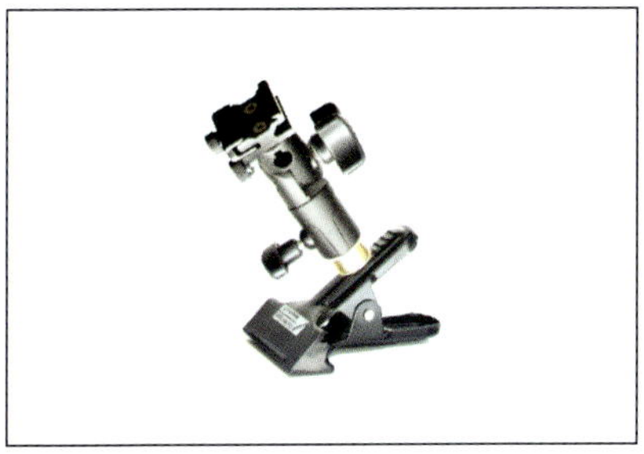

# INDEX

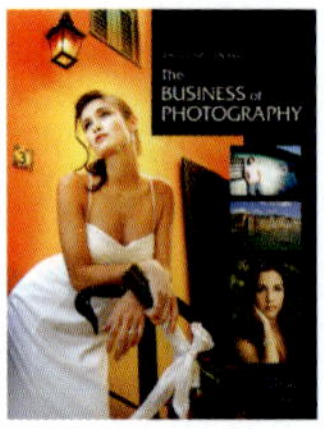


TUCCI AND USMANI'S

## The Business of Photography

*Damon Tucci and Rosena Usmani*

Take your business from flat to fantastic using the foundational business and marketing strategies detailed in this book. *$34.95 list, 8.5x11, 128p, 180 color images, index, order no. 1919.*

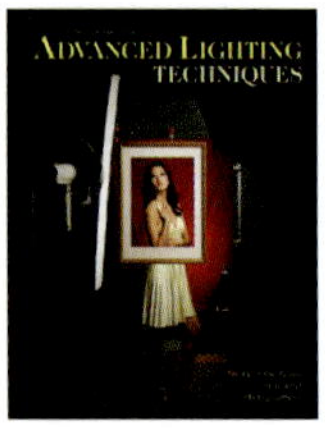


CHRISTOPHER GREY'S

## Advanced Lighting Techniques

Learn how to create twenty-five unique portrait lighting effects that other studios can't touch. Grey's popular, stylized effects are easy to replicate with this witty and highly informative guide. *$34.95 list, 8.5x11, 128p, 200 color images, 26 diagrams, index, order no. 1920.*

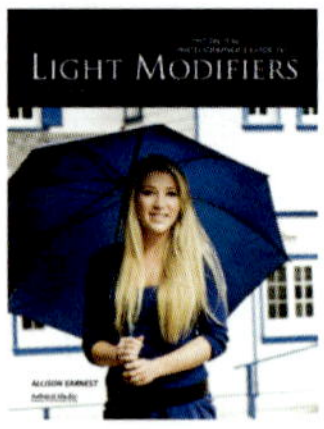


THE DIGITAL PHOTOGRAPHER'S GUIDE TO

## Light Modifiers

SCULPTING WITH LIGHT™

*Allison Earnest*

Choose and use an array of light modifiers to enhance your studio and location images. *$34.95 list, 8.5x11, 128p, 190 color images, 30 diagrams, index, order no. 1921.*

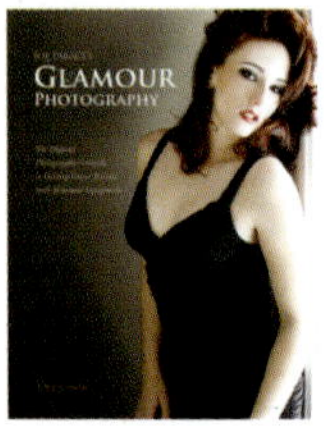


JOE FARACE'S

## Glamour Photography

Farace shows you budget-friendly options for connecting with models, building portfolios, selecting locations and backdrops, and more. *$34.95 list, 8.5x11, 128p, 180 color images, 20 diagrams, index, order no. 1922.*

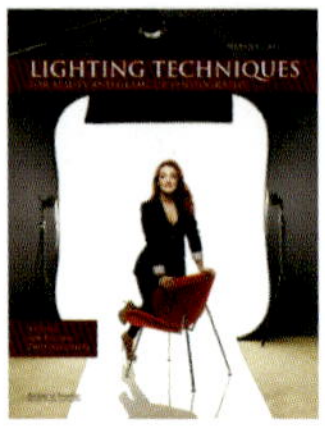


CHRISTOPHER GREY'S

## Lighting Techniques for Beauty and Glamour Photography

Create evocative, detailed shots that emphasize your subject's beauty. Grey presents twenty-six varied approaches to classic, elegant, and edgy lighting. *$34.95 list, 8.5x11, 128p, 170 color images, 30 diagrams, index, order no. 1924.*

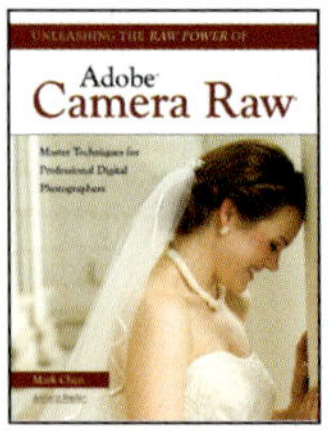


UNLEASHING THE RAW POWER OF

## Adobe® Camera Raw®

*Mark Chen*

Digital guru Mark Chen teaches you how to perfect your files for unprecedented results. *$34.95 list, 8.5x11, 128p, 100 color images, 100 screen shots, index, order no. 1925.*

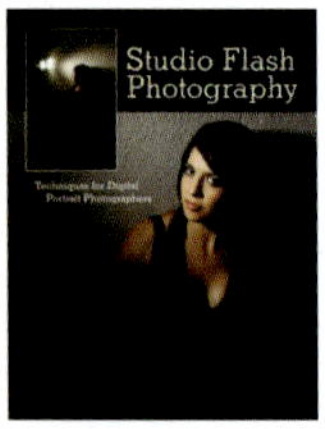


JEFF SMITH'S

## Studio Flash Photography

This common-sense approach to strobe lighting shows working photographers how to master solid techniques and tailor their lighting setups to individual subjects. *$34.95 list, 8.5x11, 128p, 150 color images, index, order no. 1928.*

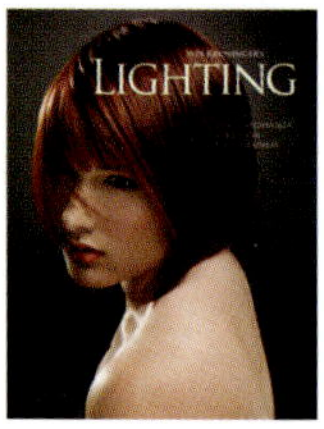


WES KRONINGER'S

## Lighting Design Techniques

FOR DIGITAL PHOTOGRAPHERS

Design portrait lighting setups that blur the lines between fashion, editorial, and traditional portrait styles. *$34.95 list, 8.5x11, 128p, 80 color images, 60 diagrams, index, order no. 1930.*

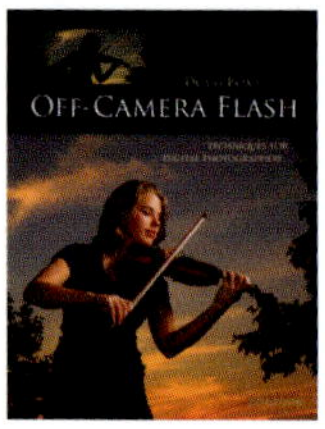


DOUG BOX'S

## Off-Camera Flash

TECHNIQUES FOR DIGITAL PHOTOGRAPHERS

Master off-camera flash, alone or with light modifiers. Box teaches you how to create perfect portrait, wedding, and event shots, indoors and out. *$34.95 list, 8.5x11, 128p, 345 color images, index, order no. 1931.*

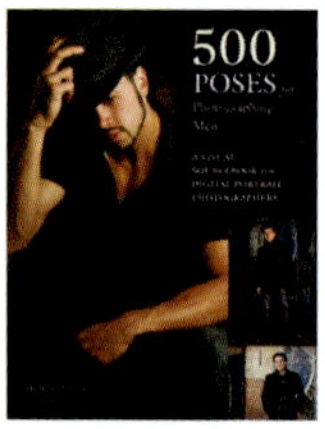


## 500 Poses for Photographing Men

*Michelle Perkins*

Overcome the challenges of posing male subjects with this visual sourcebook, showcasing an array of head-and-shoulders, three-quarter, full-length, and seated and standing poses. *$34.95 list, 8.5x11, 128p, 500 color images, index, order no. 1934.*

## MORE PHOTO BOOKS ARE AVAILABLE

**Amherst Media®**
PO BOX 586
BUFFALO, NY 14226 USA

Individuals: If possible, purchase books from an Amherst Media retailer. Contact us for the dealer nearest you, or visit our web site and use our dealer locater. To order direct, visit our web site, or send a check/money order with a note listing the books you want and your shipping address. All major credit cards are also accepted. For domestic and international shipping rates, please visit our web site or contact us at the numbers listed below. New York state residents add 8.75% sales tax.

*Dealers, distributors & colleges:* Write, call, or fax to place orders. For price information, contact Amherst Media or an Amherst Media sales representative. Net 30 days.

(800) 622-3278 or (716) 874-4450
Fax: (716) 874-4508

*All prices, publication dates, and specifications are subject to change without notice. Prices are in U.S. dollars. Payment in U.S. funds only.*

WWW.AMHERSTMEDIA.COM
FOR A COMPLETE CATALOG OF BOOKS AND ADDITIONAL INFORMATION